GREAT
COOKING
FROM
The GREAT LAKES

D1717253

Telephone *Pioneers* of America
ANSWERING THE CALL OF THOSE IN NEED

Credits

Cookbook Committee:
Joyce Frydel
Helen Keeney
Mary Ann Sprow

We wish to thank Sandy Nealy for art work that is included
in this publication.

This cookbook is a collection of our favorite recipes,
which are not necessarily original recipes.

Published by: Favorite Recipes® Press
P. O. Box 305142
Nashville, Tennessee 37230

Copyright© Great Lakes Chapter #90 Telephone Pioneers of America
3566 Michael Ave. S.W.
Grand Rapids, Michigan 49509

Library of Congress Number: 92-28197
ISBN: 0-87197-348-0

Printed in the United States of America
First Printing: 1992   20,000 copies

MADE FROM RECYCLED PAPER

Contents

Great Lakes Pioneering

The Association named the Telephone Pioneers of America was founded in 1911.

The Telephone Pioneers of America, with over 800,000 members, is the world's largest industry related volunteer organization. This group is comprised of both active and retired employees of the telecommunication industry in both the USA and Canada.

The members, along with their families, proudly contribute more than 28,000,000 volunteer hours yearly to their respective communities.

The symbol of this organization is a triangle. Each of the three sides represents their principal objectives.

1. **Fellowship**—this comes first and is the foundation upon which loyalty and service rest.

2. **Loyalty**—represented by the left side of the triangle marks the relationship of our members to each other.

Answering the Call of Those in Need

3. **Service**—signified by the right side of the emblem, is an outgrowth of both fellowship and loyalty. Through service, pioneering contributes to the well being and happiness of those it reaches within the organization, throughout the industry and within the community.

The Great Lakes Chapter #90, headquartered in Grand Rapids, is divided into 3 councils: Central, Northern and Southern. The councils are divided into 19 clubs.

Central	Northern	Southern
Bay	Escanaba	Battle Creek
Cadillac/Manistee	Houghton/Hancock	Benton Harbor
Flint	Iron Mountain	Grand Rapids/Grand Valley
Petoskey	Ironwood	Jackson
Saginaw	Marquette County	Kalamazoo
Traverse City	Menominee	Lansing
	Sault Ste. Marie	

These clubs are involved in a multitude of projects including:

Activities in veterans facilities
Providing teddy bears to police agencies
Tree planting
Flower planting
Red Ribbon Campaign—"Say No to Drugs"
Handicap bowling
Cleaning highways
Blind baseball

The list goes on and on.

The Great Lakes Chapter, with a membership of 9,000, volunteers in excess of 20,000 hours per month to their communities. This is time and energy that we as taxpayers can't afford to buy, and it's given with sheer love and enthusiasm by the Telephone Pioneers of America.

These activities are made possible by fundraising projects, such as the sale of this cookbook.

We would like to thank all of those who helped to make this book possible by contributing their prized recipes.

Yours in Pioneering,
Joyce Frydel—Lansing Club
Mary Ann Sprow—Jackson Club
Helen Keeney—Lansing Club

Nutritional Guidelines

The editors have attempted to present these family recipes in a form that allows approximate nutritional values to be computed. Persons with dietary or health problems or whose diets require close monitoring should not rely solely on the nutritional information provided. They should consult their physicians or a registered dietitian for specific information.

Abbreviations for Nutritional Analysis

Cal — Calories
Prot — Protein
Carbo — Carbohydrates
Dietary Fiber — Fiber
T Fat — Total Fat
Chol — Cholesterol
Sod — Sodium
gr — gram
mg — milligrams

Nutritional information for these recipes is computed from information derived from many sources, including materials supplied by the United States Department of Agriculture, computer databanks and journals in which the information is assumed to be in the public domain. However, many specialty items, new products and processed foods may not be available from these sources or may vary from the average values used in these analyses. More information on new and/or specific products may be obtained by reading the nutrient labels. Unless otherwise specified, the nutritional analysis of these recipes is based on all measurements being level.

- **Artificial sweeteners** vary in use and strength so should be used "to taste," using the recipe ingredients as a guideline. Sweeteners using aspartame (NutraSweet and Equal) should not be used as a sweetener in recipes involving prolonged heating which reduces the sweet taste. For further information, refer to package information.

- **Alcoholic ingredients** have been analyzed for the basic ingredients, although cooking evaporates the alcohol thus decreasing caloric content.

- **Buttermilk, sour cream** and **yogurt** are types available commercially.

- **Cake mixes** which are prepared using package directions include 3 eggs and 1/2 cup oil.

- **Chicken**, cooked for boning and chopping, has been roasted; this method yields the lowest caloric values.

- **Cottage cheese** is cream-style with 4.2% creaming mixture. Dry-curd cottage cheese has no creaming mixture.

- **Eggs** are all large. To avoid raw eggs that may carry salmonella as in eggnog or 6-week muffin batter, use an equivalent amount of commercial egg substitute.

- **Flour** is unsifted all-purpose flour.

- **Garnishes**, serving suggestions and other optional additions and variations are not included in the analysis.

- **Margarine** and **butter** are regular, not whipped or presoftened.

- **Milk** is whole milk, 3.5% butterfat. Lowfat milk is 1% butterfat. Evaporated milk is whole milk with 60% of the water removed.

- **Oil** is any type of vegetable cooking oil. Shortening is hydrogenated vegetable shortening.

- **Salt** and other ingredients to taste as noted in the ingredients have not been included in the nutritional analysis.

- If a choice of ingredients has been given, the nutritional analysis information reflects the first option. If a choice of amounts has been given, the nutritional analysis reflects the greater amount.

Food Guide Pyramid
A Guide to Daily Food Choices

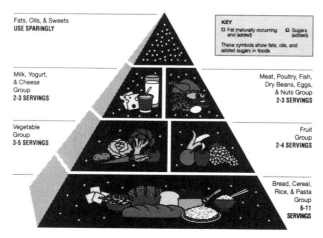

RED RIBBON CAMPAIGN

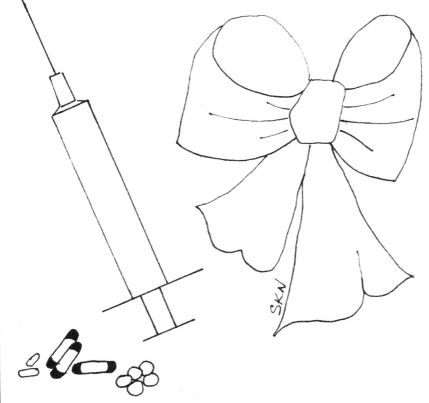

SKN

"Say No To Drugs"

Appetizers and Beverages

Crunchy Carrot Balls

3 ounces cream cheese, softened
1/2 cup shredded Cheddar cheese
1 teaspoon honey

1 cup finely shredded carrots
1/2 cup Grape Nuts
2 tablespoons finely chopped parsley

Beat cream cheese, Cheddar cheese and honey in mixer bowl until well mixed. Stir in carrots. Chill, covered, for 30 minutes. Shape into fourteen 1-inch balls. Chill, covered, until firm. Roll in mixture of cereal and parsley before serving; chill. **Yield: 14 servings.**

Approx Per Serving: Cal 57; Prot 2 g; Carbo 5 g; Fiber 1 g;
    T Fat 3 g; 54% Calories from Fat; Chol 11 mg; Sod 74 mg.

Nellie Thompson, Romulus

Cheese Ball

16 ounces cream cheese, softened
1 5-ounce jar Roka bleu cheese,
  softened
2 5-ounce jars Old English cheese,
  softened

1 teaspoon garlic salt
1 tablespoon Worcestershire sauce
2 tablespoons red wine vinegar
1 2-ounce package chopped walnuts

Beat cream cheese, bleu cheese, Old English cheese, garlic salt, Worcestershire sauce and vinegar in bowl until smooth. Chill until slightly firm. Shape into ball. Roll in chopped walnuts. Chill until serving time. **Yield: 30 (1-ounce) servings.**

Approx Per Serving: Cal 108; Prot 4 g; Carbo 2 g; Fiber <1 g;
    T Fat 10 g; 81% Calories from Fat; Chol 27 mg; Sod 275 mg.

Donna J. Hopp, Rogers City

Bev's Cheese Ball

16 ounces cream cheese, softened
4 ounces pastrami, shredded
1/2 cup chopped Bermuda onion

Minced garlic to taste
1/2 cup chopped walnuts

Combine cream cheese, pastrami, onion and garlic in bowl; mix well. Chill, covered, overnight. Shape into ball. Roll in walnuts to coat. Arrange on serving plate with crackers. May also use as dip or sandwich spread. **Yield: 28 (1-ounce) servings.**

Approx Per Serving: Cal 86; Prot 2 g; Carbo 1 g; Fiber <1 g;
    T Fat 8 g; 84% Calories from Fat; Chol 21 mg; Sod 99 mg.

Beverly Wykes, Ishpeming

Party Cheese Ball

5 ounces Roquefort cheese
6 ounces cream cheese, softened
1/2 cup shredded Cheddar cheese

1 teaspoon Worcestershire sauce
Juice of 1 onion
8 ounces pecans, crushed

Combine cheeses, Worcestershire sauce and onion juice in blender container. Process until smooth. Shape mixture into ball; place in bowl lined with waxed paper. Chill overnight. Roll in crushed pecans 1 hour before serving. Garnish with parsley or watercress sprigs. **Yield: 15 (1-ounce) servings.**

Approx Per Serving: Cal 191; Prot 5 g; Carbo 3 g; Fiber 1 g;
    T Fat 18 g; 83% Calories from Fat; Chol 25 mg; Sod 231 mg.

Amy Hoult, Rochester

Chili Cheese Log

3 ounces cream cheese, softened
2 cups shredded sharp Cheddar
    cheese
1 tablespoon lemon juice

Garlic salt to taste
1 teaspoon paprika
1 teaspoon chili powder

Beat cream cheese, Cheddar cheese, lemon juice and garlic salt in mixer bowl until fluffy. Shape into log. Sprinkle with mixture of paprika and chili powder. Chill, covered, until serving time. **Yield: 20 (1-ounce) servings.**

Approx Per Serving: Cal 61; Prot 3 g; Carbo <1 g; Fiber <1 g;
    T Fat 5 g; 77% Calories from Fat; Chol 17 mg; Sod 84 mg.

Dorothy De Feyta, Holland

Smoky Salmon Ball

1 16-ounce can red salmon, drained,
    flaked
8 ounces cream cheese, softened
1 tablespoon lemon juice
2 teaspoons grated onion

1 teaspoon prepared horseradish
1/4 teaspoon salt
1/4 teaspoon liquid smoke
1/2 cup chopped pecans
3 tablespoons parsley flakes

Combine salmon, cream cheese, lemon juice, onion, horseradish, salt and liquid smoke in bowl; mix well. Chill until firm. Shape into ball; roll in mixture of pecans and parsley. Chill until serving time. Serve with crackers.
Yield: 30 (1-ounce) servings.

Approx Per Serving: Cal 61; Prot 4 g; Carbo 1 g; Fiber <1 g;
    T Fat 5 g; 72% Calories from Fat; Chol 16 mg; Sod 124 mg.

Colleen Bastian, Escanaba

Salmon Party Balls

1 16-ounce can red salmon, drained, flaked
8 ounces cream cheese, softened
2 teaspoons grated onion
1 tablespoon lemon juice
2 teaspoons prepared horseradish
2 teaspoons salt
1/2 cup chopped walnuts
3 tablespoons parsley

Combine salmon, cream cheese, onion, lemon juice, horseradish and salt in bowl; mix well. Chill, covered, for several hours to overnight. Shape into small balls; roll in mixture of walnuts and parsley. Chill until serving time. **Yield: 30 servings.**

Approx Per Serving: Cal 61; Prot 4 g; Carbo 1 g; Fiber <1 g;
    T Fat 5 g; 70% Calories from Fat; Chol 16 mg; Sod 249 mg.

Nellie Thompson, Romulus

Shrimp Ball

3 ounces cream cheese, softened
2 tablespoons mayonnaise
1 tablespoon catsup
1 teaspoon prepared mustard
1 teaspoon finely chopped onion
Garlic salt to taste
1/2 6-ounce can shrimp, drained
1/4 cup chopped parsley

Combine cream cheese, mayonnaise, catsup, mustard, onion and garlic salt in bowl; mix well. Fold in shrimp. Shape into ball; arrange on serving plate. Sprinkle with parsley. May beat with mixer to form smooth spread. **Yield: 10 (1-ounce) servings.**

Approx Per Serving: Cal 62; Prot 3 g; Carbo 1 g; Fiber <1 g;
    T Fat 5 g; 77% Calories from Fat; Chol 26 mg; Sod 80 mg.

Helen E. Jacobs, Lansing

Bar Cheese à la Win Shooter's

16 ounces Velveeta cheese
1 cup margarine, softened
8 ounces cream cheese, softened
1 5-ounce bottle of prepared horseradish
1/4 cup melted, strained bacon drippings
2 tablespoons onion juice
1/8 teaspoon Tabasco sauce
2 drops each of red and yellow food coloring

Combine all ingredients in glass mixer bowl. Microwave on Medium-High until melted, stirring occasionally. Beat at high speed until smooth. May store several weeks in refrigerator or up to 6 months in freezer. **Yield: 40 (1-ounce) servings.**

Approx Per Serving: Cal 117; Prot 3 g; Carbo 1 g; Fiber <1 g;
    T Fat 12 g; 87% Calories from Fat; Chol 25 mg; Sod 250 mg.

Doris Ratell, Tawas City

Jezebel Sauce

1   15-ounce jar apple jelly
1   15-ounce jar apricot preserves
1   5-ounce jar prepared horseradish

1   1-ounce can dry mustard
8 ounces cream cheese, softened

Combine jelly, preserves, horseradish and mustard in bowl; mix well. Place cream cheese on serving plate. Pour 1 cup sauce over cream cheese. Serve with crackers. May store remaining sauce in refrigerator for up to 1 year. **Yield: 36 servings.**

Approx Per Serving: Cal 92; Prot 1 g; Carbo 18 g; Fiber <1 g;
        T Fat 2 g; 23% Calories from Fat; Chol 7 mg; Sod 26 mg.

Sheila McMeel, Lansing

Cheese Spread

2 pounds Velveeta cheese, cubed
1 pound bacon, crisp-fried, crumbled
8 ounces mayonnaise

8 ounces prepared horseradish
Salt to taste

Melt cheese in saucepan, stirring frequently. Combine with bacon, mayonnaise, horseradish and salt in bowl; mix well. Chill overnight. Serve with crackers. May add 1 ounce beer, wine or liquor and sprinkle with paprika.
Yield: 60 (1-ounce) servings.

Approx Per Serving: Cal 103; Prot 5 g; Carbo 1 g; Fiber <1 g;
        T Fat 9 g; 80% Calories from Fat; Chol 20 mg; Sod 155 mg.

Nancy J. Furney, Kalamazoo

Liverwurst Spread

8 ounces liverwurst
4 slices crisp-fried bacon, crumbled
1 tablespoon chopped chives

1 tablespoon dark rum
3 tablespoons butter, softened

Mash liverwurst in bowl with fork until smooth. Add bacon, chives, rum and butter; mix well. Serve with toast or crackers. **Yield: 8 (1-ounce) servings.**

Approx Per Serving: Cal 153; Prot 5 g; Carbo 1 g; Fiber <1 g;
        T Fat 14 g; 85% Calories from Fat; Chol 58 mg; Sod 173 mg.

Shirley A. Cook, Lansing

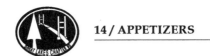

Mushroom Spread

4 slices bacon
8 ounces mushrooms, chopped
1/2 cup chopped onion
1 clove of garlic, minced
2 tablespoons flour
1/4 teaspoon salt

1/8 teaspoon pepper
8 ounces cream cheese, cubed
2 teaspoons Worcestershire sauce
1 teaspoon soy sauce
1/2 cup sour cream

Fry bacon in skillet until crisp. Drain, reserving 2 tablespoons drippings. Crumble bacon and set aside. Sauté mushrooms, onion and garlic in reserved drippings in skillet until tender. Stir in flour, salt and pepper. Add cream cheese, Worcestershire sauce and soy sauce; mix well. Cook over low heat until heated through and cream cheese is melted, stirring constantly. Stir in sour cream. Serve warm with rye bread or crackers. **Yield: 26 (1-ounce) servings.**

Approx Per Serving: Cal 61; Prot 1 g; Carbo 2 g; Fiber <1 g;
T Fat 6 g; 81% Calories from Fat; Chol 19 mg; Sod 92 mg.

Mary Helen Riggle, Charlevoix

Seafood Cracker Spread

16 ounces cream cheese, softened
2 tablespoons minced onion
1/4 teaspoon Worcestershire sauce

1/4 teaspoon seasoned salt
1   6-ounce can crab meat
1   12-ounce jar cocktail sauce

Combine cream cheese, onion, Worcestershire sauce, salt and crab meat in bowl; mix well. Shape into mound on serving plate. Cover with cocktail sauce. Serve with crackers. **Yield: 25 (1-ounce) servings.**

Approx Per Serving: Cal 86; Prot 3 g; Carbo 4 g; Fiber <1 g;
T Fat 6 g; 67% Calories from Fat; Chol 26 mg; Sod 190 mg.

Fran Lubic, Kalamazoo

Shrimp Spread

8 ounces cream cheese, softened
3 green onions, chopped

1   4-ounce can tiny shrimp
Garlic powder to taste

Combine cream cheese, green onions, shrimp and garlic powder in bowl; mix well. Serve with crackers or garlic toast. **Yield: 12 (1-ounce) servings.**

Approx Per Serving: Cal 76; Prot 3 g; Carbo 1 g; Fiber <1 g;
T Fat 7 g; 79% Calories from Fat; Chol 35 mg; Sod 273 mg.

Betty Boyd, Hemlock

Avocado Dip

2 avocados
2 tablespoons lemon juice
3 green onions, chopped
1 tomato, chopped

1 4-ounce can chopped green
   chilies, drained
1/2 teaspoon garlic powder
1/4 teaspoon salt

Mash avocados with lemon juice in bowl. Combine with green onions, tomato, green chilies, garlic powder and salt in bowl using pastry blender. Spoon into serving bowl. Serve with chips or cucumber slices. **Yield: 30 (1-ounce) servings.**

Approx Per Serving: Cal 24; Prot <1 g; Carbo 2 g; Fiber 1 g;
       T Fat 2 g; 71% Calories from Fat; Chol 0 mg; Sod 46 mg.

Mary Keeney, Lansing

Crab Dip

8 ounces cream cheese, softened
1/2 cup mayonnaise
1/2 cup catsup
1 teaspoon grated onion

2 teaspoons lemon juice
1 6-ounce package frozen crab meat,
   thawed

Combine cream cheese, mayonnaise, catsup, onion, lemon juice and crab meat in bowl; mix well. Spoon into serving bowl. **Yield: 23 (1-ounce) servings.**

Approx Per Serving: Cal 80; Prot 2 g; Carbo 2 g; Fiber <1 g;
       T Fat 7 g; 81% Calories from Fat; Chol 21 mg; Sod 142 mg.

Lucile Keckritz, Lansing

Chipped Beef Dip

1 cup sour cream
6 ounces cream cheese, softened
4 ounces dried beef, minced
2 dill pickles, finely chopped

1 teaspoon Worcestershire sauce
2 teaspoons prepared horseradish
Lemon juice and pepper to taste

Beat sour cream and cream cheese in mixer bowl until light and fluffy. Stir in dried beef, pickles, Worcestershire sauce, horseradish, lemon juice and pepper; mix well. Spoon into serving bowl; chill. Serve with chips or crackers.
Yield: 18 (1-ounce) servings.

Approx Per Serving: Cal 72; Prot 3 g; Carbo 1 g; Fiber <1 g;
       T Fat 6 g; 77% Calories from Fat; Chol 26 mg; Sod 339 mg.

Karen Doty, Eau Claire

Braunschweiger Dip

8 ounces braunschweiger, at room
  temperature
1 tablespoon mayonnaise-type salad
  dressing

8 ounces cream cheese, softened
1/4 cup finely chopped onion
3 hard-boiled eggs, chopped

Beat braunschweiger, salad dressing and cream cheese in mixer bowl until fluffy. Stir in onion and eggs. Shape into ball in serving bowl. Chill until serving time. Serve with crackers. **Yield: 20 (1-ounce) servings.**

Approx Per Serving: Cal 96; Prot 3 g; Carbo 1 g; Fiber <1 g;
    T Fat 9 g; 81% Calories from Fat; Chol 62 mg; Sod 178 mg.

Mary Ann Sprow, Lansing

Cheese and Sausage Dip

2 pounds bulk sausage
2 pounds Velveeta cheese, cubed
1   13-ounce can evaporated milk

1   2-ounce jar chopped pimento,
    drained
1 envelope Italian salad dressing mix

Brown sausage in skillet over medium high heat, stirring until sausage is crumbly; drain well. Combine cheese and evaporated milk in skillet. Cook over low heat until cheese is melted, stirring constantly. Stir in cooked sausage, pimento and salad dressing mix. Serve warm with tortilla chips. **Yield: 40 (1-ounce) servings.**

Approx Per Serving: Cal 137; Prot 8 g; Carbo 2 g; Fiber <1 g;
    T Fat 11 g; 73% Calories from Fat; Chol 33 mg; Sod 496 mg.

Nancy J. Furney, Kalamazoo

Golden Garden Dip

8 ounces Velveeta cheese, cubed
1/4 cup milk
1/2 cup sour cream
2 tablespoons finely chopped onion

2 tablespoons finely chopped green
  bell pepper
2 tablespoons finely chopped
  pimento

Combine cheese and milk in saucepan. Cook over low heat until cheese is melted and sauce is smooth, stirring constantly. Add sour cream, onion, green pepper and pimento; mix well. Chill in bowl until serving time. Serve with assorted fresh vegetables. **Yield: 26 (1-tablespoon) servings.**

Approx Per Serving: Cal 44; Prot 2 g; Carbo 1 g; Fiber <1 g;
    T Fat 4 g; 75% Calories from Fat; Chol 11 mg; Sod 128 mg.

Evelyn Helmer, Lansing

Nacho Cheese Sauce and Tortilla Chips

1 onion, cut into quarters
1/2 cup butter
Finely chopped chili peppers to taste
1 teaspoon minced garlic
1 teaspoon cumin

1 28-ounce can tomatoes, drained
2 pounds Velveeta cheese, cubed
1 50-count package corn tortillas
Oil for deep frying

Process onion in blender or food processor until finely chopped. Sauté onion in butter in skillet until tender. Add chili peppers, garlic and cumin. Cook over low heat, stirring occasionally. Process tomatoes in blender or food processor until finely chopped. Add to onion mixture with cheese. Simmer until cheese melts and sauce thickens, stirring constantly. Serve warm in slow-cooker or chafing dish. Cut tortillas into quarters. Deep-fry in hot oil until light brown and crisp; drain. Serve with cheese sauce. **Yield: 72 (1-ounce) servings.**

Approx Per Serving: Cal 106; Prot 4 g; Carbo 10 g; Fiber 2 g;
T Fat 6 g; 49% Calories from Fat; Chol 15 mg; Sod 210 mg.
Nutritional information does not include oil for deep frying.

Naomi S. Coronado, Madison Heights

Jan's Favorite Nacho Dip

2 pounds ground beef
1 15-ounce can Mexican-style
stewed tomatoes, mashed
16 ounces Velveeta cheese, cubed

16 ounces Mexican-style Velveeta
cheese, cubed
1 8-ounce can tomato sauce
1/2 teaspoon chili powder

Brown ground beef in skillet, stirring until crumbly; drain. Add tomatoes, cheeses, tomato sauce and chili powder. Cook over low heat until cheese is melted, stirring frequently. May serve in slow-cooker to keep warm. May also add red pepper for extra spicy dip. **Yield: 70 (1-ounce) servings.**

Approx Per Serving: Cal 72; Prot 5 g; Carbo 2 g; Fiber <1 g;
T Fat 5 g; 64% Calories from Fat; Chol 19 mg; Sod 241 mg.

Janice Bailey, Lansing

*Vary dips by substituting yogurt for sour cream or
Neufchâtel cheese for cream cheese.*

Parmesan-Spinach Dip

1 10-ounce package frozen chopped
   spinach, thawed, drained
1 cup grated Parmesan cheese
1 onion, chopped
1 clove of garlic, chopped

4 ounces cream cheese, softened
1 cup mayonnaise
Salt and pepper to taste
1/2 cup grated Parmesan cheese
1 teaspoon paprika

Combine spinach, 1 cup Parmesan cheese, onion, garlic, cream cheese, mayonnaise, salt and pepper in bowl; mix well. Spoon into greased casserole. Sprinkle with 1/2 cup Parmesan cheese and paprika. Bake at 350 degrees until bubbly. Serve with crackers or bread. **Yield: 35 (1-ounce) servings.**

Approx Per Serving: Cal 76; Prot 2 g; Carbo 1 g; Fiber <1 g;
     T Fat 7 g; 83% Calories from Fat; Chol 10 mg; Sod 117 mg.

Marilyn Rogers, Lansing

Shrimp Dip

8 ounces cream cheese, softened
1/3 cup sour cream
1 teaspoon onion juice
11/2 teaspoons Worcestershire sauce

1 teaspoon Dijon mustard
3 to 4 drops of Tabasco sauce
3/4 cup chopped cooked shrimp

Beat cream cheese and sour cream in mixer bowl until light and fluffy. Add onion juice, Worcestershire sauce, mustard and Tabasco sauce; mix well. Fold in shrimp. Chill until serving time. Serve with chips or crackers. **Yield: 15 (1-ounce) servings.**

Approx Per Serving: Cal 80; Prot 4 g; Carbo 1 g; Fiber 0 g;
     T Fat 7 g; 74% Calories from Fat; Chol 48 mg; Sod 95 mg.

Diane Rothenthaler, Grand Rapids

Texas Caviar

2 15-ounce cans black-eyed peas,
   drained
2 tomatoes, peeled, chopped
1 red onion, chopped
1/8 teaspoon salt

2 15-ounce cans white hominy,
   drained
1/2 green bell pepper, finely chopped
1 12-ounce jar picante sauce
Hot pepper sauce to taste

Combine all ingredients in bowl; mix well. Chill for 2 to 3 hours. Spoon into serving bowl. Serve with tortilla chips. **Yield: 100 (1-ounce) servings.**

Approx Per Serving: Cal 14; Prot 1 g; Carbo 3 g; Fiber 1 g;
     T Fat <1 g; 7% Calories from Fat; Chol <1 mg; Sod 72 mg.

Kay Collins, Lansing

Tex-Mex Dip

3 ripe avocados
2 tablespoons lemon juice
1/2 teaspoon salt
1/4 teaspoon pepper
1 cup sour cream
1/2 cup mayonnaise-type salad dressing
1 envelope taco seasoning mix

2 10-ounce cans jalapeño bean dip
1 bunch green onions, chopped
3 tomatoes, seeded, chopped
2 3-ounce cans black olives,
   drained, chopped
8 ounces sharp Cheddar cheese,
   shredded

Mash avocados with lemon juice, salt and pepper in medium bowl until smooth. Mix sour cream, salad dressing and taco mix in small bowl. Layer bean dip, avocado mixture, sour cream mixture, green onions, tomatoes, olives and cheese on shallow serving platter. Serve with tortilla chips. **Yield: 80 (1-ounce) servings.**

Approx Per Serving: Cal 51; Prot 1 g; Carbo 3 g; Fiber 1 g;
    T Fat 4 g; 69% Calories from Fat; Chol 5 mg; Sod 145 mg.

Carolyn Devers, Laingsburg

Vegetable Dip

2/3 cup mayonnaise
2/3 cup sour cream
1 teaspoon seasoned salt
1 teaspoon dillweed
1/2 teaspoon Worcestershire sauce

1/2 teaspoon MSG
1 tablespoon parsley flakes
1 tablespoon minced onion
2 drops of Tabasco sauce

Beat mayonnaise and sour cream in bowl until smooth. Stir in remaining ingredients. Chill overnight. Serve with fresh vegetables. **Yield: 12 (1-ounce) servings.**

Approx Per Serving: Cal 115; Prot 1 g; Carbo 1 g; Fiber <1 g;
    T Fat 12 g; 95% Calories from Fat; Chol 13 mg; Sod 365 mg.

Ruth Flanagan, Rockford

Apple Dip

1 14-ounce can sweetened
   condensed milk
1 cup butterscotch chips

1/2 teaspoon cinnamon
1 teaspoon white vinegar

Combine condensed milk and butterscotch chips in saucepan. Cook over low heat until chips are melted, stirring constantly. Add cinnamon and vinegar, stirring to blend. Serve warm with sliced apples. **Yield: 20 servings.**

Approx Per Serving: Cal 107; Prot 2 g; Carbo 16 g; Fiber <1 g;
    T Fat 5 g; 38% Calories from Fat; Chol 7 mg; Sod 26 mg.

Ann Hull, Charlotte

Caramel Apple Dip

8 ounces cream cheese, softened
1 teaspoon caramel extract
1 teaspoon vanilla extract

¼ cup sugar
⅔ cup packed brown sugar

Beat cream cheese with flavorings, sugar and brown sugar in mixer bowl until light and fluffy. Chill until serving time. Serve with apple slices. May sprinkle dip with chopped nuts. **Yield: 16 (1-ounce) servings.**

Approx Per Serving: Cal 95; Prot 1 g; Carbo 12 g; Fiber 0 g;
    T Fat 5 g; 46% Calories from Fat; Chol 16 mg; Sod 46 mg.

Winifred Johnson, Marquette

Easy Fruit Dip

8 ounces cream cheese, softened

1   7-ounce jar marshmallow creme

Combine cream cheese and marshmallow creme in bowl, beating until smooth. Serve with sliced bananas, apples, pineapple and strawberries. May add a few drops of red food coloring. **Yield: 15 (1-ounce) servings.**

Approx Per Serving: Cal 95; Prot 1 g; Carbo 11 g; Fiber 0 g;
    T Fat 5 g; 49% Calories from Fat; Chol 17 mg; Sod 52 mg.

Vikki Bittner, Grand Rapids

Piña Colada Fruit Dip

8 ounces cream cheese, softened
2 envelopes piña colada drink mix
3 tablespoons sugar

1 tablespoon rum
1 tablespoon milk

Combine cream cheese, drink mix, sugar, rum and milk in mixer bowl; beat well. Chill in refrigerator for 1 hour before serving. Serve with fresh fruit. **Yield: 10 (1-ounce) servings.**

Approx Per Serving: Cal 98; Prot 2 g; Carbo 4 g; Fiber 0 g;
    T Fat 8 g; 74% Calories from Fat; Chol 25 mg; Sod 68 mg.
    Nutritional information does not include piña colada drink mix.

Harriett De Vries, Kalamazoo

Antipasto

2 cups oil
1½ cups vinegar
1 quart dill pickles, drained, chopped
6 4-ounce cans chopped olives
4 onions, chopped
4 green bell peppers, chopped
3 stalks celery, chopped

½ head cauliflower, chopped
1 8-ounce can chopped mushrooms, drained
2 6-ounce cans tomato paste
1 12-ounce bottle of catsup
4 6-ounce cans tuna, drained
2 tablespoons salt

Bring all ingredients to a boil in large saucepan; reduce heat. Cook over low heat for 15 minutes or until vegetables are tender, stirring occasionally. Pour into 5 sterilized 1-quart jars leaving ½ inch headspace; seal with 2-piece lids. Serve cold with crackers. **Yield: 150 (1-ounce) servings.**

Approx Per Serving: Cal 47; Prot 2 g; Carbo 2 g; Fiber 1 g;
T Fat 4 g; 71% Calories from Fat; Chol 3 mg; Sod 237 mg.

Violet Latin, Traverse City

West Coast Crab Appetizers

8 ounces processed cheese spread
¾ cup butter
1 4-ounce can chopped mushrooms, drained

16 ounces crab meat, shredded
2 6-count packages English muffins, split, toasted, cut into quarters

Melt cheese and butter over low heat in saucepan, stirring frequently. Stir in mushrooms and crab meat. Arrange muffin quarters on baking sheet. Spread with crab meat mixture. Broil 5 inches from heat source until light brown. **Yield: 12 servings.**

Approx Per Serving: Cal 337; Prot 16 g; Carbo 28 g; Fiber 2 g;
T Fat 17 g; 47% Calories from Fat; Chol 80 mg; Sod 874 mg.

Joyce Olson, Mesa, Arizona

Cheese Curds

16 ounces skim-milk mozzarella cheese, cubed
2 eggs, beaten

Salt to taste
1 cup herb-seasoned bread crumbs

Dip cheese cubes in mixture of eggs and salt; roll in bread crumbs. Arrange in baking pan sprayed with nonstick cooking spray. Bake at 425 degrees for 20 minutes. **Yield: 32 servings.**

Approx Per Serving: Cal 57; Prot 5 g; Carbo 3 g; Fiber <1 g;
T Fat 3 g; 47% Calories from Fat; Chol 21 mg; Sod 102 mg.

June B. Brown, Bradenton, Florida

Cheese-Stuffed Mushrooms

20 fresh mushrooms
6 slices bacon
1 small onion, finely chopped

2 tablespoons mayonnaise-type salad
   dressing
½ cup shredded Cheddar cheese

Remove stems from mushrooms, reserving caps; chop stems finely. Fry bacon in skillet until crisp; crumble and set aside. Drain skillet, reserving 2 tablespoons bacon drippings. Sauté chopped mushroom stems and onion in reserved bacon drippings for 3 minutes; drain. Combine with bacon, salad dressing and cheese in small bowl; mix well. Spoon mixture into mushroom caps. Arrange on ungreased baking sheet. Bake at 350 degrees for 15 to 20 minutes or until cheese is melted. **Yield: 20 servings.**

Approx Per Serving: Cal 35; Prot 2 g; Carbo 2 g; Fiber <1 g;
   T Fat 2 g; 62% Calories from Fat; Chol 5 mg; Sod 59 mg.

Sally Taylor, Marquette

Chicken Wings

24 chicken wings
¼ cup packed brown sugar
1 5-ounce bottle of soy sauce

½ teaspoon garlic powder
1 teaspoon Dijon mustard

Rinse chicken wings and pat dry; discard tips. Mix remaining ingredients in shallow bowl. Add chicken wings, turning to coat. Marinate in refrigerator for 2 hours. Arrange in baking pan. Bake at 375 degrees for 1 hour. May add sherry, ginger, chopped green onions or Chinese spices to marinade. **Yield: 24 servings.**

Approx Per Serving: Cal 113; Prot 9 g; Carbo 3 g; Fiber <1 g;
   T Fat 7 g; 54% Calories from Fat; Chol 29 mg; Sod 372 mg.

Astrid Bailey, Menominee

Bourbon Franks

1 cup catsup
1 cup packed brown sugar
¾ cup bourbon

2 16-ounce packages frankfurters,
   cut into quarters

Combine catsup, brown sugar and bourbon in bowl. Add frankfurters. Spoon into 9x13-inch baking pan. Bake at 275 degrees for 1 to 3 hours, stirring often. Serve warm in chafing dish with wooden picks. **Yield: 40 servings.**

Approx Per Serving: Cal 115; Prot 3 g; Carbo 9 g; Fiber <1 g;
   T Fat 7 g; 52% Calories from Fat; Chol 12 mg; Sod 328 mg.

Joan Howard, Grand Rapids

Spicy Sun Hot Dog Bites

1 cup tomato sauce
¹/₄ cup grated Parmesan cheese
1 tablespoon oil
¹/₄ teaspoon oregano

¹/₄ teaspoon salt
1 pound hot dogs, cut into 1-inch
   pieces

Combine tomato sauce, cheese, oil, oregano and salt in saucepan; mix well. Simmer until thickened, stirring frequently. Add hot dogs. Simmer until heated through. Serve warm in chafing dish with wooden picks. **Yield: 30 servings.**

Approx Per Serving: Cal 58; Prot 2 g; Carbo 1 g; Fiber <1 g;
   T Fat 5 g; 79% Calories from Fat; Chol 8 mg; Sod 249 mg.

Hazel M. Bergeron, Sault Ste. Marie

Hanky Pankys

1 pound ground beef
1 pound Italian sausage, casing
   removed
16 ounces Velveeta cheese, cubed

¹/₂ teaspoon crushed red pepper
¹/₂ teaspoon oregano
1 teaspoon garlic powder
1 loaf party rye bread

Brown ground beef and sausage in skillet, stirring until crumbly; drain. Add cheese, red pepper, oregano and garlic powder. Cook over low heat until cheese is melted, stirring frequently. Spread over slices of rye bread; arrange on broiler pan. Broil 5 inches from heat source for 2 minutes or until brown. **Yield: 72 servings.**

Approx Per Serving: Cal 56; Prot 3 g; Carbo 2 g; Fiber <1 g;
   T Fat 4 g; 63% Calories from Fat; Chol 13 mg; Sod 154 mg.

Lois Elliott, Escanaba

Turkey Hanky Pankys

1 pound ground turkey
1 pound hot sausage
1 tablespoon Worcestershire sauce
¹/₂ teaspoon garlic salt

Salt and pepper to taste
16 ounces Velveeta cheese, cubed
1 loaf party rye bread

Brown ground turkey and sausage in skillet, stirring until crumbly; drain. Add Worcestershire sauce, garlic salt, salt, pepper and cheese. Cook over low heat until cheese is melted, stirring frequently. Spread over slices of rye bread; arrange on broiler pan. Broil 5 inches from heat source until cheese bubbles. May freeze on baking sheet and store in plastic bags until needed. **Yield: 72 servings.**

Approx Per Serving: Cal 54; Prot 3 g; Carbo 2 g; Fiber <1 g;
   T Fat 4 g; 61% Calories from Fat; Chol 12 mg; Sod 172 mg.

Marie Fineout, Cheboygan

Party Meatballs

2 pounds ground beef
1 envelope onion soup mix
1 egg, beaten
2 teaspoons MSG

½ cup bread crumbs
2   14-ounce bottles of hot catsup
1   10-ounce jar currant jelly

Combine first 5 ingredients in bowl; mix well. Shape into 1½-inch balls; arrange on baking sheet. Bake at 350 degrees for 10 to 15 minutes or until brown; drain well. Combine catsup and jelly in slow-cooker. Cook on High until smooth, stirring occasionally. Add meatballs. Simmer on Low until serving time. **Yield: 32 servings.**

Approx Per Serving: Cal 114; Prot 6 g; Carbo 13 g; Fiber <1 g;
     T Fat 4 g; 34% Calories from Fat; Chol 25 mg; Sod 572 mg.

Alice Brechtelsbauer, Saginaw

Party Pinwheels

16 ounces cream cheese, softened
1 envelope ranch salad dressing mix
2 green onions, minced
4   12-inch flour tortillas

½ cup chopped red bell pepper
½ cup chopped celery
1   4-ounce can chopped black olives

Mix first 3 ingredients in bowl. Spread over tortillas. Sprinkle with chopped red pepper, celery and olives. Roll up and wrap tightly with plastic wrap. Chill for 2 hours. Slice off ends. Cut remainder into 1-inch slices. **Yield: 36 servings.**

Approx Per Serving: Cal 69; Prot 1 g; Carbo 4 g; Fiber <1 g;
     T Fat 6 g; 69% Calories from Fat; Chol 14 mg; Sod 139 mg.

Evelyn Fox, Grand Rapids

Cold Vegetable Pizza

1   8-count can crescent rolls
½ cup mayonnaise
8 ounces cream cheese, softened
1 envelope ranch salad dressing mix
½ cup chopped broccoli

½ cup chopped carrots
½ cup chopped green bell pepper
½ cup chopped red bell pepper
1   2-ounce can chopped black olives

Press crescent roll dough over baking sheet, sealing perforations. Bake at 375 degrees for 6 minutes; cool. Beat mayonnaise, cream cheese and salad dressing mix in mixer bowl until light and fluffy. Spread over prepared crust. Scatter vegetables and black olives over top. Cut into small squares to serve. **Yield: 48 servings.**

Approx Per Serving: Cal 54; Prot 1 g; Carbo 3 g; Fiber <1 g;
     T Fat 5 g; 76% Calories from Fat; Chol 7 mg; Sod 115 mg.

Ardith Smith, Mecosta

Rumaki

1 8-ounce can whole water
  chestnuts, drained
1 pound bacon

1/2 cup catsup
1/3 cup sugar
1 teaspoon soy sauce

Cut water chestnuts and bacon slices into halves. Wrap bacon around water chestnuts, securing with wooden picks. Arrange in foil-lined baking pan. Bake at 350 degrees for 20 minutes; drain. Combine catsup, sugar and soy sauce in small bowl; mix well. Pour over chestnuts. Bake for 10 minutes longer. **Yield: 20 servings.**

Approx Per Serving: Cal 65; Prot 2 g; Carbo 6 g; Fiber <1 g;
   T Fat 3 g; 46% Calories from Fat; Chol 6 mg; Sod 198 mg.

Cindy Fogg, Otsego

Brandied Sausages

1 pound Polish sausage, sliced
1 cup catsup
1/4 cup packed brown sugar

1 teaspoon Worcestershire sauce
1/2 teaspoon minced onion
3/4 cup brandy

Simmer sausage in skillet for 30 minutes; drain. Combine catsup, brown sugar, Worcestershire sauce, onion and brandy in saucepan; mix well. Simmer for 30 minutes. Add sausage to sauce mixture. Simmer for 30 minutes. Serve hot. **Yield: 16 servings.**

Approx Per Serving: Cal 109; Prot 3 g; Carbo 13 g; Fiber <1 g;
   T Fat 4 g; 35% Calories from Fat; Chol 11 mg; Sod 355 mg.

Kay Lake, Marquette

Sausage Appetizers

1 pound fully-cooked smoked pork
  sausage

1 6-ounce jar mustard
1 12-ounce jar peach preserves

Cut sausage links diagonally into bite-sized pieces. Combine mustard and preserves in saucepan; mix well. Add sausage. Simmer for 15 minutes. Serve in fondue pot. **Yield: 12 servings.**

Approx Per Serving: Cal 153; Prot 4 g; Carbo 21 g; Fiber <1 g;
   T Fat 6 g; 36% Calories from Fat; Chol 15 mg; Sod 410 mg.

Marlene Carter, Kingsford

Stuffed Pita Bread

1   10-ounce package frozen chopped
   spinach
1 cup sour cream
1 cup mayonnaise
1 envelope vegetable soup mix

2 teaspoons chopped green onions
1/2   8-ounce can water chestnuts,
   drained, chopped
1   6-count package pita bread, cut
   into quarters

Cook spinach using package directions; drain well. Mix with next 5 ingredients in bowl. Stuff pita quarters with mixture. Serve immediately or chill for later. May add ham, chicken or chopped beef to mixture. **Yield: 24 servings.**

Approx Per Serving: Cal 138; Prot 3 g; Carbo 11 g; Fiber 1 g;
   T Fat 10 g; 61% Calories from Fat; Chol 10 mg; Sod 260 mg.

Mike Gardner, Traverse City

Vegetable-Cheese Pita Sandwiches

1 tablespoon butter
1 cup each sliced cauliflower,
   broccoli and carrots
1/2 cup sliced green onions

1 cup chopped tomatoes
1/4 teaspoon each oregano and basil
1 cup shredded Cheddar cheese
4 pita bread rounds, cut into halves

Combine butter, cauliflower, broccoli and carrots in 2-quart microwave-safe dish; cover with plastic wrap. Microwave on High for 3 to 4 minutes or until vegetables are tender. Add green onions, tomatoes, oregano, basil and cheese; toss well. Spoon mixture into pita bread pockets. Wrap each in paper towel; place cut side up in microwave-safe dish. Microwave for 3^{1}/2 minutes. **Yield: 8 servings.**

Approx Per Serving: Cal 168; Prot 8 g; Carbo 20 g; Fiber 2 g;
   T Fat 7 g; 35% Calories from Fat; Chol 19 mg; Sod 279 mg.

Barb Buskirk, Portland

Spinach Balls

2   10-ounce packages frozen
   chopped spinach
2 cups stuffing mix
3/4 cup butter, softened

6 eggs, beaten
1 cup grated Parmesan cheese
1 teaspoon pepper

Cook spinach using package directions; drain well. Combine with stuffing mix, butter, eggs, cheese and pepper in bowl; mix well. Shape into 1-inch balls; arrange on baking sheet. Bake at 350 degrees for 10 minutes. **Yield: 48 servings.**

Approx Per Serving: Cal 57; Prot 2 g; Carbo 3 g; Fiber <1 g;
   T Fat 4 g; 65% Calories from Fat; Chol 36 mg; Sod 113 mg.

Ann Blaser, Traverse City

Zucchini Appetizers

1 cup baking mix
1/2 cup grated Parmesan cheese
1/2 teaspoon salt
Pepper to taste
1/2 teaspoon seasoned salt
1/2 cup chopped onion

2 teaspoons parsley
1/2 teaspoon oregano
1 clove of garlic, crushed
4 eggs, slightly beaten
1/2 cup oil
3 cups sliced unpeeled zucchini

Combine first 11 ingredients in large bowl; mix well. Stir in zucchini. Pour into greased 9x13-inch baking pan. Bake at 325 degrees for 25 minutes; cool. Cut into squares to serve. **Yield: 24 servings.**

Approx Per Serving: Cal 88; Prot 2 g; Carbo 4 g; Fiber <1 g;
     T Fat 7 g; 69% Calories from Fat; Chol 37 mg; Sod 181 mg.

Nancy Ramey, Saginaw

Summer Sausage

5 pounds ground beef
5 teaspoons (heaping) Tender-Quick salt
2 teaspoons mustard seed

2 1/2 teaspoons garlic salt
2 1/2 teaspoons coarsely ground pepper
2 tablespoons liquid smoke

Combine all ingredients in bowl; mix well. Chill, covered, in refrigerator overnight. Shape into logs. Place on rack in baking pan. Bake at 200 degrees for 6 to 8 hours; cool. Wrap tightly. Store in refrigerator or freezer. **Yield: 75 (1-ounce) servings.**

Approx Per Serving: Cal 62; Prot 6 g; Carbo <1 g; Fiber 0 g;
     T Fat 4 g; 63% Calories from Fat; Chol 20 mg; Sod 203 mg.

Shirley Sullivan Wellington, Zephyrhills, Florida

Salami

2 pounds ground beef
2 tablespoons Tender-Quick salt
1 teaspoon garlic powder
1 teaspoon onion powder

1 teaspoon mustard seed
1 teaspoon cracked black pepper
1/4 teaspoon cayenne pepper
1/2 cup water

Combine ground beef, salt, garlic powder, onion powder, mustard seed, black pepper, cayenne pepper and water in bowl; mix well. Chill, covered, overnight. Shape into two 4-inch rolls. Wrap in foil. Place in large pan of hot water. Bring to a boil. Cook for 1 hour; cool. **Yield: 30 (1-ounce) servings.**

Approx Per Serving: Cal 62; Prot 6 g; Carbo 0 g; Fiber 0 g;
     T Fat 4 g; 63% Calories from Fat; Chol 20 mg; Sod 369 mg.

Leo Smith, Thompsonville

Caramel Corn

1 cup margarine
2 cups packed brown sugar
1/2 cup light corn syrup
1 teaspoon salt

1/2 teaspoon baking soda
1 teaspoon vanilla extract
7 quarts popped popcorn

Melt margarine in skillet. Stir in brown sugar, corn syrup and salt. Bring to a boil. Cook for 5 minutes, stirring constantly; remove from heat. Stir in baking soda and vanilla. Pour over popped popcorn in large pan. Bake at 250 degrees for 1 hour, stirring occasionally. **Yield: 28 (1-cup) servings.**

Approx Per Serving: Cal 178; Prot 1 g; Carbo 29 g; Fiber 1 g;
    T Fat 7 g; 34% Calories from Fat; Chol 0 mg; Sod 179 mg.

Jennifer Harper, Kingsford

Popcorn Scramble

6 cups popped popcorn
2 cups rice Chex
2 cups Cheerios
1   8-ounce can salted peanuts
1/2 cup butter

1 cup packed brown sugar
1/4 cup light corn syrup
1/2 teaspoon baking soda
1 teaspoon vanilla extract

Toss popped popcorn, rice Chex, Cheerios and peanuts in large bowl. Combine butter, brown sugar and corn syrup in small saucepan. Bring to a boil over medium heat. Boil for 3 to 4 minutes, stirring occasionally. Remove from heat. Stir in baking soda and vanilla. Drizzle over popcorn mixture, tossing to coat. Spread on large baking sheet. Bake at 250 degrees for 1 hour or until golden brown, stirring often. Cool; store in airtight container. **Yield: 11 (1-cup) servings.**

Approx Per Serving: Cal 358; Prot 7 g; Carbo 44 g; Fiber 3 g;
    T Fat 19 g; 46% Calories from Fat; Chol 23 mg; Sod 294 mg.

Marion Heil, East Lansing

Oyster Crackers

1 envelope ranch salad dressing mix
1 tablespoon dillweed
1/2 teaspoon garlic powder

3/4 cup oil
1   11-ounce package oyster crackers

Combine first 4 ingredients in bowl; mix well. Pour over crackers in shallow pan. Stir every 15 minutes for 1 hour. Store in airtight container. **Yield: 10 servings.**

Approx Per Serving: Cal 284; Prot 3 g; Carbo 24 g; Fiber 1 g;
    T Fat 20 g; 63% Calories from Fat; Chol 0 mg; Sod 586 mg.

Pam Hamstra, Traverse City

Seasoned Snack Crackers

1 cup oil
1 envelope ranch salad dressing mix
2 teaspoons dillweed
1 teaspoon garlic powder
2 teaspoons lemon pepper
2 11-ounce packages oyster crackers

Mix oil, salad dressing mix, dillweed, garlic powder and lemon pepper in bowl. Pour over crackers in shallow baking pan, stirring to coat. Bake at 200 degrees for 15 to 20 minutes or until brown; cool. Store in airtight containers. **Yield: 22 servings.**

Approx Per Serving: Cal 210; Prot 3 g; Carbo 21 g; Fiber 1 g;
    T Fat 13 g; 56% Calories from Fat; Chol 0 mg; Sod 444 mg.

Rosemarie Raterink, Grand Rapids

Nibble Bait

1 5-ounce package cheese sticks
1 5-ounce package miniature
   pretzels
1 5-ounce package pretzel sticks
1 8-ounce package salted peanuts
1 12-ounce package bite-sized
   shredded wheat biscuits
1 6-ounce package shredded rice
   biscuits
2 cups margarine
1/3 cup Worcestershire sauce
2 teaspoons garlic salt
1 teaspoon onion salt
3 tablespoons chili powder

Combine cheese sticks, pretzels, pretzel sticks, peanuts, shredded wheat biscuits and shredded rice biscuits in large shallow baking pan. Melt margarine in saucepan. Add Worcestershire sauce, garlic salt, onion salt and chili powder; mix well. Pour over pretzel mixture, stirring to coat. Bake at 300 degrees for 1 hour, stirring twice; cool. Store in airtight containers. **Yield: 48 (4-ounce) servings.**

Approx Per Serving: Cal 169; Prot 4 g; Carbo 17 g; Fiber 2 g;
    T Fat 12 g; 58% Calories from Fat; Chol 1 mg; Sod 369 mg.

Amy Hoult, Rochester

Beer Peanuts

1 pound raw peanuts
1 cup sugar
1/2 cup water
1 1/2 teaspoons cinnamon

Combine peanuts, sugar and water in skillet; mix well. Cook over medium heat until liquid is absorbed, stirring occasionally. Spread on baking sheet; sprinkle with cinnamon. Bake at 300 degrees for 30 minutes, turning after 15 minutes. May omit cinnamon. **Yield: 4 (4-ounce) servings.**

Approx Per Serving: Cal 832; Prot 29 g; Carbo 70 g; Fiber 10 g;
    T Fat 54 g; 55% Calories from Fat; Chol 0 mg; Sod 10 mg.

Nina Cawley, Saginaw

Spiced Pecans

7 tablespoons butter
3 tablespoons chili powder
1 1/2 teaspoons salt

3/4 teaspoon cayenne pepper
1/2 teaspoon cinnamon
1 pound shelled pecans

Melt butter in large heavy skillet. Add chili powder, salt, cayenne pepper and cinnamon; mix well. Add pecans, stirring to coat. Remove pecans with slotted spoon to baking sheet. Bake at 350 degrees for 20 minutes. Drain on paper towels; cool. Store in airtight containers. **Yield: 16 servings.**

Approx Per Serving: Cal 238; Prot 2 g; Carbo 6 g; Fiber 2 g;
      T Fat 25 g; 87% Calories from Fat; Chol 14 mg; Sod 257 mg.

Teddy Zeedyk, Battle Creek

White Trash

1/2 cup margarine
2 cups semisweet chocolate chips
1 cup peanut butter
1 12-ounce package rice Chex

1 12-ounce can peanuts
1 15-ounce package raisins
1 1-pound package confectioners' sugar

Combine margarine, chocolate chips and peanut butter in saucepan. Cook over low heat until melted, stirring constantly. Combine cereal, peanuts and raisins in large bowl; mix well. Pour chocolate mixture over top, stirring well to coat. Pour into large plastic bag. Add confectioners' sugar; shake well to coat. **Yield: 16 (1/2-cup) servings.**

Approx Per Serving: Cal 672; Prot 13 g; Carbo 93 g; Fiber 7 g;
      T Fat 33 g; 41% Calories from Fat; Chol 0 mg; Sod 319 mg.

Juanita Kenyon, Plainwell

Bailey's Irish Cream

1/4 cup instant coffee
1 12-ounce can sweetened
   condensed milk

2 cups half and half
1/2 cup coffee-flavored liqueur
1 1/2 cups Canadian whiskey

Combine instant coffee and condensed milk in 1-quart container; mix until coffee is dissolved. Add half and half, liqueur and whiskey; mix well. Chill until serving time. **Yield: 6 (1-cup) servings.**

Approx Per Serving: Cal 494; Prot 7 g; Carbo 46 g; Fiber <1 g;
      T Fat 14 g; 26% Calories from Fat; Chol 49 mg; Sod 108 mg.

Harriett De Vries, Kalamazoo

Bloody Marys

2 quarts clamato juice
1 pint vodka
6 tablespoons fresh lemon juice
1/4 cup white wine Worcestershire
   sauce

1 teaspoon lemon pepper
1 teaspoon celery salt
1 teaspoon dillweed
1 teaspoon Tabasco sauce

Combine all ingredients in large container; mix well with wire whisk. Serve over ice with lime wedge. May substitute 3 tablespoons lime juice for 3 tablespoons lemon juice. Chill overnight to enhance the flavor. **Yield: 6 (1-cup) servings.**

Approx Per Serving: Cal 331; Prot 2 g; Carbo 38 g; Fiber <1 g;
   T Fat <1 g; 1% Calories from Fat; Chol 0 mg; Sod 1770 mg.

Esther M. Johnson, Rockford

Frozen Daiquiris

1 12-ounce can frozen lemonade
   concentrate, thawed
1 12-ounce can frozen limeade
   concentrate, thawed

2 12-ounce cans water
1 fifth white rum
1 quart 7-Up

Combine lemonade concentrate, limeade concentrate, water and white rum in large freezer container; mix well. Freeze, covered, until serving time. Spoon into daiquiri glasses. Serve with 7-Up. **Yield: 22 (1/2-cup) servings.**

Approx Per Serving: Cal 149; Prot <1 g; Carbo 20 g; Fiber <1 g;
   T Fat <1 g; 0% Calories from Fat; Chol 0 mg; Sod 6 mg.

Joan Sarvello, Marquette

Strawberry Daiquiris

1 10-ounce package frozen
   strawberries, thawed
6 ounces rum

1 6-ounce can frozen limeade
   concentrate, thawed
1 to 1 1/4 cups water

Purée strawberries in blender. Combine with rum, limeade concentrate and water in freezer container; mix well. Freeze, covered, until serving time. Spoon into daiquiri glasses. Serve with drinking straws. **Yield: 8 (1/2-cup) servings.**

Approx Per Serving: Cal 100; Prot <1 g; Carbo 14 g; Fiber 1 g;
   T Fat <1 g; 1% Calories from Fat; Chol 0 mg; Sod 1 mg.

Catherine Wojnaroski, Goetzville

Drinks

³/₄ cup sugar
1 cup water
1¹/₂ cups grapefruit juice

1 46-ounce can pineapple juice
1 quart ginger ale, chilled

Combine sugar and water in saucepan. Bring to a boil. Boil for 5 minutes, stirring occasionally. Combine with grapefruit juice and pineapple juice in large container; mix well. Chill until serving time. Pour into punch bowl. Add ginger ale, stirring gently to mix. **Yield: 16 (6-ounce) servings.**

Approx Per Serving: Cal 113; Prot <1 g; Carbo 29 g; Fiber <1 g;
    T Fat <1 g; 1% Calories from Fat; Chol 0 mg; Sod 6 mg.

Arlene E. Hatch, Hill City, Minnesota

Eggnog

12 egg yolks
1 cup sugar
1 quart milk
1 quart whipping cream

12 egg whites
2 cups whiskey
1 cup rum
Nutmeg to taste

Beat egg yolks with sugar in mixer bowl until light and lemon-colored. Add milk, cream and egg whites; beat until thickened. Add whiskey and rum; mix lightly. Chill until serving time. Ladle into cups; sprinkle with nutmeg. May add additional sugar and whiskey. **Yield: 20 (1-cup) servings.**

Approx Per Serving: Cal 356; Prot 6 g; Carbo 14 g; Fiber 0 g;
    T Fat 23 g; 57% Calories from Fat; Chol 200 mg; Sod 73 mg.

Bill Devers, Laingsburg

Gelatin Shots

1 3-ounce package fruit-flavored
    gelatin

1 cup boiling water
1 cup vodka

Dissolve gelatin in boiling water in bowl. Add vodka; mix well. Spoon into 1-ounce paper cups; place on tray. Chill until set. Squeeze bottom of paper cup and pop gelatin shot into mouth. Lemon gelatin with Tequila substituted for vodka is a good combination also. **Yield: 16 (1-ounce) servings.**

Approx Per Serving: Cal 51; Prot 1 g; Carbo 5 g; Fiber 0 g;
    T Fat 0 g; 0% Calories from Fat; Chol 0 mg; Sod 17 mg.

Pat Hyland, Iron Mountain

Kahlua

¼ cup instant coffee
2 cups boiling water
4 cups sugar

1 vanilla bean, cut into quarters
1 quart vodka

Dissolve instant coffee in boiling water in large container. Stir in sugar until dissolved. Add vanilla bean and vodka; mix well. Let stand, covered, for 30 days. May substitute brandy for vodka. **Yield: 16 (¹/₂-cup) servings.**

Approx Per Serving: Cal 320; Prot <1 g; Carbo 50 g; Fiber <1 g;
    T Fat <1 g; 0% Calories from Fat; Chol 0 mg; Sod 2 mg.

Bill Devers, Laingsburg

Banana Punch

4 cups sugar
6 cups water
1   46-ounce can pineapple juice
2   12-ounce cans frozen orange juice
    concentrate, thawed

1   12-ounce can frozen lemonade
    concentrate, thawed
5 bananas, mashed
3   2-liter lemon-lime sodas

Dissolve sugar in water in large container. Add next 4 ingredients; mix well. Ladle into freezer container, leaving 1-inch headspace. Freeze until firm. Let stand at room temperature until slightly thawed. Combine with lemon-lime sodas in punch bowl; stir gently. Ladle into punch cups. **Yield: 32 (6-ounce) servings.**

Approx Per Serving: Cal 261; Prot 1 g; Carbo 67 g; Fiber 1 g;
    T Fat <1 g; 1% Calories from Fat; Chol 0 mg; Sod 22 mg.

Catherine Wojnaroski, Goetzville

B-J Punch

2   3-ounce packages strawberry
    gelatin
¹/₂ cup sugar
2 cups boiling water
6 cups cold water
1   24-ounce can pineapple juice

1   12-ounce can frozen orange juice
    concentrate
1   12-ounce can frozen lemonade
    concentrate
1   28-ounce bottle of ginger ale,
    chilled

Dissolve gelatin and sugar in boiling water in large container. Add next 4 ingredients; mix well. Chill, covered, for 4 to 6 hours. Pour into punch bowl. Add ginger ale, stirring gently. **Yield: 24 (6-ounce) servings.**

Approx Per Serving: Cal 118; Prot 1 g; Carbo 29 g; Fiber <1 g;
    T Fat <1 g; 1% Calories from Fat; Chol 0 mg; Sod 26 mg.

Janice Sweet Fairley, Jackson

Christmas Punch

2 quarts orange juice
1 quart lemonade

2 liters cranberry juice cocktail
2 liters ginger ale, chilled

Combine orange juice, lemonade and cranberry juice cocktail in large container; mix well. Chill, covered, until serving time. Combine juice mixture and ginger ale in punch bowl; mix well. May add chipped ice and frozen cranberry juice cocktail ice ring if desired. May add spirits if desired. **Yield: 26 (6-ounce) servings.**

Approx Per Serving: Cal 117; Prot 1 g; Carbo 29 g; Fiber 1 g;
    T Fat <1 g; 2% Calories from Fat; Chol 0 mg; Sod 7 mg.

Mary Carey, Portage

Delicious Hot Punch

1 quart unsweetened orange juice
3 cups apple cider
1/4 cup sugar
1/4 cup packed brown sugar

1/4 teaspoon allspice
1/8 teaspoon ground cloves
6 tablespoons butter, softened
6 cinnamon sticks

Combine orange juice, apple cider, sugar, brown sugar, allspice and cloves in 2-quart saucepan. Bring to a boil. Reduce heat. Simmer for 5 minutes, stirring occasionally. Ladle into mugs. Top each with 1 tablespoon butter; add cinnamon stick stirrer. **Yield: 6 (1-cup) servings.**

Approx Per Serving: Cal 308; Prot 1 g; Carbo 51 g; Fiber 1 g;
    T Fat 12 g; 34% Calories from Fat; Chol 31 mg; Sod 107 mg.

Sally Taylor, Marquette

Fresca Punch

2 12-ounce cans Fresca
1 6-ounce can frozen limeade
   concentrate
4 12-ounce cans Fresca, chilled

1 46-ounce can pineapple juice,
   chilled
1 quart lime sherbet

Pour 2 cans Fresca into greased mold. Freeze until firm. Combine limeade concentrate, 4 cans Fresca and pineapple juice in punch bowl, stirring gently to mix. Unmold Fresca mold. Add to punch. Scoop out lime sherbet; add to punch. Ladle into cups. **Yield: 16 (6-ounce) servings.**

Approx Per Serving: Cal 185; Prot 1 g; Carbo 45 g; Fiber <1 g;
    T Fat 1 g; 5% Calories from Fat; Chol 4 mg; Sod 37 mg.

Fran Lubic, Kalamazoo

Lime-Pineapple Punch

2 envelopes lime drink mix
2 cups sugar
2 quarts water
1 quart ginger ale, chilled

1 46-ounce can pineapple juice, chilled
3 pints lime sherbet

Dissolve lime drink mix and sugar in water in bowl. Add ginger ale and pineapple juice; mix gently. Place lime sherbet in punch bowl. Add ginger ale mixture slowly. Ladle into cups. **Yield: 50 (1/2-cup) servings.**

Approx Per Serving: Cal 85; Prot <1 g; Carbo 20 g; Fiber <1 g;
    T Fat <1 g; 5% Calories from Fat; Chol 2 mg; Sod 12 mg.

Juanita Mansfield, Lansing

Papaya Punch

1 quart Squirt
1 quart papaya juice

1 pint rum
1 cup orange juice

Combine Squirt, papaya juice, rum and orange juice in large container. Chill until serving time. Pour into punch bowl. Ladle into cups. **Yield: 14 (6-ounce) servings.**

Approx Per Serving: Cal 149; Prot <1 g; Carbo 20 g; Fiber <1 g;
    T Fat <1 g; 1% Calories from Fat; Chol 0 mg; Sod 12 mg.

Becky Cartwright, Lansing

Strawberry Ice Cream Soda Punch

1 16-ounce package frozen
    strawberries
1/2 gallon vanilla ice cream

2 quarts strawberry soda
2 quarts ginger ale

Combine frozen strawberries, ice cream, strawberry soda and ginger ale in punch bowl. Let stand for 1 1/2 hours before serving. Stir gently. **Yield: 15 servings.**

Approx Per Serving: Cal 259; Prot 3 g; Carbo 56 g; Fiber 1 g;
    T Fat 8 g; 26% Calories from Fat; Chol 32 mg; Sod 88 mg.

Sandy Hines, Grandville

Slush

7 cups water	1 12-ounce can each frozen orange
2 cups sugar	juice concentrate and frozen
4 tea bags	lemonade concentrate
2 cups boiling water	4 28-ounce bottles of lemon-lime
2 cups whiskey	soda, chilled

Bring 7 cups water and sugar to a boil in saucepan, stirring until sugar dissolves. Cool. Steep tea bags in 2 cups boiling water for 20 minutes. Remove tea bags. Cool. Blend sugar syrup, tea, whiskey and concentrates in large container. Freeze until serving time. Add 1/2 cup mixture to 1/2 cup lemon-lime soda for each serving. **Yield: 28 (1-cup) servings.**

Approx Per Serving: Cal 179; Prot <1 g; Carbo 36 g; Fiber <1 g;
   T Fat <1 g; 0% Calories from Fat; Chol 0 mg; Sod 14 mg.

Wayne Carter, Kingsford

Pineapple Slush

1 46-ounce can pineapple juice	1/2 1-fifth vodka
1 6-ounce can frozen lemonade	6 28-ounce bottles of lemon-lime
concentrate	soda, chilled
1 12-ounce can cream of coconut	

Mix first 4 ingredients in large container. Chill, covered, until serving time. Add 1/3 cup mixture to 2/3 cup lemon-lime beverage for each serving. **Yield: 28 (1-cup) servings.**

Approx Per Serving: Cal 159; Prot <1 g; Carbo 27 g; Fiber <1 g;
   T Fat 3 g; 15% Calories from Fat; Chol 0 mg; Sod 21 mg.

Catherine Wojnaroski, Goetzville

Whiskey Slush

4 tea bags	1 12-ounce can each frozen orange
9 cups boiling water	juice concentrate and frozen
1 cup sugar	lemonade concentrate
1 fifth whiskey	1 quart sugar-free lemon-lime soda

Mix tea bags and 2 cups water in bowl. Steep until tea is very strong. Remove tea bags. Cool. Dissolve sugar in 7 cups water in bowl. Cool. Mix tea, sugar syrup, whiskey and concentrates in large container. Ladle into zip-lock bags; seal. Freeze until serving time. Stir slush; spoon into glasses. Add soda to taste. **Yield: 15 (1-cup) servings.**

Approx Per Serving: Cal 237; Prot 1 g; Carbo 33 g; Fiber <1 g;
   T Fat <1 g; 0% Calories from Fat; Chol 0 mg; Sod 2 mg.

Jacqueline Brana, Redford

EYES FOR THE NEEDY

TELEPHONE · PIONEERS
1875 · 1911
· OF AMERICA ·
ANSWERING THE CALL OF THOSE IN NEED ®

Soups

Asparagus Soup

1¹/₂ pounds fresh asparagus,
   trimmed, cut into 1-inch pieces
¹/₂ cup chopped onion

1 10-ounce can chicken broth
1¹/₂ cups half and half
Salt and pepper to taste

Simmer asparagus, onion and chicken broth in saucepan until asparagus is tender. Purée in blender. Return to saucepan. Stir in half and half, salt and pepper. Simmer over very low heat until heated through, stirring frequently. **Yield: 4 servings.**

Approx Per Serving: Cal 174; Prot 10 g; Carbo 12 g; Fiber 3 g;
   T Fat 11 g; 54% Calories from Fat; Chol 34 mg; Sod 265 mg.

Shirley A. Cook, Lansing

Barley Soup

2 pounds ground beef
12 cups beef bouillon
2 cups chopped onion

3 cups chopped carrots
1 quart tomatoes
1 cup barley

Brown ground beef in stockpot, stirring until crumbly; drain. Add remaining ingredients; mix well. Simmer for 2 hours, stirring occasionally. **Yield: 16 servings.**

Approx Per Serving: Cal 185; Prot 13 g; Carbo 15 g; Fiber 3 g;
   T Fat 8 g; 40% Calories from Fat; Chol 37 mg; Sod 690 mg.

Joan Emmons, Jackson

Baked Beef Minestrone

2 pounds lean stew beef
1 onion, chopped
2 tablespoons olive oil
1 cup water
2 cloves of garlic, minced
1 cup sliced carrots
1 cup sliced zucchini
1 cup sliced celery

1 green bell pepper, cut into strips
3 tomatoes, peeled, chopped
3 cups shredded cabbage
¹/₂ teaspoon each salt, sugar,
   rosemary, basil and thyme
¹/₄ teaspoon pepper
3 14-ounce cans beef broth
3 cups cooked shell macaroni

Brown beef and onion in olive oil in covered Dutch oven, stirring frequently; drain. Add water. Bake, covered, at 350 degrees for 1 hour. Add next 7 ingredients. Sprinkle with seasonings. Add beef broth; mix well. Bake, covered, for 1¹/₂ hours or until beef is tender. Serve over a small amount of macaroni in serving bowls. Garnish with grated Parmesan cheese. **Yield: 16 servings.**

Approx Per Serving: Cal 181; Prot 13 g; Carbo 10 g; Fiber 2 g;
   T Fat 10 g; 50% Calories from Fat; Chol 37 mg; Sod 355 mg.

Rose Joseph, Lake Ann

Bountiful Ten-Bean Soup

1 pound mixed dried beans
8 cups water
2 to 3 ham hocks
2 tablespoons minced garlic
1 cup minced onion
1 cup minced celery
1 cup chopped carrots

1 tablespoon butter
1/2 teaspoon pepper
1   16-ounce can chopped tomatoes
2 tablespoons molasses
1 tablespoon red wine vinegar
Thyme, basil and hot pepper sauce to
   taste

Rinse beans; place in large kettle. Soak in water to cover overnight; drain. Add 8 cups water and ham hocks. Bring to a boil; reduce heat. Simmer for 2½ hours. Sauté garlic, onion, celery and carrots in butter in skillet. Add to beans. Stir in pepper, tomatoes, molasses, vinegar, thyme, basil and hot pepper sauce. Simmer for 1 hour longer or until of desired consistency. May substitute 2 tablespoons brown sugar for molasses and 3 tablespoons lemon juice for vinegar. May prepare in slow cooker, simmering all day. **Yield: 16 servings.**

Approx Per Serving: Cal 154; Prot 10 g; Carbo 22 g; Fiber 6 g;
   T Fat 3 g; 19% Calories from Fat; Chol 10 mg; Sod 221 mg.

Ruth Nelson, Saginaw

Yellow Bean Soup

1 pound cubed pork
1 smoked pork hock
1 quart water
1 quart ham stock
1/2 teaspoon caraway seed
1 teaspoon dillweed
3 bay leaves

5 whole allspice
1 tablespoon ham base
1 cup chopped celery
1 cup chopped onion
2 quarts yellow wax beans
3 potatoes, cubed
3/4 cup chopped carrots

Combine cubed pork, pork hock, water and ham stock in kettle. Simmer until pork is tender. Stir in caraway seed, dillweed, bay leaves, allspice and ham base. Add celery, onion, beans, potatoes and carrots. Simmer until vegetables are tender, stirring occasionally. Remove bay leaves and allspice before serving. May add ½ cup flour and 2 cups half and half to thicken or add ½ cup sugar and ½ cup vinegar for sweet and sour soup. **Yield: 20 servings.**

Approx Per Serving: Cal 92; Prot 9 g; Carbo 9 g; Fiber 2 g;
   T Fat 3 g; 26% Calories from Fat; Chol 16 mg; Sod 373 mg.

Geri Norlock, Bay City

Green Bean Soup

3 cups cut fresh green beans	2 eggs
1 cup finely chopped onion	1/2 teaspoon salt
2 tablespoons butter	1 cup flour
3 cups chopped potatoes	2 egg whites
5 cups milk	1 cup sour cream
Salt and pepper to taste	

Sauté green beans and onion in butter in large saucepan until beans are tender-crisp. Add potatoes and enough water to cover. Simmer over low heat until potatoes are tender. Stir in milk, salt and pepper to taste. Beat eggs with 1/2 teaspoon salt in medium bowl. Stir in flour and enough water to make stiff dough. Drop by teaspoonfuls into soup. Simmer for 20 to 30 minutes or until dumplings are done. Beat egg whites with sour cream in small bowl; add to soup. Simmer until of desired consistency, stirring frequently. **Yield: 14 servings.**

Approx Per Serving: Cal 192; Prot 7 g; Carbo 21 g; Fiber 1 g;
    T Fat 9 g; 42% Calories from Fat; Chol 54 mg; Sod 156 mg.

Clara E. Hancock, Midland

Borsch

3 1/2 cups water	1 14-ounce can beef broth
Salt to taste	1 cup shredded cabbage
2 cups shredded peeled beets	1 tablespoon butter
1 cup shredded carrots	1 tablespoon lemon juice
1 cup chopped onion	

Bring water and salt to a boil in large saucepan. Add beets, carrots and onion. Cook over medium-high heat for 20 minutes. Add beef broth, cabbage and butter; mix well. Cook for 15 minutes longer. Stir in lemon juice. Serve in heated bowls garnished with sour cream or plain yogurt. **Yield: 6 servings.**

Approx Per Serving: Cal 76; Prot 3 g; Carbo 12 g; Fiber 4 g;
    T Fat 2 g; 25% Calories from Fat; Chol 5 mg; Sod 297 mg.

Teddy Zeedyk, Battle Creek

*Freeze leftover rice, barley or bulgur in ice cube trays, then
store in plastic bags in the freezer. Add a few cubes to
thicken and enrich soups.*

Broccoli Soup

1½ quarts water
16 ounces chopped broccoli
¾ cup onion
Salt to taste
2 teaspoons seasoning salt

1 teaspoon pepper
1 teaspoon garlic powder
2 cups shredded American cheese
¼ cup margarine
1   12-ounce can evaporated milk

Bring water to a boil in large saucepan. Add broccoli, onion, salt, seasoning salt, pepper and garlic powder. Cook until tender; reduce heat to medium-low. Add cheese, margarine and evaporated milk. Cook until thickened, stirring constantly. **Yield: 8 servings.**

Approx Per Serving: Cal 237; Prot 11 g; Carbo 9 g; Fiber 2 g;
      T Fat 18 g; 67% Calories from Fat; Chol 39 mg; Sod 858 mg.

Lois Sudol, Traverse City

Cream of Broccoli Soup

1   10-ounce can cream of mushroom
    soup
1   10-ounce can cream of celery soup
1   14-ounce can chicken broth

2 tablespoons minced onion
2 slices ham, chopped
1   10-ounce package frozen chopped
    broccoli, thawed

Combine soups, chicken broth, onion, ham and broccoli in saucepan; mix well. Simmer for 30 minutes or until broccoli is tender. **Yield: 4 servings.**

Approx Per Serving: Cal 183; Prot 10 g; Carbo 15 g; Fiber 3 g;
      T Fat 10 g; 48% Calories from Fat; Chol 17 mg; Sod 1631 mg.

Margaret Shurlow, Vassar

Curried Broccoli Soup

2 tablespoons butter
3 tablespoons flour
2 cups chicken broth
½ cup chopped onion

1   10-ounce package frozen chopped
    broccoli, cooked
1 teaspoon curry powder
1 cup half and half

Melt butter in saucepan. Add flour, stirring to blend. Stir in chicken broth gradually. Add onion, broccoli, curry powder and half and half; mix well. Simmer until of desired consistency, stirring frequently. **Yield: 6 servings.**

Approx Per Serving: Cal 131; Prot 5 g; Carbo 8 g; Fiber 2 g;
      T Fat 9 g; 61% Calories from Fat; Chol 26 mg; Sod 320 mg.

Alice Crocker, Bellevue

Cream of Broccoli-Cheese Soup

¼ cup butter
¼ cup flour
2 cups milk
½ 8-ounce jar Cheez Whiz
½ cup shredded Cheddar cheese

1 10-ounce can cream of potato soup
1 soup can milk
1 10-ounce package frozen chopped broccoli, cooked
Garlic powder and pepper to taste

Melt butter in saucepan. Add flour, stirring to blend. Stir in 2 cups milk gradually. Simmer until thickened, stirring constantly. Add remaining ingredients; mix well. Simmer until cheese is melted, stirring frequently. **Yield: 8 servings.**

Approx Per Serving: Cal 230; Prot 10 g; Carbo 14 g; Fiber 1 g;
     T Fat 16 g; 60% Calories from Fat; Chol 47 mg; Sod 592 mg.

Fran Lubic, Kalamazoo

Healthy Broccoli-Cheese Soup

2 tablespoons finely chopped onion
2 teaspoons reduced-calorie margarine
1 tablespoon plus 1½ teaspoons flour
1 cup water
1 cup skim milk
1 cup broccoli flowerets

1 envelope instant chicken broth and seasoning mix
½ teaspoon chopped parsley
White pepper to taste
4 ounces low-fat Monterey Jack cheese, shredded

Sauté onion in margarine in nonstick skillet for 1 to 2 minutes or until tender but not brown. Sprinkle with flour, stirring quickly until absorbed. Stir in next 5 ingredients. Simmer over low heat for 10 minutes or until broccoli is tender, stirring frequently. Process half the soup in blender until smooth. Return to saucepan; add pepper and cheese. Cook over low heat until cheese melts, stirring constantly. **Yield: 2 servings.**

Approx Per Serving: Cal 266; Prot 23 g; Carbo 16 g; Fiber 2 g;
     T Fat 13 g; 43% Calories from Fat; Chol 43 mg; Sod 1104 mg.

Helen Byers, St. Helen

Broccoli-Corn Chowder

1 10-ounce can cream of broccoli soup
½ cup half and half
1 16-ounce can whole kernel corn

2 tablespoons onion flakes
¼ teaspoon celery seed
¼ teaspoon pepper

Combine all ingredients in saucepan; mix well. Bring to a boil, stirring constantly. Remove from heat; ladle into serving bowls. **Yield: 4 servings.**

Approx Per Serving: Cal 315; Prot 6 g; Carbo 40 g; Fiber 1 g;
     T Fat 17 g; 45% Calories from Fat; Chol 11 mg; Sod 2273 mg.

Shirley A. Cook, Lansing

Carrot Soup

2 onions, chopped
2 tablespoons butter
2 large carrots, chopped
1 stalk of celery, chopped
1 potato, peeled, chopped

1 parsnip, chopped
1 turnip, chopped
4 cups chicken broth
1 5-ounce can evaporated milk

Sauté onions in butter in large saucepan for 3 minutes or until tender. Add next 6 ingredients. Simmer, covered, for 30 minutes, stirring occasionally. Pour into blender container. Process until smooth. Return to saucepan. Add evaporated milk. Simmer until heated through. Garnish with grated nutmeg. **Yield: 4 servings.**

Approx Per Serving: Cal 252; Prot 10 g; Carbo 31 g; Fiber 5 g;
    T Fat 10 g; 36% Calories from Fat; Chol 27 mg; Sod 912 mg.

Shirley A. Cook, Lansing

Cheese Soup

3 cups cubed potatoes
1/2 cup chopped carrots
1/2 cup chopped celery
1/4 cup chopped onion
1 cup water
1 chicken bouillon cube

1 tablespoon parsley flakes
1 teaspoon salt
Pepper to taste
1 1/2 cups milk
2 tablespoons flour
8 ounces cubed Velveeta cheese

Combine potatoes, carrots, celery, onion, water, bouillon, parsley, salt and pepper in saucepan. Bring to a boil. Cook for 15 minutes, stirring occasionally. Blend milk and flour in small bowl. Stir into vegetable mixture. Add cheese. Simmer until cheese is melted, stirring frequently. **Yield: 6 servings.**

Approx Per Serving: Cal 269; Prot 13 g; Carbo 24 g; Fiber 2 g;
    T Fat 14 g; 46% Calories from Fat; Chol 44 mg; Sod 1129 mg.

Jan Dorman, Traverse City

Dieter's Soup

1 46-ounce can vegetable juice cocktail
1 10-ounce can French onion soup
1 soup can water

1 16-ounce package coleslaw
1 onion, chopped
1/8 teaspoon Mrs. Dash seasoning

Combine vegetable juice cocktail, soup, water, coleslaw, onion and seasoning in saucepan; mix well. Simmer until vegetables are tender. **Yield: 8 servings.**

Approx Per Serving: Cal 94; Prot 3 g; Carbo 18 g; Fiber 3 g;
    T Fat 2 g; 19% Calories from Fat; Chol 5 mg; Sod 913 mg.

Alice Duvall, Williamston

Fish Chowder

3 potatoes, chopped
1 carrot, chopped
2 onions, chopped
1 stalk celery, chopped
4 ounces cooked ham, chopped
1 16-ounce can whole kernel corn

12 4-ounce perch fillets, cut into
  bite-sized pieces
1/2 cup sour cream
1 cup milk
Salt and pepper to taste

Parboil potatoes and carrot in water to cover in saucepan for 5 minutes. Sauté onions, celery and ham in large saucepan until tender. Add potatoes and carrots with cooking water, undrained corn and perch. Simmer for 20 minutes or until fish flakes easily, stirring frequently. Stir in sour cream, milk, salt and pepper. Simmer until heated through, stirring constantly. Garnish with fresh parsley. **Yield: 8 servings.**

Approx Per Serving: Cal 338; Prot 42 g; Carbo 27 g; Fiber 2 g;
  T Fat 7 g; 18% Calories from Fat; Chol 175 mg; Sod 471 mg.

Marian Kasper, Saginaw

Gazpacho

4 cups cold tomato juice
1 onion, minced
2 cups chopped tomatoes
1 cup minced green bell pepper
1 teaspoon honey
1 clove of garlic, crushed
1 cucumber, chopped
2 scallions, chopped
Juice of 1/2 lemon

Juice of 1 lime
2 tablespoons wine vinegar
2 tablespoons olive oil
1/4 cup chopped fresh parsley
1 teaspoon tarragon
1 teaspoon basil
1/2 teaspoon cumin
Hot sauce, salt and pepper to taste

Combine tomato juice, onion, tomatoes, green pepper, honey, garlic, cucumber, scallions, lemon and lime juices, vinegar, olive oil, parsley and seasonings in large bowl; mix well. Chill, covered, for 2 hours before serving. May purée in blender. **Yield: 6 servings.**

Approx Per Serving: Cal 108; Prot 3 g; Carbo 16 g; Fiber 4 g;
  T Fat 5 g; 37% Calories from Fat; Chol 0 mg; Sod 596 mg.

Mary Keeney, Lansing

Ham Chowder

4 carrots, chopped
4 stalks celery, chopped
1 onion, chopped
4 potatoes, cubed
5 cups water

3 cups chopped cooked ham
2 tablespoons margarine
Salt and pepper to taste
6 tablespoons flour
2½ cups milk

Combine carrots, celery, onion, potatoes and water in large saucepan. Cook over medium-high heat for 20 minutes or until vegetables are tender. Add ham, margarine, salt and pepper. Blend flour and milk in small bowl. Stir into soup gradually. Bring to a boil, stirring constantly; reduce heat. Simmer for 10 to 20 minutes, stirring frequently. Garnish with chopped parsley and paprika. **Yield: 6 servings.**

Approx Per Serving: Cal 365; Prot 25 g; Carbo 41 g; Fiber 4 g;
    T Fat 11 g; 28% Calories from Fat; Chol 52 mg; Sod 1062 mg.

Gert Budd, Saginaw

Hearty Ham and Cabbage Chowder

1 cup thinly sliced celery
½ cup chopped onion
2 cloves of garlic, minced
2 tablespoons oil
1   28-ounce can tomatoes
1   17-ounce can whole kernel corn
1   16-ounce can sliced potatoes

1   10-ounce can chicken broth
1 cup water
¼ cup catsup
¼ cup packed brown sugar
1 pound ham, cubed
3 cups thinly sliced cabbage

Sauté celery, onion and garlic in oil in 4-quart saucepan for 2 minutes. Drain tomatoes, reserving juice. Cut tomatoes into halves. Add to celery mixture with reserved juice, undrained corn, undrained potatoes, chicken broth, water, catsup, brown sugar, ham and cabbage. Bring to a boil; reduce heat. Simmer, covered, for 1 hour. Serve with crackers or bread. **Yield: 12 servings.**

Approx Per Serving: Cal 179; Prot 12 g; Carbo 23 g; Fiber 2 g;
    T Fat 5 g; 24% Calories from Fat; Chol 21 mg; Sod 936 mg.

Jeanette Schulz, Petoskey

Hamburger Soup

1 pound ground beef, browned, drained
3 carrots, chopped
3 stalks celery, chopped
3 potatoes, chopped
1 onion, chopped
1 10-ounce can French onion soup
1 14-ounce can stewed tomatoes
1 8-ounce can tomato sauce
5 teaspoons sugar
2 teaspoons instant beef bouillon
1 teaspoon salt
1/4 teaspoon pepper
5 cups water

Combine all ingredients in large soup pot. Simmer for 45 minutes or until vegetables are tender, stirring occasionally. **Yield: 12 servings.**

Approx Per Serving: Cal 161; Prot 10 g; Carbo 19 g; Fiber 2 g;
    T Fat 6 g; 32% Calories from Fat; Chol 25 mg; Sod 784 mg.

Jan Emelander, Grand Rapids

Hamburger-Barley Stew

1 pound lean ground beef
1 onion, chopped
1 28-ounce can tomatoes
1/2 cup barley
2 carrots, sliced
2 stalks celery, sliced
4 potatoes, cubed
4 cups water

Brown ground beef and onion in 4-quart saucepan, stirring frequently; drain. Add remaining ingredients; mix well. Bring to a boil, covered; reduce heat. Simmer for 50 minutes or until vegetables are tender, stirring occasionally. **Yield: 12 servings.**

Approx Per Serving: Cal 178; Prot 10 g; Carbo 23 g; Fiber 4 g;
    T Fat 6 g; 28% Calories from Fat; Chol 25 mg; Sod 142 mg.

Anna J. Sells, Battle Creek

Hamburger-Rice Soup

1 pound ground chuck, cooked
2 quarts water
1 cup chopped onion
2 cups cubed potatoes
2 cups sliced carrots
1 bay leaf
1/2 teaspoon each thyme and basil
2 cups tomatoes
1 cup chopped celery
1 cup shredded cabbage
4 beef bouillon cubes
2 tablespoons salt
1/4 teaspoon pepper
1 cup instant rice

Mix first 14 ingredients in saucepan. Simmer, covered, for 45 minutes. Discard bay leaf. Add rice. Cook for 15 minutes longer, stirring occasionally. **Yield: 14 servings.**

Approx Per Serving: Cal 129; Prot 8 g; Carbo 14 g; Fiber 2 g;
    T Fat 5 g; 33% Calories from Fat; Chol 21 mg; Sod 1186 mg.

Waneta Dragicevich, Kalamazoo

Potato and Ham Soup

6 potatoes, peeled, cubed
5 cups water
2 onions, chopped
1 carrot, chopped
1 stalk celery, chopped
4 chicken bouillon cubes
1 tablespoon parsley flakes
1/4 teaspoon thyme

1/4 teaspoon rosemary
1/4 teaspoon celery seed
1/4 teaspoon garlic salt
Salt and pepper to taste
1   13-ounce can evaporated milk
1 1/2 cups cubed ham
1/3 cup margarine

Combine potatoes, water, onions, carrot, celery, bouillon cubes, seasonings, evaporated milk, ham and margarine in large saucepan; mix well. Simmer for 45 minutes or until vegetables are tender, stirring occasionally. May store in freezer. **Yield: 8 servings.**

Approx Per Serving: Cal 302; Prot 13 g; Carbo 35 g; Fiber 3 g;
    T Fat 13 g; 38% Calories from Fat; Chol 29 mg; Sod 1140 mg.

Barb Avery, Marquette

Potato Soup

8 potatoes, cubed
2 onions, chopped
2 tablespoons butter
4 cups milk

2 eggs
Salt and pepper to taste
2 tablespoons flour

Combine potatoes, onions and just enough water to cover in saucepan. Cook until potatoes are soft; mash slightly. Stir in butter and milk gradually. Simmer over low heat, stirring occasionally. Beat eggs with salt and pepper in small bowl. Stir in flour until mixture forms thick paste. Drizzle with fork into potato mixture. Simmer for 20 minutes longer, stirring frequently. Serve with fresh bread. May add garlic salt, corn or ham. **Yield: 6 servings.**

Approx Per Serving: Cal 381; Prot 12 g; Carbo 59 g; Fiber 4 g;
    T Fat 12 g; 27% Calories from Fat; Chol 103 mg; Sod 135 mg.

Zelma Cohoon, Sault Ste. Marie

*Season cream soups and white sauces with white pepper or hot
pepper sauce instead of black pepper. White pepper
is ground from peppercorns with the outer skin removed.*

Salmon Chowder

4 slices bacon
1/2 cup chopped onion
1 5-ounce package au gratin potato mix
2 cups water
1 1/2 cups milk

1 16-ounce can whole kernel corn, drained
1 teaspoon instant chicken bouillon
1 16-ounce can salmon, drained, flaked

Sauté bacon in large saucepan until crisp. Drain, reserving 1 tablespoon pan drippings. Crumble bacon and set aside. Sauté onion in pan drippings until tender. Add potato mix, water, milk, corn, bouillon, salmon and crumbled bacon; mix well. Bring to a boil; reduce heat. Simmer for 10 minutes, stirring frequently. **Yield: 8 servings.**

Approx Per Serving: Cal 231; Prot 17 g; Carbo 27 g; Fiber 1 g;
    T Fat 8 g; 29% Calories from Fat; Chol 38 mg; Sod 1030 mg.

Clara E. Hancock, Midland

Turkey Soup

2 cups chopped cooked turkey
2 onions, chopped
2 stalks celery, chopped
3 carrots, chopped

1 cup uncooked egg noodles
6 cups turkey broth
1 cup green peas
Salt and pepper to taste

Combine first 6 ingredients in saucepan. Simmer over medium heat for 1 hour, stirring occasionally. Add peas and seasonings. Simmer for 10 minutes. **Yield: 12 servings.**

Approx Per Serving: Cal 96; Prot 11 g; Carbo 8 g; Fiber 2 g;
    T Fat 2 g; 20% Calories from Fat; Chol 23 mg; Sod 418 mg.

Peggy St. Louis, Kingsford

French Vegetable Soup

2 pounds stew beef
1/4 cup oil
1 10-ounce can onion soup
5 soup cans water
1 6-ounce can tomato paste
1 tablespoon basil
1 1/2 teaspoons salt

1/4 teaspoon pepper
8 carrots, chopped
2 cups chopped celery
1 16-ounce can kidney beans, drained
1 16-ounce can cream-style corn
1/2 cup grated Parmesan cheese

Brown stew beef in oil in kettle; reduce heat. Add next 6 ingredients. Simmer, covered, for 1 1/2 hours, stirring occasionally. Add carrots, celery, beans and corn; mix well. Simmer for 30 minutes longer. Stir in cheese just before serving. **Yield: 6 servings.**

Approx Per Serving: Cal 519; Prot 40 g; Carbo 45 g; Fiber 13 g;
    T Fat 21 g; 36% Calories from Fat; Chol 90 mg; Sod 1676 mg.

Mary Keeney, Lansing

ADOPT-A-PARK

Salads

Apple and Pineapple Salad

1   20-ounce can pineapple tidbits
5 Delicious apples, chopped
4 bananas, chopped

2 tablespoons orange breakfast drink
  mix
1 cup miniature marshmallows

Drain pineapple, reserving juice. Mix fruits in bowl. Combine reserved juice with breakfast drink mix and marshmallows in saucepan. Cook until marshmallows melt, stirring to mix well. Pour over fruits; mix gently. Chill until serving time. **Yield: 10 servings.**

Approx Per Serving: Cal 161; Prot 1 g; Carbo 41 g; Fiber 3 g;
     T Fat 1 g; 3% Calories from Fat; Chol 0 mg; Sod 9 mg.

Rose M. Holcomb, Petoskey

Taffy Apple Salad

1   16-ounce can pineapple tidbits
1/2 cup sugar
1 tablespoon flour
1 teaspoon vinegar
1 egg, beaten

8 ounces whipped topping
4 cups multicolored miniature
  marshmallows
3 cups chopped unpeeled red apples
8 ounces dry-roasted peanuts, crushed

Drain pineapple, reserving juice. Combine sugar, flour, vinegar, egg and reserved pineapple juice in saucepan. Cook until thickened and smooth, stirring constantly; remove from heat. Stir in whipped topping. Fold in marshmallows, apples, peanuts and pineapple. Spoon into serving dish. Chill until serving time. **Yield: 12 servings.**

Approx Per Serving: Cal 320; Prot 6 g; Carbo 45 g; Fiber 1 g;
     T Fat 15 g; 39% Calories from Fat; Chol 18 mg; Sod 180 mg.

Melanie Murray, Marquette

*For **Elegant Ambrosia**, combine 8-ounce cans of drained mandarin oranges and pineapple chunks, 1 cup seedless grapes, one 15-ounce can drained Royal Anne cherries, 1 cup marshmallows and 1 cup sour cream. Chill, covered, for 24 hours.*

Taffy Apple-Peanut Salad

1 cup pineapple juice
2 tablespoons vinegar
2 tablespoons flour
1 cup sugar

6 cups chopped unpeeled Granny
   Smith apples
2 cups skinless salted peanuts, chopped
16 ounces whipped topping

Combine pineapple juice, vinegar, flour and sugar in saucepan. Cook just until mixture comes to a simmer, stirring constantly. Cool to room temperature. Combine apples and peanuts in bowl. Add cooled mixture; mix well. Fold in whipped topping. Chill until serving time. **Yield: 12 servings.**

Approx Per Serving: Cal 381; Prot 7 g; Carbo 44 g; Fiber 4 g;
    T Fat 22 g; 49% Calories from Fat; Chol 0 mg; Sod 115 mg.

Nancy Edwards, South Whitley, Indiana

Apricot Salad

1 3-ounce package apricot gelatin
1 cup boiling water
1 4-ounce jar baby food apricots

2 tablespoons chopped celery
1/3 cup sour cream

Dissolve gelatin in boiling water in saucepan. Add apricots, celery and sour cream; mix well. Spoon into salad mold. Chill until firm. Unmold onto serving plate. May add nuts if desired. **Yield: 4 servings.**

Approx Per Serving: Cal 138; Prot 3 g; Carbo 25 g; Fiber <1 g;
    T Fat 4 g; 25% Calories from Fat; Chol 8 mg; Sod 83 mg.

Carolyn Reinert, Vassar

Apricot Smoothy

1 16-ounce can crushed pineapple
2 3-ounce packages apricot gelatin
3 ounces cream cheese, softened

2 4-ounce jars baby food apricots
12 ounces whipped topping

Drain pineapple, reserving juice. Add enough water to juice to measure 1 cup. Bring juice mixture to a boil in saucepan. Stir in gelatin until dissolved. Cool to room temperature. Combine with pineapple in blender container; process until smooth. Combine with cream cheese, apricots and whipped topping in bowl; mix well. Spoon into salad mold. Chill until set. Unmold onto serving plate. May substitute blended cottage cheese for whipped topping if desired. **Yield: 8 servings.**

Approx Per Serving: Cal 314; Prot 4 g; Carbo 45 g; Fiber 1 g;
    T Fat 15 g; 40% Calories from Fat; Chol 12 mg; Sod 112 mg.

Janet Adamski, Lansing

Blueberry-Gelatin Salad

2 3-ounce packages mixed fruit
   gelatin
2 cups boiling water
1 20-ounce can crushed pineapple,
   drained

1 21-ounce can blueberry pie filling
8 ounces cream cheese, softened
1/2 cup sugar
1/2 cup sour cream
1 teaspoon vanilla extract

Dissolve gelatin in boiling water in bowl. Stir in pineapple and pie filling. Spoon into serving dish. Chill until set. Combine remaining ingredients in bowl; mix well. Spread over congealed layer. Chill until serving time. **Yield: 15 servings.**

Approx Per Serving: Cal 195; Prot 3 g; Carbo 33 g; Fiber 1 g;
   T Fat 7 g; 31% Calories from Fat; Chol 20 mg; Sod 97 mg.

Joan Emmons, Jackson

Cranberry Salad

2 3-ounce packages cherry gelatin
1 cup sugar
1 cup boiling water
Juice of 1 lemon

1 cup crushed pineapple
1 cup ground cranberries
1 whole orange, ground
1 cup pineapple juice

Dissolve gelatin and sugar in boiling water in bowl. Chill until partially set. Add lemon juice, pineapple, cranberries, orange and pineapple juice; mix well. Spoon into salad mold. Chill until set. Unmold onto serving plate. **Yield: 8 servings.**

Approx Per Serving: Cal 238; Prot 2 g; Carbo 60 g; Fiber 2 g;
   T Fat <1 g; 1% Calories from Fat; Chol 0 mg; Sod 69 mg.

Cindy Fogg, Otsego

Healthy Cranberry-Pineapple Salad

1 20-ounce can juice-pack crushed
   pineapple
2 3-ounce packages strawberry gelatin
1 cup water
1 16-ounce can whole cranberry sauce

3 tablespoons lemon juice
1 teaspoon grated lemon peel
1/4 teaspoon nutmeg
2 cups liquified low-fat cottage cheese
1/2 cup chopped walnuts

Drain pineapple, reserving juice. Mix gelatin, reserved juice and water in saucepan. Bring to a boil, stirring constantly; remove from heat. Combine with next 4 ingredients in bowl. Chill until partially set. Beat in cottage cheese; fold in pineapple and walnuts. Pour into 1 1/2-quart mold; chill. Unmold onto serving plate. **Yield: 8 servings.**

Approx Per Serving: Cal 308; Prot 11 g; Carbo 56 g; Fiber 2 g;
   T Fat 6 g; 16% Calories from Fat; Chol 5 mg; Sod 315 mg.

Pat Schulte, Lansing

Fruit Salad

1   21-ounce can peach pie filling
1 cup blueberries
1 cup each red and green grapes

1 nectarine, chopped
1/2 cantaloupe, chopped
2 bananas, sliced

Chop peach slices in pie filling into bite-sized pieces. Combine with remaining ingredients in bowl; mix gently. Chill until serving time. **Yield: 12 servings.**

Approx Per Serving: Cal 106; Prot 1 g; Carbo 27 g; Fiber 2 g;
      T Fat <1 g; 3% Calories from Fat; Chol 0 mg; Sod 19 mg.

Peggy St. Louis, Kingsford

Sugar-Free Pudding and Fruit Salad

1   6-ounce package vanilla
   sugar-free instant pudding mix
1   16-ounce can lite fruit cocktail
1   16-ounce can lite sliced peaches,
   chopped

1   21-ounce can juice-pack pineapple
   chunks, drained
1   11-ounce can mandarin oranges,
   drained
1 banana, sliced

Combine dry pudding mix, and undrained fruit cocktail in glass bowl; mix well. Add undrained peaches, pineapple and mandarin oranges; mix well. Chill, covered, overnight to 24 hours. Stir in banana at serving time. **Yield: 12 servings.**

Approx Per Serving: Cal 146; Prot 2 g; Carbo 35 g; Fiber 1 g;
      T Fat 2 g; 9% Calories from Fat; Chol 0 mg; Sod 470 mg.

Marilyn Bezemek, Saginaw

Hot Fruit Salad

1   29-ounce can peaches
1   20-ounce can pineapple chunks
1   16-ounce can dark, sweet pitted
   cherries
1   11-ounce can mandarin oranges
1/2 cup margarine

3 tablespoons cornstarch
1/4 cup packed brown sugar
1 to 2 teaspoons almond extract
1/2 to 1 teaspoon vanilla extract
Cinnamon to taste

Drain peaches, pineapple, cherries and mandarin oranges, reserving 1 cup juices. Chop peaches; combine with remaining drained fruit in greased 2 1/2-quart baking dish. Combine reserved juice with margarine, cornstarch and brown sugar in saucepan. Cook until thickened and smooth, stirring constantly. Stir in flavorings and cinnamon. Pour over fruit. Bake at 325 degrees for 45 minutes. **Yield: 12 servings.**

Approx Per Serving: Cal 235; Prot 1 g; Carbo 43 g; Fiber 2 g;
      T Fat 8 g; 28% Calories from Fat; Chol 0 mg; Sod 99 mg.

Dee Sevenski, Lansing

No-Sugar-Added Fruit Salad

1   16-ounce can juice-pack pineapple
    chunks, drained
1 unpeeled apple, chopped
3 bananas, sliced

1 cup seedless grape halves
Artificial sweetener to taste
1/4 cup low-fat sour cream

Mix pineapple, apple, bananas and grapes in bowl. Combine artificial sweetener and sour cream in small bowl; mix well. Add to fruit; mix gently. **Yield: 6 servings.**

Approx Per Serving: Cal 144; Prot 1 g; Carbo 34 g; Fiber 3 g;
    T Fat 2 g; 10% Calories from Fat; Chol 4 mg; Sod 6 mg.

Joyce Frydel, Lansing

Ginger-Fruit Salad

2   3-ounce packages lemon gelatin
1/4 cup sugar
1 1/2 cups boiling water
1 tablespoon lemon juice
7 tablespoons orange juice
2 cups ginger ale

1/2 cup chopped celery
4 red apples, chopped
1   20-ounce can crushed pineapple,
    drained
1/2 cup chopped walnuts

Dissolve gelatin and sugar in boiling water in bowl. Stir in lemon juice, orange juice and ginger ale. Chill until slightly thickened. Add celery, apples, pineapple and walnuts; mix well. Spoon into glass serving dish. Chill until set. **Yield: 10 servings.**

Approx Per Serving: Cal 205; Prot 3 g; Carbo 43 g; Fiber 2 g;
    T Fat 4 g; 16% Calories from Fat; Chol 0 mg; Sod 65 mg.

Dixie L. Tackebury, Saginaw

Hawaiian Salad

1 large package vanilla pudding and
    pie filling mix
1 1/2 cups mixed pineapple and
    orange juice

2 cups pineapple chunks
2 cups mandarin oranges
1 cup grape halves
1 banana, sliced

Blend pudding mix and juice in saucepan. Bring to a boil, stirring constantly. Cool to room temperature. Stir in pineapple, oranges and grapes. Chill until serving time. Fold in banana at serving time. May add 1/2 cup chopped nuts if desired.
Yield: 8 servings.

Approx Per Serving: Cal 186; Prot 1 g; Carbo 48 g; Fiber 2 g;
    T Fat <1 g; 2% Calories from Fat; Chol 0 mg; Sod 86 mg.

Helen Noyce, Prudenville

Gelatin Salad Supreme

1   15-ounce can mandarin oranges
1   6-ounce package orange gelatin

2   4-ounce packages vanilla instant
    pudding mix

Drain mandarin oranges, reserving juice. Combine reserved juice with enough water to measure 4 cups. Bring to a boil in saucepan. Stir in gelatin until dissolved. Stir in pudding mix. Bring to a boil. Cook for 1 minute. Stir in mandarin oranges. Cool. Chill until serving time. Garnish servings with whipped topping. **Yield: 8 servings.**

Approx Per Serving: Cal 216; Prot 2 g; Carbo 54 g; Fiber 1 g;
    T Fat <1 g; 1% Calories from Fat; Chol 0 mg; Sod 260 mg.

Marilyn Rogers, Lansing

Molded Cheese Salad

1   3-ounce package pineapple gelatin
1 cup boiling water
3 ounces cream cheese
3/4 cup cold water
2 tablespoons lemon juice
1 cup shredded American cheese

1/2 cup chopped Swiss cheese
2 tablespoons chopped pimento
1 tablespoon horseradish
1 tablespoon parsley flakes or 2
    tablespoons chopped fresh parsley
1 cup whipping cream, whipped

Dissolve gelatin in boiling water in bowl. Stir in cream cheese until smooth. Add cold water and lemon juice. Chill until slightly thickened. Add next 5 ingredients; mix well. Fold in whipped cream. Spoon into salad mold. Chill until set. Unmold onto serving plate. Serve with mayonnaise and crackers. **Yield: 8 servings.**

Approx Per Serving: Cal 261; Prot 8 g; Carbo 12 g; Fiber <1 g;
    T Fat 21 g; 71% Calories from Fat; Chol 72 mg; Sod 299 mg.

Evelyn Bedore, Ironwood

Pasta and Fruit Salad

1   16-ounce can pineapple chunks
1   11-ounce can mandarin oranges
3/4 cup acini-di-pepe, cooked
3/4 cup sugar

2 eggs
2 tablespoons flour
1/4 teaspoon salt
4 ounces whipped topping

Drain pineapple and mandarin oranges, reserving juices. Combine pasta and fruit in bowl; mix well. Combine reserved juices with sugar, eggs, flour and salt in saucepan. Cook until thickened, stirring constantly. Add to fruit mixture; mix well. Chill for 4 hours or longer. Fold in whipped topping. **Yield: 6 servings.**

Approx Per Serving: Cal 309; Prot 4 g; Carbo 61 g; Fiber 2 g;
    T Fat 7 g; 19% Calories from Fat; Chol 71 mg; Sod 121 mg.

Eileen Schrader, Reese

Macaroni-Fruit Salad

1 cup uncooked macaroni
1   16-ounce can fruit cocktail
1   16-ounce can pineapple chunks
1 banana, sliced

8 ounces whipped topping
8 ounces plain yogurt
1/4 teaspoon cinnamon

Cook macaroni using package directions; drain and cool. Combine with fruit cocktail, pineapple and banana in bowl; mix well. Combine whipped topping, yogurt and cinnamon in small bowl. Add to salad; mix gently. Chill for 1 hour before serving. **Yield: 10 servings.**

Approx Per Serving: Cal 186; Prot 2 g; Carbo 31 g; Fiber 1 g;
    T Fat 7 g; 31% Calories from Fat; Chol 3 mg; Sod 20 mg.

Margorie Kesson, Harrison

Orange-Cottage Cheese Fluff

16 ounces low-fat cottage cheese
1   3-ounce package sugar-free
   orange gelatin

1   16-ounce can juice-pack crushed
   pineapple, drained
8 ounces vanilla yogurt

Beat cottage cheese in mixer bowl until smooth. Add gelatin; mix well. Stir in pineapple and yogurt. Chill until serving time. **Yield: 8 servings.**

Approx Per Serving: Cal 112; Prot 10 g; Carbo 15 g; Fiber 1 g;
    T Fat 1 g; 12% Calories from Fat; Chol 6 mg; Sod 275 mg.

Margaret Shurlow, Vassar

Pineapple Ring with Fruit

3 cups pineapple juice
1/4 cup sugar

1/2 teaspoon salt
3/4 cup cream of rice cereal

Combine pineapple juice, sugar and salt in saucepan. Bring to a boil. Sprinkle in cream of rice. Cook for 30 seconds, stirring constantly. Remove from heat; let stand, covered, for 3 minutes. Stir well; pour into greased 1-quart ring mold. Chill for 8 hours or until set. Unmold onto platter; fill center with fresh fruit. **Yield: 6 servings.**

Approx Per Serving: Cal 202; Prot 2 g; Carbo 45 g; Fiber <1 g;
    T Fat 1 g; 5% Calories from Fat; Chol 0 mg; Sod 180 mg.

Evelyn Helmer, Lansing

Queen Anne Salad

2 15-ounce jars pitted Queen Anne
   cherries
1 20-ounce can crushed pineapple
3 3-ounce packages lemon gelatin

11 ounces cream cheese, softened
2 tablespoons milk
2 cups whipping cream
1 cup finely chopped walnuts

Drain cherries and pineapple separately, reserving juices. Add enough water to reserved juices to measure 3¾ cups. Bring juice mixture to a boil in saucepan. Stir in gelatin until dissolved. Add pineapple; mix well. Chill until partially set. Beat cream cheese with milk in mixer bowl until light and smooth. Whip whipping cream in mixer bowl until soft peaks form. Fold into cream cheese. Stir in gelatin mixture, cherries and walnuts. Spoon into 12-cup mold. Chill until set. Unmold onto serving plate. **Yield: 15 servings.**

Approx Per Serving: Cal 374; Prot 5 g; Carbo 38 g; Fiber 1 g;
      T Fat 24 g; 56% Calories from Fat; Chol 66 mg; Sod 131 mg.

Marion St. John, Grawn

Red Top Salad

1 3-ounce package lime gelatin
40 miniature marshmallows
2 cups boiling water
1 cup shredded Velveeta cheese
½ cup finely chopped celery
1 16-ounce can crushed pineapple,
   drained

1 cup whipped topping
½ cup mayonnaise
1 cup chopped walnuts
1 3-ounce package strawberry
   gelatin
2 cups boiling water

Dissolve lime gelatin and marshmallows in 2 cups boiling water in bowl. Chill until partially set. Whip until smooth. Add cheese, celery, pineapple, whipped topping, mayonnaise and walnuts; mix well. Spoon into buttered 9-inch dish. Chill until set. Dissolve strawberry gelatin in 2 cups boiling water in bowl. Chill until partially set. Spoon over congealed lime layer. Chill until set. May freeze Velveeta for easier shredding. **Yield: 8 servings.**

Approx Per Serving: Cal 395; Prot 8 g; Carbo 34 g; Fiber 2 g;
      T Fat 27 g; 59% Calories from Fat; Chol 22 mg; Sod 362 mg.

Joanne Homer, Lansing

Red and White Gelatin Salad

1 3-ounce package lemon gelatin
1 cup boiling water
10 marshmallows
1 cup cold water
1 8-ounce can crushed pineapple
3 ounces cream cheese, softened
¼ cup mayonnaise-type salad
   dressing

½ cup chopped walnuts
1 cup whipping cream, whipped
1 3-ounce package strawberry
   gelatin
1 cup boiling water
1 cup cold water

Dissolve lemon gelatin in 1 cup boiling water in bowl. Stir in marshmallows until melted. Add 1 cup cold water, pineapple, cream cheese, salad dressing and walnuts; mix well. Fold in whipped cream. Spoon into salad mold. Chill until set. Dissolve strawberry gelatin in 1 cup boiling water. Stir in 1 cup cold water. Chill until partially set. Spoon over congealed layer. Chill until set. Unmold onto serving plate. **Yield: 12 servings.**

Approx Per Serving: Cal 230; Prot 3 g; Carbo 24 g; Fiber <1 g;
   T Fat 15 g; 55% Calories from Fat; Chol 36 mg; Sod 114 mg.

Helen Lorraine Moss, Marquette

Seven-Layer Gelatin Salad

1 3-ounce package lime gelatin
1 cup boiling water
½ cup cold water
2 envelopes unflavored gelatin
½ cup cold water
2 cups milk
1 cup sugar
2 cups sour cream

1 teaspoon vanilla extract
1 3-ounce package lemon gelatin
1 3-ounce package orange gelatin
1 3-ounce package strawberry
   gelatin
3 cups boiling water
1½ cups cold water

Dissolve lime gelatin in 1 cup boiling water in bowl. Stir in ½ cup cold water. Spoon into 9x13-inch dish. Chill until set. Soften unflavored gelatin in ½ cup cold water. Bring milk to a boil in saucepan. Stir in sugar until dissolved. Add unflavored gelatin mixture; stir to dissolve completely. Stir in sour cream and vanilla. Spoon 1½ cups sour cream mixture over lime gelatin. Chill until set. Prepare remaining fruit gelatins separately using 1 cup boiling water and ½ cup cold water for each. Alternate layers of 1 flavor of gelatin and 1½ cups sour cream mixture over congealed layers, chilling each layer until set and ending with strawberry gelatin. **Yield: 15 servings.**

Approx Per Serving: Cal 224; Prot 5 g; Carbo 36 g; Fiber <1 g;
   T Fat 8 g; 29% Calories from Fat; Chol 18 mg; Sod 103 mg.

Kay Lake, Marquette

Waldorf Marshmallow Salad

1 cup chopped celery
¼ cup coarsely chopped walnuts
½ cup golden raisins
2 cups chopped unpeeled Delicious
  apples

1 cup seedless red and green grapes
¼ cup orange juice
1¼ cups miniature marshmallows
⅓ cup (scant) light mayonnaise

Combine celery, walnuts, raisins, apples and grapes in bowl. Add orange juice; toss to coat well. Add marshmallows; toss gently. Fold in mayonnaise. Chill until serving time. Spoon onto lettuce-lined serving plate. **Yield: 6 servings.**

Approx Per Serving: Cal 195; Prot 2 g; Carbo 37 g; Fiber 3 g;
  T Fat 6 g; 26% Calories from Fat; Chol 4 mg; Sod 97 mg.

Beverly J. Stone, Grand Rapids

Watergate Salad

1 4-ounce package pistachio instant
   pudding mix
1 20-ounce can juice-pack crushed
   pineapple

16 ounces whipped topping
1 cup chopped walnuts

Combine pudding mix and pineapple in bowl; mix well. Fold in whipped topping and walnuts. Chill until serving time. **Yield: 12 servings.**

Approx Per Serving: Cal 248; Prot 2 g; Carbo 27 g; Fiber 1 g;
  T Fat 16 g; 55% Calories from Fat; Chol 0 mg; Sod 74 mg.

Robin Harmon, Saginaw

Corned Beef Molded Salad

2 3-ounce packages lemon gelatin
3 cups boiling water
1 cup mayonnaise-type salad dressing
2 cups chopped celery

1 small onion, chopped
1 green bell pepper, chopped
1 12-ounce can corned beef, flaked

Dissolve gelatin in boiling water in bowl. Chill until partially set. Blend in salad dressing. Add celery, onion, green pepper and corned beef; mix well. Spoon into 9x13-inch dish. Chill until set. Cut into squares. Serve in lettuce cups.
Yield: 12 servings.

Approx Per Serving: Cal 208; Prot 9 g; Carbo 19 g; Fiber 1 g;
  T Fat 11 g; 46% Calories from Fat; Chol 29 mg; Sod 487 mg.

Betty Boyd, Hemlock

Hamslaw

½ cup sour cream
2 tablespoons honey
1 or 2 tablespoons Dijon mustard
3 tablespoons chopped green onions

1 cup chopped cooked ham
2 cups shredded cabbage
1 tablespoon chopped green onions
½ cup broken pecans

Combine sour cream, honey, mustard and 3 tablespoons green onions in bowl; mix well. Chill, covered, in refrigerator. Combine ham and cabbage in bowl. Add dressing; toss to mix well. Sprinkle with 1 tablespoon green onions and pecans. **Yield: 4 servings.**

Approx Per Serving: Cal 270; Prot 12 g; Carbo 15 g; Fiber 2 g;
    T Fat 19 g; 61% Calories from Fat; Chol 32 mg; Sod 687 mg.

Shirley A. Cook, Lansing

Oriental Chicken Salad

6 egg roll skins
2 tablespoons cornstarch
Oil for deep frying
4 chicken breasts
¼ cup sugar
½ cup vegetable oil
1 tablespoon sesame oil
3 tablespoons cider vinegar
3 tablespoons wine vinegar
1 clove of garlic, crushed

3 tablespoons soy sauce
1 tablespoon MSG
1 teaspoon salt
1 teaspoon pepper
½ head iceberg lettuce, torn
½ head romaine lettuce, torn
2 bunches green onions, chopped
1 7-ounce can sliced water
   chestnuts, drained
2 tablespoons sesame seed, toasted

Cut each egg roll skin into twelve 1x3-inch strips. Dust with cornstarch. Deep-fry in hot oil until crisp and brown; drain well. Store in airtight container. Rinse chicken and pat dry. Cook in water to cover in saucepan until tender; drain. Cut chicken into bite-sized pieces, discarding skin and bones. Chill in refrigerator. Combine sugar, oils, vinegars, garlic, soy sauce, MSG, salt and pepper in jar; shake to mix well. Chill in refrigerator. Combine iceberg and romaine lettuce, green onions, water chestnuts and chicken in salad bowl. Add dressing and sesame seed; toss to mix well. Add fried egg roll skins; toss gently. Serve with hot rolls and a light dessert. **Yield: 4 servings.**

Approx Per Serving: Cal 558; Prot 30 g; Carbo 29 g; Fiber 4 g;
    T Fat 36 g; 58% Calories from Fat; Chol 72 mg; Sod 4596 mg.
    Nutritional information does not include egg roll skins and oil for deep frying.

Patricia Virch, Marquette

Deviled Eggs in Aspic

1 tablespoon unflavored gelatin	1/4 teaspoon celery salt
1 1/2 cups chicken broth	1/2 teaspoon salt
2 tablespoons vinegar	2 hard-boiled eggs, deviled, cut into
1/2 teaspoon paprika	quarters

Soften gelatin in 1/4 cup broth in saucepan. Stir in 1/4 cup additional broth. Bring to a boil, stirring to dissolve gelatin completely. Add remaining 1 cup broth. Add mixture of vinegar, paprika, celery salt and salt; mix well. Spoon into small salad mold. Chill until slightly thickened. Arrange eggs cut side down in aspic. Chill until set. Unmold onto serving plate. **Yield: 4 servings.**

Approx Per Serving: Cal 62; Prot 6 g; Carbo 1 g; Fiber <1 g;
    T Fat 3 g; 50% Calories from Fat; Chol 107 mg; Sod 685 mg.

Evelyn Bedore, Ironwood

Salmon-Stuffed Tomatoes

1 16-ounce can salmon, drained, flaked	1/4 cup sliced black olives
	6 large tomatoes
1/3 cup sliced green onions	Salt and pepper to taste
1/3 cup chopped celery	2/3 cup sour cream

Mix first 4 ingredients in bowl. Chill in refrigerator. Cut off tops of tomatoes and scoop out pulp. Chill shells. Sprinkle insides of tomato shells with salt and pepper. Add sour cream, salt and pepper to salmon mixture; mix gently. Spoon into tomato shells. Serve on salad greens; garnish with thinly sliced cucumber. **Yield: 6 servings.**

Approx Per Serving: Cal 198; Prot 17 g; Carbo 7 g; Fiber 2 g;
    T Fat 12 g; 52% Calories from Fat; Chol 50 mg; Sod 502 mg.

Sally Taylor, Marquette

Tasty Tuna Salad

2 7-ounce cans water-pack white tuna	1/2 cup golden raisins
1 cup grated carrot	1/2 cup each chopped green and red
1/2 cup chopped celery	bell pepper
1/2 bunch green onions, chopped	1/4 cup malt vinegar
1/2 cup grapes	1/2 cup oil-and-vinegar salad dressing

Flake tuna into medium bowl. Add remaining ingredients; mix well. Chill, covered, until serving time. Serve in lettuce-lined bowl. **Yield: 6 servings.**

Approx Per Serving: Cal 248; Prot 21 g; Carbo 17 g; Fiber 3 g;
    T Fat 11 g; 40% Calories from Fat; Chol 37 mg; Sod 254 mg.

Sally Taylor, Marquette

Seafood Pasta Salad

1/2 cup mayonnaise-type salad
  dressing
1/4 cup zesty Italian salad dressing
1/4 cup grated Parmesan cheese
1 1/2 cups chopped imitation crab meat
8 ounces corkscrew noodles, cooked,
  drained

1 cup broccoli flowerets, partially
  cooked
1/2 cup chopped green bell pepper
1/2 cup chopped tomato
1/4 cup sliced green onions
Freshly ground pepper to taste

Combine salad dressings and cheese in bowl; mix well. Add imitation crab meat, pasta, broccoli, green pepper, tomato and green onions; mix lightly. Chill until serving time. Top with freshly ground pepper. **Yield: 4 servings.**

Approx Per Serving: Cal 496; Prot 18 g; Carbo 61 g; Fiber 4 g;
  T Fat 22 g; 38% Calories from Fat; Chol 24 mg; Sod 921 mg.

June A. Town, Saginaw

Shrimp and Pasta Deluxe Salad

1 cup uncooked elbow macaroni
1/2 cup sour cream
1/3 cup French salad dressing
Seafood seasoning to taste
1/4 teaspoon garlic salt
3/4 teaspoon salt
Pepper to taste

1 16-ounce can sweet green peas,
  drained
2 cups cooked peeled shrimp, chilled
1/3 cup chopped celery
1/4 cup chopped onion
1/4 cup chopped pimento

Cook pasta using package directions; rinse in cold water and drain. Combine sour cream, salad dressing, seafood seasoning, garlic salt, salt and pepper in bowl. Fold in peas, shrimp, celery, onion, pimento and pasta. Spoon into large serving bowl. Chill until serving time. **Yield: 8 servings.**

Approx Per Serving: Cal 197; Prot 13 g; Carbo 15 g; Fiber 3 g;
  T Fat 10 g; 44% Calories from Fat; Chol 89 mg; Sod 617 mg.

Sue Thomas, Royal Oak

*Serve chicken or seafood salad in avocado halves, tomato
cups, melon rings or pineapple boats.*

Cucumber and Macaroni Salad

1 16-ounce package spiral pasta	1½ tablespoons garlic powder
⅔ cup canola oil	1 tablespoon parsley flakes
1½ cups sugar	1 teaspoon salt
1½ cups vinegar	½ teaspoon pepper
1 teaspoon MSG	3 medium cucumbers, sliced
2 teaspoons dry mustard	2 onions, thinly sliced

Cook pasta using package directions; drain. Combine with oil in bowl; mix well. Combine next 8 ingredients in small bowl; mix well. Add to pasta with cucumbers and onions, mix well. Chill, covered, in refrigerator overnight. **Yield: 8 servings.**

Approx Per Serving: Cal 550; Prot 8 g; Carbo 89 g; Fiber 4 g;
    T Fat 19 g; 31% Calories from Fat; Chol 0 mg; Sod 808 mg.

Judy Yeager, Grand Rapids

Garbanzo-Pasta Salad

8 ounces uncooked pasta shells	2 tablespoons red wine vinegar
¼ cup each chopped onion, chopped	⅓ cup olive oil
parsley and chopped pimento	1 19-ounce can garbanzo beans,
1 clove of garlic, finely minced	drained

Cook pasta using package directions. Rinse with cold water and drain. Combine next 5 ingredients in bowl; mix well. Let stand for 5 minutes. Add olive oil, garbanzo beans and pasta; mix well. Chill until serving time. **Yield: 6 servings.**

Approx Per Serving: Cal 358; Prot 9 g; Carbo 50 g; Fiber 2 g;
    T Fat 13 g; 34% Calories from Fat; Chol 0 mg; Sod 271 mg.

Evon Murphy, Lansing

Italian Pasta Salad

1 16-ounce package rotini	1 tablespoon Italian seasoning
8 ounces summer sausage, chopped	1 tablespoon garlic salt
8 ounces mozzarella cheese, chopped	¼ teaspoon red pepper flakes
1 green bell pepper, chopped	1 8-ounce bottle of Italian salad
½ cup chopped onion	dressing
½ cup chopped celery	

Cook pasta using package directions; drain and cool. Combine with remaining ingredients in serving bowl; mix well. Chill, covered, overnight. **Yield: 10 servings.**

Approx Per Serving: Cal 383; Prot 13 g; Carbo 39 g; Fiber 2 g;
    T Fat 22 g; 49% Calories from Fat; Chol 26 mg; Sod 955 mg.

Carol J. Valeski, Quinnesec

Layered Pasta Salad

1¹/₂ cups uncooked pasta shells
1 tablespoon oil
1 head lettuce, torn
3 hard-boiled eggs, sliced
Pepper to taste
12 ounces ham, cut into thin strips
1 10-ounce package frozen tiny
  green peas, thawed

1 cup shredded Monterey Jack cheese
1 cup mayonnaise
¹/₂ cup sour cream
2 teaspoons Dijon mustard
¹/₄ cup sliced or chopped green
  onions
¹/₂ teaspoon salt
¹/₂ teaspoon pepper

Cook pasta using package directions; drain and rinse with cold water. Toss with oil in bowl. Layer lettuce, pasta and egg slices in 3-quart dish. Sprinkle with pepper to taste. Add layers of ham, peas and cheese. Combine mayonnaise, sour cream, mustard, green onions, salt and ¹/₂ teaspoon pepper in small bowl; mix well. Spread over layers, sealing to edge of dish. Chill, covered, overnight. Toss at serving time. **Yield: 8 servings.**

Approx Per Serving: Cal 465; Prot 21 g; Carbo 15 g; Fiber 3 g;
    T Fat 36 g; 69% Calories from Fat; Chol 139 mg; Sod 1038 mg.

Agnes R. Zervan, Burt

Macaroni Salad

1 16-ounce package macaroni
¹/₄ cup sugar
¹/₄ cup vinegar
2 teaspoons mustard
2 cups mayonnaise
1 13-ounce can evaporated milk

1 onion, chopped
1 green bell pepper, chopped
1 carrot, chopped
1 stalk celery, chopped
6 hard-boiled eggs, chopped

Cook pasta using package directions; drain. Combine sugar, vinegar, mustard, mayonnaise, evaporated milk, onion, green pepper, carrot, celery and eggs in large bowl; mix well. Add pasta; mix gently. Chill for 2 hours or longer. May add cheese and radishes if desired. **Yield: 10 servings.**

Approx Per Serving: Cal 612; Prot 13 g; Carbo 47 g; Fiber 3 g;
    T Fat 42 g; 61% Calories from Fat; Chol 165 mg; Sod 349 mg.

Julie Clements, Lansing

Pasta Salad

2 gallons water
1/8 teaspoon garlic powder
1/8 teaspoon onion powder
1/4 teaspoon salt
1/4 teaspoon pepper
2 pounds uncooked rotini
8 ounces broccoli flowerets, blanched
1 cup shredded carrot
1/2 cup each chopped green and red
  bell pepper
1/2 cup chopped green onions
3/4 cup grated Parmesan cheese
1 1/2 cups cubed provolone cheese
1 cup julienned ham
2 1/2 cups ranch salad dressing
1 tablespoon ranch salad dressing
  mix
1 cup half and half

Bring water, garlic powder, onion powder, salt and pepper to a boil in large
saucepan. Add pasta. Cook for 6 or 7 minutes or just until tender; drain and rinse
with cold water. Combine with broccoli, carrot, bell peppers, green onions, cheeses,
ham, salad dressing, salad dressing mix and half and half in large bowl; mix well.
Chill until serving time. **Yield: 16 servings.**

Approx Per Serving: Cal 444; Prot 16 g; Carbo 48 g; Fiber 3 g;
  T Fat 21 g; 43% Calories from Fat; Chol 35 mg; Sod 551 mg.

Robert Miller, Lansing

Ziti Salad

8 ounces uncooked ziti
1 or 2 tomatoes, chopped
1 1/2 cups broccoli flowerets
3/4 cup thawed frozen green peas
8 ounces mozzarella cheese, shredded
1/4 cup grated Parmesan cheese
1 cup Robusto Italian salad dressing
3/4 teaspoon basil

Cook pasta using package directions; drain. Combine with tomatoes, broccoli, peas
and cheeses in bowl; mix well. Add salad dressing and basil; mix well. Chill until
serving time. May add crab meat or lobster meat if desired. **Yield: 6 servings.**

Approx Per Serving: Cal 472; Prot 16 g; Carbo 39 g; Fiber 4 g;
  T Fat 33 g; 58% Calories from Fat; Chol 32 mg; Sod 426 mg.

Sharon Conner Oliver, Holt

Artichoke Salad

1 7-ounce package chicken-flavored
   Rice-A-Roni
12 olives, sliced
2 tablespoons chopped onion
½ green bell pepper, chopped
½ cup chopped celery
¾ teaspoon curry powder
2 6-ounce jars marinated artichoke
   hearts
⅓ cup mayonnaise

Cook Rice-A-Roni using package directions. Combine with next 5 ingredients in large bowl. Drain and chop artichokes. Add to salad; mix well. Add mayonnaise, mix gently. Chill until serving time. **Yield: 6 servings.**

Approx Per Serving: Cal 278; Prot 4 g; Carbo 28 g; Fiber 4 g;
    T Fat 18 g; 56% Calories from Fat; Chol 7 mg; Sod 829 mg.

Lee Capron, Battle Creek

Beet and Cucumber Boats

4 medium beets, coarsely shredded
2 tablespoons oil
2 tablespoons cider vinegar
2 tablespoons lemon juice
1½ teaspoons salt
2 6-inch cucumbers

Combine beets with oil, vinegar, lemon juice and salt in bowl; mix well. Chill, covered, in refrigerator. Cut cucumbers into halves lengthwise. Scoop out and chop pulp, reserving shells. Combine pulp with beet mixture. Spoon into cucumber shell boats. Serve on plates lined with salad greens. **Yield: 4 servings.**

Approx Per Serving: Cal 104; Prot 2 g; Carbo 10 g; Fiber 3 g;
    T Fat 7 g; 58% Calories from Fat; Chol 0 mg; Sod 844 mg.

Nellie Thompson, Romulus

Broccoli Salad

1 cup lite mayonnaise
3 tablespoons vinegar
⅓ cup sugar
1 bunch broccoli, finely chopped
½ red onion, finely chopped
1 cup raisins
1 pound bacon, crisp-fried, crumbled
1 7-ounce can water chestnuts,
   drained, chopped

Mix mayonnaise, vinegar and sugar in bowl. Combine half the mixture with broccoli, onion and raisins in large bowl; mix well. Chill, covered, overnight. Add remaining dressing mixture, bacon and water chestnuts at serving time; toss to mix well. May substitute 1 cup sunflower seed for water chestnuts. **Yield: 8 servings.**

Approx Per Serving: Cal 290; Prot 8 g; Carbo 35 g; Fiber 3 g;
    T Fat 15 g; 44% Calories from Fat; Chol 22 mg; Sod 438 mg.

Carroll King, Brooklyn

Broccoli-Bacon-Raisin Salad

Flowerets of 1 bunch broccoli
1/2 cup chopped celery
1/2 cup sliced red onion
1 pound bacon, crisp-fried, crumbled
1/2 cup sesame seed, toasted

1/2 cup raisins
3/4 cup mayonnaise
1/4 cup sugar
1/4 cup vinegar

Mix first 4 ingredients in large bowl. Stir in sesame seed and raisins. Mix mayonnaise, sugar and vinegar in bowl. Pour over vegetable mixture. **Yield: 12 servings.**

Approx Per Serving: Cal 248; Prot 6 g; Carbo 13 g; Fiber 2 g;
     T Fat 20 g; 70% Calories from Fat; Chol 18 mg; Sod 275 mg.

Irene A. Jankoviak, Cheboygan

Cheesy Broccoli and Bacon Toss

3 cups broccoli flowerets
1/2 cup shredded Cheddar cheese
1/4 cup chopped red onion
1/2 cup mayonnaise

2 tablespoons sugar
2 teaspoons lemon juice
8 slices bacon, crisp-fried, crumbled

Combine broccoli, cheese and onion in large bowl. Mix mayonnaise, sugar and lemon juice in small bowl. Add to salad; mix well. Chill until serving time. Add bacon at serving time; toss to mix well. **Yield: 9 servings.**

Approx Per Serving: Cal 166; Prot 4 g; Carbo 5 g; Fiber 1 g;
     T Fat 15 g; 78% Calories from Fat; Chol 19 mg; Sod 206 mg.

Mary Lucas, Rockford

New Mexico Broccoli Salad

2 cups chopped broccoli
1 cup seedless grapes
1/2 cup chopped pecans
3/4 cup mayonnaise-type salad
     dressing

2 tablespoons milk
1/4 cup sugar
1 tablespoon lemon juice
2 bananas, sliced

Combine broccoli, grapes and pecans in salad bowl. Add salad dressing, milk, sugar and lemon juice; mix well. Chill until serving time. Add bananas at serving time; mix gently. **Yield: 6 servings.**

Approx Per Serving: Cal 278; Prot 3 g; Carbo 33 g; Fiber 3 g;
     T Fat 17 g; 52% Calories from Fat; Chol 8 mg; Sod 220 mg.

Elna A. Secore, Grand Blanc

Vegetable Salad

1 large bunch broccoli, chopped
6 green onions, chopped
2 cups sliced celery
1 cup sliced almonds
1 cup raisins
2 cups seedless red grapes

1 cup mayonnaise-type salad dressing
1 tablespoon vinegar
1/4 cup sugar
1/4 cup milk
1 pound bacon, crisp-fried, crumbled

Combine broccoli, onions, celery, almonds, raisins and grapes in large bowl. Add mixture of salad dressing, vinegar, sugar and milk; mix well. Chill for several hours. Toss with bacon at serving time. **Yield: 10 servings.**

Approx Per Serving: Cal 337; Prot 9 g; Carbo 35 g; Fiber 4 g;
    T Fat 20 g; 51% Calories from Fat; Chol 18 mg; Sod 421 mg.

Patti Rizzio, Marquette

Fruited Carrot Salad

2 cups shredded carrots
1   8-ounce can pineapple chunks,
    drained

1/2 cup flaked coconut
1/4 cup raisins
1/2 cup mayonnaise

Mix all ingredients in medium bowl. Chill, covered, for 2 hours. **Yield: 4 servings.**

Approx Per Serving: Cal 324; Prot 2 g; Carbo 26 g; Fiber 4 g;
    T Fat 25 g; 67% Calories from Fat; Chol 16 mg; Sod 179 mg.

Clara Jaquays, Grand Rapids

Oriental Cabbage Salad

1   3-ounce package chicken-flavored
    ramen noodles
4 cups shredded cabbage
1/4 cup sliced green onions
2 tablespoons sesame seed
3 tablespoons vinegar

2 tablespoons sugar
2 tablespoons oil
1/4 teaspoon salt
1/2 teaspoon white pepper
1/2 cup toasted slivered almonds

Crush noodles slightly; place in colander. Pour boiling water over noodles; drain well. Combine with cabbage, green onions and sesame seed in large bowl; mix well. Combine seasonings from noodles, vinegar, sugar, oil, salt and white pepper in jar; shake to mix. Pour over salad; toss to mix well. Chill, covered, for several hours to overnight. Add almonds at serving time. **Yield: 8 servings.**

Approx Per Serving: Cal 154; Prot 4 g; Carbo 13 g; Fiber 2 g;
    T Fat 11 g; 59% Calories from Fat; Chol 0 mg; Sod 232 mg.

Mabel Gothro, Grayling

Cucumber Salad

2 cucumbers
1 onion, chopped
1 tomato, chopped

1 green bell pepper, chopped
1/4 cup sliced black olives
1 cup ranch salad dressing

Score cucumbers with fork; cut into slices. Combine with onion, tomato, green pepper, olives and salad dressing in bowl; mix well. May substitute Italian or bleu cheese salad dressing for ranch dressing. **Yield: 6 servings.**

Approx Per Serving: Cal 186; Prot 2 g; Carbo 8 g; Fiber 2 g;
T Fat 17 g; 78% Calories from Fat; Chol 16 mg; Sod 232 mg.

Maralynn Tanner, Birch Run

Easy Lettuce Salad

1 head lettuce, shredded
1 cup Swiss cheese cubes
1 cup cashews
1 cup oil
3/4 cup sugar

1/3 cup vinegar
1 tablespoon minced onion
1 tablespoon poppy seed
1 tablespoon dry mustard
Salt to taste

Combine lettuce, cheese and cashews in bowl; mix well. Chill in refrigerator. Mix oil, sugar, vinegar, onion, poppy seed, dry mustard and salt in blender or food processor container; process until smooth. Chill until serving time. Add to salad; toss gently. May reduce amount of dressing used and store unused portion in refrigerator. **Yield: 6 servings.**

Approx Per Serving: Cal 636; Prot 10 g; Carbo 34 g; Fiber 2 g;
T Fat 53 g; 73% Calories from Fat; Chol 17 mg; Sod 57 mg.

Cathy DeGoede, Grand Rapids

Oriental Salad

1/2 cup oil
2 tablespoons white vinegar
1/4 cup sugar
2 teaspoons MSG
1 teaspoon salt

1/2 teaspoon pepper
1 head lettuce, torn
3 ounces slivered almonds
1/2 cup chow mein noodles
1/4 cup sesame seed

Combine oil, vinegar, sugar, MSG, salt and pepper in small bowl; mix well. Combine lettuce, almonds, noodles and sesame seed in salad bowl. Add dressing; toss to mix well. **Yield: 6 servings.**

Approx Per Serving: Cal 337; Prot 5 g; Carbo 15 g; Fiber 3 g;
T Fat 30 g; 77% Calories from Fat; Chol <1 mg; Sod 1829 mg.

Aileen McPherson, Cheboygan

Picture-Perfect Salad

2 medium tomatoes, seeded, chopped
2 small cucumbers, sliced
1 large green bell pepper, chopped
¹/₂ cup chopped purple onion
2 large tart apples, chopped

¹/₂ cup olive oil
3 tablespoons lemon juice
1 tablespoon chopped fresh mint or
    ¹/₂ teaspoon dried mint
¹/₂ teaspoon salt

Combine tomatoes, cucumbers, green pepper, onion and apples in large bowl. Mix olive oil, lemon juice, mint and salt in small bowl. Add to salad; toss to mix well. Chill, covered, in refrigerator. Serve on crisp salad greens. **Yield: 8 servings.**

Approx Per Serving: Cal 171; Prot 1 g; Carbo 13 g; Fiber 3 g;
    T Fat 14 g; 70% Calories from Fat; Chol 0 mg; Sod 138 mg.

Evon Murphy, Lansing

Potato Salad

5 pounds potatoes
Salt to taste
6 hard-boiled eggs, chopped
6 large sweet pickles, chopped
12 green onions, chopped

1 cup mayonnaise-type salad dressing
¹/₂ cup sugar
¹/₄ cup sweet pickle juice
2 to 3 tablespoons prepared mustard
Cayenne pepper to taste

Cook potatoes in water to cover in saucepan just until tender; drain. Cool, peel and chop potatoes. Combine with salt in bowl. Add eggs, pickles and green onions. Mix salad dressing, sugar, pickle juice, mustard, salt and cayenne pepper in small bowl. Add to salad; mix gently. Chill until serving time. Garnish with paprika.
Yield: 12 servings.

Approx Per Serving: Cal 335; Prot 7 g; Carbo 56 g; Fiber 4 g;
    T Fat 10 g; 26% Calories from Fat; Chol 111 mg; Sod 297 mg.

Marylyn Shadduck, Newaygo

Shredded Potato Salad

10 large potatoes
1 large onion, grated

8 ounces radishes, thinly sliced
2 cups mayonnaise

Cook potatoes in water to cover in saucepan until tender; drain. Cool, peel and shred potatoes. Combine with onion, radishes and mayonnaise in bowl; mix well. Garnish with paprika and parsley. **Yield: 12 servings.**

Approx Per Serving: Cal 369; Prot 3 g; Carbo 26 g; Fiber 2 g;
    T Fat 29 g; 70% Calories from Fat; Chol 22 mg; Sod 218 mg.

Donna Patrick, Pinckney

Yummy Potato Salad

4 cups chopped cooked potatoes
4 hard-boiled eggs, chopped
1/2 cup chopped dill pickles
1/2 cup mayonnaise

2 tablespoons vinegar
2 teaspoons celery seed
Salt and pepper to taste

Combine potatoes, eggs and pickles in large bowl. Mix mayonnaise, vinegar, celery seed, salt and pepper in small bowl. Add to salad; mix gently. Chill, covered, until serving time. Garnish with tomato wedges. **Yield: 8 servings.**

Approx Per Serving: Cal 198; Prot 4 g; Carbo 15 g; Fiber 1 g;
     T Fat 14 g; 62% Calories from Fat; Chol 115 mg; Sod 276 mg.

Loraine Metzger, Lansing

Sesame Seed Salad

1/2 cup oil
6 tablespoons vinegar
1/2 cup sugar
2 teaspoons MSG
1 teaspoon salt
1/2 teaspoon pepper

1 large head lettuce, chopped
1 bunch green onions, chopped
3 ounces slivered almonds, toasted
1/4 cup sesame seed
1 cup chow mein noodles

Combine oil, vinegar, sugar, MSG, salt and pepper in jar; shake to mix well. Chill in refrigerator. Combine lettuce, green onions, almonds and sesame seed in bowl. Chill until serving time. Add noodles and dressing; toss to mix well. **Yield: 6 servings.**

Approx Per Serving: Cal 393; Prot 6 g; Carbo 27 g; Fiber 3 g;
     T Fat 31 g; 68% Calories from Fat; Chol 1 mg; Sod 1867 mg.

Barbara Smith, Holly

Spring Salad

2 cups tomato juice
1   3-ounce package lemon gelatin
3 ounces cream cheese
1 cup mayonnaise

1 1/2 cups chopped celery
1 1/2 cups chopped green bell pepper
1 cup chopped onion
1 cup grated carrots

Bring tomato juice to a simmer in saucepan. Stir in gelatin until dissolved. Add cream cheese and mayonnaise; mix well. Cool to room temperature. Stir in celery, green pepper, onion and carrots. Spoon into medium salad mold. Chill until set. Unmold onto serving plate. **Yield: 6 servings.**

Approx Per Serving: Cal 406; Prot 4 g; Carbo 24 g; Fiber 3 g;
     T Fat 34 g; 74% Calories from Fat; Chol 37 mg; Sod 623 mg.

Florence Chase, Kalamazoo

Zucchini Salad

3 medium zucchini, chopped
3 small yellow squash, chopped
1 medium red onion, chopped
1 green bell pepper, chopped
1/4 cup red wine vinegar
2/3 cup cider vinegar

1/3 cup oil
1/4 cup sugar
2 teaspoons dry mustard
1 teaspoon salt
1/4 teaspoon pepper

Combine zucchini, squash, onion, and green pepper in bowl. Add mixture of remaining ingredients to salad; mix well. Chill, covered, for 3 to 4 hours. **Yield: 10 servings.**

Approx Per Serving: Cal 107; Prot 1 g; Carbo 11 g; Fiber 1 g;
    T Fat 8 g; 59% Calories from Fat; Chol 0 mg; Sod 216 mg.

Carolyn Devers, Laingsburg

Marinated Vegetable Salad

1 head cauliflower, broken into
    flowerets
1 stalk broccoli, chopped
8 ounces mushrooms, sliced
8 ounces green onions, chopped
1 pound carrots, sliced
1 cup oil

1/2 cup vinegar
1/2 cup sugar
2 teaspoons celery seed
1 teaspoon paprika
1 1/2 teaspoons salt
1 teaspoon pepper

Combine vegetables in salad bowl. Mix remaining ingredients in small bowl. Add to salad; mix well. Chill, covered, for 4 hours to overnight. **Yield: 12 servings.**

Approx Per Serving: Cal 232; Prot 2 g; Carbo 17 g; Fiber 3 g;
    T Fat 19 g; 68% Calories from Fat; Chol 0 mg; Sod 290 mg.

Kathy O'Rourke, Gladwin

Bacon Dressing

6 slices bacon, chopped
1 egg, beaten
1/4 cup vinegar

1/3 cup sugar
1/4 to 1/3 cup water
Salt and pepper to taste

Fry bacon in skillet; drain, reserving 1 tablespoon drippings. Combine egg, vinegar, sugar, water, salt and pepper in bowl; mix well. Add to drippings and bacon in skillet. Simmer for 2 minutes, stirring constantly. Cool slightly. Serve immediately over salad of lettuce and chopped onion. **Yield: 6 servings.**

Approx Per Serving: Cal 93; Prot 3 g; Carbo 12 g; Fiber 0 g;
    T Fat 4 g; 38% Calories from Fat; Chol 41 mg; Sod 113 mg.

Ann M. Kammerer, Traverse City

Bleu Cheese Dressing

2 cups mayonnaise
1 cup sour cream
4 ounces bleu cheese, crumbled

2 teaspoons lemon juice
1/4 teaspoon garlic powder
Garlic salt to taste

Combine mayonnaise, sour cream, bleu cheese, lemon juice, garlic powder and garlic salt in bowl; mix well. Store in refrigerator. **Yield: 16 servings.**

Approx Per Serving: Cal 253; Prot 2 g; Carbo 2 g; Fiber <1 g;
T Fat 27 g; 94% Calories from Fat; Chol 28 mg; Sod 263 mg.

Nancy Nowlin, Charlotte

French Dressing

2 cups corn oil
3/4 cup catsup
1/3 cup vinegar
2 cups sugar

2 tablespoons Worcestershire sauce
1 cup mayonnaise-type salad dressing
Salt to taste

Combine oil, catsup, vinegar, sugar, Worcestershire sauce, salad dressing and salt in jar; mix well. Store in refrigerator. **Yield: 16 servings.**

Approx Per Serving: Cal 410; Prot <1 g; Carbo 32 g; Fiber <1 g;
T Fat 32 g; 69% Calories from Fat; Chol 4 mg; Sod 257 mg.

Betty Boyd, Hemlock

Blender French Dressing

1 cup oil
3/4 cup sugar
3/4 cup catsup
1/2 cup vinegar

1 tablespoon Worcestershire sauce
2 teaspoons dry mustard
1 teaspoon paprika
2 teaspoons salt

Combine oil, sugar, catsup, vinegar, Worcestershire sauce, dry mustard, paprika and salt in blender container; process until smooth. Store in covered container in refrigerator. **Yield: 12 servings.**

Approx Per Serving: Cal 232; Prot <1 g; Carbo 18 g; Fiber <1 g;
T Fat 18 g; 69% Calories from Fat; Chol 0 mg; Sod 546 mg.

Vivian Schultz, Stephenson

Horseradish Dressing

1 cup mayonnaise
1/2 cup buttermilk
1 1/2 tablespoons horseradish

2 tablespoons minced onion
1/2 teaspoon salt
1/8 teaspoon pepper

Combine mayonnaise, buttermilk, horseradish, onion, salt and pepper in bowl; mix well. Chill for 1 hour or longer. Serve with cold meats. **Yield: 10 servings.**

Approx Per Serving: Cal 164; Prot 1 g; Carbo 2 g; Fiber <1 g;
    T Fat 18 g; 95% Calories from Fat; Chol 13 mg; Sod 247 mg.

Shirley A. Cook, Lansing

Light Salad Dressing

1/2 cup red wine vinegar
2 teaspoons Worcestershire sauce
1 tablespoon Dijon mustard
2 tablespoons lemon juice
1 cup water

2 cloves of garlic, finely chopped
4 teaspoons sugar
1/2 teaspoon salt
1/4 teaspoon freshly ground pepper

Combine vinegar, Worcestershire sauce, mustard, lemon juice, water, garlic, sugar, salt and pepper in jar; mix well. May store, covered, in refrigerator for months. **Yield: 12 servings.**

Approx Per Serving: Cal 11; Prot <1 g; Carbo 3 g; Fiber <1 g;
    T Fat <1 g; 13% Calories from Fat; Chol 0 mg; Sod 131 mg.

Marge Venable, Grand Blanc

Shipshewana Poppy Seed Dressing

1/4 cup vinegar
1/2 cup water
2 tablespoons chopped onion
1 tablespoon dry mustard

1 cup sugar
1 1/2 cups oil
1 cup sour cream
1 or 2 tablespoons poppy seed

Combine vinegar, water, onion and dry mustard in blender container; process until smooth. Add sugar, oil, sour cream and poppy seed in order listed, processing until smooth after each addition. Store in covered jar in refrigerator. **Yield: 24 servings.**

Approx Per Serving: Cal 179; Prot 1 g; Carbo 9 g; Fiber <1 g;
    T Fat 16 g; 79% Calories from Fat; Chol 4 mg; Sod 6 mg.

Lee Capron, Battle Creek

HANDICAP BOWLING

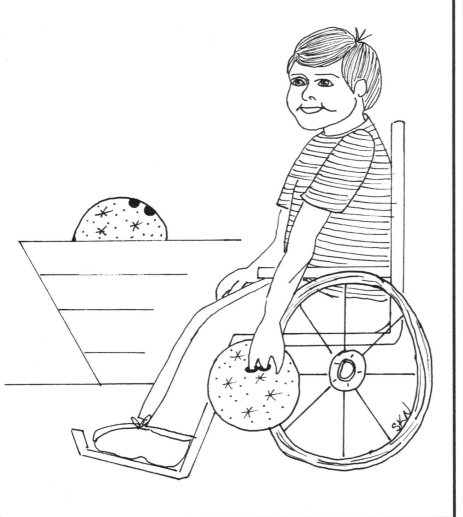

Meats

Sweet-and-Sour Barbecue

1 pound beef, cubed
1 pound pork, cubed
1 10-ounce can tomato soup
1 medium onion, chopped
¹/₄ cup sugar

¹/₃ cup vinegar
¹/₄ cup Worcestershire sauce
1 cup water
Garlic salt, celery salt, salt and
    pepper to taste

Combine beef, pork, soup, onion, sugar, vinegar, Worcestershire sauce, water, garlic salt, celery salt, salt and pepper in large roasting pan. Bake, covered, at 350 degrees for 2¹/₂ to 3 hours, stirring occasionally to break up meat and mix well. Serve on sandwich buns. May use same sauce ingredients for ribs and chicken. **Yield: 10 servings.**

Approx Per Serving: Cal 220; Prot 20 g; Carbo 11 g; Fiber <1 g;
    T Fat 10 g; 43% Calories from Fat; Chol 63 mg; Sod 309 mg.

Jennie Dopierala

Marinated Steak

1 1-pound flank steak
1 large onion, thinly sliced
2 cloves of garlic, finely chopped
¹/₂ cup oil

1 cup beer
¹/₂ cup lemon juice
2 tablespoons light brown sugar
1 tablespoon Worcestershire sauce

Score steak; place in shallow baking dish. Sauté onion and garlic in ¹/₄ cup oil in medium skillet until tender; remove from heat. Add remaining ¹/₄ cup oil, beer, lemon juice, brown sugar and Worcestershire sauce; mix well. Pour over steak. Marinate, covered, in refrigerator for 6 hours to overnight, turning occasionally. Drain, reserving marinade. Grill or broil until done to taste, basting frequently with reserved marinade. **Yield: 4 servings.**

Approx Per Serving: Cal 466; Prot 22 g; Carbo 16 g; Fiber 1 g;
    T Fat 34 g; 67% Calories from Fat; Chol 64 mg; Sod 79 mg.
    Nutritional information includes entire amount of marinade.

Sally Taylor, Marquette

Marinated Flank Steak

1/2 cup soy sauce
1/4 cup oil
2 tablespoons water
2 cloves of garlic, minced

2 teaspoons brown sugar
1 teaspoon gingerroot
1/4 teaspoon pepper
1   2-pound flank steak

Combine soy sauce, oil, water, garlic, brown sugar, gingerroot and pepper in small bowl; mix well. Score steak on both sides. Combine with marinade in sealable plastic bag. Marinate in refrigerator for 2 to 4 hours, turning occasionally. Drain, reserving marinade. Grill or broil 6 inches from heat source for 5 minutes on each side or until done to taste, basting occasionally with marinade. Slice thinly cross grain.
Yield: 6 servings.

Approx Per Serving: Cal 298; Prot 30 g; Carbo 4 g; Fiber <1 g;
    T Fat 18 g; 54% Calories from Fat; Chol 85 mg; Sod 1419 mg.
    Nutritional information includes entire amount of marinade.

Lois Roggenbeck, Saginaw

Marinated Round Steak

1 1/2 cups oil
3/4 cup soy sauce
1/4 cup Worcestershire sauce
2 tablespoons dry mustard
1/2 cup wine vinegar
1 1/2 teaspoons parsley flakes

2 cloves of garlic, crushed
1/3 cup lemon juice
2 1/4 teaspoons salt
1 tablespoon pepper
2 pounds top round steak, 1 1/2 inches
    thick

Combine oil, soy sauce, Worcestershire sauce, dry mustard, vinegar, parsley flakes, garlic, lemon juice, salt and pepper in shallow dish. Add steak. Marinate in refrigerator. Remove steak from marinade and let stand at room temperature for 1 hour. Grill for 10 minutes on each side or until done to taste. **Yield: 6 servings.**

Approx Per Serving: Cal 728; Prot 31 g; Carbo 9 g; Fiber <1 g;
    T Fat 64 g; 78% Calories from Fat; Chol 85 mg; Sod 3002 mg.
    Nutritional information includes entire amount of marinade.

Ruth Nearing, Gaylord

Teriyaki Steak

2/3 cup soy sauce
1/4 cup dry cooking sherry
1 teaspoon ginger
1/4 cup packed brown sugar

Chopped garlic to taste
1 tablespoon oil
1 pound tenderized round steak, cut
  into strips

Combine first 6 ingredients in shallow dish; mix well. Add steak. Marinate in refrigerator. Drain, reserving marinade. Thread steak strips onto skewers. Grill until done to taste, basting occasionally with marinade. **Yield: 4 servings.**

Approx Per Serving: Cal 285; Prot 24 g; Carbo 21 g; Fiber 0 g;
    T Fat 10 g; 33% Calories from Fat; Chol 64 mg; Sod 2760 mg.

Marlene Carter, Kingsford

Deep-Dish Meat Pie

1½ cups shortening
4 cups flour
1 teaspoon salt
12 to 14 tablespoons cold water
3½ cups ground cooked roast
3 potatoes, cooked, chopped

3 carrots, cooked, sliced
1/2 small onion, chopped
2 cups gravy
12 ounces sharp Cheddar cheese,
  shredded

Cut shortening into mixture of flour and salt in bowl until crumbly. Stir in water. Roll pastry 1/2 at a time on floured surface. Fit half into 9x13-inch baking dish. Combine next 5 ingredients in bowl; mix well. Layer half the roast mixture, cheese and remaining roast mixture in prepared baking dish. Top with remaining pastry. Seal edges and cut vents. Bake at 400 degrees for 1 hour. **Yield: 8 servings.**

Approx Per Serving: Cal 935; Prot 35 g; Carbo 67 g; Fiber 4 g;
    T Fat 59 g; 57% Calories from Fat; Chol 88 mg; Sod 596 mg.

Cliff Duvall, Perry

German Ribs and Kraut

4 pounds beef back ribs
4 unpeeled potatoes, chopped
1 bunch carrots, cut into 2-inch pieces

4 small onions, cut into halves
1   27-ounce can sauerkraut
Salt and pepper to taste

Layer half the ribs, potatoes, carrots, onions, and remaining ribs in 6-quart Dutch oven. Spoon sauerkraut over layers. Bake, covered, at 300 degrees for 4 hours or until ribs are tender. Season with salt and pepper. **Yield: 6 servings.**

Approx Per Serving: Cal 695; Prot 40 g; Carbo 55 g; Fiber 10 g;
    T Fat 36 g; 46% Calories from Fat; Chol 139 mg; Sod 997 mg.

Shirley A. Cook, Lansing

Easy Oven Pot Roast

1 2 to 2½-pound beef chuck roast
1 tablespoon flour
1 tablespoon oil
1 tablespoon soy sauce
⅛ teaspoon pepper

½ cup water
1 bay leaf
2 medium potatoes, cut into chunks
5 medium carrots, cut into chunks

Coat beef with flour. Brown on both sides in oil in Dutch oven. Sprinkle with soy sauce and pepper. Add water and bay leaf. Bake, covered, at 350 degrees for 1 hour. Add potatoes and carrots. Bake, covered, for 30 minutes longer or until beef and vegetables are tender. Discard bay leaf. **Yield: 6 servings.**

Approx Per Serving: Cal 348; Prot 37 g; Carbo 19 g; Fiber 3 g;
    T Fat 13 g; 35% Calories from Fat; Chol 106 mg; Sod 253 mg.

Dennis Little, Eau Claire

Quick and Easy Pot Roast

1 5-pound beef roast
2 tablespoons oil
3 10-ounce cans cream of mushroom
    soup

3 10-ounce cans onion soup
4 potatoes, peeled, cut into quarters
8 carrots

Brown roast in oil in Dutch oven. Add soups. Bake, covered, at 350 degrees for 2 hours. Add potatoes and carrots. Bake for 2 hours longer or until vegetables are tender and gravy is of desired consistency. **Yield: 10 servings.**

Approx Per Serving: Cal 531; Prot 48 g; Carbo 31 g; Fiber 3 g;
    T Fat 24 g; 40% Calories from Fat; Chol 129 mg; Sod 1513 mg.

Nancy Nowlin, Charlotte

Baked Beef Stew

2 pounds 1-inch lean beef cubes
1 cup canned tomatoes, chopped
6 carrots, cut into strips
3 medium potatoes, peeled, cut into
    quarters

½ cup thickly sliced celery
1 medium onion, sliced into rings
3 tablespoons quick-cooking tapioca
1 slice bread, crumbled
1 cup water

Combine all ingredients in large bowl; mix well. Spoon into greased 3-quart baking dish. Bake, covered, at 325 degrees for 2½ to 3 hours or until beef and vegetables are tender. **Yield: 6 servings.**

Approx Per Serving: Cal 350; Prot 32 g; Carbo 35 g; Fiber 5 g;
    T Fat 9 g; 24% Calories from Fat; Chol 85 mg; Sod 174 mg.

Virginia C. Marlatt, Howell

Busy-Day Stew

3 pounds stew beef
1 envelope dry onion soup mix
3 carrots, chopped
1 cup chopped celery
4 potatoes, chopped

2 onions, chopped
2 10-ounce cans cream of mushroom
   soup
1 soup can water
Salt and pepper to taste

Place beef in lightly greased 9x13-inch baking dish; sprinkle with soup mix. Spread vegetables over beef. Pour mixture of soup and water over layers. Season with salt and pepper. Bake, covered with foil, at 300 degrees for 4 hours. **Yield: 6 servings.**

Approx Per Serving: Cal 531; Prot 47 g; Carbo 38 g; Fiber 4 g;
    T Fat 21 g; 35% Calories from Fat; Chol 129 mg; Sod 975 mg.

Butch Ziebart, St. Joseph

Texas Deep-Dish Chili Pie

1 pound beef stew meat, cut into
    1/2-inch cubes
1 tablespoon oil
2 16-ounce cans Mexican-style
    stewed tomatoes
1 medium green bell pepper, chopped

1 envelope taco seasoning mix
1 tablespoon yellow cornmeal
1 16-ounce can kidney beans,
    drained
2 all-ready pie pastries
1/2 cup shredded Cheddar cheese

Brown beef in oil in heavy saucepan; drain. Add next 4 ingredients. Bring to a boil; reduce heat. Simmer for 20 minutes. Stir in beans. Spoon into 10-inch pie plate lined with 1 pastry. Sprinkle with 1/4 cup cheese. Top with remaining pastry. Seal edges and cut vents. Bake at 350 degrees for 30 minutes. Sprinkle with remaining cheese. Bake for 10 minutes longer. **Yield: 6 servings.**

Approx Per Serving: Cal 601; Prot 26 g; Carbo 57 g; Fiber 7 g;
    T Fat 30 g; 45% Calories from Fat; Chol 52 mg; Sod 1779 mg.

Elaine Baird, Saginaw

Beef for Tacos

1 4-pound boneless chuck roast
2 5-ounce cans chopped green chilies
1 5-ounce can salsa

1 10-ounce can beef bouillon
1/4 cup water
Chopped garlic, salt and pepper to taste

Combine all ingredients in slow cooker. Cook on High for 6 to 7 hours. Shred beef to use for tacos or burritos. **Yield: 10 servings.**

Approx Per Serving: Cal 252; Prot 35 g; Carbo 3 g; Fiber 0 g;
    T Fat 10 g; 39% Calories from Fat; Chol 102 mg; Sod 437 mg.

Estella Delaski, California

Reuben Casserole

1 16-ounce can sauerkraut, rinsed
1 12-ounce can corned beef, flaked
2¹/2 cups shredded Swiss cheese
²/3 cup mayonnaise
¹/3 cup Thousand Island salad dressing
3 slices rye bread, toasted, crumbled
2 tablespoons melted butter

Layer sauerkraut, corned beef and cheese in 9x13-inch baking dish. Spread mixture of mayonnaise and salad dressing over layers. Top with bread crumbs; drizzle with butter. Bake at 350 degrees for 30 minutes. May add layer of sliced fresh tomatoes over cheese or microwave for 13 to 15 minutes. **Yield: 6 servings.**

Approx Per Serving: Cal 626; Prot 31 g; Carbo 14 g; Fiber 2 g;
T Fat 50 g; 72% Calories from Fat; Chol 120 mg; Sod 1547 mg.

Ruth Berry, Fort Myers, Florida

Upside-Down Reuben Sandwich Casserole

1 16-ounce can sauerkraut
¹/3 cup Thousand Island salad dressing
1 12-ounce can corned beef, thinly
    sliced
8 ounces Swiss cheese, sliced
1 tablespoon butter, softened
1 small loaf party rye bread

Combine sauerkraut and salad dressing in bowl; mix lightly. Spread evenly in 9x13-inch baking dish. Layer corned beef over top. Bake at 400 degrees for 15 minutes. Layer cheese over corned beef. Spread butter on bread; arrange over casserole. Bake for 10 minutes longer. **Yield: 6 servings.**

Approx Per Serving: Cal 462; Prot 30 g; Carbo 23 g; Fiber 4 g;
T Fat 27 g; 53% Calories from Fat; Chol 94 mg; Sod 1507 mg.

Genevieve Brown, Big Rapids

Corned Beef Casserole

1 12-ounce can corned beef, flaked
1 10-ounce can cream of mushroom
    soup
1 10-ounce can cream of celery soup
1 cup milk
1 cup shredded Cheddar cheese
3 tablespoons chopped onion
1¹/2 cups uncooked macaroni
¹/4 cup chopped green bell pepper

Combine corned beef, soups, milk, cheese, onion, macaroni and green pepper in bowl; mix well. Spoon into baking dish. Bake at 350 degrees for 1 hour. May add broccoli and cauliflower if desired. **Yield: 4 servings.**

Approx Per Serving: Cal 570; Prot 37 g; Carbo 30 g; Fiber 1 g;
T Fat 33 g; 52% Calories from Fat; Chol 120 mg; Sod 2167 mg.

Oneta Ruppert, Hillsdale

Corned Beef and Cabbage

1   3 to 4-pound corned beef
1 large onion, sliced
4 cloves of garlic, cut into halves
1 teaspoon peppercorns
1 bay leaf
8 small potatoes, peeled

8 small yellow onions, peeled
8 carrots, peeled
1 head cabbage, cut into wedges
3 tablespoons mustard
1/2 cup packed brown sugar
1/2 teaspoon ground cloves

Combine corned beef and enough cold water to cover in large saucepan. Bring to a boil; skim surface. Add onion slices, garlic, peppercorns and bay leaf; reduce heat. Simmer for 3 to 4 hours or until tender. Remove beef to baking dish. Strain cooking broth into saucepan. Add potatoes, small onions, carrots and cabbage. Simmer until tender. Mix remaining ingredients in bowl. Spread over beef. Bake at 350 degrees for 20 minutes. Slice beef thinly cross grain. Serve with vegetables. **Yield: 8 servings.**

Approx Per Serving: Cal 567; Prot 30 g; Carbo 55 g; Fiber 7 g;
   T Fat 26 g; 44% Calories from Fat; Chol 131 mg; Sod 1628 mg.

Jim and Maureen Robbins, Petoskey

Corned Beef Pie

1 medium onion, chopped
2 tablespoons shortening
2 tablespoons flour

1   16-ounce can tomatoes, chopped
1   12-ounce can corned beef, flaked
1 recipe 2-crust pie pastry

Sauté onion in shortening in skillet until tender. Stir in flour. Add tomatoes and corned beef. Simmer for several minutes. Spoon into pastry-lined pie plate. Top with remaining pastry. Seal edges; cut vents. Bake at 350 degrees until top is brown. **Yield: 6 servings.**

Approx Per Serving: Cal 483; Prot 20 g; Carbo 31 g; Fiber 2 g;
   T Fat 31 g; 58% Calories from Fat; Chol 49 mg; Sod 1061 mg.

Jan Davis, Negaunee

Teriyaki Marinade for Meat

1/2 cup pineapple juice
1/4 cup packed light brown sugar
2 tablespoons soy sauce
1 tablespoon oil

3/4 teaspoon ginger
1 clove of garlic, minced
1/4 teaspoon salt

Combine all ingredients in saucepan. Simmer until flavors are blended. Use to marinate beef, pork or chicken for 12 hours or longer. **Yield: 6 servings.**

Approx Per Serving: Cal 78; Prot <1 g; Carbo 15 g; Fiber <1 g;
   T Fat 2 g; 26% Calories from Fat; Chol 0 mg; Sod 437 mg.

Brenda Buss, Grand Rapids

Barbecued Beef

1½ pounds lean ground beef
1 medium onion, chopped
1   8-ounce can tomato sauce
1 tablespoon Worcestershire sauce

½ cup catsup
¼ cup packed light brown sugar
½ teaspoon dry mustard
½ teaspoon chili powder

Brown ground beef with onion in large skillet, stirring until ground beef is crumbly; drain. Combine tomato sauce, Worcestershire sauce, catsup, brown sugar, dry mustard and chili powder in bowl; mix well. Pour over ground beef. Simmer until bubbly. Serve on sandwich buns. **Yield: 6 servings.**

Approx Per Serving: Cal 313; Prot 22 g; Carbo 20 g; Fiber 1 g;
    T Fat 16 g; 47% Calories from Fat; Chol 74 mg; Sod 562 mg.

Fred Muhlenbeck, Greer, South Carolina

Barbecued Hamburgers

1½ pounds ground beef
½ cup chopped onion
1 cup chopped celery
1 cup chopped green bell pepper
2 tablespoons Worcestershire sauce

1 cup catsup
2 tablespoons vinegar
2 tablespoons brown sugar
1 tablespoon dry mustard
Salt and pepper to taste

Brown ground beef with onion in skillet, stirring until ground beef is crumbly; drain. Add remaining ingredients; mix well. Simmer until of desired consistency. Serve on buns. **Yield: 6 servings.**

Approx Per Serving: Cal 312; Prot 22 g; Carbo 20 g; Fiber 2 g;
    T Fat 16 g; 47% Calories from Fat; Chol 74 mg; Sod 609 mg.

Tom Handley, Kalamazoo

Boston Burgers

8 ounces ground beef
¼ cup chopped onion
1   22-ounce can baked beans
¼ cup chili sauce

½ teaspoon salt
Pepper to taste
8 hamburger buns, toasted
1 cup shredded Cheddar cheese

Brown ground beef in skillet, stirring until crumbly; drain. Add onion. Cook until onion is tender. Stir in beans, chili sauce, salt and pepper. Simmer, covered, for 20 minutes. Spoon into buns; top beef mixture with cheese. **Yield: 8 servings.**

Approx Per Serving: Cal 341; Prot 17 g; Carbo 42 g; Fiber 6 g;
    T Fat 12 g; 32% Calories from Fat; Chol 39 mg; Sod 884 mg.

Shirley A. Cook, Lansing

Lemon Hamburgers

1 pound ground beef
1 teaspoon grated lemon rind
2 tablespoons lemon juice

1 teaspoon seasoned salt
⅛ teaspoon pepper

Combine ground beef, lemon rind, lemon juice, seasoned salt and pepper in bowl; mix well. Shape into patties. Grill until done to taste. **Yield: 4 servings.**

Approx Per Serving: Cal 233; Prot 21 g; Carbo 1 g; Fiber <1 g;
    T Fat 16 g; 63% Calories from Fat; Chol 74 mg; Sod 390 mg.

Evelyn Helmer, Lansing

Quick and Easy Barbecue Beef

2 pounds ground beef
1   15-ounce can Manwich sauce

1   12-ounce can Dinty Moore roast
    beef

Brown ground beef in skillet, stirring until crumbly; drain. Add sauce and canned beef; mix well. Simmer for 5 minutes. **Yield: 10 servings.**

Approx Per Serving: Cal 240; Prot 21 g; Carbo 8 g; Fiber 0 g;
    T Fat 14 g; 52% Calories from Fat; Chol 65 mg; Sod 400 mg.

Joanne Van Oort, Grand Haven

Burritos

1 pound ground beef
1 envelope taco seasoning mix
1   16-ounce can refried beans
8 flour tortillas

1   8-ounce jar brown gravy
1   8-ounce can tomato sauce
1   10-ounce can enchilada sauce
1 cup shredded Cheddar cheese

Brown ground beef in skillet, stirring until crumbly; drain. Add taco seasoning mix and beans; mix well. Simmer until heated through. Heat tortillas using package directions. Spoon beef mixture onto tortillas; roll to enclose filling. Place in 9x13-inch baking dish. Top with mixture of gravy, tomato sauce and enchilada sauce; sprinkle with cheese. Bake at 350 degrees for 25 minutes. May add lettuce and tomato if desired. **Yield: 8 servings.**

Approx Per Serving: Cal 434; Prot 23 g; Carbo 45 g; Fiber 7 g;
    T Fat 20 g; 40% Calories from Fat; Chol 52 mg; Sod 1695 mg.

Nila Stewart, Grand Rapids

Busy-Day Casserole

1 pound ground beef
1 onion, chopped
3 tablespoons uncooked rice
1 10-ounce can tomato soup

1 soup can water
1 4-ounce can mushrooms, drained
3 cups shredded cabbage

Brown ground beef with onion in skillet, stirring until ground beef is crumbly; drain. Add rice, soup, water and mushrooms; mix well. Simmer for 15 minutes. Layer over cabbage in buttered baking dish. Bake, covered, at 350 degrees for 2 hours. May substitute any variety of cream soup for tomato soup. **Yield: 6 servings.**

Approx Per Serving: Cal 225; Prot 16 g; Carbo 15 g; Fiber 2 g;
    T Fat 12 g; 46% Calories from Fat; Chol 49 mg; Sod 457 mg.

Edna A. Kolton, Saginaw

No-Burp Chili

2 pounds ground beef
1 large onion, chopped
2 banana peppers, cut into halves,
    seeded
1 15-ounce can tomato sauce

1 8-ounce can herb-seasoned tomato
    sauce
2 16-ounce cans dark red kidney
    beans
Salt and pepper to taste

Brown ground beef with onion and peppers in skillet, stirring until ground beef is crumbly; drain. Add tomato sauces, beans, salt and pepper; mix well. Simmer for 1 hour. Reheat on second day for best flavor. **Yield: 6 servings.**

Approx Per Serving: Cal 474; Prot 38 g; Carbo 33 g; Fiber 13 g;
    T Fat 22 g; 41% Calories from Fat; Chol 99 mg; Sod 1270 mg.

Robert Taylor, Marquette

Taco Chili

1 pound ground beef
1 envelope taco seasoning mix
1 20-ounce can tomato sauce

1 20-ounce can stewed tomatoes
1 16-ounce can whole kernel corn
1 20-ounce can hot chili beans

Brown ground beef in large saucepan, stirring until crumbly; drain. Add taco seasoning mix, tomato sauce, tomatoes, undrained corn and beans. Simmer until of desired consistency. Garnish servings with shredded cheese, tortilla chips, chopped onions and sour cream. **Yield: 4 servings.**

Approx Per Serving: Cal 586; Prot 35 g; Carbo 63 g; Fiber 8 g;
    T Fat 25 g; 36% Calories from Fat; Chol 98 mg; Sod 3277 mg.

Pat Hyland, Iron Mountain

Mary's Cherokee Corn and Rice Casserole

1 pound ground beef
1 teaspoon oil
3/4 cup chopped onion
2 cups cooked tomatoes
1 10-ounce can cream of mushroom
   soup
1/2 cup uncooked rice
1 16-ounce can corn, drained

3 tablespoons melted butter
1/8 teaspoon thyme
1/8 teaspoon oregano
1/2 small bay leaf, crushed
1 1/2 teaspoons salt
1/8 teaspoon pepper
1/2 cup shredded Cheddar cheese

Brown ground beef lightly in oil in skillet, stirring until crumbly; drain. Add onion. Cook until onion is tender; drain. Add tomatoes, soup, rice, corn, butter, thyme, oregano, 1/2 bay leaf, salt and pepper; mix well. Spoon into 3-quart baking dish sprayed with nonstick cooking spray. Top with cheese. Bake, covered, at 350 degrees for 45 minutes. Garnish with sliced tomatoes and sliced olives. **Yield: 6 servings.**

Approx Per Serving: Cal 441; Prot 21 g; Carbo 36 g; Fiber 3 g;
    T Fat 25 g; 49% Calories from Fat; Chol 75 mg; Sod 1250 mg.

Jean A. Steffes, Traverse City

Cheesy Beef and Noodle Casserole

1 onion, chopped
2 tablespoons oil
2 pounds ground beef
4 10-ounce cans spaghetti sauce
   with mushrooms

1 teaspoon salt
16 ounces narrow noodles, cooked,
   drained
1 pound sharp Cheddar cheese,
   shredded

Sauté onion in oil in saucepan until golden brown. Add ground beef. Cook until ground beef is brown and crumbly; drain. Add spaghetti sauce and salt. Cook until heated through. Layer noodles, meat sauce and cheese 1/2 at a time in baking dish. Bake at 325 degrees for 1 hour or until top is brown. **Yield: 8 servings.**

Approx Per Serving: Cal 869; Prot 46 g; Carbo 64 g; Fiber 2 g;
    T Fat 48 g; 49% Calories from Fat; Chol 233 mg; Sod 1396 mg.

Sue Thomas, Royal Oak

*Bleu cheese in ground beef patties and meat loaf
adds an interesting taste surprise.*

Hamburger Dressing

2 pounds ground round
1/2 cup each chopped onion and celery
12 slices bread, cubed
2   10-ounce cans cream of mushroom
   soup

1 soup can milk
1 teaspoon prepared mustard
1 teaspoon poultry seasoning
1 teaspoon salt
1/4 teaspoon pepper

Mix ground round, onion, celery, bread, 1 can soup, milk, mustard, poultry season-ing, salt and pepper in bowl. Spoon into greased 9x13-inch baking dish. Chill for 1 hour. Top with remaining soup. Bake at 350 degrees for 1 hour. **Yield: 12 servings.**

Approx Per Serving: Cal 295; Prot 18 g; Carbo 19 g; Fiber 1 g;
    T Fat 16 g; 50% Calories from Fat; Chol 53 mg; Sod 767 mg.

Gert Budd, Saginaw

Hamburger and Bean Casserole

1 pound ground beef
1 cup chopped onion
1 teaspoon vinegar
2 16-ounce cans pork and beans
1 16-ounce can kidney beans

1 cup catsup
1 cup packed brown sugar
2 tablespoons mustard
1 teaspoon salt

Brown ground beef with onion in skillet, stirring frequently; drain. Stir in remaining ingredients. Spoon into baking dish. Bake at 400 degrees for 40 minutes. **Yield: 6 servings.**

Approx Per Serving: Cal 616; Prot 27 g; Carbo 101 g; Fiber 15 g;
    T Fat 14 g; 19% Calories from Fat; Chol 60 mg; Sod 1729 mg.

Renee Prieur, Allen Park

Grandma's Hamburger and Potato Casserole

1 1/2 pounds ground beef
1 medium onion, chopped
1 tablespoon oil
1/4 cup flour

2 cups milk
5 to 6 cups sliced potatoes
Salt and pepper to taste

Brown ground beef with onion in oil in large skillet, stirring frequently. Drain, reserving 2 tablespoons drippings. Stir in flour. Add milk. Cook until thickened, stirring constantly. Spoon half the mixture into lightly greased baking dish. Add layers of potatoes, salt, pepper and remaining beef mixture. Bake, covered, at 350 degrees for 1 1/2 hours, removing cover during last 10 minutes. **Yield: 6 servings.**

Approx Per Serving: Cal 473; Prot 28 g; Carbo 43 g; Fiber 3 g;
    T Fat 21 g; 40% Calories from Fat; Chol 85 mg; Sod 108 mg.

Mark Scholten, Petoskey

Haiti Beef

1 medium onion, sliced
3 tablespoons oil
1 pound ground beef
1¹/₂ tablespoons flour
1 large green bell pepper, sliced ¹/₄ inch thick
¹/₄ cup beef broth
¹/₄ teaspoon marjoram
¹/₄ teaspoon rosemary

Salt and black pepper to taste
¹/₂ cup milk
¹/₂ cup yellow cornmeal
1¹/₂ cups milk, scalded
3 tablespoons butter
1¹/₂ teaspoons sugar
¹/₂ teaspoon salt
White pepper to taste
2 eggs

Sauté onion in oil in skillet. Add ground beef. Cook until ground beef is brown and crumbly; drain. Stir in flour, green pepper, broth, marjoram, rosemary, salt and pepper. Cook for 10 minutes or until green pepper is tender. Spoon into 1¹/₄-quart baking dish. Blend ¹/₂ cup milk and cornmeal in heavy saucepan. Stir in scalded milk. Cook until thickened, stirring constantly. Add butter, sugar, ¹/₂ teaspoon salt and white pepper; remove from heat. Beat in eggs 1 at a time. Spoon over casserole. Bake at 350 degrees for 35 minutes or until casserole is puffed and knife inserted in center comes out clean. **Yield: 6 servings.**

Approx Per Serving: Cal 406; Prot 20 g; Carbo 18 g; Fiber 2 g;
    T Fat 28 g; 62% Calories from Fat; Chol 147 mg; Sod 360 mg.

Teddy Zeedyk, Battle Creek

Mexican Lasagna Olé

1 pound ground beef
1   16-ounce can refried beans
2 teaspoons oregano
1 teaspoon garlic powder
12 uncooked lasagna noodles
2¹/₂ cups picante sauce

2¹/₂ cups water
2 cups sour cream
³/₄ cup finely sliced green onions
1   2-ounce can sliced black olives, drained
1 cup shredded Monterey Jack cheese

Brown ground beef in skillet, stirring until crumbly; drain. Add beans, oregano and garlic powder; mix well. Arrange 4 uncooked noodles in 9x13-inch baking dish. Layer beef mixture and remaining noodles ¹/₂ at a time in prepared dish. Pour mixture of picante sauce and water over layers. Bake, tightly covered with foil, at 350 degrees for 1¹/₂ hours or until noodles are tender. Combine sour cream, green onions and olives in bowl; mix well. Spoon over casserole; sprinkle with cheese. Bake, uncovered, for 5 minutes or until cheese melts. **Yield: 12 servings.**

Approx Per Serving: Cal 372; Prot 18 g; Carbo 35 g; Fiber 4 g;
    T Fat 19 g; 45% Calories from Fat; Chol 51 mg; Sod 557 mg.

Karon Fox, Three Oaks

Mexican Lasagna

2 pounds ground beef
1 small onion, chopped
1 envelope taco seasoning mix
1 8-ounce can tomato sauce

1 4-ounce can chopped green chilies
1 15-ounce can refried beans
6 flour tortillas, cut into halves
4 cups shredded Cheddar cheese

Brown ground beef with onion in skillet, stirring until ground beef is crumbly; drain. Add taco seasoning mix, tomato sauce, chilies and beans; mix well. Simmer for 10 minutes. Layer tortillas, meat sauce and cheese 1/2 at a time in 9x13-inch baking dish. Bake, covered with foil, at 350 degrees for 30 minutes. **Yield: 8 servings.**

Approx Per Serving: Cal 630; Prot 41 g; Carbo 33 g; Fiber 6 g;
    T Fat 38 g; 53% Calories from Fat; Chol 134 mg; Sod 1450 mg.

Sharon Reinholm, East Tawas

Four-Cheese Lasagna

1½ pounds ground beef
1 32-ounce jar chunky spaghetti sauce
6 uncooked lasagna noodles
8 ounces cottage cheese

2 cups shredded mozzarella cheese
2 cups shredded Cheddar cheese
1 cup grated Parmesan cheese
3/4 cup water

Brown ground beef in skillet, stirring until crumbly; drain. Stir in spaghetti sauce. Layer meat sauce, uncooked noodles and cheeses 1/2 at a time in 9x13-inch baking dish sprayed with nonstick cooking spray. Pour water over layers. Bake, covered with foil, at 350 degrees for 50 minutes. Bake, uncovered, for 15 to 20 minutes or until noodles are tender. Let stand for 10 minutes. **Yield: 8 servings.**

Approx Per Serving: Cal 645; Prot 41 g; Carbo 36 g; Fiber 1 g;
    T Fat 37 g; 52% Calories from Fat; Chol 119 mg; Sod 1197 mg.

Lucy Hallam, Kalamazoo

No-Cook Noodles Lasagna

3 pounds ground beef
1 32-ounce jar spaghetti sauce
6 uncooked lasagna noodles

24 ounces cottage cheese
4 cups shredded mozzarella cheese
1/2 cup grated Parmesan cheese

Brown ground beef in skillet, stirring until crumbly; drain. Stir in spaghetti sauce. Arrange half the uncooked noodles in 9x13-inch baking dish. Layer half the meat sauce, all the cottage cheese and half the mozzarella cheese in prepared dish. Add layers of remaining noodles, meat sauce and mozzarella cheese. Top with Parmesan cheese. Bake at 350 degrees for 1 hour or until noodles are tender. **Yield: 8 servings.**

Approx Per Serving: Cal 819; Prot 60 g; Carbo 38 g; Fiber 1 g;
    T Fat 47 g; 52% Calories from Fat; Chol 171 mg; Sod 1312 mg.

Nancy K. DeBruyn, Grand Rapids

Overnight Lasagna

1 pound ground beef
1   32-ounce jar spaghetti sauce
1 cup water
15 ounces ricotta cheese
1 egg

2 tablespoons chopped chives
1/2 teaspoon oregano
8 ounces uncooked lasagna noodles
16 ounces mozzarella cheese, sliced
1/4 cup grated Parmesan cheese

Brown ground beef in large skillet, stirring until crumbly; drain. Stir in spaghetti sauce and water. Simmer for 5 minutes. Mix ricotta cheese with egg, chives and oregano in bowl. Spread 1 1/2 cups meat sauce in ungreased 9x13-inch baking pan. Layer uncooked noodles, ricotta cheese mixture and mozzarella cheese 1/2 at a time in prepared pan. Top with remaining meat sauce; sprinkle with Parmesan cheese. Chill, covered, overnight. Bake, uncovered, at 350 degrees for 50 to 60 minutes or until noodles are tender. Let stand for 15 minutes before serving. **Yield: 8 servings.**

Approx Per Serving: Cal 619; Prot 36 g; Carbo 42 g; Fiber 1 g;
    T Fat 33 g; 48% Calories from Fat; Chol 137 mg; Sod 900 mg.

Cindy Fogg, Otsego

Zucchini Lasagna

8 ounces pork sausage
1 pound ground beef
1 large onion, chopped
1 large clove of garlic, minced
1 medium green bell pepper, chopped
1   28-ounce can tomatoes
1   8-ounce can tomato sauce
1 teaspoon salt

1/4 teaspoon pepper
1/2 teaspoon each basil, oregano and
   sage
4 large zucchini
2 teaspoons oil
Celery salt or garlic salt to taste
8 ounces mozzarella cheese, sliced
1/2 cup grated Parmesan cheese

Brown sausage in heavy saucepan over medium heat, stirring until crumbly; add beef. Cook until beef is brown and crumbly, stirring frequently; drain. Add onion and garlic. Sauté until onion is tender. Stir in green pepper, tomatoes, tomato sauce, salt, pepper, basil, oregano and sage. Simmer for 1 hour or until thickened to desired consistency, stirring occasionally. Trim ends from zucchini; cut lengthwise into 1/4-inch slices. Brush oil on both sides of zucchini. Arrange in slightly overlapping layer in oiled 10x15-inch baking pan. Sprinkle with celery salt. Bake at 400 degrees for 10 to 15 minutes or until tender-crisp. Reduce oven temperature to 350 degrees. Spread 1 cup meat sauce in 9x13-inch baking dish. Layer zucchini, overlapping slightly, remaining meat sauce and mozzarella cheese 1/2 at a time in prepared dish. Sprinkle with Parmesan cheese. Bake for 45 minutes. Let stand for 15 minutes before serving. **Yield: 8 servings.**

Approx Per Serving: Cal 334; Prot 24 g; Carbo 13 g; Fiber 3 g;
    T Fat 21 g; 56% Calories from Fat; Chol 74 mg; Sod 1008 mg.

Mary Alice Lintemuth, Lansing

Saucy Meatballs

2 pounds ground beef
1 cup cornflake crumbs
2 eggs
2 tablespoons soy sauce
2 tablespoons minced onion
1/3 cup catsup
1/2 teaspoon garlic powder

1/4 teaspoon salt
1/4 teaspoon pepper
1   16-ounce can cranberry sauce
1   12-ounce bottle of chili sauce
2 tablespoons brown sugar
1 tablespoon lemon juice

Combine ground beef, cornflake crumbs, eggs, soy sauce, onion, catsup, garlic powder, salt and pepper in bowl; mix well. Shape into small balls; arrange in 9x13-inch baking pan. Combine cranberry sauce, chili sauce, brown sugar and lemon juice in saucepan. Cook until heated through. Pour over meatballs. Bake at 350 degrees for 30 minutes. **Yield: 8 servings.**

Approx Per Serving: Cal 441; Prot 25 g; Carbo 47 g; Fiber 2 g;
     T Fat 18 g; 36% Calories from Fat; Chol 127 mg; Sod 1216 mg.

Mike Little, Eau Claire

Gourmet Meatballs

1 pound ground beef
4 ounces braunschweiger
1/2 cup soft bread crumbs
1/4 cup chopped onion
1 egg, slightly beaten
1/2 cup milk

1 teaspoon salt
Pepper to taste
2 tablespoons oil
1/4 cup mushroom soup mix
1 cup cold water

Combine ground beef, braunschweiger, bread crumbs, onion, egg, milk, salt and pepper in bowl; mix well. Shape into eighteen 1½-inch balls. Chill for 1 hour. Brown several at a time in hot oil in skillet, shaking frequently. Return browned meatballs to skillet. Add mixture of soup mix and water. Simmer, covered, for 15 minutes. Serve with noodles. **Yield: 6 servings.**

Approx Per Serving: Cal 296; Prot 18 g; Carbo 7 g; Fiber <1 g;
     T Fat 22 g; 65% Calories from Fat; Chol 102 mg; Sod 884 mg.

Shirley A. Cook, Lansing

*Use extra-lean ground round or ground beef in meat loaves
and meatballs to reduce fat and cholesterol. Extra-lean
ground beef contains about 11% fat.*

Sweet-and-Sour Meatballs

1 pound ground beef
1 egg
2 tablespoons chopped onion
1 tablespoon cornstarch
1 teaspoon salt
1/4 teaspoon pepper
3 tablespoons vinegar
1 tablespoon soy sauce

3 tablespoons cornstarch
6 tablespoons water
1/2 cup sugar
1 cup pineapple juice
1   16-ounce can pineapple chunks
1 green bell pepper, thinly sliced
1 carrot, shredded

Combine ground beef, egg, onion, 1 tablespoon cornstarch, salt and pepper in bowl; mix well. Shape into 18 meatballs. Brown on all sides in skillet; drain. Blend vinegar, soy sauce, 3 tablespoons cornstarch, water and sugar in small bowl. Bring pineapple juice to a boil in saucepan. Stir in vinegar mixture. Cook until thickened, stirring constantly. Add pineapple, green pepper, carrot and meatballs. Cook until heated through. Serve over hot cooked rice. **Yield: 4 servings.**

Approx Per Serving: Cal 516; Prot 24 g; Carbo 68 g; Fiber 2 g;
     T Fat 18 g; 30% Calories from Fat; Chol 127 mg; Sod 882 mg.

Margaret Shurlow, Vassar

Smothered Ground Beef Patties

2 pounds ground beef
2 eggs
1 small onion, chopped
1 teaspoon parsley flakes

1 1/2 cups seasoned croutons, crushed
1/4 cup (about) milk
1   10-ounce can cream of mushroom
   soup

Combine ground beef, eggs, onion, parsley flakes and crushed croutons in bowl; mix well. Add enough milk to make of desired consistency; mix well. Shape into 1-inch thick patties. Brown on both sides in skillet. Add soup. Simmer for 30 minutes. May shape into meatballs or meat loaf roll filled with chopped vegetables or dressing. **Yield: 8 servings.**

Approx Per Serving: Cal 317; Prot 24 g; Carbo 8 g; Fiber <1 g;
     T Fat 21 g; 59% Calories from Fat; Chol 129 mg; Sod 447 mg.

Lu Swaney, Fife Lake

Cajun Meat Loaf

1/2 teaspoon cumin
1/2 teaspoon nutmeg
1 bay leaf
1 1/2 teaspoons salt
1 1/2 teaspoons black pepper
1 teaspoon cayenne pepper
3/4 cup chopped onion
2 tablespoons margarine

1/2 cup chopped green bell pepper
2 cloves of garlic, minced
1 tablespoon hot pepper sauce
1 tablespoon Worcestershire sauce
1/2 cup milk
1/2 cup catsup
1 1/2 pounds ground beef
1 egg, beaten

Mix cumin, nutmeg, bay leaf, salt, black pepper and cayenne pepper in small bowl; set aside. Sauté onion in margarine in skillet until tender. Add green pepper, garlic, pepper sauce, Worcestershire sauce and seasoning mixture; mix well. Cook for 1 minute or until thickened. Stir in milk and catsup. Cook until heated through. Cool slightly; discard bay leaf. Add ground beef and egg; mix well. Shape into meat loaf; place in baking pan. Bake, covered, at 350 degrees for 30 minutes. Bake, uncovered, for 30 minutes longer or until brown. **Yield: 6 servings.**

Approx Per Serving: Cal 326; Prot 24 g; Carbo 10 g; Fiber 1 g;
    T Fat 22 g; 59% Calories from Fat; Chol 112 mg; Sod 936 mg.

Sandy Nealy, Charlotte

Cheese Meat Loaf

1 1/2 pounds ground beef
1/2 cup dry bread crumbs
1 egg, beaten
3/4 cup milk
1/4 cup chopped onion

1 1/2 teaspoons salt
1/4 teaspoon pepper
1/2 cup catsup
4 slices American cheese

Combine ground beef, bread crumbs, egg, milk, onion, salt and pepper in bowl; mix well. Pack lightly into 2-quart glass loaf dish; cover with waxed paper. Microwave on Medium-High for 5 minutes; drain and rotate dish 1/2 turn. Spread with catsup. Microwave, covered, on High for 15 minutes or until done to taste. Top with cheese. Microwave just until cheese melts. Let stand for 5 minutes. **Yield: 6 servings.**

Approx Per Serving: Cal 392; Prot 29 g; Carbo 14 g; Fiber 1 g;
    T Fat 24 g; 56% Calories from Fat; Chol 132 mg; Sod 1191 mg.

Barb Buskirk, Portland

Special Meat Loaf

1 pound ground round
2 cups cornflake crumbs
1 cup uncooked rice
1/2 cup chopped green bell pepper

1 onion, chopped
1 tomato, chopped
1 15-ounce can tomato sauce

Combine all ingredients in bowl; mix well. Shape into loaf; place in lightly greased baking dish. Bake at 375 degrees for 45 minutes or until cooked through and brown on edges. **Yield: 4 servings.**

Approx Per Serving: Cal 584; Prot 29 g; Carbo 79 g; Fiber 4 g;
    T Fat 17 g; 26% Calories from Fat; Chol 74 mg; Sod 1135 mg.

Sally Taylor, Marquette

Microwave Meat Loaf

2 pounds ground round
1 pound ground turkey
1 envelope onion soup mix

1 cup fine dry bread crumbs
2 eggs, beaten

Combine ground round and turkey in large bowl. Sprinkle with soup mix and bread crumbs. Pour eggs over top; mix well. Shape into flat round loaf 2 inches thick; place in microwave-safe dish with rack. Microwave on High for 30 minutes or until cooked through, rotating dish 1/4 turn after 15 minutes. Cover with foil, placing shiny side down. Let stand for 5 minutes. **Yield: 8 servings.**

Approx Per Serving: Cal 397; Prot 35 g; Carbo 10 g; Fiber 1 g;
    T Fat 24 g; 54% Calories from Fat; Chol 164 mg; Sod 302 mg.

Reg and Pat Martin, Big Rapids

Pizza Meat Loaf

2 pounds ground beef
1/2 envelope Italian salad dressing mix
1/2 cup chopped onion
3/4 cup bread crumbs
2 eggs

1 8-ounce can pizza sauce
2 4-ounce cans sliced mushrooms,
   drained
8 ounces mozzarella cheese, sliced
1/2 cup grated Parmesan cheese

Combine ground beef, salad dressing mix, onion, bread crumbs and eggs in bowl; mix well. Press into 9x13-inch baking dish. Top with pizza sauce, mushrooms, mozzarella cheese and Parmesan cheese. Bake at 350 degrees for 50 minutes. Cut into squares to serve. **Yield: 8 servings.**

Approx Per Serving: Cal 416; Prot 33 g; Carbo 12 g; Fiber 1 g;
    T Fat 26 g; 57% Calories from Fat; Chol 154 mg; Sod 659 mg.

Kimberly Trosien, Essexville

Sicilian Meat Roll

2 eggs, beaten
3/4 cup soft bread crumbs
2 tablespoons chopped parsley
2 tablespoons tomato juice
2 teaspoons oregano
1/4 teaspoon garlic salt
1/4 teaspoon salt
1/4 teaspoon pepper

2 pounds ground beef
1 cup shredded mozzarella cheese
4 ounces thinly sliced ham
1 8-ounce can sliced mushrooms, drained
1 cup catsup
1/2 cup shredded mozzarella cheese

Combine eggs, bread crumbs, parsley, tomato juice, oregano, garlic salt, salt and pepper in bowl. Add ground beef; mix well. Pat into rectangle on waxed paper. Sprinkle with 1 cup cheese; add ham and mushrooms, leaving narrow edges. Roll up to enclose filling; seal edges. Place seam side down in 9x13-inch baking dish. Bake at 350 degrees for 1 hour. Top with catsup and 1/2 cup cheese. Bake for 30 minutes longer. **Yield: 8 servings.**

Approx Per Serving: Cal 387; Prot 32 g; Carbo 13 g; Fiber 1 g;
    T Fat 23 g; 54% Calories from Fat; Chol 152 mg; Sod 993 mg.

Donna J. Hopp, Rogers City

Moocho Goocho

1 1/2 pounds ground beef
1 15-ounce can Manwich sauce
1 16-ounce can refried beans with chili peppers

1/2 5-ounce bottle of hot sauce
2 4-ounce cans chopped green chilies
2 pounds Velveeta cheese, chopped

Brown ground beef in skillet, stirring until crumbly; drain. Add sauce, beans, hot sauce and chilies; mix well. Simmer for 10 minutes. Stir in cheese. Simmer until cheese melts. **Yield: 8 servings.**

Approx Per Serving: Cal 694; Prot 46 g; Carbo 20 g; Fiber 5 g;
    T Fat 48 g; 62% Calories from Fat; Chol 163 mg; Sod 2446 mg.

Brenda Buss, Grand Rapids

*Bake meat loaf in greased muffin cups for a quick
way to serve a crowd.*

Oriental Hamburger Skillet

1 pound ground beef
1 cup chopped celery
1 medium onion, chopped
1 10-ounce can cream of mushroom
   soup
3 cups water

1 17-ounce can chop suey vegetables
1 17-ounce can bean sprouts
¼ cup soy sauce
1 cup uncooked instant rice
1 3-ounce can chow mein noodles

Brown ground beef in large skillet, stirring until crumbly; drain. Add celery, onion, soup and water; mix well. Simmer for 10 minutes. Stir in chop suey vegetables, bean sprouts and soy sauce. Simmer for 20 minutes. Add rice. Let stand, covered, for 7 minutes; fluff with fork. Serve with chow mein noodles. **Yield: 4 servings.**

Approx Per Serving: Cal 578; Prot 33 g; Carbo 52 g; Fiber 5 g;
      T Fat 27 g; 41% Calories from Fat; Chol 77 mg; Sod 2956 mg.

Virginia M. Shillings, Coldwater

Beef and Pork Pasties

1 pound cubed beef
8 ounces cubed pork
1 carrot, chopped
3 onions, chopped
4 potatoes, chopped
1 tablespoon salt
1 teaspoon pepper

6 tablespoons cold water
2 tablespoons melted margarine
3 cups flour
1 teaspoon salt
1 cup shortening
½ cup cold water

Combine beef, pork, carrot, onions, potatoes, 1 tablespoon salt, pepper, 6 table-spoons water and melted margarine in large bowl; mix well. Combine flour and 1 teaspoon salt in bowl. Cut in shortening until crumbly. Add ½ cup cold water stirring lightly. Divide into 6 equal portions. Roll each into 9-inch circle on floured surface. Spoon beef mixture onto circles; fold to enclose fillings. Seal edges; cut 3 vents in tops of each. Arrange on baking sheet. Bake at 425 degrees for 15 minutes. Reduce oven temperature to 375 degrees. Bake for 45 minutes longer.
Yield: 6 servings.

Approx Per Serving: Cal 846; Prot 31 g; Carbo 77 g; Fiber 5 g;
      T Fat 46 g; 49% Calories from Fat; Chol 66 mg; Sod 1520 mg.

Barbara Contois, Marquette

Cornish Pasties

1 pound ground sirloin
2¹/₄ pounds potatoes, chopped
8 ounces onions, chopped
1 tablespoon salt
Pepper to taste
6 cups flour

2 tablespoons baking powder
1 teaspoon sugar
1 tablespoon salt
1 cup minus 2 tablespoons shortening
2 cups minus 2 tablespoons milk

Combine ground sirloin, potatoes, onions, 1 tablespoon salt and pepper in bowl; mix well. Sift flour, baking powder, sugar and 1 tablespoon salt into bowl. Cut in shortening until crumbly. Add milk; mix lightly. Divide into 8 portions. Roll into circles on floured surface. Spoon filling onto circles. Fold to enclose fillings; seal edges. Place on baking sheet. Bake at 475 degrees for 10 minutes. Reduce oven temperature to 275 degrees. Bake for 1 hour longer. **Yield: 8 servings.**

Approx Per Serving: Cal 803; Prot 28 g; Carbo 105 g; Fiber 5 g;
    T Fat 30 g; 33% Calories from Fat; Chol 48 mg; Sod 1901 mg.

Etta Jo Kobie, Marquette

Meat and Vegetable Pasties

2 pounds ground beef
5 medium onions, chopped
7 large potatoes, chopped
6 large carrots, coarsely shredded
¹/₄ cup oil

Salt and pepper to taste
3 cups shortening
8 cups flour
1 tablespoon salt
2 cups (or more) cold water

Cook ground beef with onions, potatoes and carrots in oil in skillet, stirring until vegetables are partially tender. Season with salt and pepper. Add enough water to make of desired consistency. Cut shortening into flour and salt in large bowl until mixture is crumbly. Add 2 cups cold water; mix with fork to form dough. Divide into 15 portions. Roll each portion into 8x11-inch oval on lightly floured surface. Spoon filling onto ovals; fold dough over to enclose fillings. Seal edges; cut 3 small vents in each. Place on ungreased baking sheet. Bake at 375 degrees for 40 minutes. **Yield: 15 servings.**

Approx Per Serving: Cal 858; Prot 21 g; Carbo 73 g; Fiber 5 g;
    T Fat 54 g; 56% Calories from Fat; Chol 40 mg; Sod 477 mg.

Marie Fineout, Cheboygan

Pasties for-a-Crowd

5 pounds carrots, chopped
5 pounds onions, chopped
2 large turnips, chopped
10 pounds potatoes, peeled, chopped

6 pounds ground beef
Salt and pepper to taste
Pastie Crusts

Combine carrots, onions, turnips, potatoes, ground beef, salt and pepper in large bowl; mix well. Spoon into centers of Pastie Crusts. Fold to enclose fillings. Seal edges; cut vents. Place on baking sheet. Bake at 400 degrees for 1 hour. May dot with butter before baking. **Yield: 25 servings.**

Pastie Crusts

4¹/₂ cups shortening
1   5-pound package presifted flour

4 cups cold water

Cut shortening into flour in large bowl until crumbly. Add water, stirring until of desired consistency. Divide into 25 equal portions. Roll into circles on floured surface. **Yield: 25 servings.**

Approx Per Serving: Cal 1119; Prot 35 g; Carbo 125 g; Fiber 10 g;
    T Fat 54 g; 43% Calories from Fat; Chol 71 mg; Sod 114 mg.

Betty Murray, Marquette

Mexican Pizza

1 pound ground beef
1 envelope taco seasoning mix
2   8-count cans crescent rolls
16 ounces cream cheese, softened

2 tablespoons (heaping) mayonnaise
1 teaspoon (heaping) dillweed
1   16-ounce can refried beans
2 cups shredded Cheddar cheese

Brown ground beef in skillet, stirring until crumbly; drain. Stir in taco seasoning mix. Press roll dough onto large baking sheet, pressing perforations to seal. Bake using directions on roll can. Mix cream cheese, mayonnaise and dillweed in small bowl. Spread over crust. Heat refried beans in saucepan or microwave. Layer refried beans, ground beef mixture and cheese over cream cheese layer. Bake until cheese melts and pizza is heated through. **Yield: 6 servings.**

Approx Per Serving: Cal 975; Prot 38 g; Carbo 51 g; Fiber 7 g;
    T Fat 69 g; 63% Calories from Fat; Chol 174 mg; Sod 2042 mg.

Nancy K. DeBruyn, Grand Rapids

Slow-Cooker Pizza

1 12-ounce package Kluski noodles
1½ pounds ground beef
1 medium onion, chopped
1 16-ounce jar pizza sauce

1 8-ounce jar spaghetti sauce
2 cups shredded Cheddar cheese
2 cups shredded mozzarella cheese
1 4-ounce package sliced pepperoni

Cook noodles using package directions; drain. Brown ground beef with onion in skillet, stirring frequently; drain. Add pizza sauce and spaghetti sauce; mix well. Layer noodles, meat sauce, cheeses and pepperoni ½ at a time in slow cooker. Cook on High for 30 minutes or until cheese melts. **Yield: 8 servings.**

Approx Per Serving: Cal 673; Prot 39 g; Carbo 42 g; Fiber 1 g;
    T Fat 38 g; 52% Calories from Fat; Chol 112 mg; Sod 1025 mg.

Linda Haubenstricker, Birch Run

Pizza Casserole

2 pounds lean ground beef
½ cup chopped green bell pepper
½ cup chopped onion
2 10-ounce cans tomato soup
2 10-ounce cans cream of mushroom
    soup

1 soup can water
1 4-ounce can mushrooms, drained
½ teaspoon oregano
½ teaspoon garlic salt
12 ounces large noodles, cooked
7 ounces mozzarella cheese, shredded

Brown ground beef with green pepper and onion in skillet, stirring until ground beef is crumbly; drain. Stir in soups, water, mushrooms, oregano and garlic salt. Alternate layers of noodles and meat sauce in baking dish until all ingredients are used. Top with cheese. Bake at 350 degrees for 1 hour. **Yield: 8 servings.**

Approx Per Serving: Cal 594; Prot 35 g; Carbo 47 g; Fiber 1 g;
    T Fat 30 g; 45% Calories from Fat; Chol 169 mg; Sod 1419 mg.

Phyllis Gee, Lansing

Pizza Cups

12 ounces ground beef
1 15-ounce can pizza sauce

1 10-count can buttermilk biscuits
1 cup shredded mozzarella cheese

Brown ground beef in skillet, stirring until crumbly; drain. Stir in pizza sauce. Separate biscuits and press 1 biscuit into each of 10 nonstick muffin cups. Spoon meat sauce into prepared cups; sprinkle with cheese. Bake at 400 degrees for 12 minutes or until golden brown. **Yield: 10 servings.**

Approx Per Serving: Cal 190; Prot 11 g; Carbo 13 g; Fiber <1 g;
    T Fat 10 g; 49% Calories from Fat; Chol 32 mg; Sod 501 mg.

Sandy Helt, Marquette

Upside-Down Pizza

1¹/₂ pounds ground beef
1 medium onion, chopped
1   16-ounce jar pizza sauce
¹/₄ teaspoon oregano
¹/₂ teaspoon garlic salt
2 cups shredded mozzarella cheese

2 eggs
1 cup milk
1 tablespoon oil
1 cup flour
¹/₂ teaspoon salt
¹/₂ cup grated Parmesan cheese

Brown ground beef with onion in skillet, stirring frequently; drain. Stir in pizza sauce, oregano and garlic salt. Spoon into greased 9x13-inch baking pan; sprinkle with mozzarella cheese. Mix eggs, milk, oil, flour and salt in bowl. Spread over casserole; sprinkle with Parmesan cheese. Bake at 350 degrees for 30 minutes. **Yield: 8 servings.**

Approx Per Serving: Cal 425; Prot 29 g; Carbo 20 g; Fiber 1 g;
    T Fat 25 g; 54% Calories from Fat; Chol 139 mg; Sod 794 mg.

Marilyn Shearer, Flint

Easy Hamburger Quiche

¹/₂ cup reduced-calorie mayonnaise
2 eggs
¹/₂ cup low-fat milk
1 tablespoon cornstarch
8 ounces lean ground beef, cooked

1 cup shredded Cheddar cheese
¹/₂ cup shredded green onions
¹/₈ teaspoon pepper
1   9-inch unbaked pie shell

Mix mayonnaise, eggs, milk and cornstarch in bowl until smooth. Add remaining ingredients; mix well. Spoon into pie shell. Bake at 350 degrees for 35 minutes or until knife inserted in center comes out clean. Garnish with sliced tomatoes. **Yield: 6 servings.**

Approx Per Serving: Cal 393; Prot 17 g; Carbo 19 g; Fiber <1 g;
    T Fat 28 g; 64% Calories from Fat; Chol 123 mg; Sod 455 mg.

Margaret A. Voet, Marquette

Ground Beef-Sauerkraut Hot Dish

¹/₂ cup uncooked rice
1 pound ground beef
1 medium onion, chopped

4 cups stewed tomatoes
4 cups sauerkraut
Salt and pepper to taste

Cook rice using package directions. Brown ground beef with onion in skillet, stirring frequently; drain. Stir in rice and remaining ingredients. Spoon into baking dish. Bake at 275 to 300 degrees for 2 hours or until done to taste. **Yield: 6 servings.**

Approx Per Serving: Cal 257; Prot 17 g; Carbo 25 g; Fiber 3 g;
    T Fat 11 g; 37% Calories from Fat; Chol 49 mg; Sod 1565 mg.

Janet A. Roekle, Saginaw

Seven-Course Dinner

1 pound ground beef
2 cups sliced potatoes
2 cups sliced carrots
1/4 cup uncooked rice

1 cup sliced onion
1 10-ounce package frozen green
  peas, thawed
4 cups canned tomatoes

Brown ground beef in skillet, stirring until crumbly; drain. Layer potatoes, carrots, ground beef, rice, onion, peas and tomatoes in order listed in large greased baking dish. Bake, covered, at 325 degrees for 1 hour. Bake, uncovered, for 1 hour longer or until vegetables are tender. **Yield: 6 servings.**

Approx Per Serving: Cal 295; Prot 20 g; Carbo 30 g; Fiber 6 g;
    T Fat 11 g; 34% Calories from Fat; Chol 49 mg; Sod 368 mg.

Sue Stevens, East Lansing

Mushroom Sloppy Joes

1½ pounds ground beef
2 tablespoons flour
Salt and pepper to taste
2 tablespoons soy sauce

1 10-ounce can cream of mushroom
  soup
1/2 soup can water

Brown ground beef in skillet, stirring until crumbly; drain. Stir in flour, salt and pepper. Add mixture of soy sauce, soup and water; mix well. Simmer for 5 minutes or to desired consistency. Serve on sandwich buns with slices of American cheese. **Yield: 6 servings.**

Approx Per Serving: Cal 291; Prot 22 g; Carbo 6 g; Fiber <1 g;
    T Fat 20 g; 61% Calories from Fat; Chol 75 mg; Sod 791 mg.

Mrs. E. A. Shaw, Okeechobee, Florida

Sloppy Joes

1 pound ground beef
1 6-ounce can tomato paste
1 6-ounce can water
1 onion, chopped
3 tablespoons brown sugar

3 tablespoons vinegar
2 tablespoons Worcestershire sauce
1/4 cup sweet pickle relish
Salt and pepper to taste

Brown ground beef in saucepan, stirring until crumbly; drain. Add tomato paste, water, onion, brown sugar, vinegar, Worcestershire sauce, relish, salt and pepper; mix well. Simmer until of desired consistency. **Yield: 6 servings.**

Approx Per Serving: Cal 230; Prot 16 g; Carbo 19 g; Fiber 2 g;
    T Fat 11 g; 42% Calories from Fat; Chol 49 mg; Sod 197 mg.

June Adams, Sault Ste. Marie

Easy Sloppy Joes

2 pounds ground beef
1 onion, chopped
1/2 green bell pepper, chopped
1   10-ounce can tomato soup
1   14-ounce bottle of catsup

2 tablespoons vinegar
1/4 cup Worcestershire sauce
2 teaspoons chili powder
Salt and pepper to taste

Brown ground beef in skillet, stirring until crumbly; drain. Add remaining ingredients; mix well. Simmer until of desired consistency. **Yield: 8 servings.**

Approx Per Serving: Cal 323; Prot 23 g; Carbo 21 g; Fiber 2 g;
    T Fat 17 g; 46% Calories from Fat; Chol 74 mg; Sod 909 mg.

Donna Murdock, Clio

Spaghetti Pie

3 cups cooked broken spaghetti
2 eggs, beaten
1/4 cup grated Parmesan cheese
Salt and pepper to taste
2 cups small curd cottage cheese
1 1/2 pounds ground beef

1/4 cup chopped onion
1/4 cup chopped green bell pepper
Oregano to taste
1   6-ounce can tomato paste
1   15-ounce can tomatoes
2 cups shredded mozzarella cheese

Mix spaghetti, eggs, Parmesan cheese, salt and pepper in bowl. Spread in 9x13-inch baking dish. Spread with cottage cheese. Brown ground beef with onion, green pepper and oregano in skillet, stirring frequently; drain. Stir in tomato paste and tomatoes. Spread over cottage cheese, leaving narrow edge. Bake at 350 degrees for 15 minutes. Top with mozzarella cheese. Bake for 10 minutes longer. **Yield: 6 servings.**

Approx Per Serving: Cal 594; Prot 47 g; Carbo 28 g; Fiber 3 g;
    T Fat 32 g; 49% Calories from Fat; Chol 196 mg; Sod 717 mg.

Marilyn Brock, Traverse City

Spaghetti Sauce

1 pound ground beef
1/2 cup chopped onion
4 cups tomato juice

1   10-ounce can tomato soup
1 teaspoon oregano
1/4 teaspoon garlic salt

Brown ground beef with onion in skillet, stirring frequently; drain. Combine remaining ingredients in saucepan. Simmer until well blended. Add ground beef mixture. Simmer until of desired consistency. Serve over spaghetti. **Yield: 4 servings.**

Approx Per Serving: Cal 327; Prot 24 g; Carbo 21 g; Fiber 3 g;
    T Fat 17 g; 46% Calories from Fat; Chol 74 mg; Sod 1567 mg.

Paula Bedell, Munith

Hamburger Stroganoff

1/2 cup minced onion
1/4 cup margarine
1 pound ground beef
1 tablespoon flour
1 clove of garlic, minced
1/4 teaspoon MSG

1/4 teaspoon paprika
2 teaspoons salt
1/4 teaspoon pepper
1 cup concentrated cream of
   mushroom soup
1 cup sour cream

Sauté onion in margarine in saucepan. Add ground beef. Cook until ground beef is crumbly; drain. Stir in flour, garlic, MSG, paprika, salt and pepper. Cook for 5 minutes. Add soup. Cook until heated through. Stir in sour cream. Serve over noodles or hot cooked rice. **Yield: 4 servings.**

Approx Per Serving: Cal 534; Prot 25 g; Carbo 10 g; Fiber 1 g;
    T Fat 44 g; 74% Calories from Fat; Chol 100 mg; Sod 2072 mg.

Erik Little, Eau Claire

Stacker Roll Stroganoff

1 pound ground beef
1 4-ounce can mushrooms, drained
1 3-ounce can French-fried onions
1 10-ounce can cream of mushroom
  soup
1/2 cup sour cream

1 10-count can Hungry Jack biscuits
1/2 cup sour cream
1 egg
1 teaspoon celery seed
1/2 teaspoon salt

Brown ground beef in skillet, stirring until crumbly; drain. Stir in mushrooms and 1/2 can onions. Spoon into baking dish. Bring soup to a boil in saucepan. Stir in 1/2 cup sour cream. Spoon over ground beef mixture. Cut biscuits into halves. Arrange over top; sprinkle with remaining onions. Combine 1/2 cup sour cream, egg, celery seed and salt in bowl; mix well. Spoon over casserole. Bake at 375 degrees for 25 to 30 minutes or until biscuits are golden brown. **Yield: 6 servings.**

Approx Per Serving: Cal 498; Prot 21 g; Carbo 28 g; Fiber 1 g;
    T Fat 33 g; 61% Calories from Fat; Chol 104 mg; Sod 1224 mg.

Bonnie Hammond, Westland

*One of the best ways to remove fat from ground beef is to
microwave it in a colander. Place a bowl under the
colander to collect the fat as it cooks out of the ground beef.*

Mexican Stuffed Shells

1 12-ounce jar medium or mild
   picante sauce
1/2 cup water
1 8-ounce can tomato sauce
1 pound ground beef

1/2 cup shredded Monterey Jack
   cheese
1 3-ounce can French-fried onions
12 large pasta shells, cooked
1/2 cup shredded Monterey Jack cheese

Combine picante sauce, water and tomato sauce in bowl; mix well. Brown ground beef in skillet, stirring until crumbly; drain. Add 1/2 cup picante sauce mixture, 1/2 cup cheese and 1/2 can onions; mix well. Spoon mixture into pasta shells. Spoon half the remaining picante sauce mixture into 8x12-inch or 10-inch round baking dish. Arrange stuffed shells in prepared dish. Top with remaining picante sauce mixture. Bake, covered, at 350 degrees for 30 minutes. Top with 1/2 cup cheese and remaining onions. Bake, uncovered, for 5 minutes longer. **Yield: 6 servings.**

Approx Per Serving: Cal 402; Prot 23 g; Carbo 24 g; Fiber 2 g;
     T Fat 24 g; 53% Calories from Fat; Chol 67 mg; Sod 786 mg.

Elaine Baird, Saginaw

Yum-Yum Casserole

1 pound ground chuck
2 onions, chopped
5 stalks celery, chopped
1 10-ounce can cream of mushroom
   soup

1/2 soup can milk
1 3-ounce can chow mein noodles

Brown ground beef with onions in skillet, stirring until ground beef is crumbly; drain. Cook celery in a small amount of water in saucepan until tender-crisp; drain. Add to ground beef mixture with soup and milk; mix well. Spoon into baking dish. Top with noodles. Bake at 350 degrees for 30 minutes or until bubbly.
Yield: 4 servings.

Approx Per Serving: Cal 463; Prot 27 g; Carbo 27 g; Fiber 3 g;
     T Fat 28 g; 54% Calories from Fat; Chol 82 mg; Sod 912 mg.

Valerie Jarvinen, Houghton

Italian Beef and Zucchini Casserole

¹/₂ cup chopped onion	1 cup chopped peeled tomatoes
1 medium green bell pepper, chopped	Hot pepper sauce to taste
1 clove of garlic, minced	¹/₂ teaspoon oregano
1 tablespoon olive oil	¹/₂ teaspoon basil
8 ounces ground beef	Salt and pepper to taste
1 cup thinly sliced zucchini	

Sauté onion, green pepper and garlic in olive oil for 2 minutes. Add ground beef. Cook until ground beef is brown, stirring until crumbly; drain. Stir in zucchini, tomatoes, pepper sauce, oregano, basil, salt and pepper. spoon into 1-quart baking dish. Bake at 350 degrees for 30 minutes or until zucchini is tender. Garnish servings with Parmesan cheese. **Yield: 2 servings.**

Approx Per Serving: Cal 342; Prot 23 g; Carbo 11 g; Fiber 3 g;
  T Fat 23 g; 60% Calories from Fat; Chol 74 mg; Sod 76 mg.

Marcia Delaski, Skandia

Breakfast Casserole

16 slices bread	1 cup shredded Cheddar cheese
¹/₄ cup butter, softened	2 cups chopped cooked ham
4 eggs	1 cup shredded Cheddar cheese
3 cups milk	

Trim crusts from bread; spread with butter. Beat eggs and milk in bowl. Dip half the bread slices into egg mixture; arrange in single layer in 9x13-inch baking dish. Layer 1 cup cheese and all the ham in prepared dish. Dip remaining bread slices in egg mixture and arrange over layers. Sprinkle with 1 cup cheese. Pour remaining egg mixture over top. Chill for 24 hours. Let stand at room temperature for 1 hour. Bake at 350 degrees for 1 hour. **Yield: 8 servings.**

Approx Per Serving: Cal 495; Prot 27 g; Carbo 33 g; Fiber 1 g;
  T Fat 25 g; 45% Calories from Fat; Chol 183 mg; Sod 1048 mg.

Elsa Massman, Saginaw

Cauliflower and Ham au Gratin

4 cups chopped cauliflower
1¼ cups chopped cooked ham
1   10-ounce can Cheddar cheese soup
¼ cup milk

⅔ cup baking mix
2 tablespoons shredded Cheddar cheese
2 tablespoons butter, chilled
½ teaspoon paprika

Blanch cauliflower in water in saucepan; drain. Layer cauliflower and ham in 7x11-inch baking pan. Spread mixture of soup and milk over layers. Combine baking mix, cheese and butter in bowl; mix until crumbly. Sprinkle over casserole; top with paprika. Bake at 400 degrees for 20 minutes or until golden brown. **Yield: 6 servings.**

Approx Per Serving: Cal 229; Prot 13 g; Carbo 17 g; Fiber 2 g;
    T Fat 13 g; 49% Calories from Fat; Chol 41 mg; Sod 977 mg.

Michelle Richards, Lansing

Eggs Daffodil

15 slices white bread, crusts trimmed
8 eggs
3 cups milk

8 ounces cooked ham, shredded
16 ounces Velveeta cheese
¾ cup margarine

Cut bread into 1-inch cubes. Spread in buttered 9x13-inch baking pan. Beat eggs in bowl. Add milk; mix well. Pour over bread. Sprinkle with ham. Melt cheese with margarine in saucepan over low heat, stirring to mix well. Spoon over casserole. Chill for 2 hours to overnight. Bake at 350 degrees for 1 hour. **Yield: 8 servings.**

Approx Per Serving: Cal 643; Prot 32 g; Carbo 24 g; Fiber 1 g;
    T Fat 47 g; 65% Calories from Fat; Chol 295 mg; Sod 1684 mg.

Janell Sandstedt, Manistee

Cheesy Egg and Ham Bake

16 slices bread, crusts trimmed
¼ cup butter, softened
4 eggs
3 cups milk

¼ teaspoon mustard
2 pounds thinly sliced ham
4 cups shredded Cheddar cheese
2 cups cornflakes

Spread both sides of bread with butter. Beat eggs with milk and mustard in bowl. Layer bread, ham, cheese and egg mixture ½ at a time in 9x13-inch baking dish. Sprinkle with cornflakes. Chill, covered, overnight. Bake at 350 degrees for 40 minutes or until knife inserted in center comes out clean. Cut into squares to serve. **Yield: 8 servings.**

Approx Per Serving: Cal 679; Prot 52 g; Carbo 30 g; Fiber 1 g;
    T Fat 38 g; 51% Calories from Fat; Chol 256 mg; Sod 2249 mg.

Sara F. Edge, Grand Rapids

Ham and Broccoli Rolls

6 1-ounce slices thinly sliced boiled
   ham
6 slices Swiss cheese
1 10-ounce package frozen broccoli
   spears, cooked, drained
2 tablespoons margarine

2 tablespoons flour
1/4 teaspoon sweet basil
1/2 teaspoon salt
Pepper to taste
1 1/2 cups milk
1 3-ounce can French-fried onions

Top ham slices with cheese. Place broccoli spears on cheese. Roll ham and cheese to enclose broccoli; secure with wooden picks. Place in shallow baking dish. Melt margarine in saucepan. Blend in flour, basil, salt and pepper. Add milk gradually. Cook until thickened, stirring constantly. Stir in 2/3 can onions. Pour over ham rolls. Bake, covered, at 350 degrees for 25 minutes. Top with remaining onions. Bake, uncovered, for 5 minutes longer. **Yield: 6 servings.**

Approx Per Serving: Cal 333; Prot 20 g; Carbo 14 g; Fiber 1 g;
     T Fat 22 g; 59% Calories from Fat; Chol 50 mg; Sod 802 mg.

Bonnie Hammond, Westland

Ham and Broccoli Skillet Supper

1 7-ounce package tangy au gratin
   potatoes mix
3 1/2 cups water
2 cups chopped fresh broccoli
1/4 cup chopped onion

1/4 cup margarine
1 cup chopped cooked ham
1/2 cup milk
4 eggs

Bring potato slices to a boil in water in saucepan; reduce heat. Simmer, covered, for 10 minutes. Add broccoli. Simmer, covered, for 5 minutes; drain. Add onion and margarine. Sauté for 5 minutes. Add ham. Combine seasoning package from potatoes with milk in bowl; mix well. Add eggs; mix well. Pour over potato mixture in skillet. Cook, covered, over low heat for 20 to 30 minutes or until eggs are set. **Yield: 4 servings.**

Approx Per Serving: Cal 426; Prot 22 g; Carbo 42 g; Fiber 2 g;
     T Fat 22 g; 44% Calories from Fat; Chol 236 mg; Sod 1732 mg.

Barb Buskirk, Portland

*Chop leftover ham and add to macaroni and cheese, scrambled
eggs, quiche or dried beans or lentils.*

Ham and Egg Combo

½ cup mayonnaise
¼ cup flour
½ teaspoon salt
Pepper to taste
2 cups milk
4 ounces American cheese, chopped

¼ cup chopped onion
¼ cup chopped pimento
1½ cups chopped cooked ham
8 hard-boiled eggs, cut into quarters
8 English muffins, toasted

Blend mayonnaise, flour, salt and pepper in saucepan. Stir in milk gradually. Cook until thickened, stirring constantly. Add cheese, onion and pimento, stirring until cheese melts. Stir in ham and eggs; mix gently. Cook just until heated through. Serve over muffins. **Yield: 8 servings.**

Approx Per Serving: Cal 467; Prot 23 g; Carbo 34 g; Fiber 2 g;
    T Fat 26 g; 50% Calories from Fat; Chol 257 mg; Sod 1231 mg.

Mary Vitale, Jackson

Rolled Lasagna

12 ounces lasagna noodles
1 cup chopped cooked ham
1 cup chopped cooked spinach

¾ cup shredded mozzarella cheese
¾ cup ricotta cheese
1   16-ounce jar spaghetti sauce

Cook noodles using package directions; drain. Combine ham, spinach and cheeses in bowl; mix well. Spoon mixture onto noodles; roll noodles to enclose filling. Arrange in baking dish. Spoon spaghetti sauce over rolls. Bake at 350 degrees for 20 minutes. Garnish with Parmesan cheese. **Yield: 6 servings.**

Approx Per Serving: Cal 432; Prot 22 g; Carbo 57 g; Fiber 2 g;
    T Fat 13 g; 27% Calories from Fat; Chol 39 mg; Sod 788 mg.

Sally Taylor, Marquette

Ham and Cheese Quiche

2 cups shredded Swiss cheese
2 cups chopped cooked ham
½ cup chopped onion

1 cup baking mix
4 eggs
2 cups milk

Sprinkle cheese, ham and onion into greased 10-inch deep dish pie plate. Combine baking mix, eggs and milk in bowl; mix well. Pour over ham mixture; mix gently. Bake at 400 degrees for 35 to 40 minutes or until set. Let stand for 5 minutes before serving. May double recipe and bake in 9x13-inch baking dish. **Yield: 6 servings.**

Approx Per Serving: Cal 413; Prot 31 g; Carbo 20 g; Fiber <1 g;
    T Fat 22 g; 50% Calories from Fat; Chol 213 mg; Sod 1063 mg.

Norma Deyaert, Iron Mountain

Ham Fried Rice

6 slices bacon
1 large onion, chopped
1 green bell pepper, chopped
2 stalks celery, sliced diagonally
1 pound thinly sliced ham, chopped

2 eggs
3 cups cooked rice
1 cup cooked peas
1 cup torn fresh spinach
Soy sauce, salt and pepper to taste

Fry bacon in large nonstick skillet until crisp; remove with slotted spoon to drain. Stir-fry onion, green pepper and celery in bacon drippings in skillet until tender; push to 1 side of skillet. Add ham. Stir-fry until liquid evaporates from ham; push to 1 side of skillet. Add eggs to skillet. Cook until yolks are firm, chopping with spatula. Add rice, peas and spinach; mix gently. Season with soy sauce, salt and pepper. Cook until rice is light brown, stirring constantly. Crumble bacon over top. May substitute ¼ cup peanut or vegetable oil for bacon and bok choy for celery. **Yield: 4 servings.**

Approx Per Serving: Cal 496; Prot 41 g; Carbo 49 g; Fiber 4 g;
T Fat 14 g; 26% Calories from Fat; Chol 177 mg; Sod 1722 mg.

Marcia Delaski, Skandia

Swiss Hamlets

8 1-ounce thin ham slices
4 4x4-inch slices Swiss cheese
1 10-ounce package frozen broccoli
spears, thawed

1 envelope white sauce mix
¼ cup sour cream
1 tablespoon prepared mustard
¼ teaspoon dillweed

Layer 2 slices ham with 1 slice cheese. Top with broccoli. Roll ham to enclose filling; secure with wooden picks. Arrange rolls in small shallow baking dish. Prepare white sauce mix using package directions. Stir in sour cream, mustard and dillweed. Spoon over ham rolls. Bake at 350 degrees for 30 to 35 minutes or until heated through. Remove picks. Serve rolls with sauce. **Yield: 2 servings.**

Approx Per Serving: Cal 618; Prot 55 g; Carbo 22 g; Fiber 4 g;
T Fat 35 g; 50% Calories from Fat; Chol 144 mg; Sod 2198 mg.

Shirley A. Cook, Lansing

*Finely chop ham and mix with pickle relish, chopped
boiled eggs and chopped celery for a sandwich spread. Serve
in pita pockets or croissants.*

Pork Barbecue

1 small onion, chopped
1 stalk celery, chopped
1 medium green bell pepper, chopped
1/4 cup butter
1 cup catsup

1 cup water
2 tablespoons brown sugar
2 tablespoons vinegar
3 cups chopped cooked pork

Sauté onion, celery and green pepper in butter in large skillet for 5 minutes. Stir in catsup, water, brown sugar and vinegar. Bring to a boil; reduce heat. Simmer for 15 minutes. Add pork. Simmer, covered, for 30 minutes, stirring once or twice. Serve over hot cooked rice, noodles, mashed potatoes or on buns. May substitute ground beef, beef or chicken for pork. **Yield: 6 servings.**

Approx Per Serving: Cal 260; Prot 17 g; Carbo 19 g; Fiber 1 g;
 T Fat 13 g; 45% Calories from Fat; Chol 70 mg; Sod 586 mg.

Carolyn Reinert, Vassar

Hawaiian Pork

1   15-ounce can pineapple chunks
1/4 cup honey
1/3 cup soy sauce

1/4 teaspoon garlic powder
1/4 teaspoon ginger
1   5-pound boneless pork loin

Combine pineapple, honey, soy sauce, garlic powder and ginger in bowl; mix well. Pour over pork roast in roasting pan. Roast at 325 degrees for 2 to 2 1/2 hours or until cooked through. Baste every 30 minutes until last 30 minutes of cooking time, then baste every 10 minutes. **Yield: 10 servings.**

Approx Per Serving: Cal 388; Prot 46 g; Carbo 16 g; Fiber <1 g;
 T Fat 15 g; 35% Calories from Fat; Chol 139 mg; Sod 654 mg.

Judy Ebelt, Traverse City

Breaded Pork Chops

4 large pork chops
1 egg, beaten
1 cup bread crumbs

1/4 cup butter
1 cup onion soup

Dip pork chops into egg in bowl; coat with bread crumbs. Brown on both sides in butter in skillet. Add soup. Simmer, covered, over low heat for 30 minutes, turning occasionally. **Yield: 4 servings.**

Approx Per Serving: Cal 476; Prot 39 g; Carbo 23 g; Fiber 1 g;
 T Fat 25 g; 48% Calories from Fat; Chol 183 mg; Sod 904 mg.

Arlene E. Hatch, Hill City, Minnesota

Marinated Pork Chops

3/4 cup soy sauce
1/4 cup lemon juice
1 tablespoon chili sauce

1 tablespoon brown sugar
1 clove of garlic, minced
6 pork chops

Combine soy sauce, lemon juice, chili sauce, brown sugar and garlic in plastic bag. Add pork chops; seal bag. Marinate in refrigerator overnight. Drain, reserving marinade. Grill or bake pork chops until tender, basting occasionally with reserved marinade. **Yield: 6 servings.**

Approx Per Serving: Cal 262; Prot 34 g; Carbo 7 g; Fiber <1 g;
    T Fat 11 g; 37% Calories from Fat; Chol 98 mg; Sod 2174 mg.
    Nutritional information includes entire amount of marinade.

Janet Sandon, Saginaw

Oven Pork Chops

2 large potatoes, peeled, sliced 1/4
    inch thick
Pepper to taste
1 cup chopped onion

1   10-ounce can cream of mushroom
    soup
4 large pork chops
2 tablespoons oil

Layer potatoes in shallow baking dish. Sprinkle with pepper and onion. Spread soup evenly over top. Brown pork chops on both sides in oil in skillet. Place on casserole. Bake, covered, at 325 degrees for 30 minutes. Increase oven temperature to 350 degrees. Bake, covered, for 20 minutes. Bake, uncovered, for 10 minutes longer or until brown. **Yield: 4 servings.**

Approx Per Serving: Cal 448; Prot 35 g; Carbo 25 g; Fiber 2 g;
    T Fat 23 g; 46% Calories from Fat; Chol 99 mg; Sod 656 mg.

Pat Hendershot, Punta Gorda, Florida

Pork Chops and Sauerkraut

6 pork chops
Garlic powder, onion powder, salt
    and pepper to taste

2 tablespoons oil
2   16-ounce jars sauerkraut

Season pork chops with garlic powder, onion powder, salt and pepper. Brown on both sides in oil in skillet; remove to plate. Add sauerkraut to drippings in skillet. Cook until brown, stirring frequently. Arrange pork chops over sauerkraut. Cook for several minutes longer. **Yield: 6 servings.**

Approx Per Serving: Cal 297; Prot 33 g; Carbo 6 g; Fiber 3 g;
    T Fat 15 g; 46% Calories from Fat; Chol 98 mg; Sod 1077 mg.

Luci Sampier, Howard City

Baked Pork Chops

4 pork chops
½ cup flour

½ cup catsup
¼ cup packed brown sugar

Trim fat from pork chops; coat with flour. Arrange in shallow baking dish. Mix catsup and brown sugar in bowl. Spread on pork chops. Add water to ¼ thickness of pork chops. Bake, covered, at 350 degrees for 45 minutes, adding water if needed. Bake, uncovered, for 15 minutes longer. **Yield: 4 servings.**

Approx Per Serving: Cal 386; Prot 34 g; Carbo 37 g; Fiber 1 g;
T Fat 11 g; 25% Calories from Fat; Chol 98 mg; Sod 441 mg.

Dana Goudreau, Rexton

Stuffed Pork Chops

4 pork chops
1 cup chopped onion
¼ cup chopped celery with tops
1 cup cream-style corn

Salt and pepper to taste
2 cups bread crumbs
½ teaspoon sage
⅓ cup water

Brown pork chops on both sides in skillet; remove to baking dish. Add onion and celery to drippings in skillet. Sauté for 2 minutes. Add corn, salt and pepper; mix gently. Spoon mixture onto pork chops. Top with mixture of bread crumbs and sage. Pour water around chops. Bake at 375 degrees for 40 minutes. **Yield: 4 servings.**

Approx Per Serving: Cal 485; Prot 40 g; Carbo 51 g; Fiber 4 g;
T Fat 13 g; 25% Calories from Fat; Chol 100 mg; Sod 635 mg.

Shirley A. Cook, Lansing

Mexicali Pork Chop Casserole

1 onion, thinly sliced
½ each green and red bell pepper,
cut into 1-inch pieces
1 tablespoon unsalted margarine
1 16-ounce can low-sodium
tomatoes, drained, chopped

1 cup frozen whole kernel corn,
thawed, drained
¼ teaspoon marjoram
4 1-inch thick lean rib pork chops,
fat trimmed

Sauté onion, green and red bell peppers in margarine over medium heat in heavy skillet for 5 minutes. Add tomatoes, corn and marjoram. Cook over high heat for 5 minutes longer. Spoon into 1½-quart casserole. Brown pork chops in same skillet for 2 minutes on each side. Lay over vegetables. Bake, covered with foil, at 350 degrees for 12 to 15 minutes or until cooked through. **Yield: 4 servings.**

Approx Per Serving: Cal 333; Prot 35 g; Carbo 19 g; Fiber 3 g;
T Fat 13 g; 36% Calories from Fat; Chol 98 mg; Sod 103 mg.

Colleen Bastian, Escanaba

Glazed Pork Chops

2 cups soy sauce
1 cup water
1/2 cup packed brown sugar
1 tablespoon dark molasses
1 teaspoon salt
4 4-ounce pork chops

1/2 cup packed brown sugar
1/2 cup water
1 tablespoon dry mustard
1 14-ounce bottle of catsup
1 12-ounce bottle of chili sauce

Bring soy sauce, 1 cup water, 1/2 cup brown sugar, molasses and salt to a boil in saucepan. Cool to room temperature. Pour over pork chops in shallow dish. Marinate in refrigerator overnight. Place in baking pan. Bake, covered with foil, at 375 degrees for 2 hours or until tender. Reduce oven temperature to 300 degrees. Combine 1/2 cup brown sugar, 1/2 cup water and dry mustard in saucepan; mix well. Add catsup and chili sauce. Bring to a boil; remove from heat. Dip baked chops into sauce; return to baking pan. Bake for 30 minutes longer or until glazed. May grill for 15 minutes to glaze if preferred. **Yield: 4 servings.**

Approx Per Serving: Cal 706; Prot 34 g; Carbo 128 g; Fiber 3 g;
T Fat 9 g; 11% Calories from Fat; Chol 69 mg; Sod 11027 mg.
Nutritional information includes entire amount of marinade and sauce.

Jo Marshall, Traverse City

Pork Casserole

1 1/2 pounds lean pork steak
2 tablespoons butter
1 cup chopped celery
1 cup chopped onion
1 green bell pepper, chopped
1 red bell pepper, chopped
8 ounces wide noodles, cooked

1 10-ounce can tomato soup
1 soup can water
1 4-ounce can mushrooms, drained
1 7-ounce can water chestnuts,
  drained
Salt and pepper to taste
1 cup shredded Cheddar cheese

Cut pork into bite-sized pieces. Brown on all sides in butter in saucepan. Add celery, onion, green pepper, red bell pepper, noodles, soup, water, mushrooms, water chestnuts, salt and pepper; mix gently. Spoon into baking dish. Top with cheese. Bake at 325 degrees for 1 hour. May omit mushrooms and water chestnuts if preferred. **Yield: 6 servings.**

Approx Per Serving: Cal 489; Prot 35 g; Carbo 42 g; Fiber 2 g;
T Fat 20 g; 37% Calories from Fat; Chol 166 mg; Sod 640 mg.

Ilene Hilson, Hastings

Kaputza

1½ pounds pork
1 medium onion, chopped
1½ pounds Polish sausage, sliced ½
  inch thick
4 cups sauerkraut

¼ head cabbage, coarsely chopped
1   10-ounce can cream of mushroom
  soup
1 tablespoon caraway seed
Pepper to taste

Cut pork into bite-sized pieces. Cook pork with onion in heavy saucepan for 10 minutes or until pork is cooked through. Add sausage, sauerkraut, cabbage, soup, caraway seed and pepper; mix well. Simmer all day, stirring occasionally. May cook in slow cooker if preferred. **Yield: 8 servings.**

Approx Per Serving: Cal 339; Prot 27 g; Carbo 10 g; Fiber 3 g;
    T Fat 21 g; 56% Calories from Fat; Chol 85 mg; Sod 1627 mg.

Shirley A. Cook, Lansing

Unstuffed Cabbage Rolls

8 cups shredded cabbage
1   46-ounce can tomato juice
1 large onion, minced
3 tablespoons oil
12 ounces ground pork
12 ounces ground beef

1 cup uncooked rice
1 tablespoon paprika
1 tablespoon salt
½ teaspoon pepper
1   20-ounce jar sauerkraut

Spread cabbage in 11x13-inch baking pan; pour 1 cup tomato juice over cabbage. Sauté onion in oil in skillet. Add ground pork, ground beef, rice, paprika, salt and pepper; mix well. Spread over cabbage. Drain and rinse sauerkraut. Spread over meat mixture. Pour remaining tomato juice over layers. Bake at 350 degrees for 1½ hours. **Yield: 8 servings.**

Approx Per Serving: Cal 352; Prot 23 g; Carbo 34 g; Fiber 5 g;
    T Fat 15 g; 37% Calories from Fat; Chol 59 mg; Sod 1920 mg.

Virginia McCauley, Flint

Polish Meatballs

1 tablespoon chopped onion
8 ounces ground pork
8 ounces ground veal
1 egg
1 cup bread crumbs

1 teaspoon salt
1/2 teaspoon pepper
1 cup cracker meal
3 tablespoons oil

Sauté onion in small nonstick skillet. Combine with pork, veal, egg, bread crumbs, salt and pepper in bowl; mix well. Add a small amount of water if needed for desired consistency. Shape into balls. Coat with cracker meal. Fry in oil in electric skillet until brown on all sides. Remove to baking pan; add a small amount of water. Bake at 325 degrees for 40 minutes. **Yield: 4 servings.**

Approx Per Serving: Cal 500; Prot 31 g; Carbo 43 g; Fiber 1 g;
   T Fat 23 g; 41% Calories from Fat; Chol 150 mg; Sod 803 mg.

Rita Izel, Detroit

Pizza Loaf

1 loaf frozen bread dough, thawed
1 pound ground pork
1/4 cup sliced mushrooms
1 medium onion, minced
1 teaspoon salt
1/4 teaspoon pepper
1   8-ounce tomato sauce

1/2 teaspoon minced garlic
1 teaspoon paprika
1/2 teaspoon oregano
1 cup shredded Cheddar cheese
3/4 cup shredded mozzarella cheese
2 tablespoons melted margarine

Let dough rise using package directions. Brown ground pork with mushrooms, onion, salt and pepper in skillet, stirring until ground pork is crumbly; drain. Stir in tomato sauce, garlic, paprika and oregano. Bring to a boil; reduce heat. Simmer, covered, for 30 minutes. Punch dough down. Roll to 12x15-inch rectangle on floured surface. Place on greased baking sheet. Spread filling down center of dough; sprinkle with cheeses. Fold dough over filling; brush with margarine. Bake at 350 degrees for 30 minutes. **Yield: 6 servings.**

Approx Per Serving: Cal 491; Prot 32 g; Carbo 47 g; Fiber 1 g;
   T Fat 21 g; 38% Calories from Fat; Chol 87 mg; Sod 1302 mg.

Mary Herman, Gwinn

Porketta Sandwiches

1 3-pound porketta roast
1/2 cup water

12 Kaiser rolls

Remove string from roast. Combine roast with water in slow cooker. Cook on High for 6 hours or until pork shreds easily. Serve hot on Kaiser rolls. Buy porketta from Italian market or make your own: slice 3-pound boneless pork butt roast in 1 continuous piece, starting on long side. Unroll pork piece and sprinkle with granulated garlic, red pepper flakes, rosemary, dill, salt and pepper to taste. Reroll roast and sprinkle outside with same seasonings. Cook as above. **Yield: 12 servings.**

Approx Per Serving: Cal 352; Prot 30 g; Carbo 37 g; Fiber 0 g;
    T Fat 9 g; 24% Calories from Fat; Chol 69 mg; Sod 575 mg.
    Nutritional information does not include seasonings on purchased porketta.

Pat Hyland, Iron Mountain

Texas Barbecued Ribs

1/2 cup vinegar
1/2 cup Worcestershire sauce
1/2 cup melted butter
1/3 teaspoon red pepper sauce
6 pounds pork ribs
1 cup tomato juice
1/2 cup water
1/4 cup catsup

1/4 cup vinegar
2 tablespoons Worcestershire sauce
2 tablespoons brown sugar
1 tablespoon paprika
1 teaspoon dry mustard
1/4 teaspoon chili powder
1/8 teaspoon cayenne pepper
1 teaspoon salt

Combine 1/2 cup vinegar, 1/2 cup Worcestershire sauce, butter and pepper sauce in shallow dish. Add ribs, coating well. Let stand for several minutes, basting several times. Place ribs on grill over low coals sprinkled with hickory chips. Grill for 2 1/4 hours. Combine tomato juice, water, catsup, 1/4 cup vinegar, 2 tablespoons Worcestershire sauce, brown sugar, paprika, dry mustard, chili powder, cayenne pepper and salt in saucepan. Bring to a boil; reduce heat. Simmer for 15 minutes or until thickened to desired consistency. Brush over ribs. Grill for 40 minutes longer or until done to taste. Remove ribs to serving platter. Spoon remaining sauce over top. **Yield: 6 servings.**

Approx Per Serving: Cal 886; Prot 52 g; Carbo 16 g; Fiber 1 g;
    T Fat 68 g; 69% Calories from Fat; Chol 250 mg; Sod 1158 mg.

Jacqueline Brana, Redford

Country Baked Ribs

10 tablespoons soy sauce
10 tablespoons water
2 cups packed brown sugar

1 teaspoon minced garlic
5 pounds country-style pork ribs

Combine soy sauce, water, brown sugar and garlic in shallow dish; mix well. Add ribs, coating well. Marinate in refrigerator overnight. Bake at 350 degrees for 4 hours. **Yield: 6 servings.**

Approx Per Serving: Cal 928; Prot 43 g; Carbo 91 g; Fiber <1 g;
    T Fat 44 g; 42% Calories from Fat; Chol 174 mg; Sod 1889 mg.

Judy Ebelt, Traverse City

Pork Tenderloin with Asparagus Sauce

2 pounds pork tenderloin
2 tablespoons butter
1 10-ounce can cream of asparagus
    soup
1/4 cup milk

1/2 cup chopped onion
1 4-ounce can sliced mushrooms,
    drained
1/2 teaspoon curry powder
Pepper to taste

Cut pork into 8 pieces; pound to flatten. Brown on both sides in butter in skillet; remove to 2-quart baking dish. Stir mixture of soup and milk into drippings in skillet. Add onion, mushrooms, curry powder and pepper. Pour over pork. Bake at 350 degrees for 40 to 45 minutes or until tender. **Yield: 8 servings.**

Approx Per Serving: Cal 223; Prot 24 g; Carbo 5 g; Fiber 1 g;
    T Fat 12 g; 48% Calories from Fat; Chol 80 mg; Sod 143 mg.

Dorothy Martin, West Branch

Aunt Betty's Sausage-Noodle Bake

1 16-ounce package curly noodles
2 pounds kielbasa, cut into 2-inch
    pieces
8 ounces bacon, crisp-fried, crumbled
3 15-ounce cans sauerkraut,
    drained, rinsed

3 medium onions, chopped
4 4-ounce cans mushrooms, drained
Garlic powder, salt and pepper to
    taste

Cook noodles using package directions; drain. Combine with kielbasa, bacon, sauerkraut, onions, mushrooms, garlic powder, salt and pepper in bowl; mix well. Spoon into large baking pan. Bake at 350 degrees for 1 hour. **Yield: 12 servings.**

Approx Per Serving: Cal 352; Prot 16 g; Carbo 36 g; Fiber 3 g;
    T Fat 16 g; 41% Calories from Fat; Chol 100 mg; Sod 1421 mg.

Nancy Briolat, St. Ignace

Beer-Braised Bratwurst Dinner

1¹/₂ pounds bratwurst
1 small head cabbage, cut into
  wedges
1 tablespoon oil
3 medium red potatoes, coarsely
  chopped

2 medium onions, sliced ¹/₂ inch thick
1 12-ounce can beer
1 teaspoon instant chicken bouillon
1 tablespoon caraway seed
¹/₂ teaspoon salt
¹/₂ teaspoon pepper

Brown bratwurst on all sides in 12-inch skillet over medium-high heat; drain on paper towels. Combine with cabbage in shallow 3¹/₂-quart baking dish. Heat oil with drippings in skillet. Add potatoes and onions. Cook until light brown, stirring frequently. Add to baking dish. Add beer, bouillon, caraway seed, salt and pepper to drippings in skillet, stirring to deglaze. Bring to a boil over high heat. Pour into baking dish. Bake, covered, at 375 degrees for 1¹/₂ hours or until vegetables are tender. **Yield: 6 servings.**

Approx Per Serving: Cal 308; Prot 11 g; Carbo 27 g; Fiber 3 g;
    T Fat 17 g; 50% Calories from Fat; Chol 32 mg; Sod 681 mg.

Donna Lucas, McBain

Make-Ahead Brunch Casserole

1 pound sausage
1 teaspoon prepared mustard
6 slices bread, crusts trimmed
2 cups shredded Cheddar cheese
6 eggs, beaten

2 cups milk
1 teaspoon nutmeg
1 teaspoon Worcestershire sauce
Salt and pepper to taste

Brown sausage in skillet, stirring until crumbly; drain. Stir in mustard. Layer bread, sausage mixture and cheese in 9x13-inch baking dish. Beat eggs with milk, nutmeg, Worcestershire sauce, salt and pepper in bowl. Pour over layers. Chill overnight. Bake at 350 degrees for 30 to 45 minutes or until set. **Yield: 8 servings.**

Approx Per Serving: Cal 350; Prot 20 g; Carbo 11 g; Fiber <1 g;
    T Fat 25 g; 64% Calories from Fat; Chol 219 mg; Sod 687 mg.

Marge Venable, Grand Blanc

Egg and Cheese Brunch

1   32-ounce package frozen hashed
    brown potatoes, thawed
Salt and pepper to taste
8 eggs

2 cups milk
1 pound bacon, crisp-fried, crumbled
1½ cups shredded Cheddar cheese

Spread potatoes in greased 9x13-inch baking dish; sprinkle with salt and pepper. Beat eggs with milk in bowl. Pour over potatoes. Sprinkle with bacon and cheese. Bake at 375 degrees for 45 to 55 minutes or until golden brown. **Yield: 8 servings.**

Approx Per Serving: Cal 547; Prot 22 g; Carbo 36 g; Fiber 2 g;
      T Fat 36 g; 58% Calories from Fat; Chol 258 mg; Sod 536 mg.

Nancy Neuhaus, Grand Rapids

Corn Dogs

1 cup flour
1½ teaspoons baking powder
2/3 cup cornmeal
1 tablespoon sugar
½ teaspoon salt
2 tablespoons bacon drippings

1 egg, beaten
1 to 1¼ cups buttermilk
½ teaspoon baking soda
1   16-ounce package frankfurters
Oil for frying

Mix flour, baking powder, cornmeal, sugar and salt in bowl. Stir in bacon drippings. Combine egg, buttermilk and baking soda in small bowl; mix well. Add to batter; mix well. Dip frankfurters into batter, coating well. Fry in 3 to 4 inches 375-degree oil in skillet until golden brown, turning once. Drain on paper towels. Insert wooden skewers. **Yield: 10 servings.**

Approx Per Serving: Cal 276; Prot 9 g; Carbo 21 g; Fiber 1 g;
      T Fat 17 g; 57% Calories from Fat; Chol 62 mg; Sod 772 mg.
      Nutritional information does not include oil for frying.

Cyndi Sechler, Grass Valley, California

Homemade Pizzas

1 cup warm water
2 tablespoons shortening
1 teaspoon sugar
¹/₄ teaspoon salt
1 envelope dry yeast
4 cups sifted flour
1 small onion, chopped
2 tablespoons oil
1   20-ounce can tomatoes

1 bay leaf
1 teaspoon sugar
¹/₂ teaspoon oregano
1 teaspoon salt
Pepper to taste
8 ounces sliced pepperoni
8 ounces mushrooms, sliced
4 cups shredded mozzarella cheese
¹/₂ cup grated Parmesan cheese

Combine warm water, shortening, 1 teaspoon sugar and ¹/₄ teaspoon salt in large bowl. Sprinkle yeast over top. Let stand until shortening melts and yeast dissolves, stirring occasionally. Add flour gradually, mixing to form dough. Knead on floured surface until smooth and elastic. Place in greased bowl, turning to coat surface. Let rise for 1 hour or until doubled in bulk. Sauté onion in oil in skillet, Add tomatoes, bay leaf, 1 teaspoon sugar, oregano, 1 teaspoon salt and pepper. Simmer until of desired consistency; discard bay leaf. Divide dough into 2 portions. Press into 2 greased pizza pans. Spread with tomato sauce. Sprinkle with pepperoni, mushrooms and cheeses. Bake at 450 degrees for 15 to 20 minutes or until crust is golden brown. May add other toppings of choice. **Yield: 8 servings.**

Approx Per Serving: Cal 624; Prot 27 g; Carbo 53 g; Fiber 3 g;
    T Fat 33 g; 48% Calories from Fat; Chol 58 mg; Sod 1336 mg.

Aileen Pancheri, Sault Ste. Marie

Mel's Tortilla Pizza

6 flour tortillas
1   16-ounce jar pizza sauce
2 cups shredded Monterey jack
    cheese

8 ounces sliced pepperoni
1   8-ounce can sliced mushrooms
Oregano to taste

Arrange 3 tortillas over bottom and side of 8-inch baking pan, overlapping edges. Spread with half the pizza sauce, cheese, pepperoni and mushrooms. Repeat layers; sprinkle with oregano. Bake at 350 degrees for 20 minutes or until light brown. **Yield: 6 servings.**

Approx Per Serving: Cal 485; Prot 22 g; Carbo 28 g; Fiber 2 g;
    T Fat 33 g; 60% Calories from Fat; Chol 48 mg; Sod 1606 mg.

Sue Villanueva, Traverse City

Dad's Polish Sausage

15 pounds pork butts
1 bulb of garlic, chopped
3 cups (or more) water
2 teaspoons coriander

1 tablespoon marjoram
6 tablespoons noniodized canning
  salt
4 teaspoons pepper

Cut pork into 1 to 1½-inch strips, discarding most of the fat. Process garlic with water in blender until smooth. Combine seasonings in large bowl; mix well. Add garlic mixture and pork; mix well. Chill for 2 days, mixing well at least once a day. Put mixture through meat grinder fitted with medium or large knife. Stuff into sausage casings and tie in desired sizes. Cook in water to cover in saucepan for 30 minutes or until pork is no longer pink. **Yield: 60 servings.**

Approx Per Serving: Cal 163; Prot 23 g; Carbo <1 g; Fiber <1 g;
  T Fat 7 g; 42% Calories from Fat; Chol 69 mg; Sod 694 mg.

Ray Wojnaroski, Goetzville

Sauerkraut and Sausage Meal-in-a-Pot

3 pounds Polish sausage
1 28-ounce jar sauerkraut, rinsed
1 large onion, minced
½ cup oats

3 tablespoons brown sugar
4 medium potatoes, chopped
1 10-ounce can tomato soup
¼ cup peppercorns

Combine sausage, sauerkraut, onion, oats, brown sugar, potatoes, soup and peppercorns in large baking pan. Add enough water to come to top of ingredients. Bake at 250 to 275 degrees for 3½ to 4 hours or until done to taste. **Yield: 8 servings.**

Approx Per Serving: Cal 405; Prot 15 g; Carbo 34 g; Fiber 4 g;
  T Fat 24 g; 53% Calories from Fat; Chol 56 mg; Sod 1607 mg.

Pat Perry, Wyoming

Sausage and Krauterole

2 pounds sauerkraut, drained, rinsed
2 medium onions, chopped
1 tablespoon butter

2 tablespoons brown sugar
1 8-ounce can mushrooms, drained
3 8-ounce Polish sausage links

Sauté sauerkraut and onions in butter in 10-inch skillet. Add brown sugar and mushrooms. Simmer for several minutes. Spoon into oiled 9x13-inch baking dish. Top with sausage; pierce sausage with fork. Bake, covered, at 325 degrees for 1½ hours. **Yield: 6 servings.**

Approx Per Serving: Cal 286; Prot 13 g; Carbo 17 g; Fiber 4 g;
  T Fat 19 g; 58% Calories from Fat; Chol 50 mg; Sod 1869 mg.

Jean Scibior, Petoskey

Sausage Ring

3 pounds pork sausage
1/2 medium green bell pepper,
  chopped
2 medium onions, chopped

4 slices bread, crumbled
3 eggs
1 teaspoon garlic salt
1/2 teaspoon pepper

Combine sausage, green pepper, onions, bread crumbs, eggs, garlic salt and pepper in bowl; mix well. Pack into ring mold or bundt pan. Bake at 350 degrees for 1 hour; drain well. Invert onto serving plate. **Yield: 12 servings.**

Approx Per Serving: Cal 315; Prot 17 g; Carbo 8 g; Fiber 1 g;
    T Fat 24 g; 69% Calories from Fat; Chol 111 mg; Sod 1145 mg.

Sandy Hines, Grandville

Sausage and Gravy

12 ounces pork sausage
1/2 cup chopped onion
1/2 cup flour
4 cups milk

1 teaspoon instant beef bouillon
1/4 teaspoon poultry seasoning
1/8 teaspoon pepper

Brown sausage with onion in skillet, stirring until sausage is crumbly. Sprinkle with flour; stir to mix well. Cook for 1 minute, stirring constantly. Add milk gradually. Bring to a boil, stirring constantly. Add bouillon, poultry seasoning and pepper. Cook until thickened, stirring constantly. Serve over biscuits. **Yield: 6 servings.**

Approx Per Serving: Cal 242; Prot 12 g; Carbo 17 g; Fiber <1 g;
    T Fat 14 g; 52% Calories from Fat; Chol 44 mg; Sod 557 mg.

Joan Emmons, Jackson

Sausage with Tomatoes and Peppers

1 pound mild or hot pork sausage
  links, cut into 1-inch pieces
2 large yellow onions, chopped
3 tablespoons oil

3 medium tomatoes, peeled, chopped
2 large green bell peppers, cut into
  1/2-inch strips
1/4 teaspoon salt

Brown sausage pieces on all sides in heavy skillet over medium heat for 10 minutes. Remove sausage to bowl; drain skillet. Sauté onions in oil in skillet for 5 minutes. Add tomatoes, green peppers, salt and sausage. Simmer, covered, for 10 minutes; skim sauce. Serve with pasta, green salad and crusty bread. **Yield: 4 servings.**

Approx Per Serving: Cal 341; Prot 13 g; Carbo 12 g; Fiber 3 g;
    T Fat 27 g; 71% Calories from Fat; Chol 45 mg; Sod 832 mg.

Marion Underhill, Lansing

Oxtails in Peanut Butter

1¹/₂ to 2 pounds oxtails
3 or 4 cloves of garlic, crushed
1 large onion, thinly sliced
3 cups water

3 to 4 tablespoons creamy peanut
 butter
2 or 3 eggplant, cut into halves
6 ounces green beans

Cut oxtails into 2-inch pieces. Sauté garlic in nonstick saucepan until brown. Add onion. Sauté until tender. Add oxtails and water. Simmer for 1 to 1¹/₂ hours. Stir in peanut butter. Simmer for 10 minutes. Add eggplant. Simmer just until tender-crisp. Add green beans. Cook for 10 minutes. Serve with hot cooked rice. May cook oxtails in pressure cooker for 20 to 25 minutes if preferred. **Yield: 6 servings.**

Approx Per Serving: Cal 127; Prot 6 g; Carbo 17 g; Fiber 7 g;
 T Fat 6 g; 37% Calories from Fat; Chol 0 mg; Sod 52 mg.
 Nutritional information does not include oxtails.

Edwin L. Candelaria, Lansing

Braised Rabbit

1¹/₂ cups cider vinegar
1 onion, sliced
1 tablespoon dry mustard
2 teaspoons salt
¹/₂ teaspoon pepper
2 rabbits, cut up

1 cup flour
Sugar to taste
¹/₄ teaspoon nutmeg
Bacon drippings
¹/₂ cup flour
3 cups water or wine

Combine vinegar, onion, dry mustard, salt and pepper in large bowl; mix well. Add rabbit pieces. Marinate in refrigerator for several hours; drain. Mix 1 cup flour, sugar and nutmeg in paper bag. Add several pieces rabbit at a time, shaking to coat well. Brown in hot bacon drippings in skillet; remove to warm platter. Drain all but ¹/₂ cup drippings. Stir in ¹/₂ cup flour. Add water gradually. Cook over low heat until thickened, stirring constantly. Add rabbit. Simmer, covered, for 1¹/₂ to 2 hours or until tender. May bake at 250 degrees for 1¹/₂ to 2 hours if preferred.
Yield: 6 servings.

Nutritional information for this recipe is not available.

Jim Hamilton, Lansing

Use wine and tomatoes to tenderize less tender cuts of meat;
they act to break down tough fibers.

Super Venison

2 pounds venison steaks or strips
Garlic powder, onion powder, salt
   and pepper to taste
2 tablespoons oil

2 onions, sliced
1 green bell pepper, sliced
1 red bell pepper, sliced
8 ounces fresh mushrooms, sliced

Sprinkle both sides of venison with garlic powder, onion powder, salt and pepper. Brown on both sides in oil in heavy saucepan. Add onions, bell peppers and mushrooms. Cook over medium heat for 10 minutes. Simmer, covered, until venison is tender. Serve with hot cooked rice or mashed potatoes. **Yield: 6 servings.**

Approx Per Serving: Cal 204; Prot 28 g; Carbo 7 g; Fiber 2 g;
   T Fat 7 g; 31% Calories from Fat; Chol 58 mg; Sod 66 mg.

Luci Sampier, Howard City

Venison "Stoup"

1½ pounds venison, cubed
3 tablespoons bacon drippings
8 cups water

1 package beef noodle soup starter
Garlic salt to taste

Brown venison, covered, in bacon drippings in heavy 5-quart saucepan for 5 minutes, stirring occasionally. Add water and soup starter using package directions. Bring to a boil; reduce heat. Simmer, covered, for 2 hours, stirring occasionally. Season with garlic salt. May substitute vegetable soup starter for beef noodle. **Yield: 4 servings.**

Approx Per Serving: Cal 423; Prot 36 g; Carbo 36 g; Fiber 0 g;
   T Fat 14 g; 30% Calories from Fat; Chol 128 mg; Sod 1775 mg.

Bill Devers, Laingsburg

BLIND BASEBALL

Poultry and Seafood

Baked Chicken Parmesan

1   3-pound chicken
1 teaspoon salt
1/4 teaspoon pepper
1/4 teaspoon garlic salt
1/4 teaspoon paprika
1/8 teaspoon thyme

1/4 cup grated Parmesan cheese
1 tablespoon minced parsley
1/3 cup fine bread crumbs
1/3 cup water
1 tablespoon oil
1/4 cup melted margarine

Rinse chicken and pat dry; cut into serving pieces. Combine next 8 ingredients in paper bag; mix well. Place chicken pieces in bag a few at a time, shaking to coat well. Grease shallow roasting pan; pour in water. Arrange chicken pieces in prepared pan; ·drizzle with oil and melted margarine. Bake at 350 degrees for 60 to 70 minutes or until golden brown. **Yield: 4 servings.**

Approx Per Serving: Cal 511; Prot 53 g; Carbo 6 g; Fiber <1 g;
    T Fat 29 g; 53% Calories from Fat; Chol 156 mg; Sod 1096 mg.

Florence Baker, Grandville

Frankenmuth Grilled Chicken

7 pounds chicken pieces
Onion and garlic powder to taste

1 teaspoon salt
1 quart malt liquor

Rinse chicken and pat dry; sprinkle with onion and garlic powder. Mix salt and malt liquor in spray bottle. Place chicken on grill over warm coals. Grill for 1 hour or until tender, spraying with malt mixture every 5 to 10 minutes to baste. **Yield: 8 servings.**

Approx Per Serving: Cal 426; Prot 58 g; Carbo 3 g; Fiber 0 g;
    T Fat 15 g; 31% Calories from Fat; Chol 177 mg; Sod 441 mg.

Craig Kirkpatrick, Tuscola

Kay's Chicken Aloha

3 pounds chicken wings
1 cup crushed pineapple
3 tablespoons pineapple juice
1 cup packed brown sugar

2 tablespoons prepared mustard
1 teaspoon salt
Pepper to taste
3 tablespoons lemon juice

Rinse chicken wings and pat dry; discard tips. Arrange in nonstick shallow baking pan. Combine pineapple, pineapple juice, brown sugar, mustard, salt, pepper and lemon juice in bowl; mix well. Pour over chicken wings. Bake at 350 degrees for 1½ hours. **Yield: 6 servings.**

Approx Per Serving: Cal 544; Prot 30 g; Carbo 55 g; Fiber <1 g;
    T Fat 22 g; 37% Calories from Fat; Chol 97 mg; Sod 535 mg.

Susan Miner, Traverse City

Chicken-Broccoli Casserole

1 3-pound chicken, cooked	2 10-ounce cans cream of mushroom
2 10-ounce packages frozen	soup
chopped broccoli, cooked	2 6-ounce packages stuffing mix,
8 slices American cheese	prepared

Bone and cube chicken, discarding skin. Place in 9x13-inch baking dish. Layer with broccoli, cheese and soup. Sprinkle stuffing over top. Bake at 350 degrees for 45 minutes. **Yield: 6 servings.**

Approx Per Serving: Cal 693; Prot 53 g; Carbo 54 g; Fiber 3 g;
T Fat 30 g; 38% Calories from Fat; Chol 138 mg; Sod 2399 mg.

Betty Murray, Marquette

Chicken Cacciatore

1 2-pound chicken, cut into pieces	2 cloves of garlic, minced
2 tablespoons shortening	1 teaspoon oregano
1 10-ounce can tomato soup	1/4 teaspoon salt
1/4 cup water	1/2 green bell pepper, cut into strips
1/4 cup dry red wine	1/2 cup chopped onion

Rinse chicken and pat dry. Brown in shortening in skillet; drain. Add remaining ingredients. Simmer, covered, for 45 minutes, stirring occasionally. Simmer, uncovered, for 5 to 10 minutes longer or until sauce is reduced and thickened. **Yield: 6 servings.**

Approx Per Serving: Cal 229; Prot 23 g; Carbo 8 g; Fiber 1 g;
T Fat 11 g; 44% Calories from Fat; Chol 68 mg; Sod 483 mg.

Nellie Thompson, Romulus

Chicken with Forty Cloves of Garlic

40 unpeeled cloves of garlic	1/2 teaspoon sage
1 3-pound chicken, cut into pieces	1 tablespoon fresh minced parsley
1/2 cup dry white wine	4 bay leaves
1/4 cup olive oil	1 teaspoon salt
1 teaspoon thyme	1/4 teaspoon pepper

Scatter garlic in Dutch oven. Rinse chicken; pat dry. Place over garlic. Add remaining ingredients. Cover with foil and lid. Bake at 375 degrees for 1 hour, removing foil and lid during last 10 minutes to brown. Place chicken on platter; discard bay leaves. Press juice from garlic cloves into shallow bowl or over French bread. **Yield: 4 servings.**

Approx Per Serving: Cal 507; Prot 51 g; Carbo 10 g; Fiber 1 g;
T Fat 26 g; 49% Calories from Fat; Chol 152 mg; Sod 685 mg.

Astrid Bailey, Menominee

Baked Chicken and Rice

1   3-pound chicken
1/3 cup zesty Italian salad dressing
1   3-ounce can French-fried onions
2/3 cup uncooked rice

1   16-ounce package frozen mixed
     broccoli and carrots
1 3/4 cups chicken bouillon
1/2 teaspoon Italian seasoning

Rinse chicken and pat dry; arrange in 9x13-inch baking dish. Pour salad dressing over top. Bake at 400 degrees for 20 minutes. Arrange half the fried onions, rice and vegetables around and under chicken. Combine bouillon and Italian seasoning in bowl; mix well. Pour over rice and vegetables. Bake for 25 minutes. Sprinkle with remaining fried onions. Bake for 2 to 3 minutes longer. Let stand for 5 minutes before serving. **Yield: 6 servings.**

Approx Per Serving: Cal 469; Prot 38 g; Carbo 27 g; Fiber <1 g;
     T Fat 23 g; 45% Calories from Fat; Chol 102 mg; Sod 541 mg.

Jeanne Alpers, Traverse City

Souper Chicken and Rice

1 cup uncooked rice
2   10-ounce cans each cream of
     chicken soup and cream of
     mushroom soup

1/2 cup water
2 pounds chicken pieces
Paprika to taste

Combine rice, soups and water in bowl; pour into baking pan. Rinse chicken and pat dry; arrange over soup mixture. Sprinkle with paprika. Bake at 350 degrees for 1 1/2 hours or until tender. **Yield: 6 servings.**

Approx Per Serving: Cal 391; Prot 27 g; Carbo 35 g; Fiber 1 g;
     T Fat 15 g; 35% Calories from Fat; Chol 76 mg; Sod 1192 mg.

Vera Gabel, Newberry

Football Chicken

1   3-pound chicken
1 teaspoon each marjoram, thyme,
     sage, poultry seasoning, seasoned
     salt, garlic salt, paprika and pepper

1/2 cup melted margarine
1 cup crushed potato chips

Rinse chicken and pat dry; cut into serving pieces. Combine seasonings with margarine. Dip chicken into margarine mixture; roll in potato chips. Arrange on baking sheet. Bake at 375 degrees for 50 to 60 minutes or until tender. **Yield: 4 servings.**

Approx Per Serving: Cal 603; Prot 50 g; Carbo 8 g; Fiber 1 g;
     T Fat 41 g; 61% Calories from Fat; Chol 152 mg; Sod 1317 mg.

Pete and Jan Sherman, Eaton Rapids

New Country-Fried Chicken

1   3-pound chicken
1 cup flour
2 teaspoons garlic powder
1 teaspoon paprika
1/4 teaspoon poultry seasoning

1/4 teaspoon pepper
1 egg, beaten
1/2 cup milk
Oil for deep frying

Rinse chicken and pat dry; cut into serving pieces. Combine flour, garlic powder, paprika, poultry seasoning and pepper in plastic bag. Add chicken pieces, shaking to coat. Dip in mixture of egg and milk. Shake in flour mixture again. Deep-fry in hot oil for 15 to 18 minutes or until tender; drain well. **Yield: 4 servings.**

Approx Per Serving: Cal 475; Prot 55 g; Carbo 25 g; Fiber 1 g;
    T Fat 15 g; 30% Calories from Fat; Chol 209 mg; Sod 176 mg.
    Nutritional information does not include oil for deep frying.

Ruth Palmiteer, Watsonville, California

Hungarian-Style Chicken Paprika

3 onions, chopped
3 banana peppers, seeded, chopped
2 teaspoons oil
1 teaspoon salt

3 tomatoes, chopped
2 tablespoons Hungarian paprika
1   3-pound chicken

Sauté onions and peppers in oil in large skillet until tender. Add salt, tomatoes and paprika. Cook over medium heat for 15 minutes, stirring occasionally. Rinse chicken and pat dry; cut into serving pieces. Add to skillet with vegetables. Cook over low heat for 1 hour or until chicken is tender, adding water if necessary. Serve over cooked noodles or rice. **Yield: 4 servings.**

Approx Per Serving: Cal 421; Prot 52 g; Carbo 17 g; Fiber 5 g;
    T Fat 16 g; 34% Calories from Fat; Chol 152 mg; Sod 691 mg.

Laszlo Farago, Grand Rapids

*Marinate chicken breast filets in a mixture of 1/2 cup soy sauce,
minced garlic, 3/4 teaspoon ginger, 2 tablespoons sugar and
1 ounce sherry for 4 to 6 hours. Grill for 15 minutes.*

Italian Chicken over Noodles

1 pound skinless, boneless chicken
  pieces
1/2 green bell pepper, chopped
1 cup sliced fresh mushrooms
1/3 cup chopped onion

1 teaspoon basil
Pepper to taste
1 48-ounce jar spaghetti sauce
4 stalks celery, chopped
3/4 16-ounce package egg noodles

Rinse chicken and pat dry; cut into bite-sized pieces. Brown in skillet sprayed with nonstick cooking spray. Add green pepper, mushrooms, onion, basil, pepper and spaghetti sauce; mix well. Simmer, covered, for 10 minutes, stirring occasionally. Add celery. Cook for 5 minutes longer. Cook noodles using package directions; drain. Spoon chicken mixture over noodles to serve. **Yield: 4 servings.**

Approx Per Serving: Cal 825; Prot 36 g; Carbo 118 g; Fiber 6 g;
    T Fat 25 g; 27% Calories from Fat; Chol 200 mg; Sod 1787 mg.

Carolyn Ryba

Snow-on-the-Mountain

1 2-pound chicken
2 10-ounce cans cream of mushroom
  soup
1 10-ounce can cream of chicken
  soup
6 cups cooked rice
3 tomatoes, chopped
1 onion, chopped
3 cups chopped celery
1 6-ounce can black olives, drained,
  chopped
1 7-ounce jar green olives, drained,
  chopped

1 11/2-ounce can chow mein noodles
4 cups shredded Colby cheese
2 16-ounce cans crushed pineapple,
  drained
3 cups sliced almonds
4 bananas, sliced
3 11-ounce cans mandarin oranges,
  drained
4 cups Spanish peanuts
3 cups shredded coconut

Rinse chicken. Cook in water to cover in saucepan until tender. Drain, reserving 11/2 cups broth. Chop chicken, discarding skin and bones; set aside. Combine reserved broth, mushroom soup and chicken soup in saucepan. Simmer for 3 to 4 minutes or until smooth, stirring frequently. Stir in chicken; remove from heat. Layer rice, chicken mixture, tomatoes, onion, celery, black and green olives, noodles, cheese, pineapple, almonds, bananas, oranges, peanuts and coconut on large serving platter. May also add pumpkin seed and sunflower seed. **Yield: 6 servings.**

Approx Per Serving: Cal 2279; Prot 90 g; Carbo 187 g; Fiber 28 g;
    T Fat 143 g; 54% Calories from Fat; Chol 145 mg; Sod 3142 mg.

Esther Mast, Belmont

No-Peek Chicken

1 10-ounce can cream of chicken
   soup
1 10-ounce can cream of mushroom
   soup

1 soup can water
1 envelope onion soup mix
1/2 cup uncooked rice
6 chicken thighs, skinned

Combine soups, water, onion soup mix and rice in bowl; mix well. Spoon into 9x9-inch baking pan. Rinse chicken and pat dry. Place over soup mixture. Bake, covered, at 250 degrees for 1½ hours. **Yield: 6 servings.**

Approx Per Serving: Cal 260; Prot 17 g; Carbo 20 g; Fiber <1 g;
   T Fat 12 g; 43% Calories from Fat; Chol 53 mg; Sod 905 mg.

Nancy Carpenter, Jackson

West Coast Chicken

5 pounds chicken thighs, skinned
2 teaspoons salt
1/4 teaspoon pepper
1/3 cup melted butter

1 cup frozen orange juice
   concentrate, thawed
2 teaspoons ground ginger
4 teaspoons soy sauce

Rinse chicken and pat dry; arrange in greased baking pan. Combine salt, pepper, butter, orange juice concentrate, ginger and soy sauce in bowl; mix well. Pour over chicken. Marinate, covered, in refrigerator overnight. Bake, uncovered, at 350 degrees for 1 hour, basting occasionally with sauce. **Yield: 8 servings.**

Approx Per Serving: Cal 422; Prot 38 g; Carbo 14 g; Fiber <1 g;
   T Fat 23 g; 50% Calories from Fat; Chol 154 mg; Sod 895 mg.

Joyce Olson, Mesa, Arizona

Bacon-Flake Chicken Breasts

5 slices bacon, cut into halves
3 whole chicken breasts, cut into
   halves

1 cup milk
2 cups crushed cornflakes
Salt, pepper and garlic salt to taste

Place bacon in 8x10-inch microwave-safe dish. Microwave, covered with waxed paper, on High for 5 minutes; turn. Microwave for 2 to 3 minutes longer or until crisp; drain. Rinse chicken and pat dry. Dip in milk; roll in cornflakes. Arrange over cooked bacon. Pour remaining milk into dish. Microwave for 5 minutes; turn. Sprinkle with salt and pepper. Microwave for 8 minutes. Let stand for 3 minutes. Sprinkle with garlic salt before serving. **Yield: 6 servings.**

Approx Per Serving: Cal 284; Prot 31 g; Carbo 22 g; Fiber <1 g;
   T Fat 7 g; 23% Calories from Fat; Chol 82 mg; Sod 445 mg.

Janell Sandstedt, Manistee

Chicken Breasts Amandine

1/2 cup sliced almonds
1/4 cup butter
1/4 cup flour
1/4 teaspoon salt

1/8 teaspoon pepper
4 chicken breasts
1/2 cup white wine

Brown almonds in butter in skillet for 5 minutes; remove and set aside. Combine flour, salt and pepper in bowl. Rinse chicken and pat dry; coat with flour mixture. Add to skillet. Cook over medium heat until brown on both sides. Add wine. Cook, covered, over low heat for 5 to 10 minutes or until tender. Remove chicken to serving platter. Bring pan drippings to a boil. Stir in almonds; remove from heat. Spoon over chicken. **Yield: 4 servings.**

Approx Per Serving: Cal 359; Prot 30 g; Carbo 9 g; Fiber 2 g;
    T Fat 21 g; 55% Calories from Fat; Chol 103 mg; Sod 296 mg.

Judy Ebelt, Traverse City

Chicken and Asparagus

2 14-ounce cans asparagus tips, drained
3 whole chicken breast filets, cooked
3 10-ounce cans cream of mushroom soup

1 cup heavy cream
2 teaspoons curry powder
Salt and pepper to taste
3 tablespoons grated Parmesan cheese

Layer asparagus and chicken in greased 3-quart casserole. Combine soup, cream, curry powder, salt and pepper in saucepan; mix well. Cook until heated through, stirring constantly. Pour over chicken layer. Sprinkle with Parmesan cheese. Bake at 350 degrees for 30 minutes. **Yield: 6 servings.**

Approx Per Serving: Cal 451; Prot 33 g; Carbo 15 g; Fiber 2 g;
    T Fat 30 g; 58% Calories from Fat; Chol 130 mg; Sod 1583 mg.

Esther Fischrupp, Holland

Chicken Breasts with Mushroom-Wine Sauce

2 whole chicken breast filets, split
2 tablespoons flour
1/8 teaspoon pepper
2 tablespoons margarine
2 cups thinly sliced fresh mushrooms

1/4 cup chopped onion
1 cup white wine
1/4 cup chopped fresh parsley
2 cups cooked rice

Rinse chicken and pat dry. Coat with mixture of flour and pepper. Reserve remaining flour mixture. Brown chicken in margarine in skillet on both sides. Remove to warm platter. Add mushrooms and onion to skillet. Sauté until tender. Stir in reserved flour mixture and wine. Bring to a boil, stirring frequently. Add chicken and parsley; reduce heat. Simmer, covered, for 25 minutes. Serve over hot cooked rice. **Yield: 4 servings.**

Approx Per Serving: Cal 370; Prot 30 g; Carbo 31 g; Fiber 1 g;
T Fat 9 g; 22% Calories from Fat; Chol 72 mg; Sod 136 mg.

Jerold Augustine, Marshall

Chicken Cordon Bleu

6 whole chicken breast filets
8 ounces Swiss cheese, sliced
1   8-ounce package sliced cooked
    ham
3 tablespoons flour
1 teaspoon paprika

6 tablespoons butter
1/2 cup dry white wine
1 teaspoon chicken soup base
1 cup heavy cream
1 tablespoon cornstarch

Rinse chicken and pat dry. Flatten between sheets of waxed paper. Layer with slice of cheese and ham. Roll up, securing with wooden picks. Coat with mixture of flour and paprika. Brown in butter in skillet over medium heat. Add wine and soup base; reduce heat to low. Simmer, covered, for 30 minutes or until tender, adding water if necessary. Transfer chicken to warm platter; remove wooden picks. Blend cream and cornstarch in small bowl. Pour into skillet gradually. Cook until thickened, stirring constantly. Spoon over chicken. **Yield: 6 servings.**

Approx Per Serving: Cal 762; Prot 75 g; Carbo 7 g; Fiber <1 g;
T Fat 45 g; 55% Calories from Fat; Chol 285 mg; Sod 1011 mg.

Elaine Baird, Saginaw

Wonderful Chicken Divan

1 16-ounce package frozen chopped
   broccoli, thawed
3 whole chicken breast filets
2 10-ounce cans cream of chicken
   soup

1/4 cup mayonnaise
1 tablespoon lemon juice
2 cups shredded Cheddar cheese
1/2 cup bread cubes
2 teaspoons melted butter

Layer broccoli in 9x13-inch baking pan. Rinse chicken and pat dry; cut into bite-sized pieces. Arrange over broccoli. Combine soup, mayonnaise and lemon juice in saucepan. Heat until warmed through, stirring frequently. Pour over chicken; top with cheese. Toss bread cubes with melted butter. Sprinkle over cheese. Bake at 350 degrees for 40 to 50 minutes. **Yield: 6 servings.**

Approx Per Serving: Cal 485; Prot 41 g; Carbo 13 g; Fiber 2 g;
   T Fat 30 g; 55% Calories from Fat; Chol 128 mg; Sod 1134 mg.

Jo Ann E. Curtis, Forest City, Iowa

Curried Chicken Divan

2 10-ounce packages frozen
   chopped broccoli
2 cups chopped cooked chicken
1 10-ounce can cream of mushroom
   soup
1/2 teaspoon curry powder

1 teaspoon lemon juice
1 cup mayonnaise
1/2 cup shredded sharp Cheddar
   cheese
1/4 cup soft bread crumbs

Cook broccoli in saucepan for 5 minutes; drain. Layer broccoli and chicken in 8x8-inch baking dish. Combine soup, curry powder, lemon juice and mayonnaise in bowl; mix well. Spoon over chicken; sprinkle with cheese and bread crumbs. Bake, covered, at 375 degrees for 25 minutes. **Yield: 6 servings.**

Approx Per Serving: Cal 469; Prot 20 g; Carbo 11 g; Fiber 3 g;
   T Fat 40 g; 74% Calories from Fat; Chol 74 mg; Sod 721 mg.

Elizabeth Helsten, Ocala, Florida

Chicken Paprika

2 10-ounce whole chicken breasts,
    split, skinned
2 tablespoons margarine
1 onion, thinly sliced
3/4 cup tomato juice
1 tablespoon paprika

1/4 teaspoon salt
Pepper to taste
1 tablespoon cornstarch
1/2 cup plain yogurt
1 1/2 cups hot cooked noodles

Rinse chicken and pat dry. Brown in margarine in skillet for 15 minutes; remove chicken to paper towel to drain. Add onion. Sauté until tender; drain. Add tomato juice, paprika, salt, pepper and chicken. Simmer, covered, for 35 to 40 minutes. Remove chicken to serving platter; skim pan juices, reserving 1/2 cup. Blend cornstarch and yogurt in small bowl. Stir in reserved pan juices. Add yogurt mixture to skillet. Cook over medium-low heat until thickened, stirring constantly; do not boil. Serve over hot cooked noodles. **Yield: 4 servings.**

Approx Per Serving: Cal 347; Prot 37 g; Carbo 22 g; Fiber 2 g;
      T Fat 11 g; 30% Calories from Fat; Chol 113 mg; Sod 460 mg.

Kathleen Laude Janson, Vassar

Chicken Roll-Ups

3 whole chicken breasts, split, boned
8 ounces cream cheese, softened
1 tablespoon butter

2 tablespoons chives
6 slices bacon

Rinse chicken and pat dry. Spread one side with cream cheese; dot with butter. Sprinkle with chives; roll into ball. Wrap with bacon, securing with wooden picks. Place seam side down in shallow baking pan. Bake at 400 degrees for 40 minutes or until chicken is tender. **Yield: 6 servings.**

Approx Per Serving: Cal 325; Prot 31 g; Carbo 1 g; Fiber 0 g;
      T Fat 21 g; 60% Calories from Fat; Chol 124 mg; Sod 292 mg.

Judy Ebelt, Traverse City

Chicken Supreme

6 chicken breast filets
1 6-ounce package chicken-flavored
   stuffing mix
1/2 cup milk

1 10-ounce can cream of mushroom
   soup
8 ounces Swiss cheese, sliced

Rinse chicken and pat dry. Place in 9x12-inch baking dish sprayed with nonstick cooking spray. Prepare stuffing mix using package directions; spoon over chicken. Combine milk and mushroom soup in small bowl. Layer Swiss cheese over stuffing; spoon soup mixture over top. Cover with foil. Bake at 350 degrees for 1 1/4 hours. **Yield: 6 servings.**

Approx Per Serving: Cal 451; Prot 42 g; Carbo 26 g; Fiber <1 g;
    T Fat 19 g; 38% Calories from Fat; Chol 110 mg; Sod 1040 mg.

Margaret L. Cohn, St. Joseph

Chicken Taco Rice

1 pound boneless chicken breasts
2 tablespoons oil
1 13-ounce can chicken broth
1 8-ounce can tomato sauce
1 envelope taco seasoning mix
1 12-ounce can whole kernel corn,
   drained

1 red or green bell pepper, cut into
   strips
1 1/2 cups instant rice
1/2 cup shredded Cheddar cheese

Rinse chicken and pat dry; cut into strips. Stir-fry in hot oil in skillet until light brown. Add chicken broth, tomato sauce and taco seasoning mix; mix well. Bring to a boil; reduce heat. Simmer, covered, for 5 minutes. Add corn and bell pepper. Bring to a boil. Stir in rice. Remove from heat. Let stand, covered, for 5 minutes. Fluff rice with fork; sprinkle with cheese. Serve with tortilla chips and sour cream. May add salsa for spicier flavor. **Yield: 6 servings.**

Approx Per Serving: Cal 357; Prot 26 g; Carbo 39 g; Fiber 2 g;
    T Fat 11 g; 28% Calories from Fat; Chol 58 mg; Sod 1238 mg.

Carolyn Reinert, Vassar

Chicken Tarragon

4 chicken breast filets
Salt and pepper to taste
2 teaspoons tarragon vinegar

12 sheets phyllo dough
1/2 cup melted butter

Rinse chicken and pat dry. Pound with meat mallet to flatten. Season with salt and pepper; sprinkle with tarragon vinegar. Lay out 3 sheets of phyllo dough for each chicken breast. Brush with melted butter. Place one chicken breast in center of each; roll up, sealing edges. Brush with butter again. Place seam side down in ungreased baking pan. Bake at 375 degrees for 45 to 60 minutes or until golden brown. **Yield: 4 servings.**

Approx Per Serving: Cal 527; Prot 34 g; Carbo 41 g; Fiber 2 g;
T Fat 26 g; 44% Calories from Fat; Chol 134 mg; Sod 485 mg.

Norma Deyaert, Iron Mountain

Chicken Tortilla

4 chicken breasts
2   10-ounce cans cream of mushroom
soup
1   10-ounce can cream of chicken
soup
1/2 cup milk
12 corn tortillas

16 ounces Monterey Jack cheese,
shredded
1   2-ounce can sliced black olives,
drained
1   4-ounce can whole green chilies,
drained

Rinse chicken and pat dry. Place in small baking dish; cover with 1 can mushroom soup. Bake, covered with foil, at 325 degrees for 3 hours. Remove chicken, reserving soup. Cut chicken into bite-sized pieces, discarding skin and bones; set aside. Combine reserved soup, remaining 1 can mushroom soup, chicken soup and milk in bowl; mix until smooth. Spoon thin layer of sauce into large shallow baking pan. Layer tortillas, chicken, cheese, olives, chilies and remaining sauce 1/2 at a time in prepared pan. Bake at 350 degrees for 1 hour. May prepare ahead, refrigerate and heat when needed. **Yield: 6 servings.**

Approx Per Serving: Cal 679; Prot 44 g; Carbo 39 g; Fiber 5 g;
T Fat 40 g; 52% Calories from Fat; Chol 125 mg; Sod 1799 mg.

Shelby Crampton-Snider, Chino Hills, California

Chicken and Wild Rice

1 6-ounce package seasoned
   long-grain wild rice
6 chicken breasts
1 10-ounce can cream of chicken
   soup

1 10-ounce can cream of mushroom
   soup
1 10-ounce can cream of celery soup
1½ soup cans water

Scatter rice in 9x13-inch baking pan; sprinkle with contents of seasoning package. Rinse chicken and pat dry. Arrange over rice in pan. Combine soups and water in saucepan; mix well. Simmer until smooth, stirring frequently. Pour over chicken and rice. Bake at 325 degrees for 3 hours. **Yield: 6 servings.**

Approx Per Serving: Cal 385; Prot 32 g; Carbo 31 g; Fiber 1 g;
    T Fat 14 g; 34% Calories from Fat; Chol 82 mg; Sod 1778 mg.

Sue Wright, Cadillac

Chicken in Wine

3 whole chicken breast filets
Salt and pepper to taste
¼ cup butter
1 10-ounce can cream of chicken
   soup
¾ cup Sauterne wine

1 8-ounce can water chestnuts,
   drained
1 3-ounce can mushrooms, drained
2 tablespoons minced green bell
   pepper
¼ teaspoon thyme

Rinse chicken and pat dry; cut into cubes. Season with salt and pepper. Sauté in butter in skillet until light brown. Remove to shallow 8x12-inch baking dish. Add soup to pan drippings. Add wine gradually, stirring until smooth. Bring to a boil; remove from heat. Pour over chicken. Stir in water chestnuts, mushrooms, green pepper and thyme. Bake, covered with foil, at 350 degrees for 20 to 30 minutes or until heated through. Serve with hot cooked wild rice. **Yield: 4 servings.**

Approx Per Serving: Cal 442; Prot 43 g; Carbo 14 g; Fiber 2 g;
    T Fat 20 g; 41% Calories from Fat; Chol 145 mg; Sod 846 mg.

Elaine Hartwig, Gaylord

*Layer 1 cup uncooked rice, chicken pieces and 1 envelope
dry onion soup mix in a baking dish and pour 4 cups
chicken broth over the top. Bake at 375 degrees for 1 hour.*

Company Chicken

12 whole chicken breasts, skinned, split
1 cup butter
2 cups finely chopped onions
8 ounces fresh mushrooms
2 cloves of garlic, crushed
1/2 cup flour

1/2 teaspoon salt
1/2 teaspoon pepper
1/2 teaspoon thyme
2   13-ounce cans chicken broth
4 chicken bouillon cubes
2 cups Sauterne wine

Rinse chicken breasts and pat dry. Brown in hot butter in large Dutch oven. Remove and set aside. Sauté onions, mushrooms and garlic in remaining pan drippings until tender. Mix flour, salt, pepper and thyme together; stir into onion mixture. Add broth gradually, stirring well. Crumble in bouillon cubes. Bring to a boil, stirring constantly; reduce heat. Add wine and chicken. Bake, covered, at 350 degrees for 30 minutes. May divide mixture into 3 portions, placing each in foil-lined casserole. Fold foil over and freeze. Bake, covered, at 400 degrees for 40 to 60 minutes; stir. Bake, uncovered, for 15 minutes longer. **Yield: 24 servings.**

Approx Per Serving: Cal 244; Prot 28 g; Carbo 4 g; Fiber <1 g;
     T Fat 11 g; 40% Calories from Fat; Chol 93 mg; Sod 463 mg.

Nancy Linton, Lansing

Ginger Chicken Stir-Fry

4 chicken breast filets
1/2 cup oats
1/2 teaspoon ginger
1/2 teaspoon garlic powder
2 tablespoons oil
2 cups broccoli flowerets
1 green bell pepper, cut into 1-inch pieces
1 bunch scallions, chopped
1 cup cauliflowerets

1 cup snow peas
1/2 cup water chestnuts
2 tablespoons oil
2 tablespoons low-salt instant chicken bouillon
2 cups boiling water
2 tablespoons reduced-sodium soy sauce
2 tablespoons cornstarch
1 cup almonds

Rinse chicken and pat dry; cut into cubes. Process oats, ginger and garlic powder in blender. Pour into plastic bag. Add chicken, shaking well to coat. Stir-fry in 2 tablespoons hot oil in wok for 4 minutes; remove to warm platter. Stir-fry broccoli, green pepper, scallions, cauliflowerets, snow peas and water chestnuts in remaining 2 tablespoons oil. Dissolve bouillon in boiling water. Stir in soy sauce and cornstarch. Pour over vegetables. Stir-fry for 5 minutes longer. Add chicken. Cook for 3 to 4 minutes or until heated through. Remove to serving plate; sprinkle with almonds. Serve with hot cooked rice or noodles. **Yield: 4 servings.**

Approx Per Serving: Cal 608; Prot 41 g; Carbo 33 g; Fiber 10 g;
     T Fat 38 g; 53% Calories from Fat; Chol 72 mg; Sod 481 mg.

Joanne Homer, Lansing

Quick Saucy Chicken Stir-Fry

1 tablespoon oil
1 cup broccoli flowerets
1 cup cauliflowerets
3/4 cup julienned carrots
1/4 cup sliced green onions
1 clove of garlic, minced

3 chicken breast filets
1 tablespoon oil
1/2 cup mayonnaise-type salad
  dressing
1 tablespoon soy sauce
1/2 teaspoon ground ginger

Heat 1 tablespoon oil in large skillet over medium heat. Stir-fry broccoli, cauliflowerets, carrots, green onions and garlic for 4 to 5 minutes or until tender-crisp. Remove to warm platter. Rinse chicken and pat dry; cut into 1-inch pieces. Stir-fry in remaining 1 tablespoon oil for 4 minutes or until tender. Return vegetables to skillet; remove from heat. Add salad dressing, soy sauce and ginger; mix well. Serve over hot cooked rice. **Yield: 4 servings.**

Approx Per Serving: Cal 303; Prot 22 g; Carbo 12 g; Fiber 2 g;
  T Fat 19 g; 56% Calories from Fat; Chol 62 mg; Sod 528 mg.

Dorothy Balzer, Au Gres

Lemon Chicken with Thyme

4 4-ounce chicken breast filets
3 tablespoons flour
1/2 teaspoon salt
1/4 teaspoon pepper
2 tablespoons olive oil
1 onion, chopped

1 tablespoon margarine
1 cup chicken broth
2 tablespoons lemon juice
1/2 teaspoon thyme
1 tablespoon lemon juice
2 tablespoons chopped parsley

Rinse chicken and pat dry. Combine flour, salt and pepper in paper bag. Add chicken, shaking well to coat. Remove chicken, reserving flour mixture. Brown chicken in 1 tablespoon olive oil in large skillet for 5 minutes. Add remaining oil. Turn chicken. Brown for 5 minutes. Remove to warm platter; set aside. Sauté onion in margarine in skillet for 3 minutes. Add reserved flour mixture. Cook over medium heat until flour is incorporated, stirring frequently. Add chicken broth, 2 tablespoons lemon juice and thyme. Bring to a boil, stirring constantly. Return chicken to skillet; reduce heat. Cook, covered, over medium-low heat for 5 minutes or until chicken is tender. Place chicken on serving plates. Stir remaining 1 tablespoon lemon juice into sauce in skillet. Pour over chicken; sprinkle with parsley. Garnish with lemon wedges. **Yield: 4 servings.**

Approx Per Serving: Cal 273; Prot 29 g; Carbo 9 g; Fiber 1 g;
  T Fat 13 g; 44% Calories from Fat; Chol 72 mg; Sod 558 mg.

Jeanette Schulz, Petoskey

Hungarian Chicken Paprikash with Spaetzle

6 whole chicken breasts
1/4 cup butter
16 small white onions
1 cup chopped onion
1 tablespoon paprika
8 carrots, sliced diagonally in
  1 1/2-inch pieces

2 cups chicken broth
2 teaspoons salt
Spaetzle
Sour Cream Sauce

Rinse chicken and pat dry; cut into halves. Cook, covered, in half the butter in large skillet for 20 minutes or until brown. Remove to warm platter. Add whole and chopped onions, paprika and remaining butter to skillet. Sauté until tender. Add carrots. Sauté for 2 minutes. Stir in chicken broth and salt. Return chicken to skillet. Bring mixture to a boil; reduce heat. Simmer, covered, for 45 minutes. Transfer chicken to platter in warming oven, reserving pan juices. Arrange Spaetzle around chicken. Spoon Sour Cream Sauce over top. Garnish with parsley.

Spaetzle

3 1/4 cups flour
3 eggs, beaten
1 cup water

1 teaspoon salt
2 quarts water

Combine flour, eggs, water and salt in large bowl. Beat until smooth; shape into ball. Drop small pieces of dough into boiling water. Cook for 10 to 15 minutes or until spaetzle is done. Remove with slotted spoon.

Sour Cream Sauce

1/2 to 1 cup concentrated chicken
  broth from pan juices
1/3 cup flour

1/2 cup dry white wine
1 cup sour cream

Pour reserved pan juices into saucepan. Combine 1/3 cup flour and wine in small bowl. Stir into pan juices. Bring to a boil, stirring constantly; reduce heat. Simmer for 2 minutes. Stir in sour cream gradually. Simmer for 1 minute. **Yield: 8 servings.**

Approx Per Serving: Cal 695; Prot 54 g; Carbo 71 g; Fiber 8 g;
    T Fat 20 g; 27% Calories from Fat; Chol 217 mg; Sod 1210 mg.

Barbara A. Mercier, Flushing

*Use canned chicken broth, beef broth or consommé as a
quick substitute for homemade stock.*

Grilled Lemon Chicken

4 whole chicken breast filets, split
1/4 cup lemon juice
1/4 cup honey
1/8 teaspoon paprika

1/8 teaspoon cayenne pepper
1/8 teaspoon dry mustard
1 tablespoon toasted sesame seed

Rinse chicken and pat dry; place in 8x8-inch glass baking dish. Combine lemon juice, honey, paprika, cayenne pepper and mustard in small bowl; mix well. Pour over chicken. Marinate for 30 minutes, turning occasionally. Drain, reserving marinade. Grill over medium-hot coals for 30 to 40 minutes, basting frequently with reserved marinade. Sprinkle with sesame seed before serving. May broil in oven for 15 minutes on each side, basting often. **Yield: 8 servings.**

Approx Per Serving: Cal 181; Prot 27 g; Carbo 9 g; Fiber <1 g;
    T Fat 4 g; 18% Calories from Fat; Chol 72 mg; Sod 64 mg.

Gert Budd, Saginaw

Marinated Chicken Breasts

1/2 cup low-sodium soy sauce
3 tablespoons brown sugar
2 tablespoons lemon juice
2 tablespoons oil

2 tablespoons dry sherry
1/2 teaspoon garlic powder
3/4 teaspoon pepper
4 chicken breasts

Combine soy sauce, brown sugar, lemon juice, oil, sherry, garlic powder and pepper in shallow bowl; mix well. Rinse chicken and pat dry. Place in marinade, turning to coat. Marinate in refrigerator for 45 minutes to overnight. Drain, reserving marinade. Grill chicken over medium-hot coals for 30 to 45 minutes or until tender, basting occasionally with reserved marinade. **Yield: 4 servings.**

Approx Per Serving: Cal 272; Prot 30 g; Carbo 13 g; Fiber <1 g;
    T Fat 10 g; 34% Calories from Fat; Chol 72 mg; Sod 1611 mg.

Pat Lueder, Holt

Microwave Chicken Breasts

2 whole boneless chicken breasts,
  split
1   10-ounce can cream of celery soup
1/3 cup mayonnaise
2 teaspoons paprika

1/2 cup sliced green bell pepper
1/2 cup sliced red bell pepper
1/2 cup sliced green onions
1/2 cup sliced celery

Rinse chicken and pat dry. Combine celery soup, mayonnaise and paprika in 2-quart microwave-safe casserole; mix well. Microwave on High for 2 to 3 minutes or until heated through, stirring once. Stir in bell peppers, green onions and celery. Add chicken. Microwave, covered, for 10 minutes, turning chicken once. Let stand, covered, for 5 minutes. Stir before serving. Serve over hot cooked rice.
Yield: 4 servings.

Approx Per Serving: Cal 333; Prot 28 g; Carbo 8 g; Fiber 1 g;
    T Fat 21 g; 56% Calories from Fat; Chol 91 mg; Sod 717 mg.

Margaret Heighes, Holland

Microwave Chicken Breasts with Mushroom Sauce

2 tablespoons margarine
1 cup sliced fresh mushrooms
2 tablespoons finely sliced green
  onions
1/3 cup milk
3 ounces cream cheese, cubed

1/4 teaspoon chicken soup base
1/8 teaspoon salt
1/8 teaspoon pepper
4 chicken breast filets
1 tablespoon margarine

Combine 2 tablespoons margarine, mushrooms and green onions in glass dish. Microwave on High for 3 to 4 minutes, stirring once. Add milk, cream cheese, chicken soup base, salt and pepper; mix well. Microwave for 2 minutes. Stir until smooth. Microwave for 1 minute longer. Rinse chicken and pat dry. Arrange chicken in 1 tablespoon margarine in glass casserole. Microwave on High for 6 to 8 minutes or until tender. Spoon mushroom sauce over chicken. Microwave for 2 to 3 minutes longer. **Yield: 4 servings.**

Approx Per Serving: Cal 312; Prot 30 g; Carbo 3 g; Fiber <1 g;
    T Fat 20 g; 58% Calories from Fat; Chol 98 mg; Sod 366 mg.

Karen Bigford, Saginaw

Microwave Chicken Breasts Italiano

4 ounces uncooked spaghetti
3 cups water
1/4 teaspoon salt
2 tablespoons margarine
1/3 cup chopped onion
6 chicken breast filets
1   8-ounce can tomato sauce
1/8 teaspoon basil

1/8 teaspoon oregano
1/8 teaspoon salt
1/8 teaspoon pepper
1/4 cup whipping cream
1 tablespoon parsley flakes
1/2 cup shredded mozzarella cheese
1/4 cup stuffed green olives, sliced

Combine spaghetti, water and salt in large glass bowl. Microwave on High for 10 to 13 minutes or until tender, stirring occasionally. Drain and set aside. Combine margarine and onion in 9x13-inch glass baking dish. Microwave for 3 to 4 minutes. Add chicken breasts. Microwave for 8 to 10 minutes or until chicken is tender. Mix tomato sauce, basil, oregano, salt, pepper and whipping cream in bowl. Pour over chicken. Microwave for 3 to 4 minutes or until heated through. Sprinkle with parsley, mozzarella cheese and olives. Microwave for 2 to 3 minutes longer. Serve over spaghetti. **Yield: 6 servings.**

Approx Per Serving: Cal 323; Prot 32 g; Carbo 18 g; Fiber 2 g;
    T Fat 13 g; 37% Calories from Fat; Chol 93 mg; Sod 594 mg.

Karen Bigford, Saginaw

Quickie Chicken and Rice

1 cup instant rice
1/2 teaspoon margarine
1   10-ounce package frozen broccoli,
    thawed

1   10-ounce can cream of mushroom
    soup
2 chicken breasts, cooked, chopped

Cook rice with margarine in saucepan using package directions. Cook broccoli in large saucepan using package directions; drain. Add soup; mix well. Stir in chopped chicken and rice. Serve immediately or keep in warming oven. **Yield: 2 servings.**

Approx Per Serving: Cal 511; Prot 37 g; Carbo 57 g; Fiber 6 g;
    T Fat 15 g; 26% Calories from Fat; Chol 74 mg; Sod 1256 mg.

Leore Bethune, Bridgeport

San Francisco Chicken

1   6-ounce package long grain and
    wild rice mix
1   10-ounce can cream of chicken
    soup
1   10-ounce can cream of celery soup
1   10-ounce can cream of mushroom
    soup

1/4 cup French salad dressing
1/2 cup milk
1/2 cup sliced almonds
8 chicken breast filets
1/2 cup grated Parmesan cheese

Combine rice with seasoning packet, soups, salad dressing, milk and almonds in
bowl; mix well. Spoon 2/3 of the mixture into 8x12-inch casserole. Rinse chicken and
pat dry; place over rice mixture. Cover with remaining rice mixture; sprinkle with
Parmesan cheese. Bake, covered with foil, at 350 degrees for 1½ hours. Remove foil.
Bake for 30 minutes longer to brown. **Yield: 8 servings.**

Approx Per Serving: Cal 433; Prot 34 g; Carbo 26 g; Fiber 1 g;
        T Fat 21 g; 44% Calories from Fat; Chol 85 mg; Sod 1543 mg.

Elaine Hartwig, Gaylord

Stuffed Chicken Breasts in Wine Sauce

6 chicken breast filets
1 onion, chopped
Salt and pepper to taste
3 cups toasted bread cubes
1/2 teaspoon sage

2 1/4 cups chicken broth
2 cups flour
1 teaspoon salt
2 tablespoons oil
1 cup dry white wine

Rinse chicken and pat dry; pound with meat mallet to flatten. Combine onion, salt,
pepper, bread cubes and sage in bowl; mix well. Add 1/4 cup chicken broth or enough
to moisten slightly. Spread mixture on chicken. Roll up to enclose filling, securing
with string. Combine flour, 1 teaspoon salt and pepper in paper bag. Add chicken;
shake to coat. Sauté chicken in oil in skillet until light brown. Place in shallow baking
dish. Combine remaining chicken broth with wine in bowl; mix well. Pour over
chicken. Bake at 350 degrees for 1 hour. **Yield: 6 servings.**

Approx Per Serving: Cal 438; Prot 35 g; Carbo 45 g; Fiber 2 g;
        T Fat 9 g; 19% Calories from Fat; Chol 73 mg; Sod 912 mg.

June B. Brown, Bradenton, Florida

Sweet and Sour Chicken

1 pound chicken breast filets, cubed
1 tablespoon oil
3 carrots, sliced
3 stalks celery, sliced
1 green or red bell pepper, sliced
1 10-ounce package frozen pea pods
1 14-ounce can bean sprouts, drained

1 8-ounce can sliced water chestnuts, drained
1 20-ounce can chunk pineapple
2 10-ounce jars sweet and sour sauce
Salt and pepper to taste

Stir-fry chicken in hot oil in electric skillet or wok at 350 degrees until light brown. Add carrots, celery, bell pepper and pea pods. Stir-fry until tender-crisp. Add bean sprouts and water chestnuts. Stir in pineapple with juice. Cook for 1 minute, stirring frequently. Add sweet and sour sauce, salt and pepper. Stir-fry at 375 degrees for 5 minutes or until heated through, stirring occasionally. Serve over hot cooked rice. **Yield: 8 servings.**

Approx Per Serving: Cal 263; Prot 16 g; Carbo 42 g; Fiber 4 g; T Fat 4 g; 12% Calories from Fat; Chol 36 mg; Sod 241 mg.

Reg and Pat Martin, Big Rapids

Swiss Chicken

8 chicken breast filets
6 slices Swiss cheese
1 10-ounce can cream of chicken soup

1/4 cup water
1/2 cup melted butter
2 cups stuffing mix

Rinse chicken and pat dry. Place in 8x11-inch baking pan. Top with cheese. Combine soup and water in bowl; mix well. Pour over cheese layer. Mix butter and stuffing mix in bowl. Sprinkle over soup layer. Bake at 350 degrees for 1 hour or until chicken is tender. **Yield: 8 servings.**

Approx Per Serving: Cal 420; Prot 36 g; Carbo 16 g; Fiber <1 g; T Fat 23 g; 50% Calories from Fat; Chol 126 mg; Sod 727 mg.

Mary Ann Sprow, Lansing

Chicken Enchiladas

2 cups cottage cheese
1 cup chopped cooked chicken
1 cup shredded Cheddar cheese
2 tablespoons chopped chives
1 teaspoon instant chicken bouillon
12 flour tortillas

1 10-ounce can cream of chicken
   soup
1 cup sour cream
1/4 cup milk
1/2 cup shredded Cheddar cheese

Combine cottage cheese, chicken, 1 cup Cheddar cheese, chives and instant bouillon in bowl; mix well. Spoon over tortillas. Place in 9x13-inch baking pan. Combine soup, sour cream and milk in bowl; mix well. Pour over tortillas. Sprinkle with 1/2 cup Cheddar cheese. Bake at 350 degrees for 35 minutes. **Yield: 6 servings.**

Approx Per Serving: Cal 574; Prot 31 g; Carbo 47 g; Fiber 2 g;
      T Fat 31 g; 47% Calories from Fat; Chol 83 mg; Sod 1335 mg.

Therese DenBeste, Marquette

Chicken and French Green Beans

1 10-ounce package frozen
   French-style green beans
3 cups chopped cooked chicken
1 14-ounce can Chinese mixed
   vegetables, drained
1 4-ounce can mushrooms, drained
1 onion, chopped
1 10-ounce can cream of mushroom
   soup

1 8-ounce can sliced water
   chestnuts, drained
1/2 cup sharp Cheddar cheese, cubed
1/2 cup cooked rice
1/2 cup milk
1/2 teaspoon salt
1/4 teaspoon pepper
1 3-ounce can French-fried onions

Boil green beans in a small amount of water in saucepan for 5 minutes; drain. Combine with chicken, vegetables, mushrooms, onion, soup, water chestnuts, cheese, rice, milk, salt and pepper in large bowl; mix well. Spoon into large greased casserole. Bake at 350 degrees for 30 minutes. Top with French-fried onions. Bake for 10 minutes longer. **Yield: 6 servings.**

Approx Per Serving: Cal 430; Prot 29 g; Carbo 30 g; Fiber 3 g;
      T Fat 22 g; 46% Calories from Fat; Chol 76 mg; Sod 1078 mg.

Ilene Hilson, Hastings

Chicken and Rice Casserole

1 onion, chopped
3 tablespoons chopped green bell
  pepper
3 tablespoons butter
3 cups chopped cooked chicken
2 cups cooked rice

2 10-ounce cans cream of chicken
   soup
1/2 cup milk
1 1/2 cups crushed potato chips
2/3 cup blanched slivered almonds

Sauté onion and green pepper in butter in skillet. Combine chicken and rice in bowl. Stir in sautéed vegetables. Mix soup and milk in bowl; pour into chicken mixture. Line 2 1/2-quart casserole with half the crushed potato chips. Add chicken mixture. Sprinkle with remaining chips and almonds. Bake at 375 degrees for 45 minutes. Garnish with chopped parsley. **Yield: 6 servings.**

Approx Per Serving: Cal 529; Prot 29 g; Carbo 37 g; Fiber 3 g;
    T Fat 30 g; 51% Calories from Fat; Chol 88 mg; Sod 928 mg.

Kathy O'Rourke, Gladwin

Chicken-Ham Lasagna

8 ounces lasagna noodles
1/4 cup margarine
1/3 cup flour
1 tablespoon minced onion flakes
Garlic powder and pepper to taste
2 cups chicken broth
1 cup milk
1/2 cup grated Parmesan cheese

1 4-ounce can mushroom pieces,
   drained
1 10-ounce package frozen cut
   asparagus, thawed, drained
2 cups chopped cooked chicken
6 ounces mozzarella cheese, sliced
1 1/2 cups cubed cooked ham
1/2 cup grated Parmesan cheese

Cook noodles using package directions. Drain and set aside. Melt margarine in saucepan. Blend in flour. Add onion flakes, garlic powder, pepper, chicken broth and milk; mix well. Cook until bubbly, stirring constantly. Add 1/2 cup Parmesan cheese and mushrooms; mix well. Layer half the noodles, asparagus, chicken, mozzarella cheese and half the mushroom mixture in 9x13-inch baking pan. Top with ham, remaining noodles and remaining mushroom mixture. Sprinkle with remaining 1/2 cup Parmesan cheese. Bake at 350 degrees for 35 minutes. Let stand for 10 minutes before cutting. **Yield: 9 servings.**

Approx Per Serving: Cal 385; Prot 30 g; Carbo 27 g; Fiber 1 g;
    T Fat 17 g; 41% Calories from Fat; Chol 66 mg; Sod 874 mg.

Evon Murphy, Lansing

French Chicken-Broccoli Casserole

1 pound fresh broccoli, trimmed,
  steamed
3 to 4 cups chopped cooked chicken
1/4 cup cornstarch
1/4 cup water
1/3 cup melted butter
1/3 cup chicken broth
1/4 teaspoon salt
1/4 teaspoon pepper
2 cups milk
1 2-ounce jar chopped pimentos,
  drained
8 ounces Old English cheese, cubed

Alternate layers of broccoli and chicken in greased 9x13-inch baking dish. Dissolve cornstarch in water. Combine with butter, chicken broth, salt, pepper, milk and pimentos in saucepan. Cook over medium heat until thickened, stirring constantly. Add cheese. Cook until cheese is melted. Pour over layers. Bake at 350 degrees for 35 minutes or until bubbly. May substitute three 10-ounce packages frozen broccoli spears for fresh broccoli and sharp Cheddar cheese for Old English cheese. **Yield: 6 servings.**

Approx Per Serving: Cal 502; Prot 41 g; Carbo 14 g; Fiber 3 g;
    T Fat 32 g; 57% Calories from Fat; Chol 158 mg; Sod 892 mg.

Nellie K. Rogers, Cadillac

Hot Chicken Salad

3 cups chopped cooked chicken
1 8-ounce can water chestnuts,
  drained, chopped
1/2 teaspoon celery salt
3 tablespoons lemon juice
3/4 cup slivered almonds
1 4-ounce jar chopped pimentos,
  drained
Pepper to taste
1 cup mayonnaise
1/2 cup crumbled French-fried onions
1 cup shredded Cheddar cheese

Combine chicken, water chestnuts, celery salt, lemon juice, almonds, pimentos, pepper and mayonnaise in bowl; mix well. Spoon into shallow baking dish. Sprinkle with onions and cheese. Bake at 350 degrees for 30 minutes. **Yield: 6 servings.**

Approx Per Serving: Cal 829; Prot 32 g; Carbo 26 g; Fiber 3 g;
    T Fat 67 g; 72% Calories from Fat; Chol 104 mg; Sod 762 mg.

Lucile Keckritz, Lansing

Chinese Casserole

1 10-ounce can cream of celery soup
1 10-ounce can cream of mushroom soup
1 5-ounce can evaporated milk
1 3-ounce can Chinese noodles

1 14-ounce can Chinese mixed vegetables, drained
2 cups chopped cooked chicken
1/2 cup cornflake crumbs

Combine soups, evaporated milk, noodles, vegetables and chicken in bowl; mix well. Spoon into 9x15-inch baking pan. Top with cornflake crumbs. Bake at 350 degrees for 45 minutes. **Yield: 4 servings.**

Approx Per Serving: Cal 512; Prot 31 g; Carbo 42 g; Fiber 1 g;
    T Fat 26 g; 45% Calories from Fat; Chol 84 mg; Sod 1838 mg.

Juanita Colgan, Bad Axe

Quick and Easy Chop Suey

2 cups water
1 1/2 cups chopped celery
2 tablespoons margarine
1 14-ounce can Oriental mixed vegetables, drained

1 1/2 cups chopped cooked chicken
2 tablespoons water
2 tablespoons cornstarch
1 tablespoon soy sauce

Combine water, celery and margarine in skillet. Cook, covered, over high heat for 5 minutes, stirring once. Add vegetables and chicken. Cook, covered, for 5 minutes longer. Blend water, cornstarch and soy sauce in small bowl or shaker. Add to mixture; remove from heat. Let stand for 5 minutes. Serve over hot cooked rice or chow mein noodles. **Yield: 4 servings.**

Approx Per Serving: Cal 208; Prot 19 g; Carbo 11 g; Fiber 1 g;
    T Fat 10 g; 42% Calories from Fat; Chol 47 mg; Sod 1261 mg.

Grace M. Taylor, East Grand Rapids

Chicken Tetrazzini

1 7-ounce package spaghetti
1/4 cup margarine
1/4 cup flour
1/2 teaspoon salt
1/4 teaspoon pepper
1 cup chicken broth

1 cup whipping cream
2 tablespoons sherry
2 cups cubed cooked chicken
1 2-ounce jar sliced mushrooms,
  drained
1/2 cup grated Parmesan cheese

Cook spaghetti using package directions; drain. Melt margarine over low heat in 3-quart saucepan. Add flour, salt and pepper, stirring until blended. Cook until smooth and bubbly, stirring constantly; remove from heat. Stir in broth and whipping cream. Bring to a boil. Cook for 1 minute, stirring constantly. Add sherry, chicken, mushrooms and cooked spaghetti; mix well. Pour into 2-quart casserole. Sprinkle with cheese. Bake at 350 degrees for 30 minutes or until bubbly. Place under broiler to brown top. **Yield: 4 servings.**

Approx Per Serving: Cal 720; Prot 34 g; Carbo 47 g; Fiber 3 g;
    T Fat 43 g; 54% Calories from Fat; Chol 152 mg; Sod 927 mg.

Elaine Baird, Saginaw

Easy Oven Turkey Lasagna

4 ounces ground turkey
3/4 cup water
4 cups marinara sauce
8 ounces uncooked lasagna noodles

1 cup low-fat cottage cheese
3/4 cup sliced, part-skim milk
  mozzarella cheese
1/4 cup grated Parmesan cheese

Brown ground turkey in skillet, stirring until crumbly; drain. Add water and marinara sauce. Bring to a boil; remove from heat. Layer sauce, noodles, cottage cheese and mozzarella cheese 1/2 at a time in 9x13-inch baking dish, ending with sauce. Top with Parmesan cheese. Cover with foil. Bake at 375 degrees for 1 hour. Let stand for 5 to 10 minutes before cutting into squares. **Yield: 8 servings.**

Approx Per Serving: Cal 280; Prot 16 g; Carbo 35 g; Fiber 0 g;
    T Fat 9 g; 29% Calories from Fat; Chol 19 mg; Sod 1011 mg.

Eleanor Tracy, Lansing

Low-Calorie Lasagna

12 ounces ground turkey, cooked
1/2 cup chopped onion
1 green bell pepper, chopped
1 teaspoon salt
1 teaspoon garlic powder
1 teaspoon ground oregano

1/2 teaspoon pepper
1 quart canned tomatoes
1/3 cup tomato paste
2 cups water
3 ounces uncooked lasagna noodles
4 ounces mozzarella cheese, shredded

Combine cooked turkey, onion, green pepper, salt, garlic powder, oregano, pepper, tomatoes, tomato paste and water in large saucepan; mix well. Bring to a boil over medium heat; reduce heat. Simmer, covered, for 15 minutes, stirring occasionally. Pour half the sauce in 9x13-inch baking pan. Layer noodles over sauce; pour remaining sauce over noodles. Bake at 350 degrees for 40 minutes. Sprinkle with cheese. Bake for 5 minutes longer. **Yield: 6 servings.**

Approx Per Serving: Cal 253; Prot 19 g; Carbo 22 g; Fiber 3 g;
    T Fat 10 g; 36% Calories from Fat; Chol 50 mg; Sod 745 mg.

Betty Leach, Traverse City

Zesty Rice Lasagna

3 cups cooked rice
2 eggs, slightly beaten
1/2 cup grated Parmesan cheese
2 cups shredded mozzarella cheese
1/2 cup cottage cheese, drained

1 pound ground turkey
1   15-ounce jar spaghetti sauce
2 tablespoons grated Parmesan
   cheese

Combine rice, eggs and 1/4 cup Parmesan cheese in bowl; mix well and set aside. Combine remaining 1/4 cup Parmesan cheese, mozzarella cheese and cottage cheese in bowl; mix well. Brown ground turkey in skillet, stirring until crumbly; drain. Stir in spaghetti sauce. Cook until heated through. Layer rice mixture, cheese mixture and turkey mixture 1/2 at a time in greased 3-quart casserole. Sprinkle 2 tablespoons Parmesan cheese over top layer. Bake at 375 degrees for 15 to 20 minutes or until heated through. **Yield: 8 servings.**

Approx Per Serving: Cal 379; Prot 25 g; Carbo 28 g; Fiber 1 g;
    T Fat 18 g; 43% Calories from Fat; Chol 118 mg; Sod 607 mg.

Jeanette L. Schulz, Petoskey

Healthy Chili

1 pound dried red kidney beans	6 cloves of garlic, minced
2 yellow onions, chopped	3 hot chili peppers, seeded, chopped
6 tomatoes, chopped	1/4 cup chili powder
1 green bell pepper, chopped	2 pounds ground turkey
4 stalks celery, chopped	3 bay leaves

Soak kidney beans in water in bowl overnight; drain and rinse. Combine with onions, tomatoes, green pepper, celery, garlic, peppers, chili powder and enough water to cover in large saucepan. Bring to a boil; reduce heat. Brown ground turkey in skillet, stirring until crumbly; drain. Add to chili mixture with bay leaves. Simmer for 3 hours, adding water if necessary. Remove bay leaves before serving. **Yield: 8 servings.**

Approx Per Serving: Cal 439; Prot 38 g; Carbo 46 g; Fiber 16 g;
    T Fat 13 g; 25% Calories from Fat; Chol 71 mg; Sod 177 mg.

E. Eugene Russell, Leesburg, Florida

Turkey-Chili-Macaroni

1¹/₄ pounds ground turkey	2 tablespoons vinegar
1 onion, chopped	1¹/₂ teaspoons sugar
¹/₂ cup chopped green bell pepper	1 teaspoon chili powder
¹/₂ cup chopped celery	1 teaspoon garlic salt
2 tablespoons oil	6 tablespoons grated Parmesan
2¹/₂ cups chicken broth	cheese
7 ounces uncooked elbow macaroni	1¹/₂ tablespoons chopped parsley
1 15-ounce can tomato sauce	

Brown ground turkey, onion, green pepper and celery in hot oil in large saucepan, stirring occasionally. Drain and set aside, reserving pan juices. Mix broth with pan juices in saucepan. Bring to a boil. Add macaroni. Simmer for 10 minutes or until liquid is absorbed, stirring frequently. Add turkey mixture, tomato sauce, vinegar, sugar, chili powder, garlic salt and 4 tablespoons Parmesan cheese; mix well. Simmer for 10 minutes. Spoon into serving dish; sprinkle with remaining Parmesan cheese and parsley. **Yield: 4 servings.**

Approx Per Serving: Cal 601; Prot 42 g; Carbo 52 g; Fiber 5 g;
    T Fat 25 g; 37% Calories from Fat; Chol 96 mg; Sod 1920 mg.

Lois Roggenbeck, Saginaw

Alice's Turkey Loaf

1½ pounds ground turkey
½ cup chopped onion
¼ cup catsup
¼ cup oats
¼ cup stuffing mix

1 egg, slightly beaten
1 tablespoon Worcestershire sauce
½ teaspoon garlic powder
1 teaspoon salt

Combine turkey, onion, catsup, oats, stuffing mix, egg, Worcestershire sauce, garlic powder and salt in bowl; mix well. Shape into loaf; place in loaf pan. Bake at 375 degrees for 45 to 55 minutes or until brown. Cool for 10 minutes before slicing. **Yield: 6 servings.**

Approx Per Serving: Cal 247; Prot 25 g; Carbo 9 g; Fiber 1 g;
     T Fat 12 g; 46% Calories from Fat; Chol 107 mg; Sod 647 mg.

Marilyn Shearer, Flint

Ersatz Meat Loaf

1 pound ground turkey
½ pound ground turkey sausage
2 packets low-sodium beef broth
  powder
3 tablespoons Heinz 57 sauce
3 ounces egg substitute
1 onion, finely chopped
½ teaspoon pepper

½ cup cracker crumbs
½ teaspoon Worcestershire sauce
¼ cup milk
½ cup finely chopped green bell
  pepper
1 10-ounce can cream of mushroom
  soup

Combine turkey, sausage, beef broth powder, Heinz 57 sauce, egg substitute, onion, pepper, cracker crumbs, Worcestershire sauce, milk and green pepper in large bowl; mix well. Shape into loaf. Place in loaf pan sprayed with nonstick cooking spray. Bake at 350 degrees for 1 hour. Spread mushroom soup over top. Bake for 10 minutes longer. **Yield: 8 servings.**

Approx Per Serving: Cal 225; Prot 17 g; Carbo 11 g; Fiber 1 g;
     T Fat 13 g; 51% Calories from Fat; Chol 50 mg; Sod 524 mg.

Stanley Kolenda, Battle Creek

Seasoned Turkey Patties

1½ pounds ground turkey
⅓ cup dry bread crumbs
½ cup chopped onion
1 egg, beaten

1¼ teaspoons Worcestershire sauce
½ to ¾ teaspoon poultry seasoning
½ teaspoon garlic salt
½ teaspoon seasoned salt

Combine turkey, bread crumbs, onion, egg, Worcestershire sauce, poultry seasoning, garlic salt and seasoned salt in bowl; mix well. Shape into patties. Place on broiler pan. Broil 6 inches from heat source on both sides until golden brown and cooked through. May baste with chicken broth or barbecue sauce while broiling.
Yield: 8 servings.

Approx Per Serving: Cal 174; Prot 18 g; Carbo 4 g; Fiber <1 g;
T Fat 9 g; 49% Calories from Fat; Chol 80 mg; Sod 330 mg.

Balicia Duvall, Williamston

Turkey Pasties

3 pounds ground turkey
1 large onion, chopped
1 head cabbage, shredded
1 tablespoon oil

Salt and pepper to taste
3 loaves frozen bread dough, thawed
2 tablespoons melted margarine

Brown ground turkey and onion in skillet, stirring occasionally; drain. Combine cabbage, oil, salt and water to cover in saucepan. Cook until tender. Mix with turkey and onion; season with salt and pepper. Knead bread dough on floured surface. Divide into 2 equal portions. Roll into large rectangles. Line 12x18-inch baking sheet with one portion of dough. Spread filling over top; dot with margarine. Top with remaining dough. Pierce with fork in several places. Bake at 375 degrees until brown.
Yield: 36 servings.

Approx Per Serving: Cal 171; Prot 10 g; Carbo 21 g; Fiber <1 g;
T Fat 6 g; 30% Calories from Fat; Chol 24 mg; Sod 271 mg.

Leo Hancock, Midland

Turkey Potpie

2 cups chopped cooked turkey
3 cups turkey gravy
1   10-ounce package frozen mixed
   vegetables, thawed
2 or 3 potatoes, chopped
1/4 cup chopped onion

3 tablespoons cornstarch
Salt and pepper to taste
2²/₃ cups flour
³/₄ teaspoon salt
1 cup margarine
1 tablespoon (scant) ice water

Combine turkey, gravy, mixed vegetables, potatoes, onion, cornstarch, salt and pepper in saucepan; mix well. Bring to a boil; remove from heat and cool. Combine flour and salt in bowl. Cut in margarine until mixture is crumbly. Add ice water, stirring well. Roll out ²/₃ of the dough into rectangle; line bottom and sides of 9x13-inch pan. Pour filling into prepared pan. Top with remaining ¹/₃ of the dough, sealing edges and cutting vents. Bake at 400 degrees for 15 minutes. Reduce oven temperature to 350 degrees. Bake for 25 minutes longer or until golden brown.
Yield: 6 servings.

Approx Per Serving: Cal 731; Prot 26 g; Carbo 76 g; Fiber 5 g;
   T Fat 36 g; 44% Calories from Fat; Chol 38 mg; Sod 678 mg.

Lorraine Parrish, Grand Rapids

Turkey Quiche

1 recipe 1-crust pie pastry
1 cup chopped cooked turkey
1 cup skim milk
1 cup egg substitute

1/4 cup minced fresh parsley
2 tablespoons minced pimento
1/2 teaspoon sage
1/8 teaspoon pepper

Line 9-inch quiche pan with pastry. Prick entire surface with fork. Bake at 425 degrees for 8 to 10 minutes or until light brown. Spread turkey over prepared crust. Combine milk, egg substitute, parsley, pimento, sage and pepper in bowl; mix well. Pour over turkey. Bake at 350 degrees for 45 to 50 minutes or until knife inserted near center comes out clean. Let stand for 10 minutes before cutting into wedges.
Yield: 6 servings.

Approx Per Serving: Cal 241; Prot 15 g; Carbo 16 g; Fiber 1 g;
   T Fat 13 g; 48% Calories from Fat; Chol 19 mg; Sod 296 mg.

Mary Helen Riggle, Charlevoix

*Roast a larger turkey than you need. Package leftovers in
meal-sized portions and freeze for future use.*

Quick Turkey

1 pound ground turkey
1/2 cup chopped onion
1/2 cup chopped celery
1 2-ounce jar chopped pimento, drained

2 10-ounce cans cream of mushroom soup
1/2 cup milk
6 ounces chow mein noodles
1/2 cup slivered almonds

Brown ground turkey in skillet, stirring until crumbly. Add onion and celery. Cook for 5 minutes; drain. Stir in pimento, soup and milk. Add noodles. Pour into baking dish. Top with almonds. Bake at 350 degrees for 45 minutes. **Yield: 4 servings.**

Approx Per Serving: Cal 675; Prot 35 g; Carbo 43 g; Fiber 5 g;
T Fat 42 g; 55% Calories from Fat; Chol 82 mg; Sod 1699 mg.

Joan Emmons, Jackson

Ground Turkey Breakfast Sausage

1 pound ground turkey
1/2 teaspoon salt
1/4 teaspoon black pepper
1/8 teaspoon red pepper

1/2 teaspoon marjoram
1/4 teaspoon sugar
1 tablespoon cold water
1 1/2 teaspoons poultry seasoning

Combine all ingredients in bowl; mix well. Shape into patties or force through sausage stuffer using small casings. **Polish Sausage:** Omit red pepper and add 1/4 teaspoon garlic powder or 1 clove of garlic, minced. **Italian Sausage:** Add 1/4 teaspoon crushed fennel seed. **Yield: 5 servings.**

Approx Per Serving: Cal 155; Prot 18 g; Carbo <1 g; Fiber <1 g;
T Fat 9 g; 52% Calories from Fat; Chol 57 mg; Sod 292 mg.

Joyce Frydel, Lansing

Turkey Stuff

1 to 2 cups chopped cooked turkey
1 clove of garlic, minced
Ginger to taste
1 tablespoon soy sauce

1 14-ounce can Chinese mixed vegetables, drained
2 10-ounce cans cream of celery soup
1 soup can water

Combine turkey, garlic, ginger and soy sauce in skillet. Cook over medium heat for several minutes. Add vegetables, soup and water; mix well. Cook until heated through. Serve over hot cooked rice. **Yield: 4 servings.**

Approx Per Serving: Cal 295; Prot 25 g; Carbo 19 g; Fiber <1 g;
T Fat 14 g; 42% Calories from Fat; Chol 69 mg; Sod 1692 mg.

Jackie Ryan, Jackson

Easy Kids' Turkey Taco-Mac

1 pound ground turkey
1 envelope taco seasoning mix
1 14-ounce can whole tomatoes, chopped
1 cup water
1/2 cup sliced celery

8 ounces uncooked macaroni or spiral pasta
1 7-ounce package corn muffin mix
1 egg, beaten
1/3 cup milk

Brown ground turkey in skillet, stirring until crumbly. Add taco seasoning mix, undrained tomatoes, water, celery and macaroni; mix well. Bring to a boil; reduce heat. Simmer, covered, for 20 minutes. Combine muffin mix, egg and milk in bowl, stirring to mix. Spoon turkey mixture into 2 1/2-quart casserole. Drop muffin mixture by tablespoonfuls on top. Bake at 400 degrees for 15 to 20 minutes or until golden brown. Garnish with grated cheese. **Yield: 6 servings.**

Approx Per Serving: Cal 395; Prot 23 g; Carbo 50 g; Fiber 3 g;
    T Fat 11 g; 26% Calories from Fat; Chol 85 mg; Sod 929 mg.

Linda Haubenstricker, Birch Run

Fish and Asparagus Bundles

12 ounces fresh asparagus
4 1/4-inch thick filets of sole
1/4 teaspoon salt
2 tomatoes, chopped
1/2 cup sliced mushrooms
1/4 cup thinly sliced celery

1/4 cup chopped onion
1/4 cup dry white wine
1 clove of garlic, minced
1/2 teaspoon dried crushed basil
2 teaspoons minced fresh mint

Trim asparagus to 6 inches. Cook in boiling water in saucepan for 8 to 10 minutes or until tender-crisp; drain. Sprinkle fish with salt. Place asparagus in center of each filet; roll up to enclose, securing with wooden picks. Place seam side down in 10-inch nonstick skillet. Add tomatoes, mushrooms, celery, onion, wine, garlic and basil. Simmer, covered, for 8 to 10 minutes or until fish flakes easily. Remove fish to warm serving platter. Bring tomato mixture to a boil. Cook for 3 minutes, stirring constantly. Spoon over fish. Sprinkle with fresh mint. May substitute frozen fish for fresh fish. **Yield: 4 servings.**

Approx Per Serving: Cal 154; Prot 25 g; Carbo 8 g; Fiber 3 g;
    T Fat 2 g; 11% Calories from Fat; Chol 62 mg; Sod 243 mg.

Kathleen Laude Janson, Vassar

Fish with Zucchini and Green Peppers

1 pound fresh fish filets
1/2 teaspoon salt
1/8 teaspoon pepper
2 tablespoons melted margarine
1 tablespoon lemon juice

1 zucchini, cut into 1/4-inch slices
1 small green bell pepper, cut into
  1/4-inch slices
1 small red onion, thinly sliced
2 tablespoons margarine

Arrange fish in ungreased 7x12-inch baking pan. Sprinkle with salt and pepper. Mix 2 tablespoons melted margarine with lemon juice in small bowl; pour over fish. Bake at 350 degrees for 20 to 25 minutes or until fish flakes easily. Cook zucchini, green pepper and onion in 2 tablespoons margarine in skillet over medium heat for 5 to 7 minutes or until tender-crisp, stirring occasionally. Remove fish to serving plate; spoon vegetables over top. **Yield: 3 servings.**

Approx Per Serving: Cal 302; Prot 31 g; Carbo 6 g; Fiber 1 g;
    T Fat 17 g; 52% Calories from Fat; Chol 83 mg; Sod 663 mg.

Evon Murphy, Lansing

Hot and Spicy Fish

2 tablespoons oil
1/2 teaspoon hot pepper sauce
1/2 cup Italian-seasoned bread crumbs
1/4 teaspoon cayenne pepper

1/2 teaspoon oregano
1/4 teaspoon thyme
1 pound fish filets

Beat oil and pepper sauce in small bowl; set aside. Combine bread crumbs, cayenne pepper, oregano and thyme in shallow bowl; mix well. Brush filets with oil mixture; coat with bread crumb mixture. Arrange on rack in broiler pan. Broil 5 inches from heat source for 10 minutes or until fish flakes easily. **Yield: 3 servings.**

Approx Per Serving: Cal 286; Prot 31 g; Carbo 12 g; Fiber 1 g;
    T Fat 12 g; 38% Calories from Fat; Chol 83 mg; Sod 253 mg.

Sandy Nealy, Charlotte

*Grill fish filets for a quick dinner. Wrap filets in bacon
to retain their shape and prevent sticking to grill.*

Puffy Broiled Filets

1 pound fish filets
Freshly ground pepper
2 tablespoons melted margarine

1 egg white
1/4 cup tartar sauce

Arrange fish skin side down on broiler pan sprayed with nonstick cooking spray. Sprinkle with pepper; drizzle with margarine. Broil 4 inches from heat source for 10 minutes or until fish flakes easily. Beat egg white in bowl until stiff peaks form. Fold in tartar sauce. Spread over fish. Broil for 2 minutes longer or until golden brown. **Yield: 3 servings.**

Approx Per Serving: Cal 313; Prot 31 g; Carbo 1 g; Fiber <1 g;
   T Fat 20 g; 59% Calories from Fat; Chol 88 mg; Sod 475 mg.

Mrs. William Dehn, Sr., Belding

Baked Orange Roughy

2 onions, chopped
2 stalks celery, chopped
1 cup chopped tomatoes

2 tablespoons lemon juice
3 cloves of garlic, crushed
1 1/2 pounds orange roughy

Sauté onions, celery and tomatoes in skillet sprayed with nonstick cooking spray until tender. Add lemon juice and garlic. Cook for 3 minutes, stirring occasionally. Cut fish into serving pieces; arrange in baking pan sprayed with nonstick cooking spray. Pour vegetables over top. Bake, covered, at 350 degrees for 20 minutes. Serve over hot cooked rice. **Yield: 4 servings.**

Approx Per Serving: Cal 203; Prot 35 g; Carbo 10 g; Fiber 2 g;
   T Fat 2 g; 11% Calories from Fat; Chol 93 mg; Sod 166 mg.

Marge Venable, Grand Blanc

Baked Salmon Steaks

2 cups chopped celery with leaves
5 salmon steaks
2 tablespoons diet margarine
3/4 cup fresh bread crumbs

3/4 teaspoon tarragon
3/4 teaspoon rosemary
1/8 teaspoon pepper
6 lemon wedges

Arrange celery in shallow baking dish. Place salmon steaks on top. Melt margarine in skillet. Add bread crumbs, tarragon, rosemary and pepper; mix well. Spread evenly over salmon. Bake at 350 degrees for 25 minutes or until fish flakes easily. Top with lemon wedges. **Yield: 5 servings.**

Approx Per Serving: Cal 281; Prot 27 g; Carbo 13 g; Fiber 1 g;
   T Fat 13 g; 42% Calories from Fat; Chol 80 mg; Sod 267 mg.

Joann Bouwman, Zeeland

Salmon Dynamite

1 14-ounce can salmon	1 teaspoon (heaping) baking powder
1 egg, beaten	Salt and pepper to taste
1/2 cup flour	Oil for deep frying

Drain and flake salmon, reserving 1/4 cup liquid. Combine salmon, egg and flour in bowl; mix well. Combine reserved salmon liquid with baking powder in bowl; beat until foamy. Stir into salmon mixture. Drop by teaspoonfuls into hot oil. Fry until brown; drain on paper towels. **Yield: 4 servings.**

Approx Per Serving: Cal 216; Prot 23 g; Carbo 12 g; Fiber <1 g;
     T Fat 8 g; 33% Calories from Fat; Chol 104 mg; Sod 649 mg.
     Nutritional information does not include oil for deep frying.

Pat Hendershot, Cape Coral, Florida

Salmon Puff

4 eggs, slightly beaten	2 cups soft bread crumbs
1/2 cup milk	1 tablespoon minced parsley
1 10-ounce can cream of mushroom	1 small onion, minced
soup	2 tablespoons melted butter
1 14-ounce can salmon, drained,	1/2 teaspoon lemon juice
flaked	

Combine eggs, milk and soup in large bowl; mix well. Add salmon, bread crumbs, parsley, onion, butter and lemon juice; mix well. Spoon into 6x10-inch baking dish. Bake at 350 degrees for 50 minutes or until knife inserted near center comes out clean. Let stand for 5 minutes before serving. May substitute tuna for salmon, or double recipe using 1 can salmon and 1 can tuna. **Yield: 6 servings.**

Approx Per Serving: Cal 286; Prot 20 g; Carbo 14 g; Fiber 1 g;
     T Fat 16 g; 52% Calories from Fat; Chol 189 mg; Sod 913 mg.

Geraldine Gilmore, Fife Lake

*Pink salmon is ideal for loaves and patties since it breaks into
flakes. Red salmon is better for salads and casseroles
because it breaks into larger chunks.*

Tuna Biscuit Loaf

1 cup flaked tuna
1/4 cup chopped onion
1 cup cooked green beans
1 cup shredded American cheese
1/2 teaspoon salt
1/4 teaspoon pepper
1/2 teaspoon salt

2 cups flour
1 tablespoon baking powder
1/3 cup oil
2/3 cup milk
1 10-ounce can cream of mushroom
  soup
Worcestershire sauce to taste

Combine tuna, onion, green beans, cheese, 1/2 teaspoon salt and pepper in bowl; mix well. Combine remaining 1/2 teaspoon salt with flour and baking powder in small bowl. Add oil and milk, stirring until stiff dough forms. Knead on floured surface for 10 minutes. Roll into rectangle; place on baking sheet. Spread tuna mixture down center of dough in 4-inch wide band. Cut sides of dough at 1-inch intervals. Fold cut portions up alternately over tuna mixture. Bake at 425 degrees for 20 to 25 minutes or until golden brown. Heat mushroom soup and Worcestershire sauce in saucepan, stirring until smooth. Serve with loaf. May substitute 1 1/2 cups salmon for tuna or green peas for green beans. **Yield: 4 servings.**

Approx Per Serving: Cal 674; Prot 31 g; Carbo 59 g; Fiber 3 g;
    T Fat 35 g; 46% Calories from Fat; Chol 62 mg; Sod 1959 mg.

Marilyn Zimmerman, Byron Center

Overnight Casserole

2 10-ounce cans cream of mushroom
  soup
2 cups milk
2 cups flaked tuna
1 7-ounce package macaroni
8 ounces sharp Cheddar cheese,
  shredded

1 8-ounce can sliced water
  chestnuts, drained, chopped
1/4 green bell pepper, chopped
1 small onion, minced
4 hard-boiled eggs, chopped
1 teaspoon salt
1/8 teaspoon MSG

Mix soup and milk in large bowl until smooth. Add tuna, macaroni, cheese, water chestnuts, green pepper, onion, eggs, salt and MSG; mix well. Spoon into 9x13-inch casserole. Chill, covered, in refrigerator overnight. Bake at 350 degrees for 1 1/4 hours. May substitute chopped cooked chicken, shrimp, crab or ham for tuna. **Yield: 6 servings.**

Approx Per Serving: Cal 588; Prot 42 g; Carbo 43 g; Fiber 3 g;
    T Fat 27 g; 42% Calories from Fat; Chol 232 mg; Sod 1766 mg.

Beverly Ward, Sault Ste. Marie

Tuna Patties

1 6-ounce package chicken-flavored
   stuffing mix
1/2 cup hot water
1 10-ounce can cream of chicken soup

2 eggs, beaten
1 9-ounce can tuna, drained, flaked
3 tablespoons butter
1/4 cup milk

Mix seasoning packet with water in bowl. Stir in stuffing mix, half the soup, eggs and tuna. Shape into patties. Brown both sides in butter on hot griddle. Heat remaining soup with milk in saucepan; mix well. Serve over patties. **Yield: 6 servings.**

Approx Per Serving: Cal 290; Prot 20 g; Carbo 25 g; Fiber <1 g;
   T Fat 12 g; 38% Calories from Fat; Chol 116 mg; Sod 1086 mg.

Cindy Fogg, Otsego

Tuna Pasta

1 14-ounce package pasta ruffles
1 12-ounce can water-pack tuna,
   drained and flaked

1 16-ounce package frozen peas,
   thawed
1 envelope ranch salad dressing mix

Cook pasta using package directions; drain well. Combine with tuna and peas in large bowl. Prepare salad dressing using package directions. Pour over pasta mixture, tossing to coat. Chill for several hours to overnight. **Yield: 6 servings.**

Approx Per Serving: Cal 675; Prot 31 g; Carbo 66 g; Fiber 7 g;
   T Fat 32 g; 43% Calories from Fat; Chol 59 mg; Sod 838 mg.

Jeanne De Laney, Traverse City

Hot Seafood Salad

1 small green bell pepper, chopped
1/2 small onion, chopped
3 cups chopped celery
1/4 cup butter
2 cups mayonnaise
2 cups cooked flaked turbot
1 4-ounce can shrimp pieces, drained

1 cup crushed crackers
1 teaspoon Worcestershire sauce
1 teaspoon salt
Tabasco sauce to taste
1/2 cup dry bread crumbs
2 tablespoons melted butter
Paprika to taste

Sauté green pepper, onion and celery in butter in skillet until tender but not brown. Combine next 7 ingredients in bowl; mix well. Stir in sautéed vegetables. Spoon into baking dish. Top with mixture of bread crumbs and melted butter; sprinkle with paprika. Bake at 350 degrees for 20 to 25 minutes or until bubbly. **Yield: 8 servings.**

Approx Per Serving: Cal 617; Prot 14 g; Carbo 17 g; Fiber 1 g;
   T Fat 55 g; 80% Calories from Fat; Chol 84 mg; Sod 980 mg.

Evelyn Bedore, Ironwood

Shrimp and Crab Casserole

2 4-ounce cans shrimp, drained
1 7-ounce can crab meat, drained
   and flaked
1 cup chopped celery
1/4 cup chopped onion

2 10-ounce cans cream of mushroom
   soup
1 cup chow mein noodles
2 tablespoons toasted slivered
   almonds

Combine shrimp, crab meat, celery, onion and soup in bowl; mix well. Chill for 24 hours. Stir in chow mein noodles; spoon into baking dish. Sprinkle with almonds. Bake at 375 degrees for 35 to 40 minutes or until brown and bubbly. **Yield: 4 servings.**

Approx Per Serving: Cal 350; Prot 28 g; Carbo 20 g; Fiber 2 g;
      T Fat 18 g; 45% Calories from Fat; Chol 145 mg; Sod 1548 mg.

Janell Sandstedt, Manistee

Shrimp de Jonge

1 pound shrimp, peeled
10 saltine crackers
1/2 teaspoon garlic salt

1/2 teaspoon parsley
3/4 cup butter

Sauté shrimp, crackers, garlic salt and parsley in butter in skillet until shrimp turn pink. Serve hot. **Yield: 4 servings.**

Approx Per Serving: Cal 426; Prot 20 g; Carbo 6 g; Fiber <1 g;
      T Fat 36 g; 76% Calories from Fat; Chol 273 mg; Sod 847 mg.

Vikki Bittner, Grand Rapids

Shrimp Creole

1/2 cup chopped onion
1/2 cup chopped celery
1 clove of garlic, minced
3 tablespoons oil
1 16-ounce can tomatoes
1 8-ounce can tomato sauce
1 1/2 teaspoons salt

1 tablespoon Worcestershire sauce
1 teaspoon sugar
1 teaspoon chili powder
Tabasco sauce to taste
2 teaspoons cornstarch
12 ounces frozen peeled shrimp, thawed
1/2 cup chopped green pepper

Sauté onion, celery and garlic in oil in skillet until tender but not brown. Stir in next 7 ingredients. Simmer for 45 minutes, stirring frequently. Dissolve cornstarch in water. Stir into sauce. Cook until thickened, stirring constantly. Add shrimp and green pepper. Simmer, covered, for 5 minutes longer. Serve over hot rice. **Yield: 4 servings.**

Approx Per Serving: Cal 222; Prot 17 g; Carbo 15 g; Fiber 3 g;
      T Fat 12 g; 45% Calories from Fat; Chol 133 mg; Sod 1530 mg.

Albina Johnson, Grandville

Shrimp Delight

1 pound shrimp, peeled
2 tablespoons oil
1 pound fresh asparagus, trimmed
1 onion, sliced
1 cup chopped celery
1 cup sliced mushrooms

1   6-ounce can baby corn
2 cups chicken broth
2 tablespoons cornstarch
2 tablespoons soy sauce
½ cup toasted sliced almonds

Stir-fry shrimp in hot oil in wok for 3 minutes or until shrimp turn pink; set aside. Stir-fry asparagus, onion, celery and mushrooms in wok for 3 to 4 minutes. Add corn and chicken broth. Cook until mixture comes to a boil, stirring frequently. Blend cornstarch and soy sauce in bowl. Stir into hot mixture. Cook until thickened, stirring constantly. Add shrimp. Cook until heated through. Sprinkle with almonds; serve over hot cooked rice. May substitute broccoli for asparagus and may also add bamboo shoots and water chestnuts. **Yield: 4 servings.**

Approx Per Serving: Cal 332; Prot 30 g; Carbo 23 g; Fiber 5 g;
    T Fat 15 g; 40% Calories from Fat; Chol 177 mg; Sod 1245 mg.

Agnes Rock, Middleville

Grilled Shrimp

16 large shrimp, peeled
2 green bell peppers, cut into 1-inch
    pieces
1 Spanish onion, quartered, separated
1   20-ounce can chunk pineapple,
    drained

½ cup olive oil
1 cup rice wine
2 tablespoons tarragon
Bitters to taste
2 tablespoons Dijon mustard
1 tablespoon honey

Place shrimp, green peppers, onion and pineapple alternately on skewers; place in long shallow dish. Combine oil, wine, tarragon, bitters, mustard and honey in small bowl; mix well. Pour over shrimp and vegetables. Marinate in refrigerator for 4 hours. Grill over hot coals until shrimp turn pink. Serve with hot cooked brown rice. **Yield: 4 servings.**

Approx Per Serving: Cal 498; Prot 21 g; Carbo 30 g; Fiber 3 g;
    T Fat 30 g; 56% Calories from Fat; Chol 173 mg; Sod 407 mg.

Mary Vitale, Jackson

*For an **Easy Tartar Sauce**, combine 1 cup mayonnaise,*
1 teaspoon grated onion, 2 tablespoons minced dill pickles,
1 tablespoon minced parsley and 2 teaspoons chopped pimento.

Quiche by Karen

2 9-inch butter-flavored all ready
  pie pastries
1/3 cup bacon bits
3/4 of 4 ounce can shrimp pieces
1/3 cup chopped celery
1/3 cup chopped green onions
1/2 cup shredded mozzarella cheese
1/2 cup shredded Cheddar cheese
1/2 cup shredded Monterey Jack
  cheese

1/2 cup shredded Swiss cheese
4 eggs
1 1/2 cups light cream
1/2 cup whipping cream
3/4 teaspoon salt
1/4 teaspoon pepper
Nutmeg, lemon pepper, cayenne
  pepper, basil, garlic salt and
  paprika to taste

Line two 9-inch pie plates with pie pastries; place on baking sheet. Layer each prepared pie plate with bacon bits, shrimp, celery and green onions. Combine mozzarella, Cheddar, Monterey Jack and Swiss cheeses in bowl; mix well. Sprinkle over celery layer. Beat eggs with light cream, whipping cream, salt, pepper and seasonings in bowl. Pour over cheeses. Bake at 425 degrees for 15 minutes. Reduce oven temperature to 300 degrees. Bake for 30 minutes longer. Let stand for 10 minutes before slicing. May serve hot or cold. **Yield: 12 servings.**

Approx Per Serving: Cal 389; Prot 12 g; Carbo 16 g; Fiber 1 g;
    T Fat 31 g; 71% Calories from Fat; Chol 147 mg; Sod 510 mg.

Karen McLeod-Hill, Mt. Clemen

Frog Legs à la Jim

16 large frog legs
Juice of 1/2 lemon
Salt and pepper to taste

2 eggs, beaten
2 cups dry bread crumbs
Oil for deep frying

Place frog legs in boiling water with lemon juice, salt and pepper. Cook for 4 minutes; drain and pat dry. Dip into eggs; roll in bread crumbs. Deep-fry in hot oil at 370 degrees for 2 to 3 minutes; drain. Serve with onion cream sauce. **Yield: 4 servings.**

Approx Per Serving: Cal 320; Prot 104 g; Carbo 37 g; Fiber 2 g;
    T Fat 6 g; 9% Calories from Fat; Chol 109 mg; Sod 403 mg.
    Nutritional information does not include oil for deep frying.

Jim Hamilton, Lansing

CALLING CENTER

Vegetables and Side Dishes

Baked Beans

1 28-ounce can pork and beans
2 16-ounce cans California lima beans
1 16-ounce can kidney beans
1 cup packed brown sugar

2 tablespoons catsup
1 tablespoon molasses
1 tablespoon mustard
1 large sweet onion, chopped
8 ounces bacon, cut into pieces

Combine beans, brown sugar, catsup, molasses, mustard, onion and bacon in bowl; mix well. Spoon into large casserole. Bake at 300 degrees for 3 to 4 hours or until bubbly and heated through. **Yield: 15 servings.**

Approx Per Serving: Cal 236; Prot 9 g; Carbo 45 g; Fiber 10 g;
    T Fat 3 g; 12% Calories from Fat; Chol 7 mg; Sod 603 mg.

Grace Evans, Middleville

Baked Beans with Bacon

3 tablespoons chopped onion
2 tablespoons bacon drippings
3 16-ounce cans pork and beans
1/2 cup packed brown sugar

1/4 cup catsup
3/4 cup crushed gingersnaps
1 teaspoon dry mustard
6 slices bacon, crisp-fried, crumbled

Sauté onion in bacon drippings in skillet until tender. Combine with pork and beans, brown sugar, catsup, gingersnaps, dry mustard and bacon in bowl; mix well. Spoon into casserole. Bake at 325 degrees for 1 1/2 hours. **Yield: 12 servings.**

Approx Per Serving: Cal 268; Prot 8 g; Carbo 46 g; Fiber 6 g;
    T Fat 7 g; 22% Calories from Fat; Chol 24 mg; Sod 589 mg.

Dorothy Barton, Saginaw

No-Bake Beans

2 large onions, chopped
8 ounces bacon, cut into pieces

1 48-ounce jar Great Northern beans
1 1/2 cups sugar

Sauté onions and bacon in skillet until onions are transparent; drain. Add beans and sugar. Cook over low heat for 25 minutes or until most of the liquid is absorbed, stirring frequently. **Yield: 12 servings.**

Approx Per Serving: Cal 230; Prot 8 g; Carbo 44 g; Fiber 9 g;
    T Fat 3 g; 12% Calories from Fat; Chol 5 mg; Sod 485 mg.

Margaret Crouse, Mecosta

Barbecued Beans

12 slices bacon, cut into pieces
1 onion, chopped
2 16-ounce cans pork and beans
1 cup barbecue sauce

3 tablespoons brown sugar
1 tablespoon mustard
1 tablespoon Worcestershire sauce

Cook bacon in skillet until brown. Add onion. Cook until onion is tender, stirring frequently; drain. Stir in beans, barbecue sauce, brown sugar, mustard and Worcestershire sauce. Bring to a boil. Simmer for 20 minutes, stirring occasionally. **Yield: 8 servings.**

Approx Per Serving: Cal 230; Prot 10 g; Carbo 34 g; Fiber 7 g;
    T Fat 7 g; 27% Calories from Fat; Chol 16 mg; Sod 832 mg.

Eloise Robinson, Lansing

Bean Casserole with Water Chestnuts

2 16-ounce cans French-style green
   beans
1 16-ounce can bean sprouts
1 8-ounce can sliced water chestnuts

1 10-ounce can cream of mushroom
   soup
1 4-ounce can mushrooms, drained

Mix beans, bean sprouts, water chestnuts, soup and mushrooms in bowl. Spoon into casserole. Bake at 350 degrees for 1 hour. **Yield: 8 servings.**

Approx Per Serving: Cal 75; Prot 3 g; Carbo 11 g; Fiber 2 g;
    T Fat 3 g; 31% Calories from Fat; Chol <1 mg; Sod 713 mg.

Vivian Schultz, Stephenson

Bean Casserole

2 16-ounce cans pork and beans
1 16-ounce can lima beans
1 16-ounce can kidney beans
1 16-ounce can chick-peas
1¹/₂ cups chopped onions

1¹/₂ cups chopped celery
1¹/₂ cups chopped green bell pepper
1¹/₂ cups packed brown sugar
1 cup catsup

Combine beans, chick-peas, onions, celery, green pepper, brown sugar and catsup in bowl; mix well. Spoon into casserole. Bake at 350 degrees for 1¹/₂ hours or until bubbly and heated through. **Yield: 16 servings.**

Approx Per Serving: Cal 266; Prot 8 g; Carbo 58 g; Fiber 8 g;
    T Fat 1 g; 5% Calories from Fat; Chol 4 mg; Sod 668 mg.

Marcy Idalski, Posen

Dad's Bean Casserole

1 10-ounce can tomato soup	1 16-ounce can wax beans, drained
1 10-ounce can cream of mushroom soup	1 16-ounce can green beans, drained
	1 3-ounce can French-fried onions

Mix soups in saucepan. Cook over medium heat until heated through and well blended. Layer beans, onions and soups in casserole. Bake at 350 degrees for 30 to 45 minutes or until heated through. May layer mushroom pieces between onions and soups and top with 2 or 3 strips of bacon before baking. **Yield: 6 servings.**

Approx Per Serving: Cal 197; Prot 4 g; Carbo 22 g; Fiber 2 g;
 T Fat 11 g; 48% Calories from Fat; Chol 1 mg; Sod 1183 mg.

Janet Adamski, Lansing

Green Beans Amandine

1 20-ounce package frozen French-style green beans	1/2 cup slivered almonds
	1/4 cup margarine

Cook green beans using package directions; drain. Spoon into serving dish. Brown almonds in margarine in skillet. Pour over green beans; do not stir. **Yield: 6 servings.**

Approx Per Serving: Cal 159; Prot 4 g; Carbo 8 g; Fiber 4 g;
 T Fat 14 g; 72% Calories from Fat; Chol 0 mg; Sod 102 mg.

Judy Shafer, Wayland

Sour Cream Green Beans

1 onion, thinly sliced	1/4 cup flour
1/4 cup margarine	1 1/2 teaspoons salt
2 10-ounce packages frozen green beans, thawed, drained	1/4 teaspoon pepper
1 cup sour cream	1 cup shredded sharp Cheddar cheese
	1 cup soft bread crumbs

Sauté onion in margarine in skillet until tender. Combine with green beans, sour cream, flour, salt and pepper in bowl; mix well. Spoon into greased 1 1/2-quart casserole. Sprinkle with cheese. Top with crumbs. Bake at 350 degrees for 25 minutes. **Yield: 6 servings.**

Approx Per Serving: Cal 299; Prot 9 g; Carbo 17 g; Fiber 4 g;
 T Fat 22 g; 66% Calories from Fat; Chol 37 mg; Sod 811 mg.

Shirley A. Cook, Lansing

Red Beans and Rice

1 pound dried red beans
2 quarts cold water
1 ham bone
8 ounces hot sausage, thickly sliced
1 bunch green onions with tops, chopped
1 green bell pepper, chopped

2 stalks celery, chopped
3 onions, chopped
Thyme to taste
4 bay leaves
Cayenne pepper or Tabasco sauce to taste
Salt and black pepper to taste

Rinse beans. Combine with cold water, ham bone and sausage in large saucepan. Cook over medium heat. Add green onions, green pepper, celery, onions, thyme and bay leaves. Bring to a boil. Simmer for 3 hours, stirring occasionally. Mash 1/4 of the beans against side of saucepan. Simmer for 40 minutes longer, stirring frequently. Stir in cayenne pepper, salt and black pepper. Simmer for 30 minutes longer. Remove bay leaves. Serve over rice. **Yield: 12 servings.**

Approx Per Serving: Cal 191; Prot 13 g; Carbo 27 g; Fiber 9 g; T Fat 4 g; 19% Calories from Fat; Chol 11 mg; Sod 200 mg.

Mrs. William Creamer, Wyoming

Three-Bean Casserole

8 slices bacon, chopped
1 cup chopped celery
1½ cups chopped onion
1 cup water
1   6-ounce can tomato sauce
½ cup packed brown sugar
1 envelope spaghetti sauce mix

2 tablespoons prepared mustard
1 teaspoon garlic salt
2 tablespoons cider vinegar
2   16-ounce cans lima beans
1   16-ounce can kidney beans
1   28-ounce can pork and beans

Cook bacon in large skillet. Add celery and onion. Sauté until vegetables are tender; drain. Add water, tomato sauce, brown sugar, spaghetti sauce mix, prepared mustard, garlic salt and vinegar; mix well. Bring to a boil. Add beans; mix well. Spoon into 3-quart casserole. Bake at 350 degrees for 1 hour. **Yield: 10 servings.**

Approx Per Serving: Cal 308; Prot 14 g; Carbo 57 g; Fiber 15 g; T Fat 4 g; 12% Calories from Fat; Chol 10 mg; Sod 1166 mg.

Shirley A. Cook, Lansing

Bradford Beets

2 8-ounce cans crushed pineapple
2 tablespoons cornstarch
1/2 teaspoon salt
1/4 cup packed brown sugar

2 tablespoons margarine
2 16-ounce cans beets, drained
2 tablespoons lemon juice

Combine undrained pineapple, cornstarch, salt and brown sugar in saucepan. Cook until brown sugar is dissolved. Add margarine, beets and lemon juice; mix well. Cook until heated through. **Yield: 8 servings.**

Approx Per Serving: Cal 146; Prot 1 g; Carbo 30 g; Fiber 3 g;
    T Fat 3 g; 18% Calories from Fat; Chol 0 mg; Sod 482 mg.

Gladys D. Bradford, Lansing

Harvard Beets

3/4 cup sugar
2 tablespoons cornstarch
1/3 cup vinegar
1/3 cup beet juice

4 cups cooked beets
3 tablespoons butter
Salt and pepper to taste

Combine sugar, cornstarch, vinegar and beet juice in saucepan. Bring to a boil; reduce heat. Simmer for 5 minutes. Stir in beets. Cook until heated through. Stir in butter, salt and pepper. **Yield: 8 servings.**

Approx Per Serving: Cal 145; Prot 1 g; Carbo 27 g; Fiber 2 g;
    T Fat 4 g; 26% Calories from Fat; Chol 12 mg; Sod 79 mg.

Barb Miltibarger

Pickled Beets

8 quarts beets
3 1/2 cups sugar

2 cups white vinegar
2 cups water

Wash beets thoroughly, leaving buds of leaves and roots intact. Combine beets with water to cover in large saucepan. Cook over medium heat for 3 to 4 hours or until beets are tender; drain. Peel beets. Combine sugar, vinegar and 2 cups water in saucepan. Bring to a boil; reduce heat. Simmer for 5 minutes. Ladle beets into 4 hot sterilized 1-quart jars. Pour sugar mixture into jars, leaving 1/2 inch headspace; seal with 2-piece lids. Process in boiling water bath for 10 minutes. **Yield: 32 servings.**

Approx Per Serving: Cal 139; Prot 2 g; Carbo 34 g; Fiber 3 g;
    T Fat <1 g; 1% Calories from Fat; Chol 0 mg; Sod 84 mg.

Frances Robinson, Flint

Baked Broccoli

6 eggs, beaten
6 tablespoons flour
1/2 cup melted margarine
16 ounces cottage cheese

1   20-ounce package frozen chopped broccoli, thawed
2 cups shredded sharp Cheddar cheese

Beat eggs with flour and melted margarine in large bowl until smooth. Add cottage cheese, broccoli and 1 cup Cheddar cheese; mix well. Spoon into greased 9x13-inch baking dish. Top with remaining Cheddar cheese. Bake at 350 degrees for 50 minutes. **Yield: 20 servings.**

Approx Per Serving: Cal 150; Prot 9 g; Carbo 4 g; Fiber 1 g;
     T Fat 11 g; 66% Calories from Fat; Chol 79 mg; Sod 243 mg.

Dixie L. Tackebury, Saginaw

Broccoli Casserole

1 cup melted margarine
2 tablespoons flour
2 cups cottage cheese
4 eggs, beaten

2 teaspoons salt
4 ounces Velveeta cheese, cubed
2   10-ounce packages frozen broccoli, partially thawed

Mix margarine and flour in large bowl. Combine cottage cheese, eggs and salt in bowl; mix well. Stir into flour mixture. Add Velveeta cheese and broccoli; mix well. Spoon into casserole. Bake at 350 degrees for 1 hour. **Yield: 8 servings.**

Approx Per Serving: Cal 377; Prot 15 g; Carbo 7 g; Fiber 2 g;
     T Fat 32 g; 76% Calories from Fat; Chol 128 mg; Sod 1267 mg.

Karen Anderson, Grand Rapids

Broccoli and Rice Casserole

1/2 cup butter
1 teaspoon chopped onion
1 1/2 cups water
1   10-ounce package frozen broccoli cuts

1 1/2 cups minute rice
1   10-ounce can cream of mushroom soup
1   8-ounce jar Cheez Whiz

Combine butter, onion and water in saucepan. Bring to a boil. Add broccoli. Cook until heated through. Stir in rice. Remove from heat. Let stand, covered, for 5 minutes. Stir in soup and Cheez Whiz. Spoon into casserole sprayed with nonstick cooking spray. Bake at 375 degrees for 30 to 40 minutes or until heated through. **Yield: 8 servings.**

Approx Per Serving: Cal 307; Prot 9 g; Carbo 21 g; Fiber 2 g;
     T Fat 21 g; 61% Calories from Fat; Chol 50 mg; Sod 729 mg.

Jean A. Steffes, Traverse City

Broccoli and Rice

¹/₂ cup margarine
1 onion, grated
1   10-ounce can cream of chicken
   soup
¹/₂ cup evaporated milk
1   8-ounce jar Cheez Whiz

2   10-ounce packages frozen
   chopped broccoli, thawed
1 cup rice
2 cups water
1 teaspoon salt

Combine margarine, onion, soup, evaporated milk, Cheez Whiz and broccoli in double boiler. Bring to a boil; reduce heat. Simmer for 10 minutes. Combine rice, water and salt in saucepan. Cook until rice is tender and water is absorbed. Combine broccoli mixture and rice in bowl. Spoon into 9x13-inch baking dish. Bake, covered with foil, at 300 degrees for 45 minutes or until bubbly. Serve with chicken or ham. **Yield: 10 servings.**

Approx Per Serving: Cal 287; Prot 9 g; Carbo 24 g; Fiber 2 g;
   T Fat 18 g; 54% Calories from Fat; Chol 20 mg; Sod 840 mg.

Fran Hodges, Grand Rapids

Broccoli and Rice Quiche

¹/₂ cup instant rice, cooked
1 egg, beaten
1¹/₂ ounces sharp Cheddar cheese,
   shredded
1¹/₂ cups chopped cooked broccoli
³/₄ cup mushrooms
Chopped onion to taste

2 eggs, beaten
¹/₄ cup skim milk
1 tablespoon reduced-calorie
   margarine
1¹/₂ ounces sharp Cheddar cheese,
   shredded

Mix rice, 1 egg and 1¹/₂ ounces cheese in bowl. Press into 9-inch quiche pan sprayed with nonstick cooking spray. Combine broccoli, mushrooms, onion, 2 eggs, skim milk and margarine in bowl; mix well. Spoon into prepared pan. Bake at 375 degrees for 20 minutes. Sprinkle with 1¹/₂ ounces cheese. Bake for 10 minutes longer. **Yield: 3 servings.**

Approx Per Serving: Cal 303; Prot 18 g; Carbo 20 g; Fiber 3 g;
   T Fat 17 g; 50% Calories from Fat; Chol 243 mg; Sod 310 mg.

Berdina Holford, Jackson

Crunchy Broccoli and Bean Casserole

2 10-ounce packages frozen
  chopped broccoli
1 10-ounce package frozen baby
  lima beans
1 10-ounce can cream of mushroom
  soup

1 cup sour cream
1 envelope onion soup mix
1 8-ounce can water chestnuts,
  chopped
1/2 cup melted butter
3 cups crisp rice cereal

Cook broccoli and lima beans separately using package directions; drain. Spoon into 3-quart casserole; mix well. Combine soup, sour cream, soup mix and water chestnuts in bowl; mix well. Spread over vegetables. Mix melted butter and cereal in bowl. Sprinkle over top. Bake at 325 degrees for 30 minutes. **Yield: 8 servings.**

Approx Per Serving: Cal 315; Prot 7 g; Carbo 28 g; Fiber 6 g;
  T Fat 21 g; 57% Calories from Fat; Chol 44 mg; Sod 635 mg.

Shirley A. Cook, Lansing

Broccoli Elegant

1 1/2 cups water
1/4 cup butter
1 6-ounce package corn bread
  stuffing mix
2 10-ounce packages frozen broccoli
  spears, thawed
2 tablespoons butter
2 tablespoons flour

1 teaspoon instant chicken bouillon
3/4 cup milk
3 ounces cream cheese, softened
1/4 teaspoon salt
4 green onions, sliced
1 cup shredded Cheddar cheese
Paprika to taste

Combine water, 1/4 cup butter and contents of seasoning packet from stuffing mix in saucepan. Bring to a boil. Remove from heat. Stir in stuffing crumbs. Let stand, covered, for 5 minutes. Spoon stuffing around edges of buttered 9x13-inch baking pan, leaving well in center. Place broccoli in well. Melt 2 tablespoons butter in saucepan. Stir in flour. Cook for 1 minute, stirring constantly. Add instant bouillon and milk. Cook until thickened, stirring constantly. Add cream cheese and salt; mix well. Stir in green onions. Spoon over broccoli. Sprinkle with cheese and paprika. Bake, covered with foil, at 350 degrees for 35 minutes. Bake, uncovered, for 10 minutes longer. **Yield: 12 servings.**

Approx Per Serving: Cal 174; Prot 6 g; Carbo 11 g; Fiber 2 g;
  T Fat 12 g; 62% Calories from Fat; Chol 35 mg; Sod 425 mg.

Judy Hartman, Lansing

Broccoli Scramble Casserole

1 10-ounce package frozen broccoli
  spears
6 eggs
1/3 cup milk
1/8 teaspoon pepper
2 tablespoons butter

1 10-ounce can cream of chicken soup
1/2 cup cream-style cottage cheese
1 tablespoon flour
1/4 teaspoon dried tarragon, crushed
3/4 cup soft bread crumbs
1 tablespoon melted butter

Cook broccoli using package directions; drain. Arrange with stems toward center in 6x10-inch baking dish. Combine eggs, milk and pepper in blender container. Process until well blended. Heat 2 tablespoons butter in 10-inch skillet. Pour in egg mixture. Cook over low heat until eggs are set but still glossy and moist, lifting and turning cooked portions with spatula. Spoon over broccoli. Combine soup, cottage cheese, flour and tarragon in blender container. Process until smooth. Pour into small saucepan. Cook until thickened and bubbly, stirring constantly. Pour over eggs and broccoli. Mix bread crumbs and melted butter in bowl. Sprinkle over top. Bake at 350 degrees for 20 minutes. **Yield: 4 servings.**

Approx Per Serving: Cal 349; Prot 18 g; Carbo 17 g; Fiber 2 g;
    T Fat 23 g; 60% Calories from Fat; Chol 355 mg; Sod 908 mg.

T. C. Smorgasbroads, Traverse City

Cabbage Casserole

1 8-ounce package seasoned
  stuffing mix
1/4 cup melted margarine
1 head cabbage, chopped
1 green bell pepper, chopped

1 10-ounce can cream of chicken
  soup
1 4-ounce package shredded
  Cheddar cheese

Mix stuffing mix and melted margarine in bowl. Press half the stuffing into greased 9x9-inch baking dish. Cook cabbage and green pepper in boiling salted water in saucepan until tender; drain. Stir in soup and cheese. Spoon into prepared baking dish. Top with remaining stuffing. Bake at 350 degrees for 30 minutes.
Yield: 8 servings.

Approx Per Serving: Cal 258; Prot 9 g; Carbo 26 g; Fiber 1 g;
    T Fat 14 g; 47% Calories from Fat; Chol 18 mg; Sod 927 mg.

Carroll King, Brooklyn

Sweet-Sour Red Cabbage

1 large head red cabbage, finely
   shredded
8 apples, peeled, finely chopped

1 cup vinegar
2 cups water
1 cup sugar

Mix cabbage, apples, vinegar, water and sugar in heavy saucepan; cover. Bring to a boil; reduce heat. Simmer for 3 hours. Let stand until cool. Chill until serving time. **Yield: 10 servings.**

Approx Per Serving: Cal 144; Prot <1 g; Carbo 38 g; Fiber 3 g;
    T Fat <1 g; 2% Calories from Fat; Chol 0 mg; Sod 6 mg.

Beverly J. Stone, Grand Rapids

Glazed Carrots

1/3 cup packed brown sugar
2 tablespoons butter

8 carrots, cooked, cut into halves
   lengthwise

Combine brown sugar and butter in skillet. Cook until brown sugar dissolves. Stir in carrots. Cook over medium heat for 12 minutes or until well glazed, turning frequently. **Yield: 6 servings.**

Approx Per Serving: Cal 184; Prot 2 g; Carbo 36 g; Fiber 7 g;
    T Fat 4 g; 20% Calories from Fat; Chol 10 mg; Sod 178 mg.

Sally Taylor, Marquette

Carrot Mold

1 1/2 cups grated carrots
1 cup packed brown sugar
1/2 cup butter, softened
1/2 teaspoon baking powder

1/2 teaspoon salt
1 egg, beaten
1 cup flour

Combine carrots, brown sugar, butter, baking powder, salt, egg and flour in bowl; mix well. Spoon into greased 5 1/2-cup ring mold. Bake at 350 degrees for 45 minutes. Unmold onto serving plate. Serve with cooked green peas in center. **Yield: 6 servings.**

Approx Per Serving: Cal 430; Prot 3 g; Carbo 68 g; Fiber 2 g;
    T Fat 17 g; 36% Calories from Fat; Chol 77 mg; Sod 394 mg.

Sally Taylor, Marquette

Cauliflower au Gratin

Flowerets of 1 large head cauliflower
2 tablespoons butter
1/2 cup chopped onion
11/2 cups shredded Cheddar cheese

1 cup sour cream
1/4 teaspoon salt
2 tablespoons melted butter
1/2 cup dry bread crumbs

Cook cauliflower in boiling salted water in saucepan for 10 minutes; drain. Stir in next 5 ingredients. Spoon into 11/2-quart casserole. Sprinkle mixture of melted butter and crumbs over top. Bake at 350 degrees for 30 to 35 minutes. **Yield: 12 servings.**

Approx Per Serving: Cal 158; Prot 5 g; Carbo 6 g; Fiber 1 g;
    T Fat 13 g; 71% Calories from Fat; Chol 34 mg; Sod 210 mg.

Shirley A. Cook, Lansing

Holiday Cauliflower

Flowerets of 1 large head cauliflower
1 4-ounce can sliced mushrooms
1/4 cup chopped green bell pepper
1/4 cup butter
1/3 cup flour

2 cups milk
1 teaspoon salt
1 cup shredded Swiss cheese
2 tablespoons chopped pimento

Combine cauliflower with boiling water to cover in saucepan. Cook for 10 minutes or until tender-crisp; drain. Sauté mushrooms and green pepper in butter in 2-quart saucepan until tender. Stir in flour. Add milk gradually. Add salt, cheese and pimento; mix well. Layer cauliflower and cheese mixture 1/2 at a time in buttered 2-quart casserole. Bake at 325 degrees for 15 minutes. **Yield: 8 servings.**

Approx Per Serving: Cal 178; Prot 8 g; Carbo 11 g; Fiber 2 g;
    T Fat 12 g; 59% Calories from Fat; Chol 37 mg; Sod 445 mg.

Louise Huff, Lakeland, Florida

Celery Casserole

4 cups chopped celery
1 8-ounce can sliced water chestnuts
1 10-ounce can cream of chicken
   soup

1/4 cup chopped red bell pepper
1/2 cup bread crumbs
1/4 cup slivered almonds
2 tablespoons melted butter

Cook celery with water to cover in saucepan for 8 minutes; drain. Add water chestnuts, soup and red pepper; mix well. Spoon into buttered 1-quart casserole. Top with bread crumbs and almonds. Drizzle with butter. Bake at 350 degrees for 35 minutes. **Yield: 8 servings.**

Approx Per Serving: Cal 133; Prot 3 g; Carbo 14 g; Fiber 2 g;
    T Fat 8 g; 49% Calories from Fat; Chol 11 mg; Sod 405 mg.

Leanore E. Yerrick, Wyoming

Easy Corn Relish

2 12-ounce cans whole-kernel corn
   with peppers, drained
3 tablespoons oil
1/2 cup sugar

1/2 cup vinegar
2 teaspoons minced dried onion
1/2 teaspoon salt
1/4 teaspoon celery seed

Combine corn and oil in bowl. Mix sugar, vinegar, onion, salt and celery seed in saucepan; cover. Bring to a boil; reduce heat. Simmer for 2 minutes. Stir into corn mixture. Let stand until cool. Chill thoroughly; drain. **Yield: 6 servings.**

Approx Per Serving: Cal 217; Prot 2 g; Carbo 38 g; Fiber <1 g;
    T Fat 7 g; 28% Calories from Fat; Chol 0 mg; Sod 543 mg.

Shirley A. Cook, Lansing

Corn Pudding

2 17-ounce cans cream-style corn
2 tablespoons sugar
2 eggs, beaten
2 tablespoons cornstarch
1/2 cup milk

1/4 teaspoon salt
1/4 teaspoon pepper
1/2 cup bread crumbs
2 tablespoons melted butter

Combine corn, sugar, eggs, cornstarch, milk, salt and pepper in bowl; mix well. Spoon into buttered casserole. Mix bread crumbs with melted butter in bowl. Sprinkle over corn mixture. Bake at 350 degrees until bubbly and heated through. **Yield: 10 servings.**

Approx Per Serving: Cal 156; Prot 5 g; Carbo 26 g; Fiber 2 g;
    T Fat 5 g; 28% Calories from Fat; Chol 52 mg; Sod 410 mg.

Esther Fischrupp, Holland

Oven-Fried Eggplant

1/3 cup fine dry bread crumbs
2 tablespoons grated Parmesan
   cheese

1/4 teaspoon salt
1 eggplant, cut into 1/4-inch slices
1/4 cup mayonnaise

Mix bread crumbs, cheese and salt in shallow dish. Spread both sides of eggplant with mayonnaise. Dredge in crumb mixture. Place on lightly greased baking sheet. Bake at 400 degrees for 10 to 12 minutes or until light brown. **Yield: 6 servings.**

Approx Per Serving: Cal 192; Prot 2 g; Carbo 2 g; Fiber 2 g;
    T Fat 20 g; 86% Calories from Fat; Chol 15 mg; Sod 161 mg.

Cereda McConnell, Lansing

Eggplant-Zucchini Parmigiana

1/2 cup chicken broth
1/2 cup coarsely chopped celery
1/2 cup chopped onion
1 clove of garlic, minced
2 large tomatoes, chopped
1/3 cup tomato paste
1 teaspoon dried basil, crushed
1/4 teaspoon dried rosemary, crushed
1/8 teaspoon pepper

1 eggplant, peeled, cut into 1/4-inch pieces
2 cups zucchini, diagonally sliced 1/4 inch thick
1 cup low-fat cottage cheese, drained
1/2 cup shredded part-skim mozzarella cheese
1/4 cup grated Parmesan cheese

Combine chicken broth, celery, onion and garlic in medium saucepan. Bring to a boil; reduce heat. Simmer for 5 minutes. Stir in tomatoes, tomato paste, basil, rosemary and pepper. Simmer for 15 minutes, stirring occasionally. Place eggplant and zucchini in 1 inch boiling water in large saucepan. Simmer, covered, for 4 minutes. Drain on paper towel; pat dry. Spoon eggplant mixture into 4 individual casseroles. Top with cottage cheese and tomato mixture. Sprinkle with cheeses. Bake at 350 degrees for 20 to 25 minutes or until heated through. **Yield: 4 servings.**

Approx Per Serving: Cal 186; Prot 17 g; Carbo 19 g; Fiber 6 g;
    T Fat 6 g; 26% Calories from Fat; Chol 17 mg; Sod 524 mg.

Elaine Christensen, Marquette

Collard Greens

1 1/2 quarts water
1 teaspoon crushed red pepper
1 1/2 pounds pork neck bones
8 pounds collard greens

2 teaspoons sugar
1/2 cup cider vinegar
Salt and black pepper to taste

Combine water, red pepper and neck bones in large saucepan. Bring to a boil. Boil for 1 hour. Cut stems from greens; rinse well. Add greens, sugar, vinegar, salt and black pepper to saucepan. Cook, covered, for 30 minutes or until greens are tender-crisp. **Yield: 12 servings.**

Approx Per Serving: Cal 83; Prot 7 g; Carbo 13 g; Fiber 6 g;
    T Fat 2 g; 20% Calories from Fat; Chol 5 mg; Sod 188 mg.

Jackie Adams, Lansing

Substitute crushed wheat germ for buttered crumbs for a delicious, nutritious and easy casserole topping.

Brotherhood Potatoes

1 12-serving package instant
  mashed potato mix
8 ounces cream cheese, softened
2 eggs, beaten
1/4 cup chopped green onions

2 tablespoons chopped parsley
Salt and pepper to taste
2 tablespoons butter
Paprika to taste

Prepare potatoes using package directions, omitting butter. Combine potatoes, cream cheese, eggs, green onions, parsley, salt and pepper in bowl; mix well. Spoon into buttered 3-quart casserole. Dot with butter. Sprinkle with paprika. Bake at 375 degrees for 45 minutes. **Yield: 12 servings.**

Approx Per Serving: Cal 356; Prot 9 g; Carbo 58 g; Fiber 4 g;
    T Fat 11 g; 27% Calories from Fat; Chol 65 mg; Sod 455 mg.

Dorothy Martin, West Branch

Caraway-Cheese Potatoes

4 large potatoes, peeled, thinly sliced
8 ounces mozzarella cheese, shredded
2 eggs, beaten
1²/₃ cups evaporated milk
1/2 cup water

1 teaspoon salt
1/4 teaspoon pepper
1 teaspoon caraway seed
3 tablespoons butter

Alternate layers of potatoes and cheese in buttered 2-quart casserole, ending with cheese. Mix eggs, evaporated milk, water, salt, pepper and caraway seed in bowl. Pour over potatoes. Dot with butter. Bake at 325 degrees for 1 hour or until potatoes are tender. **Yield: 6 servings.**

Approx Per Serving: Cal 374; Prot 16 g; Carbo 30 g; Fiber 2 g;
    T Fat 21 g; 50% Calories from Fat; Chol 136 mg; Sod 647 mg.

Shirley A. Cook, Lansing

Never-Fail Scalloped Potatoes

6 potatoes, peeled, sliced
1 10-ounce can cream of asparagus
  soup

1 cup half and half
1/4 teaspoon pepper

Layer potatoes in greased baking dish. Mix soup, half and half and pepper in bowl. Pour over potatoes. Bake at 350 degrees for 45 to 60 minutes or until potatoes are tender. **Yield: 6 servings.**

Approx Per Serving: Cal 230; Prot 5 g; Carbo 39 g; Fiber 3 g;
    T Fat 6 g; 24% Calories from Fat; Chol 17 mg; Sod 25 mg.

Sally Taylor, Marquette

Potato Pancakes

3 slices bacon, chopped
3 cups grated potatoes
2 eggs, beaten

2 tablespoons flour
1 teaspoon baking powder
1 teaspoon salt

Cook bacon in skillet until crisp-fried; drain, reserving drippings. Mix potatoes, eggs, flour, baking powder and salt in bowl. Drop by spoonfuls into reserved drippings on hot griddle. Sprinkle with crumbled bacon. Cook until brown, turning once. **Yield: 3 servings.**

Approx Per Serving: Cal 400; Prot 13 g; Carbo 72 g; Fiber 5 g;
    T Fat 7 g; 16% Calories from Fat; Chol 147 mg; Sod 983 mg.

Bessie Stuhr Cohoon, Beaverton

Potatoes Romanoff

6 potatoes, baked, peeled
2 cups sour cream
1 cup chopped green onions
1¹/₂ cups shredded Cheddar cheese

1¹/₂ teaspoons salt
¹/₂ teaspoon pepper
Paprika to taste

Grate potatoes into large bowl. Add sour cream, green onions, cheese, salt and pepper; mix well. Spoon into 9x13-inch baking dish. Chill for 4 hours. Bake at 350 degrees for 40 to 50 minutes. Sprinkle with paprika. **Yield: 10 servings.**

Approx Per Serving: Cal 256; Prot 8 g; Carbo 23 g; Fiber 2 g;
    T Fat 15 g; 53% Calories from Fat; Chol 38 mg; Sod 455 mg.

Shirley A. Cook, Lansing

Cheesy Spuds

2 16-ounce packages frozen hashed
    brown potatoes
1 cup sour cream
¹/₂ cup margarine

10 ounces Cheddar cheese, shredded
1 10-ounce can cream of chicken
    soup
¹/₄ cup chopped onion

Place potatoes in 9x12-inch baking dish. Mix sour cream, margarine, cheese, soup and onion in microwave-safe bowl. Microwave on Medium until mixture is heated through and cheese is melted. Pour over potatoes. Bake at 350 degrees for 1¹/₄ hours. **Yield: 15 servings.**

Approx Per Serving: Cal 314; Prot 8 g; Carbo 20 g; Fiber 1 g;
    T Fat 24 g; 66% Calories from Fat; Chol 28 mg; Sod 366 mg.

Donna Lomashewich, Wyoming

Easy Cheesy Potatoes

10 potatoes, peeled, cut into slices
1   10-ounce can Cheddar cheese soup
1 soup can water

1 onion, thinly sliced
Salt and pepper to taste

Place potatoes in 9x13-inch baking dish. Mix soup and water in bowl. Pour over potatoes. Stir in onion, salt and pepper. Bake at 350 degrees for 1½ hours or until potatoes are tender and mixture is heated through. **Yield: 15 servings.**

Approx Per Serving: Cal 123; Prot 3 g; Carbo 25 g; Fiber 2 g;
      T Fat 2 g; 12% Calories from Fat; Chol 4 mg; Sod 147 mg.

Barb Ferguson, Traverse City

Cheese Potatoes

4 cups chopped cooked potatoes
2 cups chopped ham
¼ cup melted butter
¼ cup flour

2 cups milk
1 cup cubed Velveeta cheese
¼ cup melted butter
2 cups bread crumbs

Place potatoes and ham in casserole; mix well. Combine ¼ cup melted butter, flour, milk and cheese in saucepan. Cook until cheese is melted. Pour over potato mixture. Sprinkle with mixture of ¼ cup melted butter and bread crumbs. Bake at 350 degrees for 30 to 35 minutes or until bubbly and heated through. **Yield: 8 servings.**

Approx Per Serving: Cal 417; Prot 19 g; Carbo 38 g; Fiber 2 g;
      T Fat 21 g; 46% Calories from Fat; Chol 73 mg; Sod 977 mg.

Sue Wright, Cadillac

Ranch Potatoes

8 potatoes, cut into slices
½ cup sour cream
½ cup ranch salad dressing
¼ cup bacon bits

1½ cups shredded Cheddar cheese
2 cups crushed cornflakes
¼ cup melted butter

Cook potatoes in water to cover in saucepan until tender; drain. Place in greased 9x13-inch baking dish. Combine sour cream, salad dressing, bacon bits and 1 cup cheese in bowl; mix well. Pour over potatoes. Sprinkle with remaining ½ cup cheese and mixture of cornflakes and melted butter. Bake at 350 degrees for 40 to 45 minutes or until bubbly and heated through. **Yield: 15 servings.**

Approx Per Serving: Cal 223; Prot 6 g; Carbo 24 g; Fiber 1 g;
      T Fat 12 g; 47% Calories from Fat; Chol 27 mg; Sod 286 mg.

Julie Beechner, Stephenson

Red Potato Casserole

4 pounds small red potatoes
1 16-ounce bottle ranch-bacon salad
    dressing

1 3-ounce jar bacon bits
1 16-ounce package shredded Colby
    cheese

Parboil potatoes in saucepan. Cool completely. Cut into quarters. Place in large shallow baking dish. Pour dressing over potatoes. Sprinkle with bacon bits, reserving a small amount. Bake at 325 degrees for 40 minutes. Sprinkle with cheese and reserved bacon bits. Bake until cheese is melted. **Yield: 16 servings.**

Approx Per Serving: Cal 366; Prot 13 g; Carbo 32 g; Fiber 3 g;
    T Fat 21 g; 51% Calories from Fat; Chol 38 mg; Sod 419 mg.

Beverly J. Stone, Grand Rapids

Scalloped Potatoes with Cheese

4 16-ounce cans sliced potatoes,
    drained
1 pound Velveeta cheese, sliced
2 slices cooked ham

2 tablespoons mayonnaise-type salad
    dressing
1/2 cup milk

Layer potatoes, cheese and ham in slow cooker. Top with salad dressing. Pour milk over layers. Cook on High until cheese is melted; stir. Cook on Low for 4 hours, stirring occasionally. **Yield: 12 servings.**

Approx Per Serving: Cal 255; Prot 12 g; Carbo 22 g; Fiber 2 g;
    T Fat 14 g; 47% Calories from Fat; Chol 41 mg; Sod 931 mg.

Tanya Lindsey, Traverse City

Lima-Stuffed Peppers

4 green bell peppers
8 ounces lean ground beef
1 small onion, chopped
1 tablespoon oil

2 cups drained cooked large lima
    beans
3/4 cup drained canned tomatoes
Salt and pepper to taste

Cut tops from green peppers; remove seeds and membranes. Place in saucepan with boiling water to cover. Cook for 5 minutes; remove and drain upside down. Brown ground beef with onion in oil in skillet, stirring frequently. Add beans, tomatoes, salt and pepper. Fill peppers with cooked mixture. Place in shallow baking dish. Bake at 350 degrees for 30 minutes. Serve plain or with cheese sauce. **Yield: 4 servings.**

Approx Per Serving: Cal 291; Prot 19 g; Carbo 28 g; Fiber 11 g;
    T Fat 12 g; 37% Calories from Fat; Chol 37 mg; Sod 110 mg.

Nellie Thompson, Romulus

Spinach Pie

1 10-ounce package frozen spinach soufflé, thawed
2 eggs, beaten
3 tablespoons milk
2 teaspoons chopped onion
$\frac{1}{2}$ cup drained sliced mushrooms
$\frac{3}{4}$ cup crumbled cooked Italian sausage
$\frac{3}{4}$ cup shredded Swiss cheese
1 unbaked 9-inch pie shell

Mix spinach, eggs, milk, onion, mushrooms, sausage and cheese in bowl. Spoon into pie shell. Bake at 400 degrees for 25 to 30 minutes or until set. **Yield: 6 servings.**

Approx Per Serving: Cal 358; Prot 15 g; Carbo 16 g; Fiber 2 g;
   T Fat 26 g; 66% Calories from Fat; Chol 159 mg; Sod 674 mg.

Shirley A. Cook, Lansing

Sweet and Sour Spinach

1 pound spinach
4 slices bacon, cut into eighths
1 tablespoon flour
1 tablespoon brown sugar
$\frac{1}{4}$ teaspoon dry mustard
$\frac{1}{4}$ teaspoon salt
$\frac{1}{8}$ teaspoon pepper
$\frac{1}{2}$ cup half and half
1 tablespoon cider vinegar

Wash and trim spinach. Place in 3-quart glass casserole. Microwave on High for 5 to 8 minutes or until tender-crisp, stirring once; drain. Microwave bacon in $1\frac{1}{2}$-quart glass casserole for 3 to 4 minutes or until cooked through; drain, reserving 1 tablespoon drippings. Combine reserved drippings, flour, brown sugar, dry mustard, salt and pepper in casserole; mix well. Stir in half and half. Microwave on High for 1 to $1\frac{1}{2}$ minutes or until thickened, stirring once. Add vinegar and spinach; toss. Microwave for 1 to 2 minutes or until heated through. **Yield: 8 servings.**

Approx Per Serving: Cal 77; Prot 3 g; Carbo 5 g; Fiber 2 g;
   T Fat 5 g; 59% Calories from Fat; Chol 19 mg; Sod 186 mg.

Barb Miltibarger

*Pick up chopped vegetables at the supermarket produce section
or salad bar for quick stir-fries and salads.*

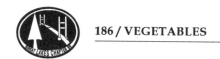

Delicious Squash

6 apples, peeled, sliced
1/2 cup butter
2 pounds butternut squash, sliced
1/2 cup butter

1/2 cup packed brown sugar
2 teaspoons cinnamon
4 cups cornflakes
1/4 cup chopped pecans

Sauté apples in 1/2 cup butter in skillet. Layer apples and squash in casserole. Melt 1/2 cup butter in skillet. Add remaining ingredients. Cook until cornflakes are coated. Spoon over squash. Bake at 350 degrees for 30 minutes. **Yield: 6 servings.**

Approx Per Serving: Cal 581; Prot 3 g; Carbo 71 g; Fiber 8 g;
    T Fat 35 g; 51% Calories from Fat; Chol 83 mg; Sod 461 mg.

Sally Taylor, Marquette

Quick Squash Casserole

3 summer squash, sliced
2 onions, sliced
1 cup sliced Polish sausage
2 tablespoons margarine

1 1/2 cups cooked rice
1/2 cup shredded Cheddar cheese
1 teaspoon dried basil
Salt and pepper to taste

Place squash and onions in microwave-safe casserole. Add sausage and margarine. Microwave on High for 6 to 8 minutes or until vegetables are tender-crisp. Stir in rice, cheese, basil, salt and pepper. Microwave for 2 to 3 minutes or until heated through. **Yield: 4 servings.**

Approx Per Serving: Cal 422; Prot 15 g; Carbo 30 g; Fiber 3 g;
    T Fat 27 g; 58% Calories from Fat; Chol 55 mg; Sod 655 mg.

Ethel Hooker, Clio

Summer Squash Casserole

1 8-ounce package herb-seasoned
    stuffing mix
1/2 cup melted butter
2 pounds summer squash, sliced

1/4 cup chopped onion
1 10-ounce can cream of chicken soup
1 cup sour cream
1 cup shredded carrots

Mix stuffing mix and melted butter in bowl. Spread half the mixture in 7x12-inch baking dish. Cook squash and onion in boiling salted water to cover in saucepan for 5 minutes; drain. Mix soup and sour cream in bowl. Stir in carrots. Add squash mixture; mix well. Spoon into prepared baking dish. Cover with remaining stuffing mixture. Bake at 350 degrees for 25 to 30 minutes or until heated through. **Yield: 6 servings.**

Approx Per Serving: Cal 444; Prot 9 g; Carbo 42 g; Fiber 3 g;
    T Fat 28 g; 55% Calories from Fat; Chol 62 mg; Sod 1180 mg.

Jan Dorman, Traverse City

Fried Tomatoes

4 half-ripened tomatoes, cut into
  3/4-inch slices, drained
1/2 cup flour
2 1/2 teaspoons sugar

2 1/2 teaspoons salt
1/4 teaspoon pepper
3/4 cup evaporated milk
Oil for frying

Dredge tomatoes in mixture of dry ingredients. Stir evaporated milk into remaining flour mixture in bowl; coat tomatoes. Fry in 1/2 inch oil in skillet until brown. **Yield: 6 servings.**

Approx Per Serving: Cal 103; Prot 4 g; Carbo 16 g; Fiber 1 g;
    T Fat 3 g; 23% Calories from Fat; Chol 9 mg; Sod 929 mg.
    Nutritional information does not include oil for frying.

Shirley A. Cook, Lansing

Tomato-Bread Casserole

1   15-ounce can chopped tomatoes
1   8-ounce loaf French bread, sliced
3 tablespoons margarine, softened
1 1/2 pounds fresh tomatoes, sliced
1 cup low-fat cottage cheese

1/4 cup olive oil
3/4 teaspoon seasoned salt
1/2 teaspoon dried oregano, crushed
1/2 teaspoon garlic powder with parsley
1/2 cup grated Parmesan cheese

Drain canned tomatoes, reserving juice. Spread bread with margarine. Place on baking sheet. Bake at 350 degrees for 7 minutes. Cut into pieces. Layer bread, tomato slices, reserved juice, cottage cheese, olive oil, canned tomatoes and seasonings 1/2 at a time in greased 9x13-inch baking dish. Sprinkle with Parmesan cheese. Bake, covered, at 350 degrees for 40 minutes. Bake, uncovered, for 5 minutes. **Yield: 10 servings.**

Approx Per Serving: Cal 204; Prot 8 g; Carbo 17 g; Fiber 2 g;
    T Fat 12 g; 51% Calories from Fat; Chol 5 mg; Sod 511 mg.

Elaine Baird, Saginaw

Tomato Pudding

2 cups packed brown sugar
1/2 teaspoon salt
1/2 cup boiling water

2   10-ounce cans tomato purée
1 cup melted margarine
12 slices bread, toasted

Combine first 4 ingredients in saucepan. Bring to a boil. Simmer for 5 minutes. Stir in margarine. Pour over bread in 2-quart casserole. Bake, covered, at 375 degrees for 30 minutes. Bake, uncovered, for 10 minutes. **Yield: 8 servings.**

Approx Per Serving: Cal 601; Prot 5 g; Carbo 94 g; Fiber 2 g;
    T Fat 25 g; 36% Calories from Fat; Chol 0 mg; Sod 661 mg.

June B. Brown, Bradenton, Florida

Wheat and Tomatoes

1 onion, chopped
1 tablespoon butter
1 16-ounce can tomatoes
1 cup water

1 cup bulgur wheat
1/2 teaspoon each allspice and cinnamon
Salt and pepper to taste
1 16-ounce can green beans, drained

Sauté onion in butter in skillet until tender. Add tomatoes, water and wheat. Stir in allspice, cinnamon, salt and pepper. Simmer, covered, for 15 minutes or until liquid is absorbed. Stir in green beans. Simmer, covered, for 5 minutes. **Yield: 8 servings.**

Approx Per Serving: Cal 116; Prot 4 g; Carbo 23 g; Fiber 6 g;
    T Fat 2 g; 15% Calories from Fat; Chol 4 mg; Sod 248 mg.

Gaye Piechowiak, Stoneham, Massachusetts

Cheesy Vegetable Casserole

1 16-ounce package frozen mixed
    vegetables, thawed, drained
8 ounces Velveeta cheese, cubed

1/4 cup margarine
1 cup crushed butter crackers
1/4 cup melted margarine

Place vegetables in 1-quart casserole. Combine cheese and 1/4 cup margarine in saucepan. Cook over medium heat until melted and blended. Pour over vegetables; mix well. Sprinkle with mixture of cracker crumbs and melted margarine. Bake at 350 degrees for 20 to 25 minutes or until heated through. **Yield: 8 servings.**

Approx Per Serving: Cal 294; Prot 9 g; Carbo 16 g; Fiber 2 g;
    T Fat 24 g; 69% Calories from Fat; Chol 27 mg; Sod 664 mg.

Pat Snider, Sault Ste. Marie

Vegetable-Cheese Puffs

4 squares puff pastry
1 teaspoon Mrs. Dash seasoning
4 tomato slices, cut into halves
4 thin slices provolone cheese
8 mushrooms, coarsely chopped

1/2 cup chopped onion
2 teaspoons minced garlic
1/2 teaspoon dried basil
2 cups whipping cream

Sprinkle pastries with seasoning. Layer half the tomatoes, cheese, remaining tomatoes, mushrooms and onion on pastries. Fold into triangles, pressing edges to seal. Place on baking sheet. Bake at 400 degrees for 10 minutes. Sauté garlic and basil in skillet until heated through. Stir in whipping cream. Cook until liquid is reduced by half. Spoon over pastries. **Yield: 4 servings.**

Approx Per Serving: Cal 796; Prot 15 g; Carbo 31 g; Fiber 1 g;
    T Fat 69 g; 77% Calories from Fat; Chol 183 mg; Sod 589 mg.

June B. Brown, Bradenton, Florida

Zucchini Casserole

1 cup melted margarine
1   8-ounce package stuffing mix
1   10-ounce package frozen chopped
    broccoli
1 cup chopped onion

1 cup sour cream
1   10-ounce can cream of mushroom
    soup
6 cups chopped cooked zucchini

Mix melted margarine and stuffing mix in bowl. Spoon half the stuffing into 9x13-inch baking pan. Combine broccoli and onion with water to cover in saucepan. Bring to a boil. Boil for 5 minutes; drain most of liquid. Mix sour cream and soup in bowl. Stir in vegetable mixture and zucchini. Spoon over stuffing in pan. Top with remaining stuffing. Bake at 350 degrees for 30 minutes or until heated through. May sprinkle with shredded Cheddar or mozzarella cheese; may substitute cream of chicken or cream of celery soup for cream of mushroom. **Yield: 12 servings.**

Approx Per Serving: Cal 298; Prot 5 g; Carbo 22 g; Fiber 3 g;
    T Fat 22 g; 64% Calories from Fat; Chol 9 mg; Sod 713 mg.

Carol Fineout, Cheboygan

If You Love Cheese

1   8-count package crescent rolls
4 ounces sharp Cheddar cheese,
    sliced
4 ounces Muenster cheese, sliced
4 ounces Swiss cheese, sliced

4 ounces Monterey Jack cheese, sliced
8 ounces cream cheese, softened
2 eggs, beaten
2 tablespoons melted butter

Press half the roll dough into 8x8-inch baking dish; seal seams. Layer cheese slices over dough. Spread with cream cheese. Pour eggs over layers. Top with remaining dough. Drizzle with melted butter. Bake at 350 degrees until golden brown. **Yield: 8 servings.**

Approx Per Serving: Cal 459; Prot 19 g; Carbo 13 g; Fiber 0 g;
    T Fat 37 g; 72% Calories from Fat; Chol 146 mg; Sod 645 mg.

Joan Wolf, Dorr

Store leftover vegetables in airtight container in freezer.
Use for quick vegetable soup.

Cottage Cheese Patties

2 eggs, beaten
1 cup creamed small curd cottage
  cheese
1 cup quick-cooking oats
1 large onion, chopped

1 teaspoon salt
1/4 teaspoon sage
1 10-ounce can cream of mushroom
  soup
1 soup can water

Mix eggs, cottage cheese, oats, onion, salt and sage in bowl. Shape into patties. Place in skillet sprayed with nonstick cooking spray. Cook until brown, turning once. Mix soup and water in bowl. Spoon over patties. Simmer for 10 minutes.
Yield: 4 servings.

Approx Per Serving: Cal 257; Prot 15 g; Carbo 24 g; Fiber 3 g;
    T Fat 12 g; 41% Calories from Fat; Chol 115 mg; Sod 1355 mg.

Mary Gordon, Lansing

Special K Roast

1 16-ounce package small curd
  cottage cheese
1 onion, chopped
1 cup chopped cashews

1 8-ounce package Special K cereal
4 eggs, slightly beaten
1/2 cup melted margarine
1/2 envelope onion soup mix

Combine cottage cheese, onion, cashews, cereal and eggs in bowl; mix well. Stir in melted margarine and soup mix. Spoon into casserole. Bake at 350 degrees for 1 hour.
Yield: 6 servings.

Approx Per Serving: Cal 538; Prot 25 g; Carbo 39 g; Fiber 2 g;
    T Fat 32 g; 53% Calories from Fat; Chol 153 mg; Sod 938 mg.

Cereda McConnell, Lansing

Mexican Cheese and Eggs

1/2 cup chopped onion
3/4 cup tomato sauce
1/2 cup water

1/4 cup salsa
1 10-ounce can cheese sauce
6 eggs

Fry onion in small nonstick skillet. Add tomato sauce, water, salsa and cheese sauce. Cook for 10 to 12 minutes or until heated through. Scramble eggs in large skillet. Stir in cheese mixture. Cook for 5 to 8 minutes or until heated through.
Yield: 6 servings.

Approx Per Serving: Cal 197; Prot 11 g; Carbo 7 g; Fiber 1 g;
    T Fat 14 g; 63% Calories from Fat; Chol 231 mg; Sod 566 mg.

Estella Delaski, California

Impossible Quiche

12 slices bacon, crisp-fried, crumbled
1 cup shredded Swiss cheese
1/3 cup finely chopped onion
1/2 cup baking mix

2 cups milk
4 eggs
1/4 teaspoon salt
1/8 teaspoon pepper

Sprinkle bacon, cheese and onion in lightly greased 10-inch quiche pan. Process mixture of remaining ingredients at high speed in blender for 1 minute. Pour into prepared pan. Bake at 350 degrees for 50 to 55 minutes or until golden brown and knife inserted near center comes out clean. Let stand for 5 minutes. **Yield: 6 servings.**

Approx Per Serving: Cal 295; Prot 17 g; Carbo 13 g; Fiber <1 g;
     T Fat 19 g; 60% Calories from Fat; Chol 181 mg; Sod 553 mg.

Evelyn Helmer, Lansing

Mother's Cheese Soufflé

1 cup butter, softened
24 slices bread, crusts trimmed
24 1-ounce slices American cheese
8 eggs

1 quart milk
1 10-ounce can mushroom soup
1 cup sour cream

Butter bread slices on both sides. Layer half the bread, cheese and remaining bread in 9x12-inch baking dish. Beat eggs with milk in bowl. Pour over layers. Chill overnight. Bake at 350 degrees for 1 hour. Combine soup and sour cream in saucepan. Cook until heated through. Spoon over soufflé. **Yield: 12 servings.**

Approx Per Serving: Cal 621; Prot 24 g; Carbo 27 g; Fiber 1 g;
     T Fat 47 g; 68% Calories from Fat; Chol 257 mg; Sod 1423 mg.

Marilyn Coombs, Jackson

Apple Fritters

2 apples, cut into small pieces
2 eggs, beaten
1 1/2 cups flour
1 teaspoon baking powder

1/8 teaspoon salt
1/2 cup sugar
3/4 cup milk
Oil for frying

Mix apples, eggs, flour, baking powder, salt, sugar and milk in bowl. Drop by tablespoonfuls into hot oil in skillet. Cook until golden brown. May roll in sugar or cinnamon sugar. **Yield: 4 servings.**

Approx Per Serving: Cal 372; Prot 10 g; Carbo 73 g; Fiber 3 g;
     T Fat 5 g; 12% Calories from Fat; Chol 113 mg; Sod 204 mg.
     Nutritional information does not include oil for frying.

Charlotte Martin, St. Joseph

Baked Pineapple

2 tablespoons cornstarch
¼ cup cold water
1 20-ounce can crushed pineapple
1 cup sugar

2 eggs, beaten
1 teaspoon vanilla extract
1 tablespoon butter

Mix cornstarch and cold water in small bowl. Combine with pineapple, sugar, eggs and vanilla in large bowl; mix well. Spoon into greased casserole. Dot with butter. Bake at 350 degrees for 1 hour. **Yield: 4 servings.**

Approx Per Serving: Cal 386; Prot 4 g; Carbo 83 g; Fiber 1 g;
    T Fat 6 g; 13% Calories from Fat; Chol 114 mg; Sod 62 mg.

Oneta Ruppert, Hillsdale

Pineapple Casserole

2 20-ounce cans pineapple chunks,
    drained
¾ cup sugar
6 tablespoons flour

1 cup shredded Cheddar cheese
½ cup melted margarine
8 ounces butter crackers, crushed

Place pineapple in 2½-quart casserole. Sprinkle with sugar and flour. Cover with cheese. Mix melted margarine and cracker crumbs in bowl. Sprinkle over cheese. Bake at 350 degrees for 30 minutes. **Yield: 8 servings.**

Approx Per Serving: Cal 468; Prot 7 g; Carbo 63 g; Fiber 2 g;
    T Fat 25 g; 45% Calories from Fat; Chol 15 mg; Sod 507 mg.

Aileen McPherson, Cheboygan

Baked Potato Topping

½ cup sour cream
¼ cup butter, softened

1½ cups shredded processed
    American cheese

Mix sour cream, butter and cheese in bowl. Serve over baked potatoes. May add chopped chives. **Yield: 4 servings.**

Approx Per Serving: Cal 322; Prot 10 g; Carbo 2 g; Fiber 0 g;
    T Fat 31 g; 85% Calories from Fat; Chol 84 mg; Sod 720 mg.

Lynn Tonka, Saginaw

Mock Apple Rings

4 pounds large ripe cucumbers
1 cup pickling lime
1/2 cup vinegar
1 teaspoon alum
1 1/2 tablespoons red food coloring

1 cup vinegar
5 cups sugar
4 ounces red-hot cinnamon candies
Whole cloves

Cut cucumbers into 1/2-inch slices and seed slices, leaving rings. Combine with lime and enough water to cover in crock. Let stand for 24 hours. Rinse and drain. Combine with 1/2 cup vinegar, alum, food coloring and water to cover in saucepan. Simmer for 2 hours; drain. Combine 1 cup vinegar, sugar and cinnamon candies in saucepan. Cook until sugar and candies dissolve, stirring to mix well. Add cucumber rings. Bring to a boil. Spoon into hot sterilized jar, leaving 1/2 inch headspace; add 4 cloves to each jar. Seal with 2-piece lids. Let stand for 30 days before serving. **Yield: 4 pints.**

Approx Per Pint: Cal 1144; Prot 2 g; Carbo 295 g; Fiber 5 g;
    T Fat 1 g; 0% Calories from Fat; Chol 0 mg; Sod 21 mg.

Marlea O'Berry, Lansing

Freezer Pickles

5 cups sugar
5 cups apple cider vinegar
1 1/2 teaspoons turmeric
1 1/2 teaspoons mustard seed

2 tablespoons salt
20 cucumbers, sliced
4 large onions, sliced

Mix first 5 ingredients in saucepan. Cook until heated through. Pour over cucumbers and onions in bowl. Refrigerate, covered, for 5 days, stirring once each day. Pack into small containers; freeze. **Yield: 16 cups.**

Approx Per Cup: Cal 312; Prot 3 g; Carbo 81 g; Fiber 5 g;
    T Fat 1 g; 2% Calories from Fat; Chol 0 mg; Sod 810 mg.

Emma M. Woodford, Paw Paw

Icebox Pickles

3 cups each sugar and vinegar
1/3 cup non-iodized salt
1 teaspoon turmeric

1 teaspoon celery seed
1 teaspoon dry mustard
2 quarts thinly sliced cucumbers

Mix sugar, vinegar, salt, turmeric, celery seed and dry mustard in bowl. Add cucumbers. Store, covered, in refrigerator for up to 1 year. **Yield: 12 cups.**

Approx Per Cup: Cal 252; Prot 2 g; Carbo 65 g; Fiber 4 g;
    T Fat 1 g; 2% Calories from Fat; Chol 0 mg; Sod 2824 mg.

Etta Holt, Holland

Microwave Bread-and-Butter Pickles

1 large cucumber, sliced
1 onion, sliced
1 cup sugar
1/2 cup white vinegar

1 teaspoon salt
1/2 teaspoon mustard seed
1/4 teaspoon celery seed
1/4 teaspoon turmeric

Combine cucumber and onion in microwave-proof bowl. Mix sugar, vinegar, salt, mustard seed, celery seed and turmeric in saucepan. Cook until heated through. Pour over cucumber and onion. Microwave on High for 7 to 8 minutes or until cucumber is translucent, stirring once. Pack into hot sterilized jars. Store in refrigerator. **Yield: 4 cups.**

Approx Per Cup: Cal 220; Prot 1 g; Carbo 57 g; Fiber 2 g;
T Fat <1 g; 1% Calories from Fat; Chol 0 mg; Sod 537 mg.

Jennie Barlett, Davison

Sun Pickles

3 heads dill
3 quarts cucumbers, thinly sliced
6 1/2 cups cold water
3 1/2 cups white vinegar
2/3 cup pickling salt

1/2 teaspoon alum
1/2 teaspoon turmeric
1/2 teaspoon mustard seed
6 cloves of garlic

Place dill in 1-gallon glass jar. Pack cucumbers into jar. Mix water, vinegar, salt, alum, turmeric, mustard seed and garlic in bowl. Pour over cucumbers. Seal jar. Let stand in sun for 3 days, shaking once per day. **Yield: 16 cups.**

Approx Per Cup: Cal 67; Prot 3 g; Carbo 17 g; Fiber 5 g;
T Fat 1 g; 6% Calories from Fat; Chol 0 mg; Sod 4231 mg.

Roseannah Keith, Grawn

*To clean blender quickly, place 3 inches of hot water and
squirt of dishwashing detergent in container. Process, covered,
on high speed for 1 minute; rinse.*

Chowchow

1 pound onions
5 green bell peppers
1 large bunch celery
1 gallon tomatoes, peeled
2 hot peppers
1 head cabbage
2 tablespoons mustard seed

2 tablespoons allspice
1/4 cup salt
1/4 cup lemon juice
2 1-pound packages brown sugar
1 tablespoon ground cloves
2 tablespoons turmeric

Grind vegetables. Mix with remaining ingredients in large bowl. Let stand, covered, overnight. Spoon into sterilized jars. Store in refrigerator. **Yield: 20 cups.**

Approx Per Cup: Cal 228; Prot 2 g; Carbo 56 g; Fiber 4 g;
    T Fat 1 g; 4% Calories from Fat; Chol 0 mg; Sod 1330 mg.

Kay Collins, Lansing

Cranberry-Ginger Chutney

1/2 cup finely chopped dried apricots
1/2 cup packed dark brown sugar
1/2 cup raisins
1 cup water
1 Granny Smith apple, peeled, cored,
    cut into 1/4-inch pieces

3 cups cranberries
1 teaspoon grated lemon rind
1/4 cup lemon juice
1/4 cup chopped crystallized ginger
1/2 teaspoon dried hot pepper flakes

Combine apricots, brown sugar, raisins and water in saucepan. Bring to a boil. Simmer for 5 minutes. Add apple, cranberries and lemon rind. Simmer for 10 minutes. Stir in lemon juice, ginger and pepper flakes. Let stand until cool. Spoon into sterilized jars. Chill for several days. **Yield: 5 cups.**

Approx Per Cup: Cal 298; Prot 2 g; Carbo 78 g; Fiber 6 g;
    T Fat <1 g; 1% Calories from Fat; Chol 0 mg; Sod 17 mg.

Teddy Zeedyk, Battle Creek

Cranberry Relish

2 cups cranberries
2 seedless oranges
2 cups chopped apples

2 cups sugar
Red food coloring to taste

Grind cranberries, oranges and apples. Mix with sugar in bowl. Stir in food coloring as desired. Chill, covered, overnight. **Yield: 8 cups.**

Approx Per Cup: Cal 239; Prot <1 g; Carbo 62 g; Fiber 3 g;
    T Fat <1 g; 1% Calories from Fat; Chol 0 mg; Sod 2 mg.

Rose Holcomb, Petoskey

Cranberry Sauce with Fruit

1 small orange
1 3-ounce package raspberry gelatin
1½ cups boiling water
1 16-ounce can cranberry sauce

1 small apple, peeled, finely chopped
⅛ teaspoon cinnamon
⅛ teaspoon cloves

Peel orange; grate rind and set aside. Chop orange into small pieces. Dissolve gelatin in boiling water in bowl. Stir in cranberry sauce. Chill until partially set. Stir in grated orange rind, chopped orange, apple, cinnamon and cloves. Spoon into mold. Chill until set. Invert onto serving plate. **Yield: 6 servings.**

Approx Per Serving: Cal 183; Prot 2 g; Carbo 46 g; Fiber 2 g;
    T.Fat <1 g; 1% Calories from Fat; Chol 0 mg; Sod 67 mg.

June Adams, Sault Ste. Marie

Deluxe Cranberry Sauce

1 pound fresh cranberries
2½ cups sugar
2 tablespoons butter

1 cup toasted chopped walnuts
Juice of 1 lemon or lime
1 10-ounce jar orange marmalade

Rinse cranberries. Spread in single layer in 9x13-inch baking pan. Sprinkle with sugar. Dot with butter. Bake, tightly covered with foil, at 350 degrees for 1 hour. Cool in pan. Combine baked mixture, walnuts, lemon juice and marmalade in bowl; mix well. Chill until serving time. **Yield: 16 servings.**

Approx Per Serving: Cal 242; Prot 1 g; Carbo 49 g; Fiber 2 g;
    T Fat 6 g; 22% Calories from Fat; Chol 4 mg; Sod 18 mg.

Nancy Neuhaus, Grand Rapids

Diet Jam

1 cup mashed strawberries
¾ cup sugar-free strawberry soft
    drink

1 3-ounce package sugar-free
    strawberry gelatin
3 envelopes artificial sweetener

Mix mashed strawberries and strawberry drink in saucepan. Bring to a boil. Simmer for 1 minute. Add gelatin, stirring until dissolved. Stir in sweetener. Pour into hot sterilized jars, leaving ½ inch headspace; seal with 2-piece lids. Store in refrigerator. **Yield: 2 cups.**

Approx Per Cup: Cal 132; Prot 3 g; Carbo 30 g; Fiber 6 g;
    T Fat 1 g; 5% Calories from Fat; Chol 0 mg; Sod 108 mg.

Anne West, Niagara, Wisconsin

Green Pepper Jelly

4 large green bell peppers
6 cups sugar
1¹/₂ cups white vinegar

1 bottle of Certo
¹/₈ teaspoon cayenne pepper
2 to 3 drops of green food coloring

Purée green peppers in blender or food processor. Combine with sugar and vinegar in large saucepan. Bring to a boil. Simmer for 10 minutes, stirring frequently. Stir in Certo, cayenne pepper and food coloring. Pack into hot sterilized jars, leaving ¹/₂ inch headspace; seal with 2-piece lids. Process in boiling water bath for 10 minutes. Serve on crackers with cream cheese. **Yield: 8 cups.**

Approx Per Cup: Cal 595; Prot 1 g; Carbo 155 g; Fiber 1 g;
    T Fat <1 g; 0% Calories from Fat; Chol 0 mg; Sod 7 mg.

Cathy DeGoede, Grand Rapids

Green Tomato Jam

4 green tomatoes
2 cups sugar

1   3-ounce package raspberry gelatin

Purée tomatoes in blender. Combine with sugar in saucepan. Bring to a boil. Simmer for 20 minutes, stirring frequently. Stir in gelatin. Cook until gelatin is dissolved. Pour into hot sterilized jars, leaving ¹/₂ inch headspace; seal with 2-piece lids. Process in boiling water bath for 10 minutes. **Yield: 4 cups.**

Approx Per Cup: Cal 494; Prot 4 g; Carbo 125 g; Fiber 0 g;
    T Fat 1 g; 1% Calories from Fat; Chol 0 mg; Sod 86 mg.

Sally Taylor, Marquette

Pineapple-Berry Relish

1   20-ounce can crushed pineapple, drained
2   16-ounce cans whole cranberry sauce

1   16-ounce package frozen whole strawberries, thawed, drained
¹/₂ cup chopped walnuts

Combine pineapple, cranberry sauce, strawberries and walnuts in bowl; mix well. Chill until serving time. **Yield: 16 servings.**

Approx Per Serving: Cal 138; Prot 1 g; Carbo 30 g; Fiber 3 g;
    T Fat 2 g; 15% Calories from Fat; Chol 0 mg; Sod 18 mg.

Marilyn Rogers, Lansing

Barbecue Sauce

2 tablespoons butter
1 onion, chopped
2 tablespoons vinegar
2 tablespoons brown sugar
1/4 cup lemon juice
1 cup catsup

3 tablespoons Worcestershire sauce
1 tablespoon mustard
1 cup water
1/2 cup chopped celery
Salt and red pepper to taste

Melt butter in saucepan. Add onion. Sauté until brown. Add vinegar, brown sugar, lemon juice, catsup, Worcestershire sauce, mustard, water, celery, salt and red pepper; mix well. Simmer for 15 minutes or until flavors are well blended. Store in refrigerator. May serve over chicken, pork or beef. **Yield: 3 cups.**

Approx Per Cup: Cal 242; Prot 3 g; Carbo 42 g; Fiber 3 g;
     T Fat 8 g; 30% Calories from Fat; Chol 21 mg; Sod 1248 mg.

Evelyn D. Colley, Big Rapids

M-J Barbecue Sauce

1 gallon barbecue sauce
1   32-ounce bottle of catsup
1   5-ounce bottle of Tabasco sauce
Juice of 1 lemon

1   1-pound package brown sugar
2 1/2 cups sugar
1/2 cup vinegar

Combine barbecue sauce, catsup, Tabasco sauce, lemon juice, brown sugar, sugar and vinegar in large saucepan; mix well. Cook over medium-low heat for 30 to 45 minutes, stirring frequently. **Yield: 16 cups.**

Approx Per Cup: Cal 448; Prot 5 g; Carbo 98 g; Fiber 3 g;
     T Fat 6 g; 12% Calories from Fat; Chol 0 mg; Sod 2681 mg.

Janice Sweet Fairley, Jackson

Bleu Cheese Butter

2 cups butter, softened
6 ounces bleu cheese, crumbled

2 teaspoons Worcestershire sauce

Cream butter in mixer bowl until light and fluffy. Add cheese and Worcestershire sauce; beat until well mixed. Store, covered, in refrigerator. Serve on hot cooked vegetables, baked potatoes, grilled steaks or hamburger buns. **Yield: 2 1/2 cups.**

Approx Per Cup: Cal 1544; Prot 16 g; Carbo 2 g; Fiber 0 g;
     T Fat 167 g; 95% Calories from Fat; Chol 448 mg; Sod 2226 mg.

Sally Taylor, Marquette

Chili Sauce

36 tomatoes
6 onions, ground
3 red bell peppers, ground
3 green bell peppers, ground
8 stalks celery, ground
3 tablespoons salt

3 cups vinegar
5 cups sugar
2 drops of oil of cinnamon
2 drops of oil of cloves
1/8 teaspoon hot pepper sauce

Cook tomatoes in large saucepan until juice comes to a boil. Remove from heat; strain into bowl. Stir in onions, peppers and celery. Add remaining ingredients; mix well. Spoon into large baking pan. Bake at 300 degrees for 4 hours. **Yield: 10 pints.**

Approx Per Pint: Cal 528; Prot 6 g; Carbo 134 g; Fiber 9 g;
    T Fat 1 g; 2% Calories from Fat; Chol 0 mg; Sod 1989 mg.

Lynn Tonka, Saginaw

Blender Hollandaise

4 egg yolks
1 1/2 teaspoons water
1 1/2 cups melted clarified butter
1/4 teaspoon white pepper

1 1/2 teaspoons fresh lemon juice
4 drops of Tabasco sauce
1/2 teaspoon salt

Combine egg yolks and water in blender container. Process at high speed for 10 seconds. Add melted butter in slow steady stream, processing constantly at low speed; mixture will thicken. Add white pepper, lemon juice, Tabasco sauce and salt; mix well with wire whisk. Use butter only at 110 degrees or less. **Yield: 2 cups.**

Approx Per Cup: Cal 1347; Prot 7 g; Carbo 1 g; Fiber <1 g;
    T Fat 149 g; 98% Calories from Fat; Chol 799 mg; Sod 1711 mg.

Robert Miller, Lansing

Mustard Sauce

1/2 cup dry mustard
1/2 cup vinegar
1/3 cup sugar
1/8 teaspoon salt

1 egg, beaten
1 1/4 cups mayonnaise-type salad
    dressing

Mix dry mustard and vinegar in bowl. Let stand for several hours to overnight. Combine with sugar, salt and egg in saucepan. Cook over medium-low heat until thickened, stirring occasionally. Cool. Stir in salad dressing. **Yield: 2 1/2 cups.**

Approx Per Cup: Cal 741; Prot 11 g; Carbo 69 g; Fiber 0 g;
    T Fat 51 g; 59% Calories from Fat; Chol 115 mg; Sod 970 mg.

Jeanne DeLaney, Traverse City

Mushroom Sauce

1 cup dry red wine
1/2 yellow onion, finely chopped
8 ounces mushrooms, thinly sliced
1/8 teaspoon crumbled dried thyme
1/8 teaspoon crumbled dried rosemary

1 1/2 cups low-sodium beef broth
1 tablespoon tomato paste
1 tablespoon cornstarch
2 tablespoons water

Combine wine, onion, mushrooms, thyme and rosemary in heavy saucepan. Bring to a boil. Cook over medium-high heat for 5 to 10 minutes or until liquid is reduced to 1/2 cup. Stir in beef broth and tomato paste. Simmer, covered, for 30 minutes. Stir in mixture of cornstarch and water. Cook until slightly thickened, stirring constantly. Serve over meat or poultry. **Yield: 2 cups.**

Approx Per Cup: Cal 796; Prot 3 g; Carbo 87 g; Fiber 3 g;
    T Fat 37 g; 41% Calories from Fat; Chol 0 mg; Sod 17 mg.

Lois Roggenbeck, Saginaw

Sweet and Spicy Mustard

1/4 cup flour
1/4 cup sugar
2 tablespoons dry mustard

5 tablespoons vinegar
1 1/2 tablespoons melted margarine
1 cup sour cream

Mix flour, sugar and dry mustard in bowl. Bring vinegar to a boil in saucepan. Stir into flour mixture. Add melted margarine; mix well. Stir in sour cream. Spoon into airtight jar. Chill for 24 hours. **Yield: 1 1/2 cups.**

Approx Per Cup: Cal 701; Prot 10 g; Carbo 63 g; Fiber 1 g;
    T Fat 48 g; 59% Calories from Fat; Chol 68 mg; Sod 217 mg.

Bernadine A. Johan, Glendale, Arizona

Salt-Less Surprise Seasoning

16 teaspoons garlic powder
8 teaspoons aniseed
8 teaspoons powdered lemon rind

8 teaspoons basil
8 teaspoons oregano

Mix garlic powder, aniseed, lemon rind, basil and oregano in bowl. Spoon into airtight glass container. Use in soups or almost any dish you wish.
Yield: 16 tablespoons.

Approx Per Tablespoon: Cal 18; Prot 1 g; Carbo 4 g; Fiber <1 g;
    T Fat <1 g; 12% Calories from Fat; Chol 0 mg; Sod 1 mg.

Julius L. Cavitch, Kalkaska

Sausage Stuffing

8 ounces lean pork sausage
1 cup chopped celery
1/2 cup chopped onion
8 cups dry bread crumbs

1 1/2 teaspoons rubbed marjoram
1/2 teaspoon salt
1/8 teaspoon pepper
1 cup (about) hot milk

Brown sausage in skillet, stirring until crumbly. Cook celery and onion in sausage drippings in skillet. Mix sausage, celery mixture, bread crumbs, marjoram, salt and pepper in bowl. Stir in just enough milk to hold stuffing together. Stuff turkey. Roast using turkey package instructions. **Yield: 10 cups.**

Approx Per Cup: Cal 405; Prot 14 g; Carbo 61 g; Fiber 4 g;
    T Fat 12 g; 27% Calories from Fat; Chol 39 mg; Sod 892 mg.

Marian Kasper, Saginaw

Turkey Dressing

1 1/2 pounds ground pork
1 cup chopped onion
1 pound butter
2   14-ounce cans chicken broth
1   10-ounce can cream of chicken soup

2 cups chopped celery
2   15-ounce packages croutons
1   7-ounce package croutons, crushed
1 teaspoon salt
4 teaspoons sage

Brown pork and onion in skillet, stirring frequently; drain. Combine butter, broth, soup and celery in large saucepan. Cook until butter is melted, stirring frequently. Combine pork mixture, soup mixture, croutons, salt and sage in bowl; mix well. Stuff turkey. Roast using turkey package instructions. Do not substitute sausage for ground pork in this recipe. **Yield: 12 cups.**

Approx Per Cup: Cal 716; Prot 25 g; Carbo 67 g; Fiber 1 g;
    T Fat 39 g; 49% Calories from Fat; Chol 120 mg; Sod 2039 mg.

Ann Hull, Charlotte

Turkey Stuffing

2 pounds bulk pork sausage
1/2 stalk celery, chopped
8 onions, chopped
1/2 bunch parsley, chopped

1 teaspoon poultry seasoning
1 loaf bread, crumbled
1 egg, beaten

Brown sausage in skillet, stiring until crumbly; drain. Add celery, onions, parsley and poultry seasoning. Simmer for 30 minutes. Combine with bread and egg in bowl; mix well. Stuff turkey. Roast using turkey package instructions. **Yield: 10 cups.**

Approx Per Cup: Cal 333; Prot 15 g; Carbo 33 g; Fiber 4 g;
    T Fat 16 g; 43% Calories from Fat; Chol 56 mg; Sod 797 mg.

Mrs. Ed Haynack, Farwell

Cajun Rice Casserole

8 ounces bacon
1 large onion, chopped
8 ounces okra, trimmed, chopped
2   16-ounce cans tomatoes
1   10-ounce can tomatoes with green
   chilies

3 tablespoons dried parsley flakes
Salt and pepper to taste
1 teaspoon garlic salt
1 teaspoon onion salt
3 cups hot cooked rice

Cook bacon in skillet until crisp-fried and crumbly. Remove bacon to paper towel to drain. Crumble bacon. Add onion to bacon drippings in skillet. Sauté until golden. Add okra, tomatoes, tomatoes with chilies, parsley, salt, pepper, garlic salt and onion salt; mix well. Simmer for 1½ hours. Spoon over rice. Top with crumbled bacon. **Yield: 6 servings.**

Approx Per Serving: Cal 358; Prot 8 g; Carbo 38 g; Fiber 4 g;
   T Fat 20 g; 49% Calories from Fat; Chol 91 mg; Sod 1360 mg.

Sally Taylor, Marquette

Dirty Rice

½ cup margarine
¾ cup vermicelli, crushed into small
   pieces
1 large onion, chopped

1 clove of garlic, minced
3   14-ounce cans consommé
1¾ cups long grain rice
3 bay leaves

Melt margarine in heavy skillet. Add vermicelli. Cook until brown, stirring constantly. Add onion, garlic and consommé; mix well. Bring to a boil. Add rice and bay leaves. Cook, covered, over high heat for 10 minutes; stir. Reduce heat to low. Cook, covered, for 25 minutes longer. Remove bay leaves. May add 1 small can shrimp, mushrooms and/or water chestnuts. **Yield: 10 servings.**

Approx Per Serving: Cal 248; Prot 8 g; Carbo 32 g; Fiber 1 g;
   T Fat 9 g; 34% Calories from Fat; Chol 0 mg; Sod 727 mg.

Doris Ratell, Tawas City

*Reheat cooked rice in a metal strainer over a pan of steaming
water; cover with foil and steam for 15 minutes.*

California Stir-Fry

2 ounces uncooked spaghetti
2 tablespoons peanut oil
1 medium onion, chopped
1 medium green bell pepper, chopped
1 or 2 cloves of garlic, minced

2 cups California blend mixed
  vegetables
1/4 to 1/3 cup water
2 cups cooked rice

Break spaghetti into 1-inch lengths. Sauté in peanut oil in skillet. Add onion and green pepper. Stir-fry until tender. Add garlic and California vegetables. Stir-fry until tender-crisp. Add water and rice; mix well. Simmer, covered, for 10 minutes, stirring occasionally. Serve with sprinkle of soy sauce and sesame oil. May cook rice with chicken bouillon cube or substitute vegetable of choice for California blend. **Yield: 6 servings.**

Approx Per Serving: Cal 199; Prot 5 g; Carbo 35 g; Fiber 4 g;
    T Fat 5 g; 22% Calories from Fat; Chol 0 mg; Sod 23 mg.

John McKenna, Lansing

Spanish Rice

1 pound ground beef
8 slices bacon
1 cup chopped onion
1/4 cup chopped green bell pepper
1 16-ounce can tomatoes
1 1/2 cups water

3/4 cup minute rice
1/2 cup catsup
1 tablespoon brown sugar
1 teaspoon salt
1/2 teaspoon Worcestershire sauce
1/8 teaspoon pepper

Brown ground beef in skillet, stirring until crumbly; drain. Cook bacon in skillet until crisp; drain, reserving half the drippings. Crumble bacon. Cook onion and green pepper in reserved drippings in skillet until tender. Stir in ground beef, tomatoes, water, rice, catsup, brown sugar and seasonings. Cook, covered, for 30 to 40 minutes or until heated through. Sprinkle with bacon. **Yield: 6 servings.**

Approx Per Serving: Cal 365; Prot 19 g; Carbo 23 g; Fiber 2 g;
    T Fat 22 g; 54% Calories from Fat; Chol 97 mg; Sod 967 mg.

Bonnie Hammond, Westland

Wild Rice with Raisins and Mushrooms

2 cups chicken broth
1 cup water
1 cup wild rice

1/2 cup seedless raisins
1   4-ounce can mushrooms

Combine broth and water in saucepan. Bring to a boil. Add rice, raisins and undrained mushrooms. Cook, covered, for 1 hour or until rice is tender. **Yield: 6 servings.**

Approx Per Serving: Cal 153; Prot 6 g; Carbo 32 g; Fiber 1 g;
    T Fat 1 g; 4% Calories from Fat; Chol <1 mg; Sod 343 mg.

Marge Venable, Grand Blanc

Country Garden Fettucini

1/4 cup margarine
2 cups chopped broccoli
2 cups sliced carrots
1 cup sliced asparagus
1 cup sliced summer squash
1/2 cup sliced green onions
3/4 cup cubed Velveeta cheese

1 cup half and half
1/2 cup water
1 1/2 cups finely chopped ham
1/2 teaspoon salt
1/4 teaspoon red pepper
4 cups cooked noodles

Melt margarine in skillet. Add broccoli, carrots, asparagus and squash. Stir-fry for 5 to 8 minutes or until tender-crisp. Add next 7 ingredients. Cook until cheese is melted and mixture is bubbly, stirring frequently. Serve over noodles. **Yield: 8 servings.**

Approx Per Serving: Cal 293; Prot 15 g; Carbo 25 g; Fiber 4 g;
    T Fat 15 g; 46% Calories from Fat; Chol 61 mg; Sod 728 mg.

Kathy Dohm-Beiser, Traverse City

Cheesy Vegetable Lasagna

2/3 cup water
1   28-ounce jar spaghetti sauce
2   4-ounce cans mushroom pieces
2 cups cottage cheese
1/2 cup grated Parmesan cheese

1   10-ounce package frozen chopped
    spinach, thawed, drained
6 lasagna noodles, cooked
2 cups shredded mozzarella cheese

Mix water, spaghetti sauce and mushrooms in medium bowl. Mix cottage cheese, Parmesan cheese and spinach in large bowl. Layer noodles, mushroom mixture, spinach mixture and mozzarella cheese 1/2 at a time in lightly greased 8x12-inch baking dish. Chill, covered, for 8 hours. Bake at 350 degrees for 1 hour. **Yield: 12 servings.**

Approx Per Serving: Cal 241; Prot 14 g; Carbo 25 g; Fiber 2 g;
    T Fat 10 g; 37% Calories from Fat; Chol 22 mg; Sod 705 mg.

Pat Lueder, Holt

Lasagna Squares

1/2 10-ounce package frozen
  chopped spinach
1/2 green bell pepper, chopped
1 small onion, chopped
1 tablespoon oil
1 28-ounce can tomatoes, puréed
2/3 cup tomato sauce
1/8 teaspoon parsley

1 1/2 teaspoons oregano
1 1/2 pounds cottage cheese
1 egg, beaten
3/4 cup grated Parmesan cheese
1 teaspoon salt
1/4 teaspoon pepper
8 ounces lasagna noodles, cooked
8 ounces mozzarella cheese, shredded

Cook spinach using package directions; drain. Sauté green pepper and onion in oil in skillet. Stir in tomatoes, tomato sauce, parsley and oregano. Simmer for 20 minutes. Combine spinach, cottage cheese, egg, 1/4 cup Parmesan cheese, salt, and pepper in bowl; mix well. Layer 1/3 of the tomato mixture, 1/3 of the noodles, half the spinach mixture, half the mozzarella cheese and 1/4 cup Parmesan cheese in 9x13-inch baking dish. Add 1/2 of the tomato mixture, 1/2 of the noodles, remaining spinach mixture, remaining noodles, remaining tomato mixture, 1/4 cup Parmesan cheese and remaining mozzarella cheese. Bake at 350 degrees for 45 minutes. Let stand for several minutes. **Yield: 8 servings.**

Approx Per Serving: Cal 368; Prot 26 g; Carbo 32 g; Fiber 2 g;
  T Fat 15 g; 37% Calories from Fat; Chol 67 mg; Sod 1166 mg.

Grace M. Taylor, East Grand Rapids

Macaroni and Cheese

8 ounces macaroni
1 teaspoon melted butter
1 egg, beaten
1 teaspoon salt
1 teaspoon dry mustard

1 tablespoon hot water
1 cup milk
3 cups shredded sharp Cheddar
  cheese

Cook macaroni in boiling water in saucepan; drain. Stir in melted butter and egg. Mix salt, dry mustard and hot water in bowl. Stir in milk. Add 2 1/2 cups cheese; mix well. Stir into macaroni. Spoon into buttered casserole. Sprinkle with remaining 1/2 cup cheese. Bake at 350 degrees for 45 minutes or until custard is set and top is crusty. **Yield: 8 servings.**

Approx Per Serving: Cal 310; Prot 16 g; Carbo 24 g; Fiber 1 g;
  T Fat 17 g; 49% Calories from Fat; Chol 77 mg; Sod 555 mg.

Sally Taylor, Marquette

Macaroni and Cheese Deluxe

1   17-ounce package macaroni
2 cups small curd cottage cheese
1 egg, slightly beaten
1 cup sour cream

8 ounces American cheese, shredded
Salt and pepper to taste
Paprika to taste

Cook macaroni using package directions; drain. Mix macaroni, cottage cheese, egg, sour cream, cheese, salt and pepper in bowl. Spoon into 9x9-inch baking dish. Sprinkle with paprika. Bake at 350 degrees for 45 minutes. **Yield: 6 servings.**

Approx Per Serving: Cal 604; Prot 29 g; Carbo 65 g; Fiber 3 g;
    T Fat 25 g; 37% Calories from Fat; Chol 99 mg; Sod 857 mg.

Carl N. Clark, Lansing

Macaroni Mousse

1½ cups scalded milk
¼ cup melted margarine
3 eggs, well beaten
1 pimento, chopped
1 cup cooked macaroni
1 green bell pepper, chopped

1 tablespoon chopped onion
½ teaspoon salt
½ cup soft bread crumbs
½ cup shredded Cheddar cheese
½ cup sliced mushrooms
½ cup soft bread crumbs

Combine milk, melted margarine, eggs, pimento, macaroni, green pepper, onion, salt, ½ cup crumbs, cheese and mushrooms in bowl; mix well. Spoon into casserole. Sprinkle with ½ cup crumbs. Place casserole in pan of hot water. Bake at 350 degrees for 40 minutes. **Yield: 4 servings.**

Approx Per Serving: Cal 355; Prot 14 g; Carbo 21 g; Fiber 1 g;
    T Fat 24 g; 61% Calories from Fat; Chol 218 mg; Sod 600 mg.

Mrs. L. Hayden, Kalamazoo

Cheese Noodles Parmesan

1   16-ounce package egg noodles
4 cups whipping cream
3 eggs

1 cup grated Parmesan cheese
1 tablespoon minced onion flakes

Cook noodles using package directions; drain. Mix whipping cream, eggs, cheese and onion flakes in bowl. Pour over hot noodles; toss to coat. Let stand, covered, for 10 minutes. Serve at room temperature. Garnish with fresh basil or parsley. **Yield: 12 servings.**

Approx Per Serving: Cal 471; Prot 11 g; Carbo 29 g; Fiber <1 g;
    T Fat 35 g; 66% Calories from Fat; Chol 233 mg; Sod 179 mg.

Deanna Eisenzimmer, Davison

Cheese and Spinach Manicotti

1 8-ounce package manicotti	1/2 cup grated Parmesan cheese
1 8-ounce can Italian tomato sauce	1 10-ounce package frozen chopped
1/4 cup chopped onion	spinach, thawed, drained
1 clove of garlic, crushed	1/2 teaspoon salt
1 tablespoon butter	1/4 teaspoon pepper
1 cup shredded mozzarella cheese	1/2 teaspoon Italian seasoning
1 cup small curd cottage cheese	1/2 cup shredded mozzarella cheese

Cook manicotti using package directions; drain. Cover bottom of 9x12-inch baking pan with 1/3 of the Italian sauce. Sauté onion and garlic in butter in small skillet until onion is tender. Combine 1 cup mozzarella, cottage cheese, Parmesan cheese, spinach, salt, pepper, Italian seasoning and onion mixture in bowl; mix well. Spoon into cooked manicotti. Arrange in pan. Cover with remaining Italian sauce. Sprinkle with 1/2 cup mozzarella cheese. Bake, covered, at 350 degrees for 40 minutes. **Yield: 8 servings.**

Approx Per Serving: Cal 249; Prot 15 g; Carbo 27 g; Fiber 3 g;
     T Fat 9 g; 34% Calories from Fat; Chol 28 mg; Sod 552 mg.

Elaine Baird, Saginaw

Father Kim's Fried Noodles

1 1-pound package spaghetti	1 8-ounce can bamboo shoots
3 tablespoons oil	Salt and pepper to taste
1 clove of garlic, minced	Finely chopped green onions to taste
2 teaspoons chopped ginger	1/2 cup water
7 ounces pork, finely chopped	1 tablespoon cornstarch
4 stalks celery, cut julienne-style	

Cook spaghetti using package directions; drain. Stir in 2 tablespoons oil. Cook spaghetti in skillet until beginning to brown, turning frequently. Remove to serving bowl. Add 1 tablespoon oil, garlic and ginger to skillet. Cook for 1 minute. Add pork, celery, bamboo shoots, salt, pepper, green onions and 1/2 cup water. Cook until heated through. Stir in mixture of cornstarch and a small amount of water. Pour over spaghetti. **Yield: 5 servings.**

Approx Per Serving: Cal 486; Prot 20 g; Carbo 73 g; Fiber 6 g;
     T Fat 12 g; 23% Calories from Fat; Chol 24 mg; Sod 52 mg.

Grace Cameron, Brethren

Spinach and Spaghetti

1 10-ounce package frozen chopped
  spinach
1 egg, beaten
1/2 cup sour cream
1/4 cup milk
2 tablespoons grated Parmesan
  cheese
2 teaspoons minced dried onion

1/2 teaspoon salt
1/8 teaspoon pepper
2 cups shredded Monterey Jack
  cheese
4 ounces spaghetti, cooked, drained
2 tablespoons grated Parmesan
  cheese

Cook spinach using package directions; drain. Combine egg, sour cream, milk, 2 tablespoons Parmesan cheese, onion, salt and pepper in bowl; mix well. Stir in Monterey Jack cheese. Add spaghetti; mix well. Turn into ungreased 6x10-inch baking dish. Sprinkle with 2 tablespoons Parmesan cheese. Bake, covered, at 350 degrees for 15 minutes. Bake, uncovered, for 15 to 20 minutes longer or until heated through. **Yield: 4 servings.**

Approx Per Serving: Cal 452; Prot 25 g; Carbo 28 g; Fiber 3 g;
    T Fat 27 g; 53% Calories from Fat; Chol 124 mg; Sod 765 mg.

Joan Keeney, Lansing

Bacon Spaghetti

8 ounces bacon, cut into quarters
1 small onion, chopped
1/2 green bell pepper, chopped
8 ounces uncooked spaghetti, broken
  into 2-inch pieces

1 16-ounce can tomatoes
1 1/2 cups boiling water
1/2 teaspoon salt
1/8 teaspoon pepper
1/4 cup grated Parmesan cheese

Sauté bacon, onion and green pepper in skillet until bacon is almost crisp; drain. Add spaghetti, tomatoes, boiling water, salt and pepper. Simmer, tightly covered, for 20 minutes, stirring occasionally. Sprinkle with cheese. **Yield: 8 servings.**

Approx Per Serving: Cal 182; Prot 8 g; Carbo 25 g; Fiber 2 g;
    T Fat 5 g; 27% Calories from Fat; Chol 9 mg; Sod 409 mg.

Howard French, Grand Rapids

PLANTING SEEDLING & FLOWERS

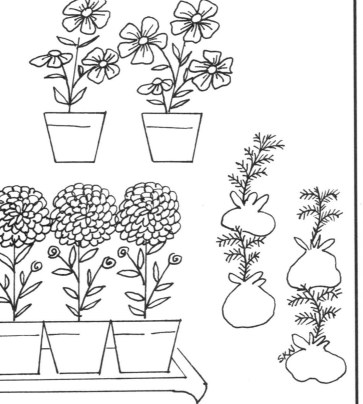

Breads

Danish Puffs

1 cup melted margarine
1½ cups cottage cheese
2 cups flour
1 cup confectioners' sugar

2 tablespoons margarine, softened
2 teaspoons maple extract
¼ cup (about) milk

Combine 1 cup margarine, cottage cheese and flour in bowl; mix well. Chill, covered, in refrigerator overnight. Divide into 3 portions. Roll each portion into a circle. Cut into 16 wedges. Roll each wedge, beginning at large end. Place on baking sheet. Bake at 350 degrees for 20 to 25 minutes. Let stand until cool. Mix confectioners' sugar, 2 tablespoons margarine and maple extract in bowl. Stir in enough milk to make of spreading consistency. Spread on cooled puffs. **Yield: 48 servings.**

Approx Per Serving: Cal 75; Prot 1 g; Carbo 7 g; Fiber <1 g;
    T Fat 5 g; 56% Calories from Fat; Chol 1 mg; Sod 77 mg.

Harriett De Vries, Kalamazoo

Almond French Toast

3 eggs, slightly beaten
⅛ teaspoon salt
1 tablespoon sugar
1½ cups milk

½ teaspoon almond extract
16   ½-inch thick slices French bread
Strawberry Butter

Combine eggs, salt, sugar, milk and almond extract in shallow dish; mix well. Dip bread in mixture, turning to coat both sides. Bake on hot well oiled griddle until golden brown, turning once. Serve with Strawberry Butter. **Yield: 8 servings.**

Strawberry Butter

1   10-ounce package frozen
    strawberries, thawed

½ cup butter, softened
¼ cup confectioners' sugar

Combine strawberries, butter and confectioners' sugar in food processor container. Process until smooth. Store in refrigerator.

Approx Per Serving: Cal 393; Prot 11 g; Carbo 46 g; Fiber 2 g;
    T Fat 18 g; 41% Calories from Fat; Chol 117 mg; Sod 582 mg.

Jo Marshall, Traverse City

Egg Beaters French Toast

1 8-ounce carton Egg Beaters
⅓ cup skim milk
1 teaspoon cinnamon

1 teaspoon vanilla extract
10 slices low-sodium bread
2 tablespoons margarine

Combine Egg Beaters, milk, cinnamon and vanilla in shallow dish. Dip bread in mixture, turning to coat both sides. Cook bread in margarine in skillet over medium heat for 3 minutes or until golden brown, turning once. **Yield: 5 servings.**

Approx Per Serving: Cal 225; Prot 12 g; Carbo 29 g; Fiber 0 g;
    T Fat 7 g; 26% Calories from Fat; Chol 1 mg; Sod 192 mg.

Loraine Metzger, Lansing

Macadamia French Toast

4 eggs
⅔ cup orange juice
⅓ cup milk
¼ cup sugar
¼ teaspoon nutmeg

½ teaspoon vanilla extract
1 8-ounce loaf Italian bread, cut
    into 1-inch slices
⅓ cup melted butter
½ cup macadamia nuts, chopped

Combine eggs, orange juice, milk, sugar, nutmeg and vanilla in bowl; mix well. Place bread in single layer in shallow dish. Pour egg mixture over bread. Chill, covered, overnight, turning once. Arrange bread slices side by side in 10x15-inch baking pan coated with butter. Sprinkle with macadamia nuts. Bake at 400 degrees for 20 to 25 minutes or until French toast tests done. May serve with syrup. **Yield: 4 servings.**

Approx Per Serving: Cal 566; Prot 14 g; Carbo 53 g; Fiber 2 g;
    T Fat 34 g; 54% Calories from Fat; Chol 257 mg; Sod 539 mg.

Dorothy Louise Zeller, St. Joseph

Beer Doughnuts

3 cups flour
2 tablespoons sugar
1 12-ounce bottle of warm beer

Oil for deep frying
½ cup sugar

Combine flour, sugar and beer in bowl; mix well. Roll dough on floured surface. Cut with doughnut cutter. Deep-fry in hot oil until golden brown. Coat with sugar. **Yield: 12 servings.**

Approx Per Serving: Cal 165; Prot 3 g; Carbo 35 g; Fiber 1 g;
    T Fat <1 g; 2% Calories from Fat; Chol 0 mg; Sod 2 mg.
    Nutritional analysis does not include oil for deep frying.

Arlene E. Hatch, Hill City, Minnesota

Banana Pancakes

1 very ripe banana, cut into pieces
1 egg
1 teaspoon margarine, softened

½ teaspoon vanilla extract
3 tablespoons flour
1 teaspoon baking powder

Combine banana, egg, margarine and vanilla in blender container. Process until smooth. Add flour and baking powder. Process until blended. Pour ¼ cup at a time into skillet sprayed with nonstick cooking spray. Bake until brown on both sides, turning once. **Yield: 2 servings.**

Approx Per Serving: Cal 154; Prot 5 g; Carbo 23 g; Fiber 1 g;
    T Fat 5 g; 29% Calories from Fat; Chol 106 mg; Sod 222 mg.

Joann Bouwman, Zeeland

Bran Pancakes

3 cups Raisin Bran cereal
2 cups All-Bran cereal
1 cup raisins
½ cup wheat germ
3 cups boiling water
2 cups whole wheat flour
1 cup nonfat dry milk powder

1⅓ cups all-purpose flour
½ cup packed brown sugar
5 teaspoons baking soda
2 teaspoons salt
7 eggs, slightly beaten
¾ cup oil
4 cups buttermilk

Combine cereals, raisins and wheat germ in large bowl. Stir in boiling water. Set aside. Combine whole wheat flour, dry milk powder, all-purpose flour, brown sugar, baking soda and salt in bowl; mix well. Add eggs, oil and buttermilk to cereal mixture; mix well. Stir in dry ingredients. Pour ¼ cup at a time onto hot lightly greased griddle. Bake until brown on both sides, turning once. Store unused batter in refrigerator. May substitute 14 egg whites or 1¾ cups egg substitute for eggs. **Yield: 24 servings.**

Approx Per Serving: Cal 254; Prot 8 g; Carbo 38 g; Fiber 5 g;
    T Fat 10 g; 32% Calories from Fat; Chol 64 mg; Sod 548 mg.

Elaine Hartwig, Gaylord

*Whip applesauce with light margarine to make
a low-calorie topping for pancakes.*

Great-Grandma's Egg Pancakes

5 eggs	7 tablespoons flour
¾ cup milk	Salt to taste

Combine eggs, milk, flour and salt in bowl; mix well. Batter will be thin. Pour a small amount at a time into buttered skillet. Cook over medium-high heat until golden brown. Turn pancake over. Cook until edges begin to curl. Cut into small pieces, using pancake turner. Serve with syrup. **Yield: 4 servings.**

Approx Per Serving: Cal 134; Prot 7 g; Carbo 13 g; Fiber <1 g;
    T Fat 6 g; 38% Calories from Fat; Chol 157 mg; Sod 68 mg.

Betty Boyd, Hemlock

Healthy Oat Pancakes

1½ cups quick-cooking oats	1 teaspoon baking soda
¼ cup uncooked oat bran cereal	1 teaspoon salt
2 cups low-fat buttermilk	1 packet artificial sweetener
4 egg whites, beaten	1 tablespoon oil
½ cup whole wheat flour	

Mix oats, cereal and buttermilk in bowl. Beat in egg whites. Sift in wheat flour, baking soda, salt and artificial sweetener; mix well. Stir in oil. Pour ¼ cup at a time onto hot lightly greased griddle. Bake until brown on both sides, turning once. May add 1 cup blueberries before baking. **Yield: 6 servings.**

Approx Per Serving: Cal 187; Prot 11 g; Carbo 28 g; Fiber 4 g;
    T Fat 5 g; 21% Calories from Fat; Chol 0 mg; Sod 634 mg.

Pat Schulte, Lansing

Whole Wheat Pancakes

1 cup whole wheat flour	½ teaspoon salt
1 cup all-purpose flour	2 eggs
4 teaspoons baking powder	2 cups milk

Combine flours, baking powder, salt, eggs and milk in bowl; mix just until moistened. Pour ¼ cup at a time onto hot lightly greased griddle. Bake until golden brown on both sides, turning once. Serve with butter and maple syrup.
Yield: 6 servings.

Approx Per Serving: Cal 222; Prot 10 g; Carbo 35 g; Fiber 3 g;
    T Fat 5 g; 21% Calories from Fat; Chol 82 mg; Sod 455 mg.

Cathy DeGoede, Grand Rapids

Oatmeal-Raisin Scones

1 cup flour
3 tablespoons brown sugar
1½ teaspoons baking powder
½ teaspoon cinnamon
⅓ cup margarine

1 cup quick-cooking oats
½ cup raisins, chopped
2 egg whites
2 tablespoons skim milk

Blend flour, brown sugar, baking powder and cinnamon in bowl. Cut in margarine until crumbly. Stir in oats and raisins. Add egg whites and milk, stirring until moistened. Pat dough in 7-inch circle on lightly floured surface. Cut into 12 wedges. Place on ungreased baking sheet. Brush with additional milk. Bake at 400 degrees for 10 to 12 minutes or until scones test done. **Yield: 12 servings.**

Approx Per Serving: Cal 146; Prot 3 g; Carbo 22 g; Fiber 1 g;
    T Fat 6 g; 34% Calories from Fat; Chol <1 mg; Sod 112 mg.

Teddy Zeedyk, Battle Creek

French Bread with Swiss Cheese

1 loaf French bread
¼ cup margarine, softened

6 ounces Swiss cheese slices
¼ cup bacon bits

Cut crust off top and sides of bread. Cut loaf into 1-inch slices to but not through bottom. Spread cut sides with margarine. Place ½ cheese slice and some bacon bits between each bread slice. Spread margarine over top and sides of bread; sprinkle any remaining bacon bits over top. Place on foil. Pull up foil to cover sides of bread, leaving top open. Bake at 400 degrees for 20 to 25 minutes. **Yield: 12 servings.**

Approx Per Serving: Cal 205; Prot 9 g; Carbo 20 g; Fiber 1 g;
    T Fat 9 g; 42% Calories from Fat; Chol 13 mg; Sod 344 mg.

Easy Mexican Corn Bread

1½ cups self-rising cornmeal
1 cup milk
½ cup oil
1   16-ounce can Mexicorn

2 eggs
1 teaspoon chili powder
½ teaspoon red pepper
1 cup shredded Monterey Jack cheese

Combine first 7 ingredients in bowl; mix well. Spoon half the batter into hot greased skillet. Sprinkle cheese over top. Spoon remaining batter over cheese. Bake at 350 degrees for 30 to 35 minutes or until corn bread tests done. **Yield: 8 servings.**

Approx Per Serving: Cal 367; Prot 10 g; Carbo 36 g; Fiber <1 g;
    T Fat 21 g; 51% Calories from Fat; Chol 70 mg; Sod 719 mg.

Anna J. Sells, Battle Creek

Mexicorn Bread

1 small onion, finely chopped
1 small banana pepper, finely
chopped
1/2 small green bell pepper, finely
chopped
1/2 small red bell pepper, finely
chopped
4 cloves of garlic, finely chopped

1/4 cup butter
1/4 cup sugar
4 teaspoons baking powder
1/2 teaspoon salt
1 cup unbleached flour
1 cup yellow cornmeal
2 eggs, slightly beaten
1 cup milk

Sauté onion, peppers and garlic in butter in skillet until tender. Remove from heat. Combine sugar, baking powder, salt, flour and cornmeal in large bowl. Whip eggs and milk together in small bowl. Stir into dry ingredients with sautéed vegetables. Spoon into greased 9x9-inch baking pan. Bake at 425 degrees for 20 to 25 minutes or until cornbread tests done. May add 2 tablespoons chili powder for variety. **Yield: 9 servings.**

Approx Per Serving: Cal 212; Prot 5 g; Carbo 31 g; Fiber 2 g;
T Fat 8 g; 33% Calories from Fat; Chol 65 mg; Sod 336 mg.

Peggy Yarrow, Flint

Mexican Corn Bread

2 eggs, slightly beaten
1 1/4 cups milk
3/4 cup shredded sharp Cheddar
cheese
1/2 cup oil
1/2 cup canned cream-style corn
1 medium onion, finely chopped

3 slices crisp-fried bacon, crumbled
2 tablespoons finely chopped
jalapeño peppers
1 1/4 cups yellow self-rising cornmeal
1/2 cup flour
1 tablespoon baking powder
1 teaspoon salt

Combine eggs, milk, cheese, oil, corn, onion, bacon and jalapeño peppers in large bowl; mix well. Stir in mixture of cornmeal, flour, baking powder and salt just until blended. Spoon into lightly buttered 10-inch ovenproof skillet. Bake at 350 degrees for 30 minutes. **Yield: 12 servings.**

Approx Per Serving: Cal 241; Prot 6 g; Carbo 22 g; Fiber 1 g;
T Fat 14 g; 54% Calories from Fat; Chol 48 mg; Sod 640 mg.

Nellie Thompson, Romulus

*Add crumbled crisp-fried bacon, cheese, green chilies or
whole kernel corn to your favorite corn bread recipe.*

Polenta

6 cups cold water
2 cups yellow cornmeal

1 tablespoon salt

Combine water, cornmeal and salt in deep saucepan. Cook over medium heat until thickened, stirring constantly. Reduce heat to medium-low. Cook for 30 minutes longer. Invert onto serving plate. May serve this old-world favorite with any meat dish. **Yield: 6 servings.**

Approx Per Serving: Cal 167; Prot 4 g; Carbo 36 g; Fiber 3 g;
   T Fat 1 g; 3% Calories from Fat; Chol 0 mg; Sod 1066 mg.

Aileen Pancheri, Sault Ste. Marie

Flour Tortillas

4 cups sifted flour
2 teaspoons salt

½ cup shortening
1 cup lukewarm water

Combine flour and salt in bowl. Cut in shortening until crumbly. Stir in lukewarm water to make stiff dough. Knead on floured surface 50 times. Divide into 12 portions. Shape each into a ball. Let stand, covered with damp cloth, for 15 minutes. Roll each ball into 8-inch circle. Cook in ungreased skillet over medium heat until golden brown, turning once. **Yield: 12 servings.**

Approx Per Serving: Cal 215; Prot 4 g; Carbo 29 g; Fiber 1 g;
   T Fat 9 g; 38% Calories from Fat; Chol 0 mg; Sod 356 mg.

Nancy Briolat, St. Ignace

Apple Coffee Cake

1½ cups oil
2 cups sugar
2 eggs
3 cups flour
1 teaspoon salt
1 teaspoon cinnamon

1 teaspoon baking soda
1 teaspoon vanilla extract
3 cups chopped apples
1 cup coconut
1 cup walnut pieces

Cream oil, sugar and eggs in bowl until light and fluffy. Add flour, salt, cinnamon, baking soda, vanilla, apples, coconut and walnuts; mix well. Spread in greased 9x12-inch baking pan. Bake at 325 degrees for 1 hour. Serve warm or cold. Garnish with whipped cream. **Yield: 12 servings.**

Approx Per Serving: Cal 608; Prot 6 g; Carbo 66 g; Fiber 3 g;
   T Fat 37 g; 53% Calories from Fat; Chol 36 mg; Sod 261 mg.

Ruby Kessinger, Eau Claire

Blueberry Coffee Cake

1/2 cup chopped walnuts
3/4 cup sugar
1 teaspoon cinnamon
5 cups flour
2 tablespoons baking powder
1 1/2 cups sugar

1 teaspoon salt
3/4 cup margarine
4 eggs
2 cups milk
2 teaspoons vanilla extract
1 1/2 cups fresh blueberries

Combine walnuts, 3/4 cup sugar and cinnamon in small bowl; mix well. Combine flour, baking powder, 1 1/2 cups sugar and salt in large bowl. Cut in margarine until crumbly. Combine eggs, milk and vanilla in bowl; mix well. Stir into flour mixture until moistened. Fold in blueberries gently. Spoon 1/3 of the batter into greased and floured 10-inch bundt pan. Layer walnut mixture and remaining batter 1/2 at a time into pan. Bake at 350 degrees for 1 hour and 10 minutes or until coffee cake tests done. Cool in pan for 15 minutes. Invert onto serving plate to cool completely.
Yield: 15 servings.

Approx Per Serving: Cal 427; Prot 8 g; Carbo 67 g; Fiber 2 g;
     T Fat 15 g; 31% Calories from Fat; Chol 61 mg; Sod 416 mg.

Althea Ondovcsik, Davison

Cardamom Coffee Bread

20 cardamom pods
7 to 8 1/2 cups flour
2 envelopes dry yeast
2/3 to 1 cup sugar
2 teaspoons salt
1 1/2 cups milk

1/2 cup water
1/2 cup butter
2 eggs
1 egg, slightly beaten
3 tablespoons sliced almonds

Crack cardamom pods open, removing seed. Crush seed. Combine 2 1/2 cups flour, yeast, sugar, salt and ground cardamom in large bowl; mix well. Combine milk, water and butter in saucepan. Cook over low heat to 130 degrees. Stir into flour mixture. Add 2 eggs. Beat at low speed until moistened. Beat at high speed for 5 minutes longer. Stir in 5 1/2 to 6 cups flour or enough to make soft dough. Add any remaining flour. Knead on lightly floured surface for 8 minutes or until smooth and elastic. Place in greased bowl, turning to coat surface. Let rise, covered, in warm place for 1 hour or until doubled in bulk. Punch dough down. Divide into 3 portions. Roll each into 18-inch rope. Shape into braids on 3 greased baking sheets; seal ends. Let rise, covered, in warm place for 20 to 30 minutes or until almost doubled. Brush gently with remaining egg; sprinkle with almonds. Bake at 350 degrees for 20 to 25 minutes or until golden brown. Cool on wire racks. May substitute 1 teaspoon ground cardamom for freshly crushed cardamom. **Yield: 36 servings.**

Approx Per Serving: Cal 170; Prot 4 g; Carbo 30 g; Fiber 1 g;
     T Fat 4 g; 22% Calories from Fat; Chol 26 mg; Sod 151 mg.

Patricia Virch, Marquette

Cinnamon Swirl Coffee Cake

1 cup butter, softened
1¼ cups sugar
2 eggs
1 cup sour cream
1 teaspoon vanilla extract
2 cups flour

1½ teaspoons baking powder
½ teaspoon baking soda
¾ cup chopped pecans
¼ cup sugar
1 teaspoon cinnamon
1¾ cups blueberries

Combine butter, 1¼ cups sugar, eggs, sour cream and vanilla in large mixer bowl. Beat at medium speed for 2 minutes. Add flour, baking powder and baking soda. Beat at low speed for 1 minute. Spread half the batter in greased 9x13-inch baking pan. Combine pecans, ¼ cup sugar and cinnamon in small bowl. Sprinkle half the mixture over batter layer. Layer remaining batter, blueberries and remaining pecan mixture over top. Bake at 350 degrees for 40 minutes. **Yield: 15 servings.**

Approx Per Serving: Cal 340; Prot 4 g; Carbo 37 g; Fiber 1 g;
    T Fat 21 g; 53% Calories from Fat; Chol 68 mg; Sod 183 mg.

Florence H. Canterbury, Burton

Crumb Coffee Cake

1 2-layer package yellow cake mix
1 4-ounce package butterscotch
   instant pudding mix
1 4-ounce package vanilla instant
   pudding mix
1 cup oil

1 cup water
4 eggs
1¼ cups packed brown sugar
1 tablespoon cinnamon
¾ to 1 cup crushed pecans

Combine cake mix, pudding mixes, oil, water and eggs in mixer bowl; beat for 2 minutes. Combine brown sugar, cinnamon and pecans in small bowl; mix well. Spread about ⅓ of the batter in greased 9x13-inch baking pan. Layer half the pecan mixture, remaining batter and remaining pecan mixture over top. Bake at 325 degrees for 50 to 55 minutes or until coffee cake tests done. **Yield: 15 servings.**

Approx Per Serving: Cal 476; Prot 4 g; Carbo 63 g; Fiber 1 g;
    T Fat 24 g; 45% Calories from Fat; Chol 57 mg; Sod 314 mg.

Mary Gabrion, Ithaca

Danish Coffee Cake

1 cup flour
1/3 teaspoon salt
1/2 cup margarine
2 tablespoons cold water
1/2 cup margarine

1 cup cold water
1 cup flour
1/8 teaspoon salt
1 tablespoon almond extract
3 eggs

Blend 1 cup flour and 1/3 teaspoon salt in bowl. Cut in 1/2 cup margarine until crumbly. Add 2 tablespoons cold water. Spread on baking sheet. Chill completely. Combine 1/2 cup margarine and 1 cup cold water in saucepan. Cook over medium heat until margarine melts. Add 1 cup flour and 1/8 teaspoon salt. Cook until mixture forms a ball, stirring constantly. Remove from heat. Stir in almond flavoring. Add eggs 1 at a time, beating well after each addition. Spread over chilled crust. Bake at 400 degrees for 10 minutes. Reduce oven temperature to 350 degrees. Bake for 40 minutes. Prick with fork. May serve plain or with thin confectioners' sugar glaze. **Yield: 15 servings.**

Approx Per Serving: Cal 188; Prot 3 g; Carbo 13 g; Fiber <1 g;
 T Fat 13 g; 65% Calories from Fat; Chol 43 mg; Sod 221 mg.

Lois Elliott, Escanaba

Easy Coffee Cake

2 8-count cans crescent rolls
16 ounces cream cheese, softened
1 cup sugar

1 egg
1 teaspoon vanilla extract

Spread half the crescent rolls in bottom of 9x13-inch baking pan coated with nonstick cooking spray. Beat cream cheese, sugar, egg and vanilla in mixer bowl until light and fluffy. Spread in prepared pan. Top with remaining crescent rolls. Bake at 350 degrees for 25 to 30 minutes. May drizzle with glaze. **Yield: 12 servings.**

Approx Per Serving: Cal 337; Prot 5 g; Carbo 32 g; Fiber 0 g;
 T Fat 21 g; 56% Calories from Fat; Chol 59 mg; Sod 425 mg.

Ruth Rummel, Reese

Hungarian Coffee Cake

1 cup margarine, softened
1¹/₂ cups sugar
2 eggs
1 teaspoon vanilla extract
2 cups sifted flour
¹/₂ teaspoon baking soda

¹/₂ teaspoon baking powder
¹/₂ teaspoon salt
1 cup sour cream
³/₄ cup chopped pecans
2 tablespoons sugar
12 maraschino cherries, chopped

Cream margarine, 1¹/₂ cups sugar, eggs and vanilla in bowl until light and fluffy. Sift flour, baking soda, baking powder and salt together. Add to creamed mixture with sour cream; mix well. Combine pecans, 2 tablespoons sugar and cherries in small bowl; mix well. Layer batter and pecan mixture ¹/₂ at a time into greased and floured tube pan. Place in cold oven. Turn oven to 350 degrees. Bake for 55 to 60 minutes or until coffee cake tests done. Cool completely on wire rack. Turn onto serving plate. **Yield: 16 servings.**

Approx Per Serving: Cal 316; Prot 3 g; Carbo 34 g; Fiber 1 g;
T Fat 19 g; 53% Calories from Fat; Chol 33 mg; Sod 254 mg.

Beverly Ward, Sault Ste. Marie

Swedish Coffee Bread

1 tablespoon plus 1 teaspoon dry
yeast
1 teaspoon sugar
¹/₂ cup lukewarm water
2 cups milk
¹/₂ cup butter

1 cup plus 2 teaspoons sugar
2 teaspoons salt
1¹/₂ teaspoons crushed cardamom
seed
3 eggs, well beaten
8¹/₂ cups bread flour

Dissolve yeast and 1 teaspoon sugar in lukewarm water. Combine milk, butter, 1 cup plus 2 teaspoons sugar, salt and cardamom seed in saucepan. Cook over medium heat until steaming hot, stirring frequently. Let stand until lukewarm. Combine with yeast mixture and eggs in large mixer bowl; mix well. Add flour. Knead for 8 to 10 minutes. Let rise, covered, in warm place until doubled in bulk. Divide dough into 3 portions. Roll each into 18-inch rope. Shape into braid on baking sheet; seal ends. Bake at 350 degrees for 35 minutes. **Yield: 36 servings.**

Approx Per Serving: Cal 168; Prot 4 g; Carbo 29 g; Fiber 1 g;
T Fat 4 g; 20% Calories from Fat; Chol 27 mg; Sod 152 mg.

Esther Erickson, Negaunee

Party Coffee Cake

2 cups sugar
1 cup margarine, softened
6 eggs, slightly beaten
1 tablespoon vanilla extract
2 cups sour cream
4 cups flour
1/2 teaspoon salt

1 1/2 teaspoons baking powder
1 teaspoon baking soda
1/2 1-pound package light brown
    sugar
1 cup chopped pecans
2 teaspoons cinnamon

Cream sugar and margarine in bowl until light and fluffy. Add eggs, vanilla and sour cream; mix well. Add mixture of flour, salt, baking powder and baking soda gradually, mixing well after each addition. Combine brown sugar, pecans and cinnamon in small bowl. Layer batter and brown sugar mixture 1/3 at a time into lightly greased tube pan. Bake at 350 degrees for 1 hour and 15 minutes. May add about 6 maraschino cherries with each brown sugar layer. **Yield: 16 servings.**

Approx Per Serving: Cal 509; Prot 7 g; Carbo 66 g; Fiber 1 g;
    T Fat 25 g; 43% Calories from Fat; Chol 93 mg; Sod 331 mg.

Pat Idalski, Hamtramck

Sour Cream Coffee Cake

3/4 cup margarine, softened
1 1/2 cups sugar
2 eggs
1 teaspoon vanilla extract
2 1/2 to 3 cups flour
1 teaspoon baking soda

1 teaspoon baking powder
1/4 teaspoon salt
2 cups sour cream
2 tablespoons brown sugar
1/2 cup chopped walnuts
1 1/2 teaspoons cinnamon

Cream margarine, sugar, eggs and vanilla in bowl until light and fluffy. Add flour, baking soda, baking powder, salt and sour cream; mix well. Combine brown sugar, walnuts and cinnamon in small bowl; mix well. Spoon half the batter into greased and floured tube pan. Top with brown sugar mixture and remaining batter. Bake at 350 degrees for 1 hour. **Yield: 16 servings.**

Approx Per Serving: Cal 338; Prot 5 g; Carbo 41 g; Fiber 1 g;
    T Fat 18 g; 47% Calories from Fat; Chol 39 mg; Sod 232 mg.

Rosemary Cramton, St. Charles

Overnight Coffee Cake

1 1-pound package frozen dinner
   rolls
1 4-ounce package vanilla pudding
   and pie filling mix

1/2 cup packed brown sugar
1 teaspoon cinnamon
1/2 cup melted margarine
1 cup chopped pecans

Arrange rolls in greased bundt pan. Sprinkle with mixture of pudding mix, brown sugar and cinnamon. Drizzle with margarine. Sprinkle pecans over top. Cover lightly with waxed paper. Let rise 8 hours or overnight. Bake at 350 degrees for 30 minutes. Invert onto serving plate. May substitute butterscotch pudding for vanilla pudding. **Yield: 16 servings.**

Approx Per Serving: Cal 244; Prot 3 g; Carbo 31 g; Fiber 1 g;
   T Fat 13 g; 46% Calories from Fat; Chol <1 mg; Sod 273 mg.

Carolyn Devers, Laingsburg
Carroll King, Brooklyn

Zucchini-Spice Coffee Cake

1 1/2 cups flour
1 1/4 cups quick-cooking oats
1 cup packed brown sugar
1 teaspoon baking soda
1 teaspoon cinnamon
1/4 teaspoon salt
1/4 teaspoon nutmeg
2 cups shredded zucchini
1/2 cup margarine, softened

1/4 cup sour cream
1 teaspoon vanilla extract
2 eggs
3/4 cup sugar
1/2 cup flour
1/2 cup quick-cooking oats
1/2 teaspoon cinnamon
1/4 cup margarine, softened

Combine 1 1/2 cups flour, 1 1/4 cups oats, brown sugar, baking soda, 1 teaspoon cinnamon, salt, nutmeg, zucchini, 1/2 cup margarine, sour cream, vanilla and eggs in large mixer bowl. Mix until moistened. Beat at medium speed for 2 minutes. Pour into greased and floured 9x13-inch baking pan. Combine sugar, 1/2 cup flour, 1/2 cup oats, 1/2 teaspoon cinnamon and 1/4 cup margarine in bowl; mix well. Sprinkle over batter. Bake at 350 degrees for 30 to 40 minutes or until coffee cake tests done. **Yield: 12 servings.**

Approx Per Serving: Cal 388; Prot 6 g; Carbo 60 g; Fiber 2 g;
   T Fat 14 g; 33% Calories from Fat; Chol 38 mg; Sod 273 mg.

Betty Dewitt, Houghton Lake

Belly Busters

2 1-pound packages frozen dinner
   rolls
1 cup whipping cream

1 cup sugar
1 tablespoon cinnamon

Arrange rolls in 9x13-inch baking pan. Let rise until doubled in bulk. Combine whipping cream, sugar and cinnamon in bowl; mix well. Pour over dough. Bake at 350 degrees for 30 minutes or until golden brown. **Yield: 12 servings.**

Approx Per Serving: Cal 360; Prot 6 g; Carbo 55 g; Fiber 2 g;
     T Fat 13 g; 32% Calories from Fat; Chol 27 mg; Sod 421 mg.

Barbara Thelen, Lansing

Apple Bread

1/2 cup oil
1 cup sugar
2 tablespoons sour milk
1 teaspoon baking soda
2 eggs
2 cups flour

1/2 teaspoon salt
2 cups finely chopped apples
2 tablespoons butter, softened
2 tablespoons flour
2 tablespoons brown sugar
1 teaspoon cinnamon

Mix first 8 ingredients in bowl until moistened. Spoon into loaf pan. Combine butter, flour, brown sugar and cinnamon in bowl in order listed, mixing well after each addition. Sprinkle over batter. Bake at 325 degrees for 1 hour. **Yield: 12 servings.**

Approx Per Serving: Cal 273; Prot 3 g; Carbo 39 g; Fiber 1 g;
     T Fat 12 g; 38% Calories from Fat; Chol 41 mg; Sod 188 mg.

Pat Knapp, Big Rapids

Applesauce-Lemon Bread

3 cups flour
2 cups sugar
1 teaspoon baking soda
1 tablespoon cinnamon
1 teaspoon salt
1¼ cups oil

4 eggs, beaten
2 cups applesauce
1/4 to 1/3 cup finely chopped candied
   lemon peel
1 cup raisins

Mix first 5 ingredients in bowl. Stir in oil and remaining ingredients until moistened. Spoon into 2 loaf pans. Bake at 350 degrees for 1 hour or until bread tests done. Cool in pans for 5 minutes. Invert onto wire rack. **Yield: 24 servings.**

Approx Per Serving: Cal 282; Prot 3 g; Carbo 41 g; Fiber 1 g;
     T Fat 13 g; 39% Calories from Fat; Chol 36 mg; Sod 137 mg.

Ethel Hooker, Clio

Apricot Bread

1½ cups apricot nectar
¾ cup dried apricots, chopped
¾ cup raisins
1 tablespoon margarine, softened
1 egg, beaten

⅓ cup milk
1 cup whole wheat flour
1 cup all-purpose flour
2 teaspoons baking soda
⅛ teaspoon salt

Combine apricot nectar, apricots and raisins in saucepan. Cook over medium heat for 8 to 10 minutes or until apricots are soft. Strain, reserving liquid. Mix margarine, egg, milk and reserved liquid in bowl. Add flours, baking soda and salt, stirring until moistened. Stir in apricot and raisin mixture. Spoon into loaf pan. Bake at 350 degrees for 45 to 50 minutes. **Yield: 12 servings.**

Approx Per Serving: Cal 158; Prot 4 g; Carbo 33 g; Fiber 3 g;
   T Fat 2 g; 11% Calories from Fat; Chol 19 mg; Sod 182 mg.

Frances Peeks, Holland

Betty's Banana Bread

1 cup sugar
½ cup margarine, softened
2 eggs
1 teaspoon vanilla extract
1 to 2 bananas, mashed
½ cup sour cream

1½ cups flour
1 teaspoon baking soda
½ teaspoon salt
1 teaspoon sugar
1 teaspoon cinnamon

Cream 1 cup sugar and margarine in large bowl until light and fluffy. Add eggs and vanilla; mix well. Beat bananas and sour cream in bowl. Add to creamed mixture; mix well. Sift in mixture of flour, baking soda and salt. Beat by hand for 10 minutes. Spoon into greased and floured loaf pan. Sprinkle with mixture of 1 teaspoon sugar and cinnamon. Bake at 350 degrees for 1 hour. May add ½ cup nuts and ½ cup raisins that have been softened in water to batter before baking. **Yield: 12 servings.**

Approx Per Serving: Cal 243; Prot 3 g; Carbo 34 g; Fiber 1 g;
   T Fat 11 g; 39% Calories from Fat; Chol 40 mg; Sod 264 mg.

Pam Bossche, Wyoming

Banana Bread

1¹/₂ cups sugar
3 tablespoons margarine, softened
1 cup mashed bananas
1 egg
2 cups flour

1 teaspoon baking soda
¹/₄ teaspoon salt
¹/₂ cup sour milk
1 cup chopped pecans

Cream sugar, margarine, bananas and egg in large bowl until light and fluffy. Sift in flour, baking soda and salt; mix well. Stir in milk and pecans. Spoon into loaf pan. Bake at 350 degrees for 50 minutes. **Yield: 12 servings.**

Approx Per Serving: Cal 294; Prot 4 g; Carbo 48 g; Fiber 2 g;
T Fat 11 g; 32% Calories from Fat; Chol 19 mg; Sod 158 mg.

Dorothy Morrin, Lansing

Banana-Oatmeal Bread

¹/₂ cup shortening
1 cup sugar
2 eggs
¹/₂ teaspoon vanilla extract
1 cup flour
1 cup oats

¹/₂ teaspoon salt
1 teaspoon baking soda
¹/₂ teaspoon cinnamon
1¹/₂ cups mashed ripe bananas
¹/₄ cup milk
¹/₂ cup raisins

Combine shortening, sugar, eggs, vanilla, flour, oats, salt, baking soda, cinnamon, bananas, milk and raisins in order listed, mixing well after each addition. Spoon into greased loaf pan. Bake at 350 degrees for 50 to 60 minutes. May cover bread for first 5 minutes after removing from oven to keep in moisture. **Yield: 12 servings.**

Approx Per Serving: Cal 273; Prot 4 g; Carbo 42 g; Fiber 2 g;
T Fat 11 g; 34% Calories from Fat; Chol 38 mg; Sod 175 mg.

Sue Stevens, East Lansing

Blueberry-Banana Bread

2½ cups baking mix
¾ cup packed light brown sugar
1 teaspoon cinnamon
½ teaspoon baking soda
½ teaspoon salt
1 cup mashed ripe bananas

¾ cup fresh blueberries
½ cup chopped pecans
½ cup sour cream
2 eggs
1 teaspoon vanilla extract

Combine baking mix, brown sugar, cinnamon, baking soda and salt in large mixer bowl; mix well. Add bananas, blueberries, pecans, sour cream, eggs and vanilla, stirring just until moistened. Spoon into buttered loaf pan. Bake at 350 degrees for 55 to 60 minutes or until wooden pick inserted near center comes our clean. Cool in pan for 10 minutes. Remove to wire rack to cool completely. **Yield: 12 servings.**

Approx Per Serving: Cal 268; Prot 4 g; Carbo 41 g; Fiber 1 g;
    T Fat 10 g; 34% Calories from Fat; Chol 40 mg; Sod 479 mg.

Sally Taylor, Marquette

Brown Bread

2 cups raisins
2 cups water
2 teaspoons baking soda
1 cup packed brown sugar
2 tablespoons shortening
1 tablespoon molasses

¾ cup All-Bran cereal
1 egg
1 teaspoon vanilla extract
2¾ cups flour
¼ teaspoon salt

Combine raisins, water and baking soda in large saucepan. Simmer for 10 minutes. Let stand until cool. Add brown sugar, shortening, molasses, cereal, egg, vanilla, flour and salt; mix well. Fill four 15-ounce cans ½ full. Bake at 350 degrees for 1 hour. **Yield: 16 servings.**

Approx Per Serving: Cal 224; Prot 4 g; Carbo 50 g; Fiber 3 g;
    T Fat 2 g; 9% Calories from Fat; Chol 13 mg; Sod 195 mg.

Mary Keeney, Lansing

*Make bread pudding out of unusual breads such as raisin
bread, brown bread, sweet rolls or croissants.*

Dutch Oven Bread

2 envelopes yeast
3 cups lukewarm water
2/3 cup melted shortening, cooled

1/4 cup sugar
2 teaspoons salt
7 to 8 cups flour

Combine yeast, lukewarm water, shortening, sugar and salt in large bowl; mix well. Let stand for 10 minutes. Add enough flour to make stiff dough. Knead on floured surface until smooth and elastic. Place in greased bowl, turning to coat surface. Let rise, covered, in warm place until doubled in bulk. Knead again. Place in greased Dutch oven. Let rise until doubled in bulk. Butter inside of Dutch oven lid. Bake, covered, at 375 degrees for 10 minutes. Remove lid. Bake for 35 minutes. Cool on wire rack. **Yield: 16 servings.**

Approx Per Serving: Cal 341; Prot 7 g; Carbo 57 g; Fiber 2 g;
    T Fat 9 g; 25% Calories from Fat; Chol 0 mg; Sod 268 mg.

Kay Collins, Lansing

Finnish Graham-Oatmeal Bread

1 envelope yeast
1 cup lukewarm water
1 cup quick-cooking oats
4 cups water
1/4 cup margarine
1 tablespoon salt
2 tablespoons sugar

1 cup milk
2 cups stone-ground graham flour
1/2 cup coarse rye flour
1 teaspoon caraway seed
14 cups all-purpose flour
2 teaspoons oil

Dissolve yeast in 1 cup lukewarm water. Combine oats and 4 cups water in large saucepan. Boil for 1 minute. Add margarine, salt, sugar and milk. Cook until milk is scalded. Add 8 or 9 ice cubes to cool mixture to lukewarm. Stir in yeast mixture. Stir in graham flour, rye flour and caraway seed. Let stand for 5 minutes. Add all-purpose flour gradually, stirring constantly. Knead dough on floured surface until smooth and elastic, kneading in oil. Place in greased bowl, turning to coat surface. Let rise, covered, in warm place until doubled in bulk. Punch dough down. Let rise until doubled in bulk. Divide dough into 5 portions. Shape into loaves. Place in 5 greased loaf pans. Let rise, covered, until doubled in bulk. Bake at 375 degrees for 15 minutes. Reduce oven temperature to 350 degrees. Bake for 45 minutes longer. Cool on wire rack. **Yield: 60 servings.**

Approx Per Serving: Cal 141; Prot 4 g; Carbo 27 g; Fiber 2 g;
    T Fat 2 g; 10% Calories from Fat; Chol 1 mg; Sod 118 mg.

Marcia De Laski, Skandia

Gooseberry Bread

2 cups flour
1 cup sugar
1½ teaspoons baking powder
1 teaspoon baking soda
1 teaspoon salt
Juice of 1 orange
2 tablespoons melted butter

¾ cup boiling water
1 egg, beaten
1 cup chopped pecans
Grated rind of 1 orange
1 cup fresh gooseberries, cut into
    halves

Sift flour, sugar, baking powder, baking soda and salt together into large bowl 2 times. Add mixture of orange juice, butter, water and egg, stirring just until moistened. Stir in pecans, grated orange rind and gooseberries. Spoon into greased loaf pan. Let stand for 20 minutes. Bake at 350 degrees for 1 hour. **Yield: 12 servings.**

Approx Per Serving: Cal 239; Prot 4 g; Carbo 37 g; Fiber 2 g;
    T Fat 9 g; 34% Calories from Fat; Chol 23 mg; Sod 310 mg.

Ethel Hooker, Clio

Oatbran Bread

2 cups apple cider
1 cup raisins
1 cup oatbran
1 cup oats
1 cup oat flour

1 teaspoon baking soda
1 teaspoon cinnamon
½ teaspoon nutmeg
1 cup finely chopped pecans

Combine apple cider and raisins in saucepan. Bring to a boil over medium heat. Reduce heat to low. Simmer for 5 minutes. Let stand until cool. Mix oatbran, oats, oat flour, baking soda, cinnamon, nutmeg and pecans in large bowl. Add cooled cider mixture; mix well. Spoon into greased loaf pan. Bake at 350 degrees for 40 to 50 minutes. Cool in pan for 10 minutes. Remove to wire rack to cool completely. Store, tightly covered, in refrigerator. **Yield: 12 servings.**

Approx Per Serving: Cal 204; Prot 5 g; Carbo 35 g; Fiber 4 g;
    T Fat 8 g; 31% Calories from Fat; Chol 0 mg; Sod 73 mg.

Frances Peeks, Holland

Pork and Bean Bread

1 cup raisins
1 cup boiling water
3 eggs
1 cup oil
2 cups sugar
1   16-ounce can pork and beans
3 cups flour

1 teaspoon cinnamon
1/2 teaspoon baking powder
1 teaspoon baking soda
1/2 teaspoon salt
1 cup chopped walnuts
1 teaspoon vanilla extract

Combine raisins and water in bowl. Set aside. Beat eggs, oil, sugar and pork and beans in bowl until beans are crushed. Add flour, cinnamon, baking powder, baking soda and salt; mix well. Fold in raisin mixture, walnuts and vanilla. Spoon into 3 greased loaf pans. Bake at 325 degrees for 50 to 60 minutes. **Yield: 16 servings.**

Approx Per Serving: Cal 428; Prot 7 g; Carbo 59 g; Fiber 3 g;
    T Fat 20 g; 41% Calories from Fat; Chol 42 mg; Sod 239 mg.

Barb Kubont, Escanaba

Tasty Pumpkin Bread

3 1/2 cups flour
1 teaspoon baking powder
2 teaspoons baking soda
2 teaspoons salt
1/2 teaspoon ground cloves
1/2 teaspoon nutmeg
1/2 teaspoon allspice
3 cups sugar

1 cup oil
4 eggs
1   16-ounce can pumpkin
2/3 cup water
2 cups raisins
1/2 cup chopped candied cherries
1/2 cup chopped walnuts
2/3 cup chopped dates

Mix flour, baking powder, baking soda, salt, cloves, nutmeg and allspice in bowl. Cream sugar and oil in large mixer bowl until light and fluffy. Add eggs, pumpkin and water; mix well. Add dry ingredients; mix well. Fold in raisins, cherries, walnuts and dates. Spoon into 3 loaf pans. Bake at 350 degrees for 1 hour. Cool in pans for 15 minutes. Remove to wire rack to cool completely. **Yield: 36 servings.**

Approx Per Serving: Cal 232; Prot 3 g; Carbo 40 g; Fiber 1 g;
    T Fat 8 g; 30% Calories from Fat; Chol 24 mg; Sod 183 mg.

Loraynne Leaby, Sault Ste. Marie

Pumpkin Bread

2²/₃ cups sugar
4 eggs
²/₃ cup butter, softened
2 cups pumpkin
²/₃ cup water

3¹/₃ cups flour
¹/₂ teaspoon baking powder
2 teaspoons baking soda
1¹/₂ teaspoons salt
1 to 1¹/₄ teaspoons cinnamon

Cream sugar, eggs and butter in large mixer bowl until light and fluffy. Add pumpkin, water, flour, baking powder, baking soda, salt and cinnamon; mix well. Spoon into four 3x7-inch loaf pans. Bake at 375 degrees for 33 minutes. **Yield: 16 servings.**

Approx Per Serving: Cal 320; Prot 5 g; Carbo 56 g; Fiber 1 g;
    T Fat 9 g; 26% Calories from Fat; Chol 74 mg; Sod 397 mg.

Marion Muhlenbeck, Greer, South Carolina

Toasty Poppy Seed Bread

1 2-layer package yellow cake mix
1 4-ounce package toasted coconut
   instant pudding mix
2 tablespoons poppy seed

4 eggs
¹/₂ cup oil
1 cup hot water

Combine cake mix, pudding mix, poppy seed, eggs, oil and water in large bowl; mix well. Spoon into 2 greased and floured loaf pans. Bake at 350 degrees for 40 to 50 minutes. **Yield: 24 servings.**

Approx Per Serving: Cal 166; Prot 2 g; Carbo 23 g; Fiber <1 g;
    T Fat 8 g; 41% Calories from Fat; Chol 36 mg; Sod 174 mg.

Dorothy Beauch, Saginaw

Poppy Seed Bread

1 2-layer package yellow cake mix
1 4-ounce package coconut instant
   pudding mix
1 cup hot water

3 eggs
¹/₄ cup poppy seed
¹/₂ cup oil

Combine cake mix, pudding mix, water, eggs, poppy seed and oil in large bowl; mix well. Spoon into 2 greased and floured loaf pans. Bake at 350 degrees for 40 to 50 minutes. **Yield: 24 servings.**

Approx Per Serving: Cal 209; Prot 2 g; Carbo 23 g; Fiber <1 g;
    T Fat 8 g; 34% Calories from Fat; Chol 27 mg; Sod 172 mg.

Nancy Neuhaus, Grand Rapids

Glazed Poppy Seed Bread

3 eggs
2¹/₂ cups sugar
1¹/₃ cups oil
1¹/₂ cups milk
1¹/₂ teaspoons vanilla extract
1¹/₂ teaspoons almond extract
2 tablespoons poppy seed

3 cups flour
¹/₂ teaspoon salt
1¹/₂ teaspoons baking powder
¹/₂ cup orange juice
1 cup confectioners' sugar
2 to 4 tablespoons melted butter

Beat eggs, sugar, oil and milk in mixer bowl until smooth. Add flavorings and poppy seed; mix well. Sift in flour, salt and baking powder. Stir just until moistened. Spoon into 2 greased and floured loaf pans. Bake at 325 degrees for 1 hour. Pierce tops of hot loaves. Pour mixture of orange juice, confectioners' sugar and butter over tops. Bake for 15 minutes longer. **Yield: 24 servings.**

Approx Per Serving: Cal 308; Prot 3 g; Carbo 39 g; Fiber <1 g;
     T Fat 16 g; 45% Calories from Fat; Chol 34 mg; Sod 97 mg.

Kathy Clemo, Iron Mountain

Squash Bread

²/₃ cup margarine, softened
2²/₃ cups packed brown sugar
4 eggs
¹/₂ teaspoon baking powder
¹/₂ teaspoon salt
1 teaspoon cinnamon

2 teaspoons baking soda
¹/₂ teaspoon allspice
2 cups chopped cooked squash
3¹/₃ cups flour
1 cup chopped walnuts

Beat margarine, brown sugar, eggs, baking powder, salt, cinnamon, baking soda and allspice in bowl until light and fluffy. Add squash and flour; mix well. Stir in walnuts. Spoon into greased wide-mouthed canning jars. Bake at 325 degrees for 45 minutes. Cool upside down on wire rack. May store in jars sealed with waxed paper and ring lids. **Yield: 24 servings.**

Approx Per Serving: Cal 270; Prot 4 g; Carbo 44 g; Fiber 1 g;
     T Fat 9 g; 30% Calories from Fat; Chol 36 mg; Sod 204 mg.

Cathy DeGoede, Grand Rapids

*Add 1 cup chopped dates, dried apricots, raisins or figs
to your favorite bread recipe.*

Aunt Syl's Raisin-Nut Bread

2 cups raisins
2 cups water
2 teaspoons baking soda
2 eggs
1¹/₂ cups sugar

¹/₈ teaspoon salt
1¹/₂ teaspoons vanilla extract
3 cups flour
1 cup chopped walnuts

Combine raisins, water and baking soda in saucepan. Bring to a boil over medium heat. Remove from heat when mixture begins to foam. Let stand until cool. Cream eggs, sugar, salt and vanilla in mixer bowl until light and fluffy. Add raisin mixture alternately with flour, mixing well after each addition. Fold in walnuts. Spoon into 2 greased and floured 20-ounce cans. Bake at 350 degrees for 1 hour. Serve with butter or cheese. **Yield: 16 servings.**

Approx Per Serving: Cal 279; Prot 5 g; Carbo 54 g; Fiber 2 g;
    T Fat 6 g; 18% Calories from Fat; Chol 27 mg; Sod 132 mg.

Marcia De Laski, Skandia

Rhubarb Bread

1 cup sour milk
1 teaspoon baking soda
1 teaspoon salt
1 teaspoon vanilla extract
1 cup packed brown sugar
¹/₂ cup oil

1 egg
2¹/₂ cups flour
1¹/₂ cups chopped rhubarb
1 tablespoon melted butter
¹/₂ cup sugar

Combine milk, baking soda, salt and vanilla in small bowl; mix well. Combine brown sugar, oil and egg in mixer bowl; mix well. Add milk mixture alternately with flour, mixing well after each addition. Stir in rhubarb. Spoon into greased and floured loaf pan. Sprinkle with mixture of melted butter and sugar. Bake at 350 degrees for 1 hour. Serve warm with butter. **Yield: 12 servings.**

Approx Per Serving: Cal 325; Prot 4 g; Carbo 52 g; Fiber 1 g;
    T Fat 12 g; 32% Calories from Fat; Chol 23 mg; Sod 280 mg.

Sally Taylor, Marquette

Zucchini Bread

3 cups flour
1 teaspoon cinnamon
1 teaspoon baking powder
1 teaspoon baking soda
1 teaspoon salt
3 eggs
1 cup packed brown sugar

1 cup sugar
1 cup oil
2 cups shredded zucchini
1 teaspoon vanilla extract
1 cup chopped walnuts
1 cup chopped dates

Sift flour, cinnamon, baking powder, baking soda and salt together. Beat eggs in mixer bowl. Stir in brown sugar, sugar, oil, zucchini and vanilla. Add sifted dry ingredients; stir until moistened. Stir in walnuts and dates. Spoon into 2 greased and floured loaf pans. Bake at 325 degrees for 1 hour. **Yield: 24 servings.**

Approx Per Serving: Cal 278; Prot 4 g; Carbo 38 g; Fiber 2 g;
     T Fat 13 g; 41% Calories from Fat; Chol 27 mg; Sod 152 mg.

Janell Sandstedt, Manistee

Banana-Zucchini Bread

3 eggs
1 cup oil
1 tablespoon vanilla extract
1 cup packed brown sugar
1 teaspoon salt
2 teaspoons baking soda
1/4 teaspoon baking powder

1 cup sugar
2 cups flour
1 tablespoon cinnamon
2 cups shredded zucchini
2 bananas, mashed
1 cup chopped walnuts

Combine eggs, oil, vanilla, brown sugar, salt, baking soda, baking powder, sugar, flour, cinnamon, zucchini, bananas and walnuts in bowl; mix well. Spoon into greased and floured loaf pan. Bake at 350 degrees for 1 hour. Cool in pan for 10 minutes. Remove to wire rack to cool completely. **Yield: 12 servings.**

Approx Per Serving: Cal 499; Prot 6 g; Carbo 63 g; Fiber 2 g;
     T Fat 26 g; 46% Calories from Fat; Chol 53 mg; Sod 352 mg.

Hazel E. Kilderhouse, Traverse City

Walnut-Zucchini Bread

3 eggs
2 cups sugar
1 cup oil
1 tablespoon vanilla extract
2 cups shredded zucchini
2 cups flour

1 tablespoon cinnamon
2 teaspoons baking soda
1/4 teaspoon baking powder
1 teaspoon salt
1 cup chopped walnuts

Beat eggs in mixer bowl until foamy. Add sugar, oil and vanilla; beat until thick and lemon-colored. Stir in zucchini, flour, cinnamon, baking soda, baking powder and salt. Fold in walnuts. Spoon into 2 greased and floured loaf pans. Bake at 350 degrees for 1 hour. Cool on wire rack. **Yield: 24 servings.**

Approx Per Serving: Cal 229; Prot 3 g; Carbo 26 g; Fiber 1 g;
    T Fat 13 g; 50% Calories from Fat; Chol 27 mg; Sod 174 mg.

Nova Little, Eau Claire

English Muffin Bread

5¹/₂ cups flour
2 envelopes dry yeast
1 tablespoon sugar
2 teaspoons salt

1/4 teaspoon baking soda
2 cups milk
1/4 to 1/2 cup water

Combine 3 cups flour, yeast, sugar, salt and baking soda in large mixer bowl; mix well. Combine milk and water in saucepan. Cook over low heat to 125 degrees. Add to flour mixture; mix well. Stir in remaining flour; mix well. Spoon into 2 loaf pans. Let rise for 45 minutes or until dough rises to top of pans. Bake at 400 degrees for 25 minutes. **Yield: 24 servings.**

Approx Per Serving: Cal 120; Prot 4 g; Carbo 24 g; Fiber 1 g;
    T Fat 1 g; 7% Calories from Fat; Chol 3 mg; Sod 196 mg.

Frances DeNooyer, Delton
Judy Lippens, Escanaba

Cardamom Bread

2 cups evaporated milk
2 cups milk
1¹/₂ cups sugar
1 tablespoon salt
Crushed seed of 26 cardamom pods
3 envelopes dry yeast

6 eggs
1¹/₂ cups melted margarine
12 cups flour
1 egg, beaten
2 tablespoons water

Scald evaporated milk and 2 cups milk in saucepan. Stir in sugar, salt and cardamom. Cool to lukewarm. Dissolve yeast in milk mixture. Beat 6 eggs in large bowl. Add milk mixture; mix well. Add margarine and half the flour; mix well. Stir in remaining flour. Let dough rest for 10 to 15 minutes. Knead on floured surface for 10 minutes. Place in greased bowl, turning to coat surface. Let rise, covered, in warm place until doubled in bulk. Punch dough down. Let rise for 30 minutes. Divide into 5 portions. Shape each portion into 3 ropes; braid, sealing ends. Place on greased baking sheet. Let rise for 45 minutes. Bake at 375 degrees for 30 minutes. Brush with mixture of 1 egg and water. Sprinkle with additional sugar. Bake for 5 minutes longer. **Yield: 60 servings.**

Approx Per Serving: Cal 178; Prot 4 g; Carbo 26 g; Fiber 1 g;
       T Fat 6 g; 33% Calories from Fat; Chol 28 mg; Sod 181 mg.

Patti Heikkinen, Pickford

Refrigerator Rolls

2 envelopes dry yeast
2 cups lukewarm water
¹/₂ cup sugar
2 teaspoons salt

¹/₄ cup shortening
1 egg
6¹/₂ to 7 cups flour

Dissolve yeast in lukewarm water in large bowl. Stir in sugar, salt, shortening and egg. Add enough flour to make soft dough. Chill, covered, for 2 hours or longer. Shape into rolls. Place on baking sheet. Let rise, covered, for 1¹/₂ to 2 hours or until doubled in bulk. Bake at 400 degrees for 12 to 15 minutes or until golden brown. May store dough in refrigerator for 1 week. **Yield: 30 servings.**

Approx Per Serving: Cal 138; Prot 3 g; Carbo 26 g; Fiber 1 g;
       T Fat 2 g; 14% Calories from Fat; Chol 7 mg; Sod 145 mg.

Helen Keeney, Lansing

Saffron Bread

4 cups boiling water
1 to 2 packages saffron
2 envelopes dry yeast
1/2 cup lukewarm water
16 ounces raisins

2 cups margarine, softened
1 cup sugar
1 tablespoon salt
12 cups flour

Pour 4 cups boiling water over saffron in large bowl. Let stand, covered, for 1 hour. Dissolve yeast in 1/2 cup lukewarm water in small bowl. Soak raisins in hot water in bowl until soft; drain. Add yeast mixture, raisins, margarine, sugar, salt and flour to saffron mixture; mix well. Knead dough on floured surface until smooth and elastic. Place in greased bowl, turning to coat surface. Let rise, covered, in warm place until doubled in bulk. Shape into loaves on baking sheets. Let rise until doubled in bulk. Bake at 350 degrees for 30 to 40 minutes. **Yield: 48 servings.**

Approx Per Serving: Cal 331; Prot 7 g; Carbo 58 g; Fiber 1 g;
    T Fat 8 g; 22% Calories from Fat; Chol 0 mg; Sod 224 mg.
    Nutritional information does not include saffron.

Joan Sarvello, Marquette

Bohemian Fruit Slices

1 envelope dry yeast
1/4 cup lukewarm water
1 teaspoon sugar
2 cups sifted flour
1/2 teaspoon salt

3/4 cup butter
2 egg yolks
1   21-ounce can blueberry pie filling
1/2 cup confectioners' sugar

Dissolve yeast in lukewarm water with sugar in bowl. Sift flour and salt into bowl. Cut in butter until crumbly. Add egg yolks and yeast mixture, stirring until soft ball forms. Divide dough into 2 portions. Roll each into 9x13-inch rectangle on floured surface. Spread each with half the pie filling. Roll as for jelly rolls. Place on greased baking sheet. Make 1/2-inch deep cut lengthwise in center of each roll. Bake at 375 degrees for 22 minutes. Sift confectioners' sugar over warm rolls. Cut into diagonal slices. May substitute any fruit-based pie filling for blueberry pie filling. **Yield: 16 servings.**

Approx Per Serving: Cal 188; Prot 2 g; Carbo 24 g; Fiber 1 g;
    T Fat 9 g; 44% Calories from Fat; Chol 50 mg; Sod 152 mg.

Jessie Wojnaroski, Goetzville

Hot Cross Buns

1 envelope dry yeast
1 1/2 cups lukewarm water
1 cup unseasoned lukewarm mashed
  potatoes
2/3 cup sugar
2/3 cup shortening
2 eggs
1 1/2 teaspoons salt

6 to 7 cups flour
1 1/2 cups raisins
2/3 cup chopped citron
1/2 teaspoon nutmeg
2 egg whites, slightly beaten
1 1/2 cups confectioners' sugar
4 teaspoons water
1/2 teaspoon vanilla extract

Dissolve yeast in lukewarm water in large bowl. Stir in potatoes, sugar, shortening, eggs, salt and 3 cups flour; beat until smooth. Add enough remaining flour to make soft dough. Knead on floured surface for about 5 minutes or until smooth and elastic. Place in greased bowl, turning to coat surface. Chill, tightly covered, for 8 hours or longer. Knead in raisins, citron and nutmeg. Shape into 48 balls. Place 2 inches apart on greased baking sheet. Snip cross in top of each bun. Let rise, covered, for 1 hour or until doubled in bulk. Brush tops of buns with egg whites. Bake at 375 degrees for 20 minutes. Cool on wire rack. Frost with mixture of confectioners' sugar, 4 teaspoons water and vanilla. **Yield: 48 servings.**

Approx Per Serving: Cal 150; Prot 3 g; Carbo 28 g; Fiber 1 g;
     T Fat 3 g; 20% Calories from Fat; Chol 9 mg; Sod 95 mg.

Hannah Gabel, Newberry

Quick Cinnamon Rolls

1 envelope dry yeast
1/2 cup lukewarm milk
1 teaspoon salt
1 tablespoon sugar
1 egg

2 tablespoons shortening
2 to 2 1/4 cups sifted flour
1 tablespoon butter, softened
1/4 cup sugar
1 teaspoon cinnamon

Dissolve yeast in mixture of lukewarm milk, salt and 1 tablespoon sugar in medium saucepan. Add egg, shortening and enough flour to make stiff dough. Knead on floured surface until smooth and elastic. Let rise, covered with damp cloth, for 25 to 35 minutes. Pat dough into 7x12-inch rectangle. Spread with butter; sprinkle with 1/4 cup sugar and cinnamon. Roll as for jelly roll, beginning at wide end. Cut into 12 slices. Arrange in greased 9-inch round baking pan. Bake at 400 degrees for 12 to 14 minutes. May frost with confectioners' sugar icing. **Yield: 12 servings.**

Approx Per Serving: Cal 140; Prot 3 g; Carbo 22 g; Fiber 1 g;
     T Fat 4 g; 27% Calories from Fat; Chol 22 mg; Sod 197 mg.

Barbara Nabozny, Jackson

Sticky Buns

1 envelope dry yeast
2 cups lukewarm water
1/2 cup sugar
2 teaspoons salt
2 eggs
1/2 cup shortening

7 to 7 1/2 cups flour
1 cup (about) packed brown sugar
1 1/2 teaspoons cinnamon
2 tablespoons melted butter
1/4 cup packed brown sugar
1/2 teaspoon cinnamon

Dissolve yeast in mixture of lukewarm water, sugar and salt in large bowl. Stir in eggs and shortening. Add flour 1/2 at a time, mixing well after each addition. Place in greased bowl, turning to coat surface. Let rise for 1 1/2 hours. Punch dough down. Let rise for 40 minutes. Divide dough into 2 portions. Roll each portion into rectangle. Sprinkle with 1 cup brown sugar and 1 1/2 teaspoons cinnamon. Roll as for jelly rolls. Cut into 1-inch slices. Arrange rolls in 9x13-inch baking pan coated with melted butter, 1/4 cup brown sugar and 1/2 teaspoon cinnamon. Let rise until doubled in bulk. Bake at 350 degrees for 25 minutes. May adjust amounts of brown sugar and cinnamon to suit personal taste. **Yield: 24 servings.**

Approx Per Serving: Cal 265; Prot 5 g; Carbo 48 g; Fiber 1 g;
    T Fat 6 g; 21% Calories from Fat; Chol 20 mg; Sod 199 mg.

Aileen Pancheri, Sault Ste. Marie

Apple Muffins

1 1/2 cups packed brown sugar
2/3 cup oil
1 egg
1 cup buttermilk
1 teaspoon baking soda
1 teaspoon salt

1 teaspoon vanilla extract
2 1/2 cups flour
1 1/2 cups chopped apples
1/2 cup chopped pecans
2 tablespoons melted margarine
2 tablespoons brown sugar

Combine 1 1/2 cups brown sugar, oil and egg in large bowl; mix well. Combine buttermilk, baking soda, salt and vanilla in small bowl. Add to brown sugar mixture alternately with flour, mixing well after addition. Fold in apples and pecans. Fill paper-lined muffin cups 2/3 full. Brush tops with melted margarine; sprinkle with 2 tablespoons brown sugar. Bake at 325 degrees for 30 minutes. **Yield: 18 servings.**

Approx Per Serving: Cal 275; Prot 3 g; Carbo 40 g; Fiber 1 g;
    T Fat 12 g; 39% Calories from Fat; Chol 12 mg; Sod 208 mg.

Nancy Carpenter, Jackson

Banana-Walnut Muffins

1¹/₂ cups flour
³/₄ cup sugar
³/₄ cup chopped walnuts
1¹/₂ teaspoons baking soda
¹/₄ teaspoon salt

1¹/₄ cups mashed ripe bananas
¹/₂ cup melted butter
1 egg
2¹/₂ tablespoons milk

Mix flour, sugar, walnuts, baking soda and salt in large bowl. Combine bananas, butter, egg and milk in medium bowl; mix well. Add to flour mixture, mixing just until moistened. Spoon ¹/₂ cup batter into each of 12 greased muffin cups. Bake at 350 degrees for 25 minutes. **Yield: 12 servings.**

Approx Per Serving: Cal 251; Prot 4 g; Carbo 31 g; Fiber 1 g;
    T Fat 13 g; 46% Calories from Fat; Chol 39 mg; Sod 220 mg.

Shirley A. Cook, Lansing

Lemon-Poppy Seed Muffins

1 cup sugar
2 cups flour
¹/₂ teaspoon salt
1 to 3 tablespoons poppy seed
¹/₄ teaspoon baking soda
¹/₂ cup melted margarine

2 eggs, beaten
1 teaspoon vanilla extract
1 teaspoon grated lemon rind
1 cup lemon yogurt
1 teaspoon lemon extract

Mix sugar, flour, salt, poppy seed and baking soda in large bowl. Add margarine, eggs, vanilla, lemon rind, yogurt and lemon extract, stirring until moistened. Fill paper-lined muffin cups ²/₃ full. Bake at 375 degrees for 20 minutes.
Yield: 18 servings.

Approx Per Serving: Cal 168; Prot 3 g; Carbo 24 g; Fiber <1 g;
    T Fat 7 g; 36% Calories from Fat; Chol 24 mg; Sod 158 mg.

Gert Budd, Saginaw

Substitute ¹/₂ cup maple syrup for ¹/₂ cup milk in your favorite recipe for maple syrup muffins.

Fresh Peach Muffins

2 eggs
1/2 cup honey
1/2 cup melted margarine
1 cup chopped peaches
1/2 cup yogurt

1 teaspoon baking soda
1 cup oats
1 1/2 cups whole wheat flour
1/4 cup oats
1 tablespoon brown sugar

Mix eggs, honey, margarine and peaches in bowl. Mix yogurt and baking soda in bowl. Add to egg mixture; mix well. Add 1 cup oats and wheat flour, stirring just until moistened. Fill greased muffin cups 2/3 full. Top with mixture of 1/4 cup oats and brown sugar. Bake at 375 degrees for 20 minutes. May substitute any fresh fruit for peaches. **Yield: 12 servings.**

Approx Per Serving: Cal 229; Prot 5 g; Carbo 33 g; Fiber 3 g;
T Fat 10 g; 37% Calories from Fat; Chol 37 mg; Sod 175 mg.

Balicia Duvall, Williamston

Peanut Butter-Banana Muffins

1 1/2 cups flour
1/2 cup sugar
2 teaspoons baking powder
1/2 teaspoon salt
1 egg, slightly beaten

1/2 cup milk
1/4 cup oil
3/4 cup mashed bananas
3/4 cup peanut butter chips
1/2 cup chopped walnuts

Mix flour, sugar, baking powder and salt in bowl. Add egg, milk, oil and bananas, stirring just until moistened. Fold in peanut butter chips and walnuts. Fill greased muffin cups 2/3 full. Bake at 400 degrees for 20 to 25 minutes. **Yield: 12 servings.**

Approx Per Serving: Cal 245; Prot 6 g; Carbo 30 g; Fiber 1 g;
T Fat 12 g; 43% Calories from Fat; Chol 19 mg; Sod 182 mg.

Evelyn Helmer, Lansing

Raspberry-Nut Muffins

2 cups flour
1/2 cup sugar
2 teaspoons baking powder
1/2 teaspoon salt
1/2 cup walnut pieces
1 egg

1 cup skim milk
1/2 cup melted margarine, cooled
1 teaspoon vanilla extract
1 cup fresh or thawed frozen
  raspberries

Combine flour, sugar, baking powder, salt and walnuts in large bowl. Beat egg in small bowl. Add milk, margarine and vanilla; mix well. Add to dry mixture; mix well. Fold in raspberries. Spoon into greased muffin cups. Bake at 425 degrees for 20 to 25 minutes or until muffins test done. **Yield: 12 servings.**

Approx Per Serving: Cal 229; Prot 4 g; Carbo 28 g; Fiber 2 g;
  T Fat 11 g; 45% Calories from Fat; Chol 18 mg; Sod 250 mg.

Kathy Clemo, Iron Mountain

Blueberry-Bran Muffins

1 1/4 cups flour
1 tablespoon baking powder
1/2 teaspoon salt
3/4 cup packed brown sugar
2 1/2 cups bran flakes cereal

1 1/4 cups milk
1 egg
1/3 cup oil
1 cup blueberries
1 cup walnut pieces

Mix flour, baking powder, salt and brown sugar in bowl. Combine cereal and milk in large bowl. Let stand for 2 minutes or until cereal softens. Stir in egg and oil. Add dry ingredients, stirring just until moistened. Fold in blueberries and walnuts. Fill paper-lined muffin cups 3/4 full. Bake at 400 degrees for 25 minutes.
Yield: 21 servings.

Approx Per Serving: Cal 167; Prot 3 g; Carbo 23 g; Fiber 1 g;
  T Fat 8 g; 44% Calories from Fat; Chol 12 mg; Sod 156 mg.

Helen Nothelfer, Saginaw

Ready-Bake Bran Muffins

3 cups 100% bran cereal
1 cup boiling water
2 eggs, slightly beaten
2 cups buttermilk
1/2 cup oil

1 cup chopped currants
2 1/2 teaspoons baking soda
1/2 teaspoon salt
1 cup sugar
2 1/2 cups flour

Combine cereal and water in large bowl; mix well. Cool to lukewarm. Add eggs, buttermilk, oil and currants; mix well. Add mixture of baking soda, salt, sugar and flour, stirring just until moistened. Fill greased muffin cups 2/3 full. Bake at 425 degrees for 20 minutes. May store batter in refrigerator for 2 weeks. **Yield: 24 servings.**

Approx Per Serving: Cal 174; Prot 4 g; Carbo 30 g; Fiber 4 g;
    T Fat 6 g; 28% Calories from Fat; Chol 18 mg; Sod 216 mg.

Lydia Engstrom, Reed City

Ralph's Health Muffins

1 1/2 cups whole wheat flour
1 1/2 cups wheat and bran cereal,
    finely crushed
1 tablespoon baking powder
1/2 teaspoon salt
1/2 teaspoon cinnamon
1/2 teaspoon ground cloves
1/2 teaspoon pumpkin pie spice
1/2 teaspoon ginger
1   4-ounce package vanilla pudding
    and pie filling mix

1 medium orange, cut into wedges
1/2 cup honey
1/2 cup melted butter
2 eggs
1 cup raisins
1/2 cup chopped dates
1 cup walnut pieces
1 cup skim milk

Mix wheat flour, cereal, baking powder, salt, cinnamon, cloves, pumpkin pie spice, ginger and pudding mix in large bowl. Combine orange wedges, honey, butter, eggs, raisins, dates, walnuts and milk in blender container. Process until smooth. Add to dry ingredients, stirring until moistened. Spoon into nonstick muffin cups. Bake at 350 degrees for 20 minutes. **Yield: 24 servings.**

Approx Per Serving: Cal 182; Prot 3 g; Carbo 28 g; Fiber 2 g;
    T Fat 8 g; 36% Calories from Fat; Chol 28 mg; Sod 185 mg.

Ralph E. Phillips, Allendale

LAP ROBES FOR NURSING HOMES

Desserts

Apple Crumble

1 quart apples, peeled, sliced
3/4 cup packed light brown sugar
Cinnamon to taste
1/4 cup water

1 cup flour
1/2 cup packed light brown sugar
1 teaspoon salt
1/3 cup butter

Arrange apple slices in baking dish sprayed with nonstick cooking spray. Combine 3/4 cup brown sugar, cinnamon and water in bowl; mix well. Spread over apples. Combine flour, 1/2 cup brown sugar and salt in bowl. Cut in butter until crumbly. Sprinkle over apples. Bake at 350 degrees for 50 minutes or until apples are tender. **Yield: 6 servings.**

Approx Per Serving: Cal 451; Prot 2 g; Carbo 90 g; Fiber 3 g;
    T Fat 11 g; 21% Calories from Fat; Chol 27 mg; Sod 466 mg.

Helen Hoermann, Grand Haven

Apple Crush

5 to 6 cups sliced peeled apples
1 cup sifted flour
1/2 to 1 cup sugar
1 teaspoon baking powder

3/4 teaspoon salt
1 egg
1/3 cup butter
1/2 teaspoon cinnamon

Place apples in greased 6x10-inch baking dish. Combine flour, sugar, baking powder, salt and egg in bowl; mix with fork until crumbly. Sprinkle over apples; dot with butter. Sprinkle with cinnamon. Bake at 350 degrees for 30 to 40 minutes or until apples are tender. **Yield: 10 servings.**

Approx Per Serving: Cal 220; Prot 2 g; Carbo 38 g; Fiber 2 g;
    T Fat 7 g; 28% Calories from Fat; Chol 38 mg; Sod 252 mg.

Ruth Andrus, Kalamazoo

*Make **Apple Empañadas** by filling flour tortillas with a mixture of 1 can of apple pie filling, 1/4 cup melted butter and 2 teaspoons cinnamon. Fold and secure with toothpicks. Deep-fry and sprinkle with cinnamon-sugar.*

Apple Pan Dowdy

8 cups sliced apples
Salt to taste
Cinnamon to taste
1 cup sugar
1/4 cup melted butter
1 cup milk

2 cups flour
2 teaspoons baking powder
1 cup packed brown sugar
2 tablespoons cornstarch
1 cup boiling water

Arrange apples in greased 9x13-inch baking dish. Sprinkle with salt and cinnamon. Combine sugar, butter, milk, flour and baking powder in mixer bowl; mix well. Spread over apples. Sprinkle with mixture of brown sugar and cornstarch. Pour boiling water over top. Bake at 350 degrees for 1 hour. **Yield: 10 servings.**

Approx Per Serving: Cal 385; Prot 4 g; Carbo 81 g; Fiber 3 g;
    T Fat 6 g; 14% Calories from Fat; Chol 16 mg; Sod 128 mg.

Lois Walls, Reed City

Apple Crisp

1 1/2 cups flour
3/4 cup quick-cooking oats
1/4 teaspoon salt
1/2 teaspoon cinnamon
Artificial sweetener to equal 1/4 cup
    sugar
1/2 cup low-fat margarine

6 apples, peeled, thinly sliced
1 teaspoon cinnamon
1/4 teaspoon nutmeg
1/4 teaspoon salt
Artificial sweetener to equal 1/2 cup
    sugar

Combine flour, oats, salt, 1/2 teaspoon cinnamon and artificial sweetener to equal 1/4 cup sugar in bowl; mix well. Cut in margarine until crumbly. Reserve 3/4 cup mixture. Press remaining mixture into greased 9x9-inch baking dish. Combine apples with remaining cinnamon, nutmeg, salt and artificial sweetener in bowl; toss to mix. Spread over crumb crust; sprinkle with reserved crumbs. Bake at 375 degrees for 25 minutes or until apples are tender. **Yield: 8 servings.**

Approx Per Serving: Cal 218; Prot 4 g; Carbo 37 g; Fiber 3 g;
    T Fat 7 g; 26% Calories from Fat; Chol 0 mg; Sod 270 mg.

Joyce Frydel, Lansing

Baked Apples

6 apples, cored
³/₄ cup packed brown sugar
¹/₂ cup raisins

¹/₂ cup chopped walnuts
1 cup maple syrup

Arrange apples in baking pan. Fill cores with brown sugar, raisins and walnuts. Pour maple syrup over apples. Bake at 350 degrees for 1 hour. **Yield: 6 servings.**

Approx Per Serving: Cal 447; Prot 2 g; Carbo 101 g; Fiber 5 g;
      T Fat 7 g; 13% Calories from Fat; Chol 0 mg; Sod 27 mg.

Sally Taylor, Marquette

Banana Split Cake

16 graham crackers, crushed
1 6-ounce package sugar-free
   vanilla instant pudding mix
4 bananas, sliced
8 ounces whipped topping

2 cups strawberries
2 8-ounce cans crushed pineapple,
   drained
1 3-ounce can coconut

Spread graham cracker crumbs in 9x13-inch baking dish. Prepare pudding mix using package directions. Spread over crumb shell. Chill in refrigerator until firm. Layer bananas, whipped topping, strawberries, pineapple and coconut over pudding mix. Chill until serving time. **Yield: 16 servings.**

Approx Per Serving: Cal 265; Prot 6 g; Carbo 43 g; Fiber 2 g;
      T Fat 9 g; 28% Calories from Fat; Chol 0 mg; Sod 577 mg.

Nila Stewart, Grand Rapids

Blueberry Dessert

1 recipe graham cracker crust
16 ounces whipped topping
1 14-ounce can sweetened
   condensed milk

¹/₃ cup lemon juice
1 to 1¹/₄ quarts blueberries
¹/₂ cup chopped pecans

Prepare graham cracker crust mixture using package or recipe directions. Press into greased 9x13-inch dish. Chill until firm. Combine whipped topping, condensed milk and lemon juice in bowl; mix well. Fold in blueberries. Spread in prepared dish; sprinkle with pecans. Chill until serving time. **Yield: 15 servings.**

Approx Per Serving: Cal 328; Prot 4 g; Carbo 40 g; Fiber 2 g;
      T Fat 18 g; 48% Calories from Fat; Chol 9 mg; Sod 153 mg.

Helen Nothelfer, Saginaw

Blueberry-Peach Trifle

1 14-ounce can sweetened
   condensed milk
1½ cups cold water
2 tablespoons grated lemon rind
1 4-ounce package vanilla instant
   pudding mix

2 cups whipped topping
4 cups cubed pound cake
1 pound fresh peaches, peeled,
   coarsely chopped
2 cups fresh blueberries

Combine condensed milk, cold water and lemon rind in mixer bowl; mix well. Add pudding mix; beat until well mixed. Chill in refrigerator for 5 minutes. Fold in whipped topping. Spoon 2 cups pudding mixture into 4-quart glass serving bowl. Layer half the cake, peaches, half the remaining pudding mixture, remaining cake, blueberries and remaining pudding mixture in prepared bowl. Chill in refrigerator for 4 hours or longer. **Yield: 20 servings.**

Approx Per Serving: Cal 171; Prot 3 g; Carbo 29 g; Fiber 1 g;
    T Fat 6 g; 30% Calories from Fat; Chol 32 mg; Sod 109 mg.

Gloria J. Debri, Grand Rapids

My Blue Heaven

1 16-ounce can fruit cocktail,
   drained
1 16-ounce can sliced peaches,
   drained

1 11-ounce can mandarin oranges,
   drained
1 21-ounce can blueberry pie filling

Combine fruit cocktail, peaches, mandarin oranges and blueberry pie filling in bowl; mix well. Spoon into serving bowl or serve in tart shells. **Yield: 12 servings.**

Approx Per Serving: Cal 105; Prot 1 g; Carbo 28 g; Fiber 2 g;
    T Fat <1 g; 0% Calories from Fat; Chol 0 mg; Sod 21 mg.

Jo Marshall, Traverse City

*For an easy refreshing dessert, shape scoops of lemon or orange
sherbet into balls and roll in flaked coconut; freeze until
firm. Serve over sliced strawberries or peaches.*

Butterscotch Torte

1¹/₄ cups flour
¹/₂ cup butter
¹/₂ cup chopped pecans
8 ounces cream cheese, softened
1 cup confectioners' sugar

9 ounces whipped topping
2 4-ounce packages butterscotch
  instant pudding mix
3¹/₂ cups cold milk

Combine flour, butter and pecans in bowl; mix well. Press into 9x13-inch baking dish. Bake at 350 degrees for 15 minutes. Cool to room temperature. Beat cream cheese, confectioners' sugar and 1 cup whipped topping in mixer bowl until smooth. Spread on cooled crust. Combine pudding mix and milk in bowl; beat for 2 minutes. Spread over cream cheese layer. Top with remaining whipped topping. Chill until serving time. Garnish with additional pecans or chocolate shavings.
Yield: 15 servings.

Approx Per Serving: Cal 347; Prot 5 g; Carbo 38 g; Fiber 1 g;
    T Fat 21 g; 52% Calories from Fat; Chol 41 mg; Sod 226 mg.

Michelle Richards, Lansing

Stuffed Cantaloupe

1 small cantaloupe
2 tablespoons fresh lemon juice
1 cup firm yogurt
2 to 3 tablespoons honey

¹/₂ teaspoon vanilla extract
1 cup fresh blueberries
¹/₂ cup toasted slivered almonds

Cut cantaloupe crosswise into halves; discard seed. Cut thin slice from each end so cantaloupe halves will stand evenly. Place each half on serving plate; drizzle with lemon juice. Combine yogurt, honey, vanilla and blueberries in bowl; stir gently to mix. Spoon into cantaloupe halves; sprinkle with almonds. May substitute strawberries for blueberries. **Yield: 2 servings.**

Approx Per Serving: Cal 495; Prot 13 g; Carbo 70 g; Fiber 8 g;
    T Fat 22 g; 38% Calories from Fat; Chol 15 mg; Sod 83 mg.

Jean A. Steffes, Traverse City

*Create a quick dessert with fresh fruit slices, a dollop of sour cream
or yogurt and a sprinkle of brown sugar or coconut.*

Cherries and Cream Roll

1 cup sifted cake flour
1 teaspoon baking powder
1/4 teaspoon salt
3 eggs
3/4 cup sugar
1 tablespoon thawed frozen orange
   juice concentrate

2 tablespoons water
1/2 cup confectioners' sugar
1 21-ounce can cherry pie filling
2 cups whipping cream
1/2 cup confectioners' sugar
1/2 teaspoon almond extract

Grease 10x15-inch baking pan; line with greased waxed paper. Sift cake flour, baking powder and salt into bowl. Beat eggs in medium bowl at high speed until thickened. Beat in sugar 1 tablespoon at a time. Add orange juice concentrate and water. Beat at low speed until smooth. Add cake flour mixture gradually, beating until batter is smooth; do not overbeat. Spoon into prepared baking pan. Bake at 375 degrees for 12 minutes or until center springs back when lightly touched. Loosen edges with knife. Invert immediately onto towel sprinkled with 1/2 cup confectioners' sugar; remove waxed paper. Trim 1/4 inch from all sides with sharp knife. Roll up in towel; let stand on wire rack until cool. Drain pie filling in colander. Whip cream in medium bowl until soft peaks form. Beat in 1/2 cup confectioners' sugar and almond extract. Unroll cooled cake. Spread with half the whipped cream mixture. Top with 3/4 of the pie filling. Roll as for jelly roll to enclose filling. Place seam side down on serving plate. Spread with remaining whipped cream mixture. Top with remaining pie filling. Garnish with candy mint leaves. **Yield: 10 servings.**

Approx Per Serving: Cal 394; Prot 4 g; Carbo 53 g; Fiber 1 g;
   T Fat 19 g; 43% Calories from Fat; Chol 129 mg; Sod 143 mg.

Jean A. Steffes, Traverse City

Cherry Dessert

1 cup flour
1/2 cup sugar
1 teaspoon baking powder
1/4 teaspoon salt
1/4 cup shortening

1/2 cup milk
1/2 teaspoon vanilla extract
1 16-ounce can juice-pack cherries
1/2 cup sugar

Mix flour, 1/2 cup sugar, baking powder and salt in bowl. Add shortening, milk and vanilla; mix well. Spoon into greased 8x8-inch baking pan. Drain cherries, reserving juice. Spread cherries over batter; sprinkle with 1/2 cup sugar. Bring cherry juice to a boil in saucepan. Pour over top. Bake at 375 degrees for 40 to 45 minutes or until dessert tests done. Serve warm with ice cream, whipped cream or whipped topping. **Yield: 6 servings.**

Approx Per Serving: Cal 334; Prot 4 g; Carbo 61 g; Fiber 1 g;
   T Fat 9 g; 25% Calories from Fat; Chol 3 mg; Sod 155 mg.

Betty L. Menhennick, Marquette

Champagne Dessert

1 2-layer package white cake mix
1 4-ounce package vanilla instant
   pudding mix
3 ounces cream cheese, softened

1 20-ounce can crushed pineapple,
   drained
8 ounces whipped topping

Prepare and bake cake mix using package directions for 9x13-inch baking dish. Cool. Prepare pudding mix using package directions. Add cream cheese; mix well. Pour over cooled cake. Layer pineapple and whipped topping over pudding mix mixture. Chill in refrigerator for 6 hours before serving. May garnish with chopped nuts, cherries or pineapple. May remove a portion of the cake batter and use to make 6 cupcakes if cake layer is too deep. **Yield: 15 servings.**

Approx Per Serving: Cal 376; Prot 5 g; Carbo 58 g; Fiber <1 g;
    T Fat 15 g; 35% Calories from Fat; Chol 10 mg; Sod 288 mg.

Helen Lorraine Moss, Marquette

Yogurt Cheesecake

2 cups graham cracker crumbs
1/2 cup melted margarine
1/2 cup sugar
9 ounces cream cheese, softened
4 eggs
1 cup sugar

1 teaspoon grated lemon rind
4 teaspoons (rounded) vanilla yogurt
2 cups sour cream
1/2 cup sugar
1 teaspoon vanilla extract

Combine graham cracker crumbs, melted margarine and 1/2 cup sugar in bowl; mix well. Press into 9x13-inch baking dish. Beat cream cheese in mixer bowl until light. Beat in eggs 1 at a time. Add 1 cup sugar, lemon rind and yogurt; mix well. Pour into prepared baking dish. Bake at 350 degrees for 40 minutes. Combine sour cream, 1/2 cup sugar and vanilla in bowl; mix well. Spread over hot cheesecake. Bake at 425 degrees for 10 minutes longer. Cool slightly. Chill in refrigerator until serving time. Cut with hot knife rinsed in hot water. **Yield: 15 servings.**

Approx Per Serving: Cal 373; Prot 5 g; Carbo 41 g; Fiber <1 g;
    T Fat 22 g; 51% Calories from Fat; Chol 89 mg; Sod 256 mg.

Michele Brechtelsbauer, Troy

Miniature Cheesecakes

1 1-pound package vanilla wafers
16 ounces cream cheese, softened
2 eggs

¼ cup sugar
2 teaspoons vanilla extract
1 21-ounce can cherry pie filling

Place 1 vanilla wafer in each of 20 paper-lined muffin cups. Combine cream cheese, eggs, sugar and vanilla in mixer bowl; beat until smooth. Fill each muffin cup ¾ full. Top with pie filling. Bake at 375 degrees for 12 to 15 minutes or until cheesecakes test done. May substitute any flavor pie filling for cherry. **Yield: 20 servings.**

Approx Per Serving: Cal 230; Prot 4 g; Carbo 27 g; Fiber 1 g;
    T Fat 12 g; 48% Calories from Fat; Chol 60 mg; Sod 168 mg.

Rocky Rothenthaler, Grand Rapids

Chocolate Pizza

2 cups semisweet chocolate chips
14 ounces white almond bark
2 cups miniature marshmallows
1 cup crisp rice cereal
1 cup peanuts
1 6-ounce jar red maraschino
   cherries, drained

3 tablespoons chopped green
   maraschino cherries
⅓ cup coconut
2 ounces white almond bark
1 teaspoon oil

Combine chocolate chips and 14 ounces almond bark in microwave-safe bowl. Microwave on High for 2 minutes; stir. Microwave for 1 to 2 minutes longer or until smooth, stirring every 30 seconds. Stir in marshmallows, cereal and peanuts. Spread in greased 12-inch pizza pan. Cut red cherries into halves. Sprinkle red and green cherries over mixture; top with coconut. Combine remaining 2 ounces almond bark and oil in microwave-safe bowl. Microwave on High for 30 seconds or until smooth, stirring every 15 seconds. Drizzle over coconut. Chill until firm. Cut into wedges. May store at room temperature. **Yield: 12 servings.**

Approx Per Serving: Cal 486; Prot 9 g; Carbo 54 g; Fiber 4 g;
    T Fat 31 g; 53% Calories from Fat; Chol 6 mg; Sod 74 mg.

Karen Wilhelm, Traverse City

Chocolate Punch Bowl Dessert

1 2-layer package chocolate cake mix
2 4-ounce packages milk chocolate
   or chocolate fudge instant pudding
   mix

$\frac{1}{2}$ cup Amaretto
3 cups milk
6 1-ounce Heath bars, crushed
16 ounces whipped topping

Prepare and bake cake mix using package directions for 9x13-inch cake pan. Cool cake to room temperature and crumble. Combine pudding mix, liqueur and milk in bowl; beat until smooth. Layer cake pieces, pudding mix mixture, crushed candy and whipped topping $\frac{1}{3}$ at a time in punch bowl. Chill, covered, overnight. May substitute 2 teaspoons vanilla extract for liqueur or bake cake in layers and split layers into halves. **Yield: 20 servings.**

Approx Per Serving: Cal 404; Prot 4 g; Carbo 56 g; Fiber <1 g; T Fat 18 g; 41% Calories from Fat; Chol 5 mg; Sod 247 mg.

Dixie L. Tackebury, Saginaw

Chocolate Sauce

1 cup sugar
1 cup baking cocoa

1 cup corn syrup
1 cup water

Combine sugar, baking cocoa, corn syrup and water in heavy saucepan; mix well. Cook for several minutes or until of desired consistency. Use as topping for ice cream. May cook for a shorter time and use 1 tablespoon sauce in each cup or glass of milk for chocolate milk or hot chocolate. **Yield: 16 servings.**

Approx Per Serving: Cal 119; Prot 1 g; Carbo 30 g; Fiber 2 g; T Fat 1 g; 7% Calories from Fat; Chol 0 mg; Sod 11 mg.

Zelma Cohoon, Sault Ste. Marie

Coconut Cream Dessert

60 butter crackers, crushed
$\frac{1}{2}$ cup melted margarine
2 4-ounce packages coconut cream
   instant pudding mix

1 quart vanilla ice cream, softened
1$\frac{1}{2}$ cups milk
8 ounces whipped topping

Mix cracker crumbs and margarine in bowl. Spread half the mixture in 9x13-inch dish. Combine pudding mix, ice cream and milk in bowl; mix until smooth. Spread in prepared dish. Spread with whipped topping; sprinkle with remaining crumb mixture. Chill until serving time. **Yield: 15 servings.**

Approx Per Serving: Cal 305; Prot 3 g; Carbo 36 g; Fiber <1 g; T Fat 19 g; 52% Calories from Fat; Chol 19 mg; Sod 337 mg.

Jo Marshall, Traverse City

Cream Cheese-Fruit Dessert

2 envelopes whipped topping mix
8 ounces cream cheese, softened
2 tablespoons confectioners' sugar
1 16-ounce can crushed pineapple, drained
1 16-ounce can fruit cocktail, drained
1 15-ounce can mandarin oranges, drained
2 cups miniature marshmallows
1 cup chopped pecans

Prepare whipped topping mix using package directions. Add cream cheese gradual- ly, beating until light. Beat in confectioners' sugar. Fold in pineapple, fruit cocktail, mandarin oranges, marshmallows and pecans. Chill for several hours to overnight. **Yield: 16 servings.**

Approx Per Serving: Cal 210; Prot 3 g; Carbo 24 g; Fiber 1 g;
    T Fat 13 g; 51% Calories from Fat; Chol 18 mg; Sod 65 mg.

Betty Boyd, Hemlock

Date-Nut Dessert

1 cup chopped dates
1/4 cup water
1 teaspoon baking soda
1/2 cup shortening
1 cup sugar
1/2 teaspoon salt
1 egg, beaten
1 1/2 cups flour
1/2 cup milk
1/2 cup chopped pecans

Combine dates, water and baking soda in bowl; mix well. Let stand for several minutes. Cream shortening, sugar and salt in mixer bowl until light and fluffy. Add egg, date mixture, flour and milk; mix well. Stir in pecans. Spoon into baking dish. Bake at 350 degrees for 30 minutes. **Yield: 12 servings.**

Approx Per Serving: Cal 283; Prot 3 g; Carbo 41 g; Fiber 2 g;
    T Fat 13 g; 40% Calories from Fat; Chol 19 mg; Sod 168 mg.

Mary Ann Thurston, Cadillac

*For a delicious topping for desserts, mix 1 cup sour cream and
1/2 cup packed brown sugar. Chill for 1 hour or longer
and mix well before serving.*

Dump Dessert

1 20-ounce can crushed pineapple
1 2-layer package yellow cake mix
1/2 cup margarine

1 cup chopped pecans
16 ounces whipped topping

Spread undrained pineapple in baking dish. Sprinkle with cake mix. Dot with margarine; sprinkle with pecans. Bake at 350 degrees for 1 hour. Cool on wire rack. Spread with whipped topping. Chill until serving time. **Yield: 15 servings.**

Approx Per Serving: Cal 379; Prot 3 g; Carbo 45 g; Fiber 1 g;
    T Fat 22 g; 52% Calories from Fat; Chol 0 mg; Sod 272 mg.

A. L. Butenschden, Saginaw

Éclair Dessert

1 12-ounce package honey graham
    crackers
2 4-ounce packages vanilla instant
    pudding mix
8 to 9 ounces whipped topping
3 1/2 cups milk

2 envelopes liquid baking chocolate
1 1/2 cups confectioners' sugar
1/4 cup milk
2 teaspoons light corn syrup
3 tablespoons melted butter
1 teaspoon vanilla extract

Layer 1/3 of the crackers in buttered 9x13-inch dish. Combine pudding mix, whipped topping and milk in mixer bowl; beat until smooth. Layer pudding mixture and remaining crackers 1/2 at a time in prepared dish. Combine baking chocolate, confectioners' sugar, milk, corn syrup, butter and vanilla in bowl; mix well. Spread over layers. Chill for 24 to 48 hours. May omit corn syrup, substitute 1/4 cup margarine for butter, 6 tablespoons baking cocoa for liquid chocolate, water for milk and increase confectioners' sugar to 2 cups if desired. **Yield: 15 servings.**

Approx Per Serving: Cal 333; Prot 4 g; Carbo 52 g; Fiber 1 g;
    T Fat 13 g; 34% Calories from Fat; Chol 15 mg; Sod 290 mg.

Virginia C. Marlatt, Howell
Laura Scofield, St. Joseph

Fruit Delight

3 cups graham cracker crumbs
1/2 cup margarine, softened
8 ounces cream cheese, softened
8 packets artificial sweetener
3 tablespoons milk

12 ounces whipped topping
4 large bananas, sliced
2 1-ounce packages sugar-free
   vanilla instant pudding mix

Mix cracker crumbs and margarine in bowl. Reserve 1/4 cup mixture for topping. Press remaining mixture into 9x13-inch dish. Beat cream cheese with artificial sweetener in bowl. Add milk and 2 cups whipped topping. Spread over crumb layer. Top with bananas. Prepare pudding mix using package directions. Spread over bananas. Chill until serving time. Spread with remaining whipped topping; sprinkle with reserved topping mixture. **Yield: 15 servings.**

Approx Per Serving: Cal 352; Prot 5 g; Carbo 38 g; Fiber 1 g;
    T Fat 21 g; 54% Calories from Fat; Chol 17 mg; Sod 442 mg.

Denise Toogood, Coopersville

Black-and-White Fluff

1 cup whipping cream
1/2 teaspoon lemon extract
1 1/2 cups cooked prunes

2 bananas
12 marshmallows

Whip cream in mixer bowl until soft peaks form. Fold in lemon extract. Reserve a small amount of whipped cream for topping. Cut prunes, bananas and marshmallows into small pieces. Fold into remaining whipped cream. Chill dessert and reserved whipped cream until serving time. Top servings with reserved whipped cream. **Yield: 6 servings.**

Approx Per Serving: Cal 274; Prot 2 g; Carbo 36 g; Fiber 3 g;
    T Fat 15 g; 47% Calories from Fat; Chol 54 mg; Sod 29 mg.

Aileen Pancheri, Sault Ste. Marie

Holland Rusk Dessert

20 Holland rusks, crushed
½ cup melted butter
½ cup sugar
4 egg yolks, beaten
½ cup sugar
2 tablespoons flour

2 cups milk
1 teaspoon vanilla extract
4 egg whites
¼ teaspoon cream of tartar
1 tablespoon sugar
¼ cup crushed walnuts

Combine rusk crumbs, butter and ½ cup sugar in bowl; mix well. Reserve a small amount of mixture for topping. Press remaining mixture into 9x9-inch baking pan. Combine egg yolks, ½ cup sugar, flour and milk in double boiler; mix well. Cook until thickened, stirring constantly. Stir in vanilla. Cool to room temperature. Spoon into prepared pan. Beat egg whites with cream of tartar and 1 tablespoon sugar in mixer bowl until stiff peaks form. Spread over top of dessert. Sprinkle with reserved crumbs and walnuts. Bake at 325 degrees until light brown. Chill until serving time. **Yield: 8 servings.**

Approx Per Serving: Cal 407; Prot 9 g; Carbo 48 g; Fiber <1 g;
    T Fat 21 g; 45% Calories from Fat; Chol 146 mg; Sod 207 mg.

Mary Ann Thurston, Cadillac

Frozen Ice Cream Dessert

1 cup chopped pecans
½ cup butter
1 cup packed brown sugar

1 cup coconut
2 cups crushed crisp rice cereal
½ gallon vanilla ice cream, softened

Brown pecans in butter in skillet. Combine brown sugar, coconut and cereal in bowl. Add to pecans; mix well. Press half the mixture into 9x13-inch dish. Spread with ice cream. Top with remaining cereal mixture. Freeze until firm. **Yield: 15 servings.**

Approx Per Serving: Cal 357; Prot 4 g; Carbo 41 g; Fiber 1 g;
    T Fat 21 g; 51% Calories from Fat; Chol 48 mg; Sod 168 mg.

Helen Byers, St. Helen

Ice Cream Dessert

1½ cups cornflake crumbs
1 cup packed brown sugar
1 cup coconut

½ cup melted butter
½ gallon vanilla ice cream, softened

Combine cornflake crumbs, brown sugar, coconut and butter in bowl; mix well. Pat half the mixture into 9x13-inch dish. Spread ice cream in prepared dish. Top with remaining crumbs. Freeze until firm. May drizzle with caramel or chocolate ice cream topping if desired. **Yield: 15 servings.**

Approx Per Serving: Cal 315; Prot 3 g; Carbo 43 g; Fiber 1 g;
    T Fat 15 g; 43% Calories from Fat; Chol 48 mg; Sod 207 mg.

Lucile Keckritz, Lansing

Frozen Oreo Dessert

24 Oreo cookies, crushed
¼ cup melted margarine
½ gallon vanilla ice cream, softened
1   16-ounce can chocolate syrup
½ cup margarine

1   14-ounce can sweetened
    condensed milk
16 ounces whipped topping
½ cup chopped walnuts

Mix cookie crumbs with ¼ cup margarine in bowl. Press over bottom of buttered 9x13-inch dish. Freeze for 30 minutes. Spread with ice cream. Freeze for 45 minutes. Combine chocolate syrup, ½ cup margarine and condensed milk in saucepan. Bring to a boil over low heat. Simmer for 5 minutes. Cool to room temperature. Spread over ice cream. Freeze for 45 minutes. Top with whipped topping and walnuts. Freeze overnight. **Yield: 15 servings.**

Approx Per Serving: Cal 578; Prot 7 g; Carbo 68 g; Fiber 1 g;
    T Fat 33 g; 49% Calories from Fat; Chol 41 mg; Sod 311 mg.

Marilyn Rogers, Lansing

Oreo Ice Cream

3 egg yolks
4 teaspoons vanilla extract
2 tablespoons water
1   14-ounce can sweetened
    condensed milk

2 cups whipping cream
1 cup Oreo cookie crumbs

Beat egg yolks with vanilla and water in mixer bowl. Add condensed milk; mix well. Whip cream in mixer bowl until soft peaks form. Fold into egg yolk mixture. Fold in cookie crumbs. Spoon into dish. Freeze until firm. **Yield: 12 servings.**

Approx Per Serving: Cal 312; Prot 5 g; Carbo 27 g; Fiber <1 g;
    T Fat 21 g; 60% Calories from Fat; Chol 119 mg; Sod 106 mg.

Ed Nadeau, Traverse City

Lemon-Angel Dessert

1 loaf-size angel food cake
2   4-ounce packages lemon pudding
    and pie filling mix

12 ounces whipped topping
1/2 cup chopped walnuts

Break cake into small pieces; spread in 9x13-inch dish. Cook pudding mix using package directions. Spread over cake. Chill in refrigerator. Top with whipped topping; sprinkle with walnuts. Chill until serving time. **Yield: 15 servings.**

Approx Per Serving: Cal 261; Prot 5 g; Carbo 37 g; Fiber <1 g;
    T Fat 12 g; 38% Calories from Fat; Chol 12 mg; Sod 249 mg.

Jeanne L. Alpers, Traverse City

Lemon Snow

2   3-ounce packages lemon gelatin
3 1/2 cups boiling water

1   21-ounce can lemon pie filling
8 ounces whipped topping

Dissolve gelatin in boiling water in bowl. Chill until partially set. Stir in pie filling and whipped topping. Spoon into serving dish. Chill until firm. May spoon into graham cracker shell if preferred. **Yield: 12 servings.**

Approx Per Serving: Cal 160; Prot 2 g; Carbo 29 g; Fiber 1 g;
    T Fat 5 g; 26% Calories from Fat; Chol 0 mg; Sod 65 mg.

Marion Heil, East Lansing

Lemon Delight

1 cup flour
3/4 cup chopped walnuts
1/2 cup margarine, softened
1 cup confectioners' sugar
12 ounces whipped topping

8 ounces cream cheese, softened
2   4-ounce packages lemon instant
    pudding mix
3 cups milk
1/4 cup chopped walnuts

Mix flour, 3/4 cup walnuts and margarine in bowl. Press into 9x13-inch baking dish. Bake at 350 degrees for 20 minutes. Cool to room temperature. Combine confectioners' sugar, 1 cup whipped topping and cream cheese in mixer bowl; mix until smooth. Spread over cooled crust. Combine pudding mix and milk in mixer bowl. Beat at low speed until thickened and smooth. Spread over cream cheese layer. Top with remaining whipped topping and 1/4 cup walnuts. Chill until serving time. **Yield: 15 servings.**

Approx Per Serving: Cal 378; Prot 5 g; Carbo 38 g; Fiber 1 g;
    T Fat 24 g; 55% Calories from Fat; Chol 23 mg; Sod 244 mg.

Judy Shafer, Wayland

Lorna Doone Dessert

1   8-ounce package Lorna Doone
    cookies, crushed
1/2 cup melted butter
2   4-ounce packages vanilla instant
    pudding mix

1 1/2 cups milk
1 quart vanilla ice cream, softened
8 ounces whipped topping
3   1-ounce Heath bars, crushed

Mix cookie crumbs and butter in bowl. Press into 9x13-inch dish. Bake at 350 degrees for 10 minutes. Cool to room temperature. Combine pudding mix and milk in bowl; mix until smooth. Add ice cream; mix well. Spread over crumb layer. Top with whipped topping; sprinkle with crushed candy. Chill until serving time. **Yield: 15 servings.**

Approx Per Serving: Cal 357; Prot 3 g; Carbo 39 g; Fiber <1 g;
    T Fat 22 g; 54% Calories from Fat; Chol 48 mg; Sod 272 mg.

Alice Campbell, Otisville

Honey Meringue

2 egg whites   1 cup honey
1/8 teaspoon salt

Beat egg whites with salt in mixer bowl until soft peaks form. Add honey in fine
stream, beating constantly at high speed for 2 1/2 minutes or until stiff peaks form.
Use as topping for cake or pudding. **Yield: 8 servings.**

Approx Per Serving: Cal 133; Prot 1 g; Carbo 35 g; Fiber 0 g;
     T Fat 0 g; 0% Calories from Fat; Chol 0 mg; Sod 48 mg.

Sally Taylor, Marguette

Mousse in-a-Minute

1   4-ounce package instant pudding   1 1/2 cups cold milk
    mix   1 to 1 1/2 cups whipped topping

Combine pudding mix and milk in bowl; mix until smooth. Fold in whipped topping. Chill until serving time. Top servings with additional whipped topping. May
use any flavor pudding mix. **Yield: 4 servings.**

Approx Per Serving: Cal 251; Prot 3 g; Carbo 37 g; Fiber <1 g;
     T Fat 10 g; 36% Calories from Fat; Chol 12 mg; Sod 235 mg.

Judy Hartman, Lansing

Pumpkin Mousse

1 1/4 cups cold milk   1   4-ounce package vanilla instant
1 cup canned pumpkin   pudding mix
1 teaspoon grated orange rind   1 cup whipped topping
1/4 teaspoon each cinnamon, nutmeg   1/4 cup chopped pecans
    and ginger

Combine milk, pumpkin, orange rind, cinnamon, nutmeg and ginger in mixer bowl.
Add pudding mix. Beat at low speed for 1 to 2 minutes or until smooth. Fold in
whipped topping and pecans. Spoon into dessert glasses. Chill until serving time.
Garnish with additional whipped topping and pecans. May substitute butterscotch
pudding mix for vanilla or use sugar-free pudding mix if preferred.
Yield: 6 servings.

Approx Per Serving: Cal 188; Prot 3 g; Carbo 27 g; Fiber 1 g;
     T Fat 8 g; 39% Calories from Fat; Chol 7 mg; Sod 153 mg.

Mary Herman, Gwinn

Mud Dessert

1 cup sugar
1/2 cup melted margarine
2 eggs
1/3 cup flour
1/3 cup baking cocoa

1 teaspoon vanilla extract
1/4 teaspoon salt
1 cup walnuts
1/4 cup fudge topping

Combine sugar, margarine, eggs, flour, baking cocoa, vanilla and salt in bowl; mix with wooden spoon until smooth. Stir in walnuts. Spoon into greased 8-inch baking dish. Bake at 350 degrees for 25 minutes or until wooden pick inserted between center and edge of layer comes out clean. Pierce holes in baked layer with wooden pick. Pour fudge topping over top. Cool to room temperature. Cut into wedges to serve. Serve with whipped cream, ice cream or whipped topping. **Yield: 8 servings.**

Approx Per Serving: Cal 374; Prot 5 g; Carbo 38 g; Fiber 2 g;
 T Fat 24 g; 55% Calories from Fat; Chol 53 mg; Sod 231 mg.

June Brassar, Sault Ste. Marie

Black Forest Parfaits

1 21-ounce can cherry pie filling
3 ounces cream cheese, softened
2 cups cold milk

1 4-ounce package chocolate instant
 pudding mix
1/2 cup chocolate wafer crumbs

Reserve 6 cherries from pie filling. Combine cream cheese and 1/2 cup milk in mixer bowl; beat until smooth. Add remaining 1 1/2 cups milk and pudding mix; beat for 1 to 2 minutes or until smooth. Layer half the pudding mixture, cookie crumbs, remaining pie filling and remaining pudding mixture in dessert dishes. Top with reserved cherries. Chill until serving time. Garnish with additional cookie crumbs if desired. **Yield: 6 servings.**

Approx Per Serving: Cal 311; Prot 5 g; Carbo 55 g; Fiber 2 g;
 T Fat 9 g; 26% Calories from Fat; Chol 27 mg; Sod 305 mg.

Michelle Richards, Lansing

For easy but elegant desserts, spoon cream sherry over a chilled grapefruit or Crème de Menthe over vanilla ice cream.

Peach Cobbler

9 medium peaches
2 tablespoons lemon juice
1/4 cup sugar
3 tablespoons sugar

1 recipe baking mix drop biscuits
1/8 teaspoon nutmeg
2 teaspoons sugar

Immerse peaches in boiling water in saucepan for 1 minute. Rinse under cold water and remove skins. Slice peaches into 2-quart baking dish or deep 10-inch pie plate. Add lemon juice and 1/4 cup sugar; toss to mix well. Bake, covered with foil, at 400 degrees for 15 minutes or until bubbly. Add 3 tablespoons sugar to baking mix dough. Drop by heaping tablespoonfuls onto peaches. Sprinkle with mixture of nutmeg and 2 teaspoons sugar. Bake for 30 minutes longer or until topping is golden brown. Let cool for several minutes before serving. **Yield: 8 servings.**

Approx Per Serving: Cal 254; Prot 4 g; Carbo 48 g; Fiber 2 g;
     T Fat 6 g; 20% Calories from Fat; Chol 3 mg; Sod 455 mg.

Irene Momier, Saginaw

Peach Crumb Dessert

1   4-ounce package butterscotch
  instant pudding mix
1/2 cup sugar
1/4 cup butter
1 cup chopped walnuts
1/8 teaspoon each cinnamon and
  nutmeg

2/3 cup milk
1 egg, beaten
2 1/4 cups baking mix
1/4 teaspoon almond extract
1 cup chopped peeled peaches

Combine pudding mix, sugar and butter in bowl; mix with pastry blender until crumbly. Stir in walnuts. Combine 1 cup crumb mixture with cinnamon and nutmeg in small bowl; set aside. Add milk, egg, baking mix and almond extract to remaining crumb mixture; mix well. Fold in 3/4 cup peaches. Spoon into greased and floured 9-inch baking pan. Spread remaining 1/4 cup peaches over top; sprinkle with reserved crumbs. Bake at 350 degrees for 45 to 50 minutes or until light brown. Remove to wire rack to cool. Garnish with confectioners' sugar. **Yield: 8 servings.**

Approx Per Serving: Cal 441; Prot 6 g; Carbo 58 g; Fiber 2 g;
     T Fat 22 g; 43% Calories from Fat; Chol 45 mg; Sod 609 mg.

Jason Uhrik, Stevensville

Peach Thing

3 cups flour
3 tablespoons sugar
1 cup oil
1/4 cup plus 1 1/2 teaspoons milk
1 1/2 teaspoons salt
8 peaches, peeled, sliced
1 1/3 cups sugar

1/4 cup flour
2 tablespoons tapioca
1 teaspoon vanilla extract
1/4 cup butter
1/2 cup chopped pecans
2 tablespoons sugar

Combine 3 cups flour, 3 tablespoons sugar, oil, milk and salt in bowl; mix well. Spread 2/3 of the mixture over bottom and 1 inch up sides of 9x13-inch baking pan. Combine peaches with 1 1/3 cups sugar, 1/4 cup flour, tapioca and vanilla in bowl; mix well. Spoon into prepared pan; dot with butter. Sprinkle remaining flour mixture over top. Sprinkle with pecans and 2 tablespoons sugar. Bake at 450 degrees for 10 minutes. Reduce temperature to 350 degrees. Bake for 40 minutes longer. **Yield: 15 servings.**

Approx Per Serving: Cal 392; Prot 4 g; Carbo 50 g; Fiber 2 g;
    T Fat 21 g; 47% Calories from Fat; Chol 9 mg; Sod 29 mg.

Fran Lubic, Kalamazoo

Baked Pear Halves

2 large pears
Juice of 1 lemon
1/2 cup water
1 tablespoon honey

1/4 cup graham cracker crumbs
1 tablespoon melted diet margarine
1/4 teaspoon cinnamon

Peel pears and cut into halves lengthwise. Scoop out cores with teaspoon. Rub with lemon juice. Place cored side up in lightly greased 8x8-inch baking dish. Add water to dish; drizzle with honey. Bake, covered with foil, at 425 degrees for 15 to 20 minutes or until tender. Sprinkle with mixture of graham cracker crumbs, margarine and cinnamon. Bake for 10 minutes longer. **Yield: 4 servings.**

Approx Per Serving: Cal 112; Prot 1 g; Carbo 24 g; Fiber 3 g;
    T Fat 3 g; 19% Calories from Fat; Chol 0 mg; Sod 81 mg.

Joann Bouwman, Zeeland

Pineapple Fluff

1 16-ounce can juice-pack crushed
   pineapple
2 cups plain yogurt

1 4-serving package sugar-free
   pistachio instant pudding mix

Combine undrained pineapple, yogurt and pudding mix in bowl; mix well. Chill until serving time. **Yield: 8 servings.**

Approx Per Serving: Cal 126; Prot 4 g; Carbo 23 g; Fiber 1 g;
   T Fat 3 g; 22% Calories from Fat; Chol 7 mg; Sod 490 mg.

Betty Boyd, Hemlock

Prune Dumplings

2 cups pitted prunes
1 cup self-rising flour
1 tablespoon sugar

1 egg
1/2 cup (about) milk
1/2 cup raisins

Cook prunes in large amount of water in saucepan until tender. Combine flour, sugar and egg in bowl. Add enough milk to make a stiff dough. Add raisins; mix well. Drop by spoonfuls into boiling prune mixture. Simmer for 10 minutes or until dumplings are cooked through. **Yield: 4 servings.**

Approx Per Serving: Cal 417; Prot 8 g; Carbo 95 g; Fiber 10 g;
   T Fat 3 g; 7% Calories from Fat; Chol 57 mg; Sod 373 mg.

Bessie Stuhr Cohoon, Beaverton

Apple Pudding

1/4 cup flour
3/4 cup sugar
1/4 teaspoon baking powder
1 egg, beaten

2 cups chopped peeled apples
1/2 cup chopped walnuts
Cinnamon to taste
Vanilla extract to taste

Mix flour, sugar and baking powder in bowl. Add egg; mix well. Stir in apples and walnuts. Add cinnamon and vanilla; mix well. Spoon into greased 8x8-inch baking pan. Bake at 350 degrees for 25 minutes. Serve with whipped cream.
Yield: 6 servings.

Approx Per Serving: Cal 217; Prot 3 g; Carbo 37 g; Fiber 2 g;
   T Fat 7 g; 29% Calories from Fat; Chol 36 mg; Sod 27 mg.

Marie Fineout, Cheboygan

Apple Pudding with Sauce

1/4 cup butter, softened
1 cup sugar
1 egg
2 cups chopped or thinly sliced
  peeled apples
1 cup flour
1 teaspoon baking soda
1 teaspoon cinnamon

3/4 teaspoon nutmeg
1/4 teaspoon salt
1 teaspoon vanilla extract
3/4 cup chopped walnuts
1/2 cup butter
1 cup sugar
1/2 cup light cream
2 teaspoons vanilla extract

Cream 1/4 cup butter and 1 cup sugar in mixer bowl until light. Beat in egg. Stir in apples. Add mixture of flour, baking soda, cinnamon, nutmeg and salt; mix well. Stir in 1 teaspoon vanilla and walnuts. Spoon into greased 8x8-inch baking pan. Bake at 350 degrees for 45 minutes. Combine 1/2 cup butter, 1 cup sugar and cream in double boiler. Cook for 10 to 15 minutes or until thickened, stirring constantly; do not boil. Stir in 2 teaspoons vanilla. Serve hot with warm pudding. **Yield: 6 servings.**

Approx Per Serving: Cal 727; Prot 6 g; Carbo 92 g; Fiber 2 g;
  T Fat 40 g; 48% Calories from Fat; Chol 120 mg; Sod 441 mg.

Florence McLain, Marshall

Bread Pudding

3 eggs
1 1/2 cups sugar
1/2 cup margarine
2 cups milk

1 1/2 teaspoons cinnamon
1/4 teaspoon nutmeg
1 1/2 teaspoons vanilla extract
1/4 loaf day-old bread, crumbled

Combine eggs and sugar in mixer bowl; beat until smooth. Add margarine, milk, cinnamon, nutmeg and vanilla; mix well. Stir in bread crumbs. Spoon into baking dish. Bake at 350 degrees for 1 hour. Serve with sauce if desired. **Yield: 6 servings.**

Approx Per Serving: Cal 468; Prot 7 g; Carbo 63 g; Fiber <1 g;
  T Fat 21 g; 41% Calories from Fat; Chol 117 mg; Sod 344 mg.

Shirley Sullivan Wellington, Zephyrhills, Florida

*Substitute low-fat yogurt for milk and cream
in puddings and other desserts.*

Raisin-Bread Pudding

1 cup dry bread crumbs
4 cups milk, scalded
³/₄ cup sugar
1 tablespoon butter

4 eggs, at room temperature, slightly
  beaten
1 tablespoon vanilla extract
1 cup raisins

Process bread crumbs in blender until fine. Combine with scalded milk in bowl; mix well. Let stand for 5 minutes. Add sugar and butter; mix well. Add gradually to mixture of eggs and vanilla in bowl, stirring to mix well. Stir in raisins. Spoon into greased 1¹/₂-quart baking dish. Place in larger pan of hot water. Bake at 350 degrees for 1 hour or until set. Serve with Whiskey Sauce which has been spooned over top and broiled until bubbly. **Yield: 6 servings.**

Approx Per Serving: Cal 413; Prot 13 g; Carbo 67 g; Fiber 2 g;
    T Fat 12 g; 25% Calories from Fat; Chol 170 mg; Sod 257 mg.
    Nutritional information does not include Whiskey Sauce.

Karla Couture, Coleman

Whiskey Sauce

¹/₂ cup butter
1 cup confectioners' sugar

1 egg, beaten
¹/₄ cup (or more) whiskey

Combine butter and confectioners' sugar in double boiler. Cook over simmering water until confectioners' sugar dissolves and mixture is very hot. Remove pan from heat. Stir a small amount of hot mixture into egg; stir egg into hot mixture. Remove top of double boiler from hot water. Beat until cool. Stir in whiskey. Serve over bread pudding. **Yield: 6 servings.**

Approx Per Serving: Cal 247; Prot 1 g; Carbo 20 g; Fiber 0 g;
    T Fat 16 g; 63% Calories from Fat; Chol 77 mg; Sod 141 mg.

Karla Couture, Coleman

*Prevent a "skin" from forming on custards and puddings by
placing a piece of plastic wrap directly on the surface
after removing from heat.*

Rice Pudding

4 cups milk
4 cups water
1/4 cup margarine
1 1/4 cups sugar

1 1/4 cups uncooked rice
2 eggs, beaten
3/4 teaspoon vanilla extract
Cinnamon to taste

Bring milk, 4 cups water, margarine and sugar to a boil in large saucepan; reduce heat. Stir in rice. Cook until rice is tender. Combine eggs with enough water to measure 1 cup. Add to rice with vanilla; mix well. Cook until thickened, stirring constantly. Spoon into 9x13-inch dish; sprinkle with cinnamon. Chill until serving time. **Yield: 12 servings.**

Approx Per Serving: Cal 247; Prot 5 g; Carbo 40 g; Fiber <1 g;
    T Fat 8 g; 27% Calories from Fat; Chol 47 mg; Sod 92 mg.

Carol Lyons, Horton

Easy Rice Pudding

4 cups milk
4 cups water
1/4 cup margarine
1 cup sugar

1 cup uncooked rice
1 teaspoon salt
3 eggs, beaten
1 teaspoon vanilla extract

Bring milk, water, margarine and sugar to a boil in saucepan. Stir in rice and salt. Cook over medium heat for 35 minutes or until rice is tender, stirring occasionally. Stir a small amount of hot mixture into eggs; stir eggs and vanilla into hot mixture. Spoon into serving dish; chill. **Yield: 8 servings.**

Approx Per Serving: Cal 336; Prot 8 g; Carbo 50 g; Fiber <1 g;
    T Fat 12 g; 32% Calories from Fat; Chol 96 mg; Sod 412 mg.

Nancy Carpenter, Jackson

Microwave Rice Pudding

2 cups cooked rice
1 1/3 cups milk
1/2 cup packed brown sugar
3 eggs, beaten

1 tablespoon margarine, softened
1 teaspoon vanilla extract
1 teaspoon cinnamon

Combine all ingredients in 2 1/2-quart glass dish. Microwave, covered, on Medium for 13 to 15 minutes or until of desired consistency, stirring every 5 minutes. Let stand for 10 minutes before serving. May add raisins if desired. **Yield: 8 servings.**

Approx Per Serving: Cal 187; Prot 5 g; Carbo 31 g; Fiber <1 g;
    T Fat 5 g; 24% Calories from Fat; Chol 86 mg; Sod 67 mg.

Nancy Briolat, St. Ignace

Quick Rice Pudding

½ cup instant rice
3 cups milk
1 4-ounce package vanilla pudding
   and pie filling mix

3 tablespoons raisins
¼ teaspoon cinnamon

Combine rice, milk, pudding mix, raisins and cinnamon in 2-quart glass dish; mix well. Microwave, covered with waxed paper, on Medium for 11 to 13 minutes or until thickened, stirring 3 times. Let stand for several minutes. **Yield: 8 servings.**

Approx Per Serving: Cal 129; Prot 4 g; Carbo 22 g; Fiber <1 g;
    T Fat 3 g; 22% Calories from Fat; Chol 12 mg; Sod 110 mg.

Sally Taylor, Marquette

Recycled Rice Pudding

1 cup cooked rice
4 eggs, beaten
½ cup sugar

3 cups milk
1 teaspoon nutmeg
1 teaspoon vanilla extract

Combine rice, eggs, sugar, milk, nutmeg and vanilla in bowl; mix well. Spoon into baking dish. Bake at 300 degrees for 45 minutes or until knife inserted in center comes out clean. May substitute brown sugar for half the sugar. **Yield: 4 servings.**

Approx Per Serving: Cal 343; Prot 13 g; Carbo 46 g; Fiber <1 g;
    T Fat 12 g; 31% Calories from Fat; Chol 238 mg; Sod 146 mg.

Zelma Cohoon, Sault Ste. Marie

Date-Nut Pudding

2 tablespoons margarine, softened
1 cup sugar
2 eggs
2 tablespoons flour
½ cup water

1 teaspoon baking powder
1 cup milk
8 ounces dates, chopped
1 cup chopped walnuts

Cream margarine and sugar in mixer bowl until light and fluffy. Beat in eggs. Blend flour with water in small bowl. Add to batter with baking powder and milk; mix well. Stir in dates and walnuts. Spoon into greased 8x8-inch baking pan. Bake at 375 degrees for 30 minutes. Serve with whipped topping. May double recipe and bake in 9x13-inch baking dish. **Yield: 8 servings.**

Approx Per Serving: Cal 342; Prot 5 g; Carbo 52 g; Fiber 3 g;
    T Fat 15 g; 37% Calories from Fat; Chol 57 mg; Sod 108 mg.

E. Fern Garter, Grand Rapids

Incredible Noodle Pudding

16 ounces uncooked wide egg
  noodles
4 quarts water
1/2 cup margarine
1 cup sugar
4 eggs
8 ounces pot-style cottage cheese
2 cups sour cream
2 cups milk

2 apples, peeled, chopped
1 8-ounce can peaches, drained
5 ounces orange marmalade
1/2 cup raisins
1 teaspoon vanilla extract
1/2 cup crushed cornflakes
1/4 cup margarine
4 teaspoons sugar
2 teaspoons cinnamon

Cook noodles in 4 quarts water in large saucepan for 5 minutes; drain. Add 1/2 cup margarine; mix to coat well. Process 1 cup sugar and eggs in blender until smooth. Add cottage cheese, sour cream and milk; mix well. Combine with apples, peaches, marmalade, raisins and vanilla in bowl; mix well. Add to noodles; mix gently. Spoon into large baking dish. Sprinkle with cornflakes; dot with 1/4 cup margarine. Sprinkle with mixture of 4 teaspoons sugar and cinnamon. Bake at 350 degrees for 1 hour. **Yield: 15 servings.**

Approx Per Serving: Cal 444; Prot 10 g; Carbo 57 g; Fiber 1 g;
    T Fat 20 g; 41% Calories from Fat; Chol 130 mg; Sod 253 mg.

June B. Brown, Bradenton, Florida

Raspberry Delight

1/2 cup melted margarine
1/3 cup confectioners' sugar
12 graham crackers, crushed
8 ounces cream cheese, softened
2 1/2 cups whipped topping
1/3 cup confectioners' sugar
1 teaspoon vanilla extract

2 10-ounce packages frozen
  raspberries
1 cup water
1 cup sugar
1/3 cup cornstarch
1/4 cup cold water

Mix margarine, 1/3 cup confectioners' sugar and cracker crumbs in bowl. Pat into 9x13-inch dish. Combine cream cheese, whipped topping, 1/3 cup confectioners' sugar and vanilla in mixer bowl; mix well. Spread in prepared dish. Bring raspberries, 1 cup water and sugar to a boil in saucepan, stirring frequently. Stir in mixture of cornstarch and 1/4 cup cold water. Bring to a boil, stirring constantly. Cook for 1 minute longer, stirring constantly. Pour over layers in dish. Chill until serving time. **Yield: 15 servings.**

Approx Per Serving: Cal 291; Prot 2 g; Carbo 39 g; Fiber 2 g;
    T Fat 15 g; 46% Calories from Fat; Chol 17 mg; Sod 154 mg.

Pauline Bradley, Calumet

Nen's Rhubarb Dessert

1 2-layer package yellow cake mix
3 cups chopped rhubarb

1½ cups sugar
1 cup half and half

Prepare cake mix using package directions. Spoon into 10x15-inch baking pan. Top with rhubarb; sprinkle with sugar. Pour half and half over top. Bake at 350 degrees for 30 to 35 minutes or until rhubarb is tender. Cut into squares; serve with whipped topping or ice cream. Store in refrigerator. **Yield: 15 servings.**

Approx Per Serving: Cal 351; Prot 4 g; Carbo 64 g; Fiber 1 g;
    T Fat 10 g; 25% Calories from Fat; Chol 6 mg; Sod 175 mg.

Aurelia Champlin, Sault Ste. Marie

Strawberry Pizza

½ cup butter, softened
1 cup sugar
1 egg
¼ cup milk
2 cups flour
1 teaspoon baking powder

¼ teaspoon vanilla extract
11 ounces cream cheese, softened
½ cup sugar
1 teaspoon vanilla extract
6 cups sliced strawberries

Cream butter and 1 cup sugar in mixer bowl until light. Add egg, milk, flour, baking powder and ¼ teaspoon vanilla; mix to form dough. Chill, covered, overnight. Press dough into greased 14-inch round pan. Bake at 375 degrees for 15 to 20 minutes or until light brown. Cool to room temperature. Beat cream cheese, ½ cup sugar and 1 teaspoon vanilla in mixer bowl until fluffy. Spread on cooled crust. Top with strawberries. Chill until serving time. Cut into wedges to serve. **Yield: 16 servings.**

Approx Per Serving: Cal 289; Prot 4 g; Carbo 39 g; Fiber 3 g;
    T Fat 14 g; 41% Calories from Fat; Chol 51 mg; Sod 135 mg.

Michelle Richards, Lansing

Super Sundae Dessert

1 14-ounce can sweetened
   condensed milk
2 21-ounce cans strawberry pie filling

1 16-ounce can crushed pineapple,
   drained
16 ounces whipped topping

Combine condensed milk, pie filling, pineapple and whipped topping in bowl; mix well. Spoon into freezer pan. Freeze until firm. Garnish servings with salted peanuts. **Yield: 12 servings.**

Approx Per Serving: Cal 340; Prot 4 g; Carbo 57 g; Fiber 2 g;
    T Fat 13 g; 32% Calories from Fat; Chol 11 mg; Sod 82 mg.

T. C. Smorgasbroads, Traverse City

TEDDY BEARS

Cakes

Applesauce Cake

1¹/₂ cups sugar
¹/₂ cup shortening
2 eggs
³/₄ teaspoon salt
¹/₂ teaspoon cinnamon
¹/₂ teaspoon cloves
¹/₂ teaspoon nutmeg
¹/₂ teaspoon allspice

2 tablespoons baking cocoa
1¹/₂ teaspoons baking soda
2 cups flour
³/₄ cup raisins
³/₄ cup chopped dates
³/₄ cup chopped walnuts
1¹/₂ cups unsweetened applesauce
1   8-ounce can crushed pineapple

Cream sugar and shortening in mixer bowl until light and fluffy. Beat in eggs 1 at a time. Add salt, cinnamon, cloves, nutmeg, allspice, baking cocoa and baking soda; beat well. Add flour; mix well. Plump raisins in hot water to cover in bowl; drain. Stir raisins, dates, walnuts, applesauce, crushed pineapple and liquid into batter. Spoon into greased and floured 9x13-inch cake pan. Bake at 350 degrees for 40 to 45 minutes or until cake tests done. Serve with whipped topping or favorite frosting. **Yield: 15 servings.**

Approx Per Serving: Cal 372; Prot 4 g; Carbo 66 g; Fiber 3 g;
      T Fat 12 g; 32% Calories from Fat; Chol 28 mg; Sod 201 mg.

Patricia A. McComb, Topinabee

Banana Cake

1 cup shortening
1¹/₂ cups sugar
2 eggs, beaten
2 cups sifted flour
1 teaspoon baking soda

2 teaspoons baking powder
¹/₂ teaspoon salt
1 cup sour milk
1 cup mashed bananas
1 teaspoon vanilla extract

Cream shortening and sugar in mixer bowl until light and fluffy. Add eggs; mix well. Add flour, baking soda, baking powder, salt and milk; beat well. Stir in bananas and vanilla. Spoon into greased and floured cake pan. Bake at 350 degrees for 40 to 45 minutes or until cake tests done. Remove to wire rack to cool. **Yield: 16 servings.**

Approx Per Serving: Cal 271; Prot 3 g; Carbo 34 g; Fiber 1 g;
      T Fat 14 g; 47% Calories from Fat; Chol 29 mg; Sod 175 mg.

Jennie Hill Barlett, Davison

Kona Banana Cake

½ cup shortening
1 cup sugar
2 eggs
1 cup mashed bananas

1¼ cups flour
¾ teaspoon baking soda
½ teaspoon salt
½ teaspoon vanilla extract

Cream shortening and sugar in mixer bowl until light and fluffy. Beat in eggs 1 at a time. Add bananas; mix well. Add flour, baking soda, salt and vanilla; beat well. Spoon into greased and floured 9x9-inch cake pan. Bake at 350 degrees for 30 to 35 minutes or until cake tests done. May serve warm or at room temperature. Garnish with whipped topping. **Yield: 6 servings.**

Approx Per Serving: Cal 436; Prot 5 g; Carbo 62 g; Fiber 1 g;
    T Fat 19 g; 39% Calories from Fat; Chol 71 mg; Sod 305 mg.

Donna Holmes, Lansing

Butter Bundt Cake

1 2-layer package yellow cake mix
1 4-ounce package vanilla instant
    pudding mix
4 eggs
¾ cup water
¾ cup oil
1 teaspoon butter flavoring
1 teaspoon vanilla extract

½ cup chopped pecans
¼ cup sugar
2 tablespoons cinnamon
1 cup confectioners' sugar
½ teaspoon vanilla extract
1 tablespoon butter flavoring
3 teaspoons milk

Combine cake mix, pudding mix, eggs, water, oil, 1 teaspoon butter flavoring and 1 teaspoon vanilla in mixer bowl; beat for 8 minutes. Combine pecans, sugar and cinnamon in bowl; mix well. Layer half the batter, all the pecan mixture and remaining batter in greased and floured bundt pan. Bake at 350 degrees for 45 minutes or until cake tests done. Remove to serving plate to cool. Combine confectioners' sugar, ½ teaspoon vanilla, 1 tablespoon butter flavoring and milk in bowl; mix well. Drizzle over cooled cake. **Yield: 16 servings.**

Approx Per Serving: Cal 344; Prot 3 g; Carbo 45 g; Fiber <1 g;
    T Fat 17 g; 44% Calories from Fat; Chol 53 mg; Sod 262 mg.

Dani Peterson, Lansing

California Walnut Torte

3¹/₄ cups walnuts
3 tablespoons flour
1 teaspoon baking powder
¹/₄ teaspoon salt

6 egg yolks, beaten
1 cup sugar
6 egg whites, stiffly beaten
1 cup whipping cream, whipped

Grease two 8-inch round cake pans. Line with waxed paper; grease waxed paper. Chop 1 tablespoon walnuts coarsely; set aside. Press remaining walnuts through grinder until finely ground. Combine ground walnuts, flour, baking powder and salt in bowl; mix well. Combine egg yolks and sugar in mixer bowl. Beat at high speed until thick and lemon colored. Fold walnut mixture and egg yolks into stiffly beaten egg whites in bowl. Spoon into prepared pans. Bake at 350 degrees for 25 to 30 minutes or until layers test done. Cool in pans for 5 minutes. Remove to wire rack; remove waxed paper. Cool completely. Spread whipped cream between layers and on top of cooled cake. Sprinkle with reserved walnuts. **Yield: 12 servings.**

Approx Per Serving: Cal 388; Prot 8 g; Carbo 25 g; Fiber 2 g;
   T Fat 30 g; 67% Calories from Fat; Chol 134 mg; Sod 112 mg.

Mary Carey, Portage

Caramel Surprise

1 2-layer package Swiss chocolate
   cake mix
1 14-ounce can sweetened
   condensed milk

1 14-ounce package caramels
¹/₂ cup chopped walnuts
1 cup chocolate chips

Prepare cake mix using package directions. Spoon half the batter into greased and floured 9x13-inch cake pan. Bake at 350 degrees for 15 minutes. Combine condensed milk and caramels in saucepan. Cook over low heat until caramels are melted, stirring frequently. Pour caramel mixture over hot cake; sprinkle with walnuts and chocolate chips. Top with remaining batter. Bake at 350 degrees for 15 minutes longer. Cool in cake pan. Garnish with whipped topping. **Yield: 15 servings.**

Approx Per Serving: Cal 523; Prot 7 g; Carbo 85 g; Fiber 1 g;
   T Fat 20 g; 33% Calories from Fat; Chol 10 mg; Sod 262 mg.

Juanita Mansfield, Lansing

Carrot-Applesauce Cake

4 eggs, beaten
3/4 cup oil
2 cups sugar
1 teaspoon vanilla extract
1²/₃ cups applesauce
3 cups shredded carrots
2³/₄ cups flour

1 tablespoon baking soda
1 teaspoon salt
1 tablespoon cinnamon
1 teaspoon nutmeg
1 cup golden raisins
1 cup chopped walnuts

Combine eggs, oil, sugar, vanilla, applesauce and carrots in mixer bowl; beat well. Mix flour, baking soda, salt, cinnamon and nutmeg together. Add to egg mixture; mix well. Stir in raisins and half the walnuts. Spoon into greased and floured 9x13-inch cake pan; sprinkle with remaining walnuts. Bake at 350 degrees for 45 minutes or until cake tests done. **Yield: 15 servings.**

Approx Per Serving: Cal 420; Prot 6 g; Carbo 62 g; Fiber 3 g;
    T Fat 18 g; 37% Calories from Fat; Chol 57 mg; Sod 336 mg.

Helen DeGraff, Grand Rapids

Carrot and Pineapple Cake

1¹/₂ cups oil
2 cups sugar
3 eggs
2 cups grated carrots
1 cup drained crushed pineapple
2¹/₂ cups flour
1 teaspoon baking soda
¹/₂ teaspoon salt

1 teaspoon cinnamon
1 teaspoon vanilla extract
1 cup chopped pecans
1 1-pound package confectioners' sugar
¹/₂ cup butter, softened
3 ounces cream cheese, softened

Cream oil, sugar and eggs together in mixer bowl. Add carrots and pineapple; mix well. Sift in flour, baking soda, salt and cinnamon, beating constantly. Stir in vanilla and pecans. Pour into greased and floured 9x13-inch cake pan. Bake at 350 degrees for 45 minutes or until cake tests done. Cool slightly. Combine confectioners' sugar, butter and cream cheese in mixer bowl; beat until smooth. Spread on cake. **Yield: 15 servings.**

Approx Per Serving: Cal 670; Prot 5 g; Carbo 84 g; Fiber 2 g;
    T Fat 37 g; 48% Calories from Fat; Chol 65 mg; Sod 215 mg.

Martha Boog, Lansing

Incredible Carrot and Coconut Cake

1½ cups corn oil
2 cups sugar
3 eggs, beaten
2 cups flour
2 teaspoons cinnamon
2 teaspoons baking soda
1 teaspoon salt

1 8-ounce can crushed pineapple
1 cup coconut
2 cups shredded carrots
1 cup chopped walnuts
3 ounces cream cheese, softened
2 cups confectioners' sugar
¼ cup margarine, softened

Combine oil, sugar and eggs in mixer bowl; beat well. Add flour, cinnamon, baking soda and salt; mix well. Stir in pineapple, coconut, carrots and walnuts. Spoon into ungreased 9x13-inch cake pan. Bake at 350 degrees for 1 hour or until cake tests done. Cool slightly. Combine cream cheese, confectioners' sugar and margarine in mixer bowl; beat until smooth, adding a small amount of milk if needed to make of spreading consistency. Spread over cake. **Yield: 15 servings.**

Approx Per Serving: Cal 573; Prot 5 g; Carbo 64 g; Fiber 2 g;
    T Fat 35 g; 53% Calories from Fat; Chol 49 mg; Sod 326 mg.

Diane Juskewicz, Grand Rapids

Carrot and Walnut Cake

2 cups flour
2 cups sugar
2 8-ounce jars junior baby food
    carrots
2 teaspoons baking soda
2 teaspoons baking powder
2 teaspoons cinnamon
⅔ cup corn oil

4 eggs, beaten
¾ cup chopped walnuts
1 1-pound package confectioners'
    sugar
½ cup margarine, softened
8 ounces cream cheese, softened
1 teaspoon vanilla extract
Juice of ½ lemon

Combine flour, sugar, baby food carrots, baking soda, baking powder, cinnamon, oil and eggs in mixer bowl; beat well. Stir in walnuts. Spoon into greased and floured 9x13-inch cake pan. Bake at 350 degrees for 45 minutes or until cake tests done. Cool slightly. Combine confectioners' sugar, margarine, cream cheese, vanilla and lemon juice in mixer bowl; beat until creamy. Spread over cake. **Yield: 15 servings.**

Approx Per Serving: Cal 566; Prot 6 g; Carbo 80 g; Fiber 1 g;
    T Fat 26 g; 41% Calories from Fat; Chol 73 mg; Sod 304 mg.

Karla Couture, Coleman

Almond Cream Chocolate Cake

1 2-layer package pudding-recipe
  Devil's food cake mix
1 cup sour cream
3/4 cup milk
1/2 cup butter, softened
3 eggs
1 teaspoon cinnamon

1/2 teaspoon nutmeg
1/2 teaspoon almond extract
3 ounces cream cheese, softened
1/4 teaspoon confectioners' sugar
1/4 to 1/2 teaspoon almond extract
3/4 cup whipping cream, whipped
Almond Cream Chocolate Frosting

Combine cake mix, sour cream, milk, butter, eggs, cinnamon, nutmeg and 1/2 teaspoon almond extract in mixer bowl; mix at low speed. Beat at high speed for 2 minutes. Spread in 3 greased and floured round cake pans. Bake at 350 degrees for 25 to 35 minutes or until layers test done. Cool in pans for 10 minutes. Remove to wire rack to cool completely. Combine cream cheese, confectioners' sugar and remaining almond extract in bowl; beat until light and fluffy. Fold in whipped cream. Chill cream cheese filling, covered, in refrigerator until cake layers are cool. Spread filling between cake layers. Spread Almond Cream Chocolate Frosting on side and top of cake. Garnish with chocolate curls. Chill in refrigerator. Let stand at room temperature for 30 minutes before serving. Store in refrigerator.
Yield: 15 servings.

Approx Per Serving: Cal 510; Prot 7 g; Carbo 52 g; Fiber 1 g;
    T Fat 32 g; 55% Calories from Fat; Chol 110 mg; Sod 497 mg.

Almond Cream Chocolate Frosting

2 ounces unsweetened chocolate
1/4 cup butter
3 ounces cream cheese, softened
2 1/2 cups confectioners' sugar

1/2 to 1 teaspoon almond extract
1/2 teaspoon salt
3 to 4 tablespoons whipping cream
2/3 cup finely chopped almonds

Melt chocolate and butter in saucepan over low heat, stirring constantly. Combine chocolate mixture with cream cheese in mixer bowl; beat well. Add confectioners' sugar, almond extract and salt; mix well. Add enough whipping cream to make frosting of spreading consistency. Stir in almonds. **Yield: 15 servings.**

Approx Per Serving: Cal 191; Prot 2 g; Carbo 22 g; Fiber 1 g;
    T Fat 12 g; 51% Calories from Fat; Chol 20 mg; Sod 116 mg.

Linda Haubenstricker, Birch Run

Chocolate Cake

2²/₃ cups flour
6 tablespoons baking cocoa
2 teaspoons salt
2 teaspoons baking soda
2 cups sugar

2 cups water
2 teaspoons vanilla extract
2 tablespoons white vinegar
1 cup vegetable oil

Combine flour, baking cocoa, salt, baking soda and sugar in mixer bowl; mix well. Add water, vanilla, vinegar and oil, beating well. Pour into greased and floured 9x13-inch cake pan. Bake at 350 degrees for 30 minutes or until cake tests done. **Yield: 15 servings.**

Approx Per Serving: Cal 320; Prot 3 g; Carbo 45 g; Fiber 1 g;
    T Fat 15 g; 42% Calories from Fat; Chol 0 mg; Sod 395 mg.

Carolyn Devers, Laingsburg

Chocolate-Cream Cheese Cake

6 ounces cream cheese, softened
½ cup butter, softened
1 teaspoon vanilla extract
1½ 1-pound packages
    confectioners' sugar, sifted
⅓ cup milk, at room temperature
4 ounces unsweetened chocolate,
    melted, cooled

¼ cup butter, softened
3 eggs
2¼ cups flour
1 teaspoon baking powder
1 teaspoon baking soda
1 teaspoon salt
1¼ cups milk

Combine cream cheese, ½ cup butter and vanilla in mixer bowl; beat well. Add confectioners' sugar alternately with ⅓ cup milk, beating well after each addition. Add chocolate; mix well. Reserve 2 cups chocolate mixture for frosting. Chill, covered, in refrigerator. Add ¼ cup butter to remaining chocolate mixture; mix well. Beat in eggs 1 at a time. Sift flour, baking powder, baking soda and salt together. Add to chocolate mixture alternately with 1¼ cups milk, beating well after each addition. Spoon into 2 greased and floured 9-inch round cake pans. Bake at 350 degrees for 30 minutes. Cool in pans for 10 minutes. Remove to wire rack to cool completely. Let frosting stand at room temperature for 15 minutes. Spread frosting between layers and over top and side of cake. **Yield: 16 servings.**

Approx Per Serving: Cal 441; Prot 6 g; Carbo 68 g; Fiber 2 g;
    T Fat 18 g; 36% Calories from Fat; Chol 78 mg; Sod 333 mg.

June Crampton, Freeland

Heavenly Chocolate Cake

1 2-layer package chocolate cake mix
1 4-ounce package chocolate instant
   pudding mix
4 eggs
1 cup sour cream
1/2 cup water
1/2 cup oil
2 cups chocolate chips

Combine cake mix and pudding mix in mixer bowl. Beat in eggs 1 at a time. Add sour cream, water and oil; beat well. Stir in chocolate chips. Pour into greased and floured tube pan. Bake at 350 degrees for 50 to 60 minutes or until cake tests done. Cool in pan for several minutes. Remove to serving plate. Garnish with confectioners' sugar and strawberries. **Yield: 16 servings.**

Approx Per Serving: Cal 381; Prot 4 g; Carbo 46 g; Fiber 1 g;
    T Fat 22 g; 49% Calories from Fat; Chol 60 mg; Sod 272 mg.

Sally Taylor, Marquette

Ho Ho Cake

1 2-layer package chocolate cake mix
1/2 cup margarine, softened
2/3 cup shortening
1 cup sugar
1 5-ounce can evaporated milk
1 teaspoon vanilla extract
1/2 16-ounce can chocolate frosting

Prepare and bake cake mix using package directions for 9x13-inch cake pan. Cool slightly. Cream margarine, shortening and sugar in mixer bowl until light and fluffy. Add evaporated milk; beat at high speed for 10 minutes. Add vanilla; mix well. Spread on cake. Place in freezer until firm. Heat frosting in saucepan until melted. Drizzle over top of cake. **Yield: 15 servings.**

Approx Per Serving: Cal 509; Prot 4 g; Carbo 66 g; Fiber 0 g;
    T Fat 27 g; 46% Calories from Fat; Chol 3 mg; Sod 281 mg.

Kenna Dobson, Ishpeming

Split 2 chocolate cake layers and fill with mixture of 16 ounces whipped topping, 8 ounces softened cream cheese, 4 cups confectioners' sugar, 2 cups miniature chocolate chips and 1/2 cup nuts.

Hot Fudge Pudding Cake

³/₄ cup sugar
1 cup flour
3 tablespoons baking cocoa
2 teaspoons baking powder
¹/₄ teaspoon salt
¹/₂ cup milk

¹/₃ cup melted margarine
1¹/₂ teaspoons vanilla extract
¹/₂ cup sugar
¹/₂ cup packed light brown sugar
¹/₄ cup baking cocoa
1¹/₄ cups hot water

Combine ³/₄ cup sugar, flour, 3 tablespoons baking cocoa, baking powder and salt in mixer bowl. Add milk, melted margarine and vanilla; mix well. Spoon into greased and floured 9x9-inch cake pan. Mix ¹/₂ cup sugar, brown sugar and ¹/₄ cup baking cocoa in bowl. Sprinkle over batter. Pour hot water over top. Do not stir. Bake at 350 degrees for 40 minutes or until center is set. Let stand for 15 minutes. Spoon into serving dish, scooping up sauce from bottom of pan. May top with ice cream. **Yield: 12 servings.**

Approx Per Serving: Cal 223; Prot 2 g; Carbo 42 g; Fiber 1 g;
     T Fat 6 g; 24% Calories from Fat; Chol 1 mg; Sod 169 mg.

Barb Buskirk, Portland

Crème de Cacao Chocolate Cake

1   2-layer package white cake mix
3 tablespoons Crème de Cacao
1   16-ounce jar chocolate fudge
    topping

2 to 3 tablespoons Crème de Cacao
12 ounces whipped topping
¹/₄ cup Crème de Cacao
1   16-ounce chocolate candy bar

Prepare and bake cake mix with 3 tablespoons Crème de Cacao using package directions for 9x13-inch cake pan. Cool. Combine fudge topping and Crème de Cacao in bowl; mix well. Spread on cake. Combine whipped topping and ¹/₄ cup Crème de Cacao in bowl; mix well. Spread over fudge topping. Cut chocolate candy bar with scraper into curls. Sprinkle on top of cake. **Yield: 15 servings.**

Approx Per Serving: Cal 619; Prot 7 g; Carbo 85 g; Fiber 2 g;
     T Fat 28 g; 41% Calories from Fat; Chol 6 mg; Sod 232 mg.

Michelle Richards, Lansing

Cinnamon Cake

1 2-layer package yellow cake mix
1 tablespoon vanilla extract

Cinnamon to taste
¼ cup melted margarine

Prepare and bake yellow cake mix with vanilla and cinnamon using package directions for 2 round cake pans and light no-oil recipe. Remove layers to wire rack. Brush top of hot cake layers with melted margarine; sprinkle with cinnamon. **Yield: 12 servings.**

Approx Per Serving: Cal 237; Prot 3 g; Carbo 37 g; Fiber 0 g;
    T Fat 8 g; 30% Calories from Fat; Chol 55 mg; Sod 355 mg.

Ruth Christensen, Marquette

Coconut-Almond-Carrot Ring Cake

1½ cups flour
1½ teaspoons baking powder
½ teaspoon salt
1 teaspoon cinnamon
1 cup sugar
1 cup oil
2 eggs

1 cup finely grated carrots
½ cup chopped almonds
½ cup raisins
⅔ cup flaked coconut
1 16-ounce can cream cheese frosting
2 cups flaked coconut

Mix flour, baking powder, salt and cinnamon together. Cream sugar and oil in mixer bowl until light and fluffy. Add flour mixture; mix well. Beat in eggs 1 at a time. Stir in carrots, almonds, raisins and ⅔ cup coconut. Spoon into greased 9-inch bundt pan. Bake at 350 degrees for 35 minutes. Cool in pan for 15 minutes. Remove to serving plate. Frost with cream cheese frosting; sprinkle with remaining 2 cups coconut. **Yield: 16 servings.**

Approx Per Serving: Cal 441; Prot 4 g; Carbo 49 g; Fiber 3 g;
    T Fat 27 g; 53% Calories from Fat; Chol 44 mg; Sod 164 mg.

Nancy Carpenter, Jackson

Coconut Cake

1 2-layer package yellow cake mix
1/4 cup oil
3 eggs, beaten
1 cup sour cream
3/4 cup water
2 cups sugar
1/2 cup water

4 egg whites, at room temperature
1/4 teaspoon cream of tartar
2 cups confectioners' sugar
1 teaspoon vanilla extract
1 6-ounce package frozen coconut,
   thawed

Combine cake mix, oil, eggs, sour cream and 3/4 cup water in mixer bowl; mix well. Spoon into 3 greased and floured 8-inch round cake pans. Bake using cake mix package directions. Cool in pans for 5 minutes. Remove to wire rack to cool completely. Combine 2 cups sugar and 1/2 cup water in saucepan. Cook over medium heat to 234 to 240 degrees on candy thermometer, soft-ball stage. Beat egg whites with cream of tartar until soft peaks form. Add hot syrup gradually in mixer bowl, beating until stiff peaks form. Fold in confectioners' sugar and vanilla. Spread frosting between layers and over top and side of cake, sprinkling layers and top with coconut. **Yield: 12 servings.**

Approx Per Serving: Cal 563; Prot 6 g; Carbo 97 g; Fiber 2 g;
    T Fat 18 g; 28% Calories from Fat; Chol 62 mg; Sod 343 mg.

Bobbie N. Perkins, Jackson, Tennessee

Cranberry Loaf Cakes

1 2-layer package yellow cake mix
1 4-ounce package lemon instant
   pudding mix
4 eggs
1 cup sour cream

1/4 cup oil
1/2 cup chopped pecans
1 16-ounce can whole cranberry
   sauce, chopped

Combine cake mix, pudding mix, eggs, sour cream, oil and pecans in mixer bowl; mix well. Beat for 4 minutes. Fold in cranberry sauce. Spoon into 2 greased and floured 5x9-inch loaf cake pans. Bake at 350 degrees for 50 to 55 minutes or until cakes test done. Cool in pans. Remove to serving plates. **Yield: 24 servings.**

Approx Per Serving: Cal 208; Prot 2 g; Carbo 31 g; Fiber 1 g;
    T Fat 9 g; 37% Calories from Fat; Chol 40 mg; Sod 185 mg.

Carroll King, Brooklyn

Crumb Cake

1 2-layer package yellow cake mix
1 cup melted margarine
1½ cups flour
1 cup sugar
2½ teaspoons cinnamon
1 teaspoon nutmeg
¾ cup finely chopped walnuts
2 tablespoons confectioners' sugar

Prepare cake using package directions for 9x13-inch cake pan. Bake at 375 degrees for 25 minutes. Combine melted margarine, flour, sugar, cinnamon and nutmeg in bowl; mix until crumbly. Stir in walnuts. Sprinkle over hot cake. Bake at 375 degrees for 15 minutes longer or until cake tests done. Cool. Sprinkle with confectioners' sugar. **Yield: 15 servings.**

Approx Per Serving: Cal 394; Prot 4 g; Carbo 54 g; Fiber 1 g;
   T Fat 19 g; 42% Calories from Fat; Chol 0 mg; Sod 353 mg.

Audrey M. Aros, Sault Ste. Marie

Mrs. Dowell's Five-Flavor Cake

1 cup butter, softened
½ cup vegetable oil
3 cups sugar
5 eggs, beaten
3 cups flour
½ teaspoon baking powder
1 cup milk
1 teaspoon each coconut, rum, butter, lemon and vanilla extracts
1 cup sugar
½ cup water
1 teaspoon each coconut, rum, lemon, vanilla and almond extracts

Cream butter, oil and 3 cups sugar in mixer bowl until light and fluffy. Add eggs; beat well after each addition. Add mixture of flour and baking powder alternately with milk, beating well. Add coconut, rum, butter, lemon and vanilla flavorings. Spoon into greased and floured 10-inch bundt pan. Bake at 325 degrees for 1¼ hours or until cake tests done. Combine 1 cup sugar, ½ cup water and coconut, rum, lemon, vanilla and almond extracts in heavy saucepan. Cook until sugar is melted, stirring constantly. Spoon half the glaze over hot cake. Cool cake in pan for 10 minutes. Remove to serving plate. Spoon remaining glaze over cake.
Yield: 16 servings.

Approx Per Serving: Cal 483; Prot 5 g; Carbo 69 g; Fiber 1 g;
   T Fat 21 g; 39% Calories from Fat; Chol 100 mg; Sod 137 mg.

Eloise Robinson, Lansing

Fantastic Fruitcake

2 cups raisins	1 teaspoon cinnamon
2 cups water	1 teaspoon salt
1/2 cup shortening	1 teaspoon baking soda
2 cups sugar	1 cup water
2 eggs	4 cups flour
1/2 teaspoon cloves	1 cup chopped pecans
1/2 teaspoon nutmeg	1 cup chopped candied fruit peel

Combine raisins and 2 cups water in saucepan. Bring to a boil; reduce heat. Simmer for 15 minutes, stirring occasionally. Remove from heat. Let stand until cool. Cream shortening and sugar in mixer bowl until light and fluffy. Beat in eggs 1 at a time. Add cloves, nutmeg, cinnamon, salt and mixture of baking soda and 1 cup water; mix well. Add flour; beat well. Stir in raisins with liquid, pecans and fruit peel. Spoon into greased and floured tube pan. Bake at 350 degrees for 1 hour. Reduce oven temperature to 325 degrees. Bake for 20 minutes longer. Cool in pan for 15 minutes. Remove to wire rack to cool completely. **Yield: 16 servings.**

Approx Per Serving: Cal 433; Prot 5 g; Carbo 78 g; Fiber 3 g;
    T Fat 13 g; 25% Calories from Fat; Chol 27 mg; Sod 197 mg.

Althea J. Ondovcsik, Davison

Fruit Cocktail Cake

2 cups flour	1/2 cup chopped pecans
2 teaspoons baking soda	1/2 cup margarine
1 1/2 cups sugar	3/4 cup sugar
2 eggs, beaten	1 5-ounce can evaporated milk
1 16-ounce can fruit cocktail	1 cup coconut
1/2 cup packed brown sugar	1 teaspoon vanilla extract

Combine flour, baking soda and 1 1/2 cups sugar in mixer bowl; mix well. Add eggs; beat well. Stir in fruit cocktail. Mix brown sugar and pecans together in bowl. Stir into batter. Pour into greased and floured 5x9-inch loaf cake pan. Bake at 350 degrees for 45 minutes or until cake tests done. Cool in pan for several minutes. Remove to serving plate. Combine margarine, 3/4 cup sugar, evaporated milk, coconut and vanilla in saucepan. Bring to a boil, stirring frequently. Boil for 3 minutes, stirring frequently. Pour over warm cake. **Yield: 12 servings.**

Approx Per Serving: Cal 450; Prot 5 g; Carbo 76 g; Fiber 2 g;
    T Fat 15 g; 29% Calories from Fat; Chol 39 mg; Sod 260 mg.

Kay Collins, Lansing

Gumdrop Fruitcakes

2 cups shortening
1 cup sugar
1 cup packed brown sugar
4 eggs
4 cups flour
1/2 teaspoon baking powder
2 teaspoons allspice
2 teaspoons cinnamon

2 teaspoons nutmeg
2 cups applesauce
2 teaspoons baking soda
1 cup chopped dates
1 cup raisins
1 cup small gumdrops
1 cup chopped walnuts

Cream shortening, sugar and brown sugar in mixer bowl until light and fluffy. Beat in eggs 1 at a time. Mix flour, baking powder, allspice, cinnamon and nutmeg together. Add to creamed mixture; mix well. Stir in mixture of applesauce and baking soda, dates, raisins, gumdrops and walnuts. Spoon into 3 greased and floured 5x9-inch loaf cake pans. Bake at 300 degrees for 1 hour. Cool in pans for several minutes. Remove to wire rack to cool completely. **Yield: 36 servings.**

Approx Per Serving: Cal 280; Prot 3 g; Carbo 37 g; Fiber 1 g;
T Fat 14 g; 45% Calories from Fat; Chol 24 mg; Sod 64 mg.

Joan Sarvello, Marquette

Fuzzy Navel Cake

1   2-layer package yellow cake mix
1/2 cup oil
1   4-ounce package vanilla instant
    pudding mix
4 eggs
3/4 cup peach schnapps

1/2 cup orange juice
1/2 teaspoon orange extract
1 cup confectioners' sugar
1/4 cup peach schnapps
2 tablespoons orange juice

Combine cake mix, oil, pudding mix and eggs in mixer bowl; beat well. Add 3/4 cup peach schnapps and 1/2 cup orange juice; mix well. Spoon into greased and floured bundt pan. Bake at 350 degrees for 45 to 50 minutes or until cake tests done. Combine confectioners' sugar, remaining 1/4 cup peach schnapps and orange juice in mixer bowl; beat until smooth. Pierce holes in hot cake; drizzle glaze over cake. Cool in pan for 2 hours. Remove to serving plate. **Yield: 16 servings.**

Approx Per Serving: Cal 335; Prot 3 g; Carbo 50 g; Fiber <1 g;
T Fat 11 g; 29% Calories from Fat; Chol 53 mg; Sod 263 mg.

Vi Kloko, St. Joseph

Mace Cake

1 cup butter, softened	1/2 teaspoon (or more) baking soda
1 cup sugar	1 tablespoon (heaping) mace
5 eggs	1 teaspoon cream of tartar
1 cup sugar	1 cup milk
3 cups flour	1 cup chopped black walnuts

Cream butter and 1 cup sugar in mixer bowl until light and fluffy. Beat in eggs 1 at a time. Sift 1 cup sugar, flour, baking soda, mace and cream of tartar together. Add to creamed mixture alternately with milk, beating well after each addition. Stir in walnuts. Spoon batter into greased and floured 10-inch tube pan. Bake at 350 degrees for 1 hour and 10 minutes or until cake tests done. Cool in pan on wire rack for 15 minutes. Remove to serving plate. **Yield: 16 servings.**

Approx Per Serving: Cal 366; Prot 7 g; Carbo 45 g; Fiber 1 g;
    T Fat 19 g; 45% Calories from Fat; Chol 100 mg; Sod 152 mg.

Lorraine B. Watson, Benton Harbor

Oatmeal Cake

1 1/4 cups boiling water	1 1/2 cups flour
1 cup oats	1 teaspoon vanilla
1/2 cup margarine, softened	1 cup chopped pecans
1 cup sugar	1/2 cup packed brown sugar
1 cup packed brown sugar	1/2 cup canned evaporated milk
2 eggs	6 tablespoons margarine
1 teaspoon cinnamon	1 teaspoon vanilla extract
1 teaspoon baking soda	1 cup coconut
1 teaspoon salt	

Combine boiling water and oats in bowl; mix well. Cream 1/2 cup margarine, sugar and 1 cup brown sugar in mixer bowl until light and fluffy. Beat in eggs 1 at a time. Add cinnamon, baking soda and salt; beat well. Add oats mixture, flour, 1 teaspoon vanilla and pecans; mix well. Spoon into greased and floured 8x8-inch cake pan. Bake at 350 degrees for 40 minutes. Cool in pan for several minutes. Remove to serving plate to cool completely. Combine remaining 1/2 cup brown sugar, evaporated milk and remaining 6 tablespoons margarine in saucepan. Cook until sugar is melted, stirring frequently. Remove from heat. Stir in remaining 1 teaspoon vanilla and coconut. Spread frosting over top and side of cake. **Yield: 12 servings.**

Approx Per Serving: Cal 518; Prot 6 g; Carbo 72 g; Fiber 3 g;
    T Fat 24 g; 41% Calories from Fat; Chol 39 mg; Sod 442 mg.

Alice Duvall, Williamston

Orange Snack Cake

1 cup oats
1¹/₂ cups boiling water
2 cups flour
1 teaspoon baking powder
1 teaspoon baking soda
1 teaspoon cinnamon
¹/₄ teaspoon salt
¹/₂ cup margarine, softened
¹/₂ cup sugar
³/₄ cup packed brown sugar

3 egg whites
¹/₄ cup thawed frozen orange juice
   concentrate
1 teaspoon vanilla extract
¹/₄ cup margarine
³/₄ cup packed brown sugar
2 tablespoons thawed frozen orange
   juice concentrate
¹/₂ cup finely chopped walnuts

Spray 9x13-inch cake pan with nonstick cooking spray. Combine oats and boiling water in bowl; mix well. Mix flour, baking powder, baking soda, cinnamon and salt together. Cream margarine, sugar and ³/₄ cup brown sugar in mixer bowl until light and fluffy. Beat in egg whites. Add ¹/₄ cup orange juice concentrate and vanilla; beat well. Add flour mixture alternately with oats mixture, beating well after each addition. Spoon into prepared pan. Bake at 350 degrees for 25 minutes or until cake tests done. Combine ¹/₄ cup margarine, ³/₄ cup brown sugar and 2 tablespoons orange juice concentrate in bowl; mix well. Stir in walnuts. Spread over top of hot cake. Broil for 1 minute, watching carefully to prevent burning. **Yield: 15 servings.**

Approx Per Serving: Cal 333; Prot 4 g; Carbo 53 g; Fiber 1 g;
   T Fat 12 g; 32% Calories from Fat; Chol 0 mg; Sod 243 mg.

Betty Dewitt, Houghton Lake

Pineapple Upside-Down Cake

¹/₂ cup butter
³/₄ cup packed brown sugar
1 8-ounce can juice-pack pineapple
   slices
¹/₂ cup pecan halves
¹/₄ cup maraschino cherries

1 cup flour
1 teaspoon baking powder
¹/₈ teaspoon salt
3 egg yolks
1 cup sugar
3 egg whites, stiffly beaten

Melt butter and brown sugar in saucepan, stirring frequently. Pour into tube pan. Drain pineapple, reserving 5 tablespoons juice. Arrange pineapple slices, pecans and maraschino cherries in brown sugar mixture. Mix flour, baking powder and salt together. Beat egg yolks, sugar and reserved pineapple juice together in mixer bowl. Add flour mixture; mix well. Fold in egg whites gently. Spoon into tube pan. Bake at 350 degrees for 40 minutes. Cool in pan on wire rack. Invert onto serving plate. **Yield: 15 servings.**

Approx Per Serving: Cal 241; Prot 3 g; Carbo 37 g; Fiber 1 g;
   T Fat 10 g; 36% Calories from Fat; Chol 59 mg; Sod 110 mg.

Katherine Brokob, Farwell

Pineapple Rum Cake

2 eggs
1²/₃ cups sugar
1 teaspoon vanilla extract
2 tablespoons rum
1 20-ounce can juice-pack crushed
  pineapple

2¹/₄ cups flour
1¹/₂ teaspoons baking soda
1 teaspoon salt
1 teaspoon cinnamon
Rum Frosting

Beat eggs and sugar in mixer bowl until thick and lemon colored. Add vanilla, rum, pineapple and juice; mix well. Sift flour, baking soda, salt and cinnamon together. Add to batter; mix well. Spread batter in greased and floured 12x17-inch cake pan. Bake at 350 degrees for 25 minutes. Spread Rum Frosting over hot cake. **Yield: 15 servings.**

Approx Per Serving: Cal 366; Prot 4 g; Carbo 59 g; Fiber 1 g;
    T Fat 13 g; 31% Calories from Fat; Chol 30 mg; Sod 311 mg.

Rum Frosting

¹/₂ cup margarine
1 cup sugar
¹/₄ cup evaporated milk

1 teaspoon vanilla extract
1 tablespoon rum
1 cup chopped pecans

Combine margarine, sugar and evaporated milk in saucepan. Bring to a rolling boil over medium heat, stirring occasionally. Cook for 2 minutes, stirring frequently. Remove from heat. Stir in vanilla, rum and pecans. **Yield: 15 servings.**

Approx Per Serving: Cal 167; Prot 1 g; Carbo 15 g; Fiber 1 g;
    T Fat 12 g; 62% Calories from Fat; Chol 1 mg; Sod 76 mg.

Leanore E. Yerrick, Wyoming

Hawaiian Dream Cake

1 7-ounce package Jiffy cake mix
8 ounces cream cheese, softened
2 cups milk
1 4-ounce package vanilla instant
  pudding mix

1 20-ounce can crushed pineapple,
  drained
8 ounces whipped topping

Prepare cake mix using package directions for 9x13-inch cake pan. Bake at 350 degrees for 15 minutes. Cool cake in pan. Combine cream cheese and ¹/₂ cup milk in bowl; beat well. Add remaining milk and pudding mix. Beat at low speed for 5 minutes. Spread over cooled cake. Cover with pineapple; top with whipped topping. May sprinkle with chopped nuts. Chill in refrigerator. **Yield: 15 servings.**

Approx Per Serving: Cal 222; Prot 3 g; Carbo 27 g; Fiber <1 g;
    T Fat 12 g; 46% Calories from Fat; Chol 31 mg; Sod 193 mg.

Mark Hayden, St. Joseph

Hawaiian Cake

2 cups sugar
1/2 cup oil
2 eggs
2 cups flour
2 teaspoons baking soda

1　20-ounce can juice-pack crushed
　　pineapple
1 cup chopped pecans
1 cup coconut
Cream Cheese Frosting

Cream sugar and oil in mixer bowl until light and fluffy. Beat in eggs 1 at a time. Add mixture of flour and baking soda; mix well. Stir in pineapple and juice, pecans and coconut. Spoon into greased and floured 9x13-inch cake pan. Bake at 350 degrees for 45 minutes. Cool. Spread Cream Cheese Frosting on cake. May sprinkle with additional coconut. **Yield: 15 servings.**

Approx Per Serving: Cal 492; Prot 5 g; Carbo 61 g; Fiber 2 g;
　　T Fat 27 g; 47% Calories from Fat; Chol 45 mg; Sod 237 mg.

Cream Cheese Frosting

8 ounces cream cheese, softened
1/2 cup margarine, softened

1 1/2 cups confectioners' sugar
2 teaspoons vanilla extract

Combine cream cheese, margarine and confectioners' sugar in mixer bowl. Beat at high speed until smooth and creamy. Add vanilla; beat well. **Yield: 15 servings.**

Approx Per Serving: Cal 155; Prot 1 g; Carbo 13 g; Fiber 0 g;
　　T Fat 11 g; 65% Calories from Fat; Chol 17 mg; Sod 116 mg.

Julia M. Rieger, Traverse City

Mexican Fruitcake

2 cups sugar
2 eggs
2 cups flour
1 teaspoon baking soda
1　20-ounce can crushed pineapple

1 cup chopped walnuts
8 ounces cream cheese, softened
1 teaspoon butter, softened
2 cups confectioners' sugar
1 teaspoon vanilla extract

Beat sugar and eggs in mixer bowl until thick and lemon colored. Add mixture of flour and baking soda; mix well. Stir in pineapple and walnuts. Spoon into nonstick tube pan. Bake at 350 degrees for 35 minutes or until cake tests done. Cool in pan for several minutes. Remove to serving plate to cool completely. Combine cream cheese, butter and confectioners' sugar in mixer bowl; beat until smooth and creamy. Add vanilla; mix well. Spread on cooled cake. **Yield: 15 servings.**

Approx Per Serving: Cal 372; Prot 5 g; Carbo 65 g; Fiber 1 g;
　　T Fat 11 g; 27% Calories from Fat; Chol 46 mg; Sod 113 mg.

Marquita Sommer, Eau Claire

Mexican Wedding Cake

2 cups sugar
2 eggs
2 cups flour
2 teaspoons baking soda
1   20-ounce can juice-pack crushed
   pineapple
1 cup chopped walnuts

2 teaspoons vanilla extract
8 ounces cream cheese, softened
¹/₂ cup margarine, softened
1 cup confectioners' sugar
1 teaspoon vanilla extract
1 cup finely chopped walnuts

Beat sugar and eggs in mixer bowl until thick and lemon colored. Add flour, baking soda and pineapple with juice; mix well. Stir in 1 cup walnuts and 2 teaspoons vanilla. Spoon into greased and floured 9x13-inch cake pan. Bake at 350 degrees for 35 to 45 minutes or until cake tests done. Cool in cake pan. Combine cream cheese, margarine and confectioners' sugar in mixer bowl; beat until smooth and creamy. Add vanilla; mix well. Spread over cooled cake. Sprinkle with remaining 1 cup walnuts. May bake cake in greased and floured bundt pan. Cool for 15 minutes in pan; remove to serving plate. Spread half the amount of frosting over warm cake. Sprinkle with remaining walnuts. **Yield: 15 servings.**

Approx Per Serving: Cal 440; Prot 6 g; Carbo 57 g; Fiber 2 g;
   T Fat 22 g; 44% Calories from Fat; Chol 45 mg; Sod 238 mg.

Margaret Bell, Marquette
Joan Coyne, Charlevoix

Poppy Seed Cake

1 cup margarine, softened
1¹/₂ cups sugar
4 egg yolks
2 cups flour
1 teaspoon baking soda

1 cup sour cream
1 tablespoon vanilla extract
¹/₈ to ¹/₄ cup poppy seed
4 egg whites, stiffly beaten

Cream margarine and sugar in mixer bowl until light and fluffy. Beat in egg yolks. Add flour, baking soda and sour cream; mix well. Add vanilla and poppy seed; beat well. Fold in egg whites gently. Spoon into greased bundt pan. Bake at 350 degrees for 45 minutes or until cake tests done. Cool in pan for 10 minutes. Remove to wire rack to cool completely. May also be baked in 2 loaf pans. **Yield: 15 servings.**

Approx Per Serving: Cal 316; Prot 4 g; Carbo 34 g; Fiber 1 g;
   T Fat 18 g; 51% Calories from Fat; Chol 64 mg; Sod 222 mg.

Karen McLeod-Hill, Mt. Clemens

Pound Cake

1 cup margarine, softened
2 cups sugar
6 eggs

2 cups sifted flour
1¹/₂ teaspoons vanilla extract

Cream margarine and sugar in mixer bowl until light and fluffy. Beat in eggs 1 at a time. Add flour; beat well. Beat in vanilla. Spoon into greased and floured tube pan. Bake at 350 degrees for 1¹/₄ hours or until cake tests done. Cool in pan for several minutes. Remove to wire rack to cool completely. May substitute egg substitute for eggs. **Yield: 15 servings.**

Approx Per Serving: Cal 300; Prot 4 g; Carbo 39 g; Fiber <1 g;
    T Fat 15 g; 43% Calories from Fat; Chol 85 mg; Sod 171 mg.

Jennie Hill Barlett, Davison

My Favorite Pound Cake

2 cups butter, softened
2 cups sugar
³/₄ cup evaporated milk

6 eggs
4 cups sifted flour
2 teaspoons black walnut flavoring

Cream butter and sugar in mixer bowl until light and fluffy. Add evaporated milk, eggs and flour ¹/₃ at a time, beating well after each addition. Add flavoring; mix well. Spoon into greased and floured tube pan. Bake at 325 degrees for 1¹/₄ hours or until cake tests done. Cool in pan for several minutes. Remove to wire rack to cool completely. **Yield: 15 servings.**

Approx Per Serving: Cal 482; Prot 7 g; Carbo 52 g; Fiber 1 g;
    T Fat 28 g; 52% Calories from Fat; Chol 155 mg; Sod 249 mg.

Althea J. Ondovcsik, Davison

*Allow for variation in oven temperature by setting the timer for the
minimum time indicated in the recipe. Test by inserting a
tester or toothpick into the center of the cake. If the
tester comes out clean, the cake is done.*

Choco Dot Pumpkin Cake

2 cups sifted flour
2 teaspoons baking powder
1 teaspoon baking soda
1/2 teaspoon salt
1 1/2 teaspoons cinnamon
1/2 teaspoon ground cloves
1/4 teaspoon each allspice and ginger

2 cups sugar
4 eggs
2 cups canned pumpkin
1 cup vegetable oil
1 cup All-Bran cereal
1 cup semisweet chocolate chips
1 cup raisins

Sift flour, baking powder, baking soda, salt, cinnamon, cloves, allspice, ginger and sugar together. Beat eggs in mixer bowl until foamy. Add pumpkin, oil and cereal; mix well. Add flour mixture, mixing just until combined. Stir in chocolate chips and raisins. Spread in greased and floured tube pan. Bake at 350 degrees for 1 hour and 10 minutes or until cake tests done. Cool completely in pan. Remove to serving plate. May drizzle with confectioners' sugar glaze or heated vanilla frosting. May substitute chopped nuts for raisins. **Yield: 15 servings.**

Approx Per Serving: Cal 424; Prot 5 g; Carbo 61 g; Fiber 4 g;
    T Fat 21 g; 41% Calories from Fat; Chol 57 mg; Sod 258 mg.

Carolyn Devers, Laingsburg

Pumpkin Cake Roll

3/4 cup flour
1 teaspoon baking powder
2 teaspoons cinnamon
1 teaspoon ginger
1 teaspoon nutmeg
1/2 teaspoon salt
3 eggs, beaten
1 cup sugar

2/3 cup pumpkin
1 teaspoon lemon juice
1/2 cup confectioners' sugar
8 ounces cream cheese, softened
1/4 cup margarine, softened
1 cup confectioners' sugar
1/2 teaspoon vanilla extract

Mix flour, baking powder, cinnamon, ginger, nutmeg and salt together. Beat eggs and sugar in mixer bowl until thick and lemon colored. Add pumpkin and lemon juice; beat well. Fold in flour mixture. Spread on greased 10x15-inch jelly roll pan. Bake at 375 degrees for 15 minutes or until cake tests done. Sprinkle 1/2 cup confectioners' sugar on towel. Invert cake onto towel. Roll in towel immediately. Place cake roll on tray. Chill in refrigerator for 2 hours. Combine cream cheese, margarine and 1 cup confectioners' sugar in mixer bowl; beat until smooth and creamy. Add vanilla; beat well. Unroll cake. Spread filling over cake; roll cake to enclose filling. Wrap in waxed paper. Chill in refrigerator until serving time. **Yield: 15 servings.**

Approx Per Serving: Cal 221; Prot 3 g; Carbo 32 g; Fiber <1 g;
    T Fat 10 g; 38% Calories from Fat; Chol 59 mg; Sod 188 mg.

Billie Jo Duvall, Perry

Pumpkin Pie Cake

1½ cups sugar
1 teaspoon salt
2 teaspoons pumpkin pie spice
1   16-ounce can pumpkin
1   13-ounce can Milnot

4 eggs, beaten
1   2-layer package yellow cake mix
¾ cup melted margarine
1 cup chopped pecans

Combine sugar, salt, pumpkin pie spice, pumpkin, Milnot and eggs in mixer bowl; beat well. Pour into ungreased 9x13-inch cake pan. Sprinkle cake mix over mixture; drizzle with margarine. Sprinkle with pecans. Bake at 350 degrees for 50 to 60 minutes or until cake tests done. Garnish with whipped cream. **Yield: 15 servings.**

Approx Per Serving: Cal 406; Prot 5 g; Carbo 54 g; Fiber 1 g;
    T Fat 20 g; 43% Calories from Fat; Chol 57 mg; Sod 495 mg.

Bertha Kauppila, Kohler, Wisconsin

Mom's Boiled Raisin Cake

2 cups sugar
2 cups water
1 cup shortening
1 pound raisins
1 teaspoon ground cloves

1 teaspoon cinnamon
3½ cups flour
2 teaspoons baking soda
¾ teaspoon salt
1 cup chopped walnuts

Combine sugar, water, shortening, raisins, cloves and cinnamon in saucepan. Bring to a boil. Cook for 5 minutes, stirring occasionally. Cool to room temperature. Sift flour, baking soda and salt into bowl. Add cooled raisin mixture; mix well. Stir in walnuts. Pour into greased tube pan. Bake at 375 degrees for 1 hour or until cake tests done. Cool in pan for several minutes. Invert onto serving plate.
Yield: 16 servings.

Approx Per Serving: Cal 442; Prot 5 g; Carbo 70 g; Fiber 3 g;
    T Fat 18 g; 35% Calories from Fat; Chol 0 mg; Sod 208 mg.

Jean A. Steffes, Traverse City

*For a great Halloween Jack-o'-Lantern Cake, bake
2 Choco Dot Pumpkin Cakes in identical bundt pans. Stack
smooth sides together. Frost between and
outside of cakes and decorate.*

Rhubarb Cake

½ cup shortening
1½ cups packed brown sugar
1 egg
½ teaspoon salt
2 cups flour
1 teaspoon baking soda

1 teaspoon vanilla extract
1 cup sour milk
1½ cups chopped rhubarb
¼ cup sugar
1 tablespoon cinnamon

Cream shortening and brown sugar in mixer bowl until light and fluffy. Add egg and salt; beat well. Reserve 2 tablespoons flour. Mix remaining flour and baking soda together. Add to creamed mixture with vanilla and milk; mix well. Add reserved flour to rhubarb in bowl; toss to coat. Stir into batter. Spoon into greased and floured 9x13-inch cake pan. Sprinkle with mixture of sugar and cinnamon. Bake at 375 degrees for 35 to 40 minutes or until cake tests done. **Yield: 15 servings.**

Approx Per Serving: Cal 255; Prot 3 g; Carbo 44 g; Fiber 1 g;
    T Fat 8 g; 28% Calories from Fat; Chol 16 mg; Sod 150 mg.

Helen Finner, Sault Ste. Marie

Salad Dressing Cake

1½ cups sugar
¼ cup baking cocoa
1 cup mayonnaise-type salad dressing
1 cup warm water

2 teaspoons baking soda
2 cups flour
1 teaspoon vanilla extract
½ cup (or more) chopped walnuts

Combine sugar, baking cocoa, salad dressing and water in mixer bowl; beat well. Add mixture of baking soda and flour; mix well. Add vanilla. Stir in walnuts. Spoon into greased and floured 9x13-inch cake pan. Sprinkle with additional walnuts if desired. Bake at 350 degrees for 40 minutes. **Yield: 15 servings.**

Approx Per Serving: Cal 229; Prot 3 g; Carbo 38 g; Fiber 1 g;
    T Fat 8 g; 31% Calories from Fat; Chol 4 mg; Sod 222 mg.

Nancy Nowlin, Charlotte

Add ½ cup mayonnaise to any 2-layer cake mix for moistness.

Seven-Up Cake

1½ cups margarine, softened
3 cups sugar
5 eggs

3 cups flour
¾ cup 7-Up
2 teaspoons vanilla or lemon extract

Cream margarine and sugar in mixer bowl until light and fluffy. Beat in eggs 1 at a time. Add flour; mix well. Add 7-Up and flavoring; mix well. Pour into greased and floured tube pan. Bake at 325 degrees for 1¼ hours or until cake tests done. Cool in pan for several minutes. Remove to serving plate. **Yield: 16 servings.**

Approx Per Serving: Cal 414; Prot 5 g; Carbo 57 g; Fiber 1 g;
    T Fat 19 g; 41% Calories from Fat; Chol 67 mg; Sod 225 mg.

Janice Sweet Fairley, Jackson

Sunshine Cake

1 cup sifted cake flour
½ cup sugar
6 egg whites
¼ teaspoon salt
½ teaspoon cream of tartar

4 egg yolks
½ cup sugar
½ teaspoon lemon extract
Lemon Frosting

Sift cake flour and ½ cup sugar together 3 times. Beat egg whites in mixer bowl until soft peaks form. Add salt and cream of tartar, beating until stiff peaks form. Beat egg yolks in mixer bowl until light and lemon colored. Add ½ cup sugar and lemon extract; beat well. Fold in egg whites gently. Fold in flour mixture. Spoon into greased and floured tube pan. Bake at 325 degrees for 50 to 60 minutes or until cake tests done. Cool in pan for several minutes. Invert onto serving plate to cool completely. Spread Lemon Frosting over cake. **Yield: 16 servings.**

Approx Per Serving: Cal 192; Prot 3 g; Carbo 37 g; Fiber <1 g;
    T Fat 4 g; 18% Calories from Fat; Chol 60 mg; Sod 73 mg.

Lemon Frosting

2½ cups confectioners' sugar
⅛ teaspoon grated lemon rind
3 tablespoons lemon juice
Salt to taste

3 tablespoons melted butter
1 tablespoon (or more) whipping
cream

Combine confectioners' sugar, lemon rind, lemon juice, salt and butter in mixer bowl; mix well. Add cream; beat well. May add additional cream to make of spreading consistency. **Yield: 16 servings.**

Approx Per Serving: Cal 95; Prot <1 g; Carbo 19 g; Fiber <1 g;
    T Fat 3 g; 23% Calories from Fat; Chol 7 mg; Sod 19 mg.

Arlene Sherman, Lansing

Zucchini Cake

4 eggs
3 cups sugar
1 cup corn oil
3 cups grated zucchini
3 cups flour
1½ teaspoons baking powder
1 teaspoon baking soda

1 teaspoon salt
1½ teaspoons cinnamon
1 cup chopped pecans
1 cup raisins
3 ounces cream cheese, softened
2 cups confectioners' sugar
1 tablespoon margarine, softened

Combine eggs, sugar, oil and zucchini in mixer bowl; mix well. Mix flour, baking powder, baking soda, salt and cinnamon together. Add to creamed mixture; beat well. Stir in pecans and raisins. Pour into greased and floured bundt pan. Bake at 350 degrees for 1½ hours or until cake tests done. Cool in pan for several minutes. Remove to serving plate. Cool. Combine cream cheese, confectioners' sugar and margarine in mixer bowl; beat until smooth and creamy. Spread over cooled cake. **Yield: 16 servings.**

Approx Per Serving: Cal 541; Prot 6 g; Carbo 81 g; Fiber 2 g;
    T Fat 23 g; 37% Calories from Fat; Chol 59 mg; Sod 261 mg.

Nancy Ramey, Saginaw

Banana Cupcakes

4 cups mashed bananas
2 eggs, beaten
1½ cups sugar
½ cup oil
1 teaspoon vanilla extract

2 cups flour
2 teaspoons baking soda
1 teaspoon salt
½ cup chopped pecans

Combine bananas, eggs, sugar, oil and vanilla in mixer bowl; mix well. Mix flour, baking soda and salt together. Add to banana mixture; mix just until dry ingredients are moistened. Stir in pecans. Fill nonstick muffin cups ¾ full. Bake at 325 degrees for 20 to 25 minutes or until cupcakes test done. May frost with chocolate fudge or cream cheese frosting. **Yield: 24 servings.**

Approx Per Serving: Cal 184; Prot 2 g; Carbo 30 g; Fiber 1 g;
    T Fat 7 g; 33% Calories from Fat; Chol 18 mg; Sod 164 mg.

Marcia De Laski, Skandia

Chocolate Cupcakes

1/2 cup baking cocoa
1 cup hot water
1²/3 cups flour
1/2 teaspoon baking powder
1 teaspoon baking soda

1/2 teaspoon salt
2 eggs
1¹/2 cups sugar
1/2 cup shortening

Mix baking cocoa and hot water together in bowl until smooth. Cool. Mix flour, baking powder, baking soda and salt together. Beat eggs and sugar together in mixer bowl. Add shortening; beat well. Add cocoa mixture; beat well. Add flour mixture. Beat at medium speed for 2 minutes, scraping sides of bowl. Fill paper-lined muffin cups 1/2 full. Bake at 400 degrees for 15 to 20 minutes or until cupcakes test done. **Yield: 24 servings.**

Approx Per Serving: Cal 129; Prot 2 g; Carbo 20 g; Fiber 1 g;
    T Fat 5 g; 35% Calories from Fat; Chol 18 mg; Sod 92 mg.

Mary J. Konoski, Flint

Double-Chocolate Cupcakes

1¹/2 cups flour
1/2 cup sugar
1/4 cup baking cocoa
1 teaspoon baking soda
1/2 teaspoon salt
1/2 cup unsweetened orange juice
1/3 cup water

3 tablespoons oil
1 tablespoon vinegar
1 teaspoon vanilla extract
1/3 cup semisweet miniature
    chocolate chips
1 teaspoon confectioners' sugar

Combine flour, sugar, baking cocoa, baking soda and salt in bowl; mix well. Make a well in center. Combine orange juice, water, oil, vinegar and vanilla in bowl; mix well. Pour into well in flour mixture, stirring just until moistened. Fold in chocolate chips. Fill paper-lined muffin cups 2/3 full. Bake at 375 degrees for 12 minutes or until cupcakes test done. Cool. Sprinkle with confectioners' sugar. **Yield: 12 servings.**

Approx Per Serving: Cal 154; Prot 2 g; Carbo 25 g; Fiber 1 g;
    T Fat 6 g; 32% Calories from Fat; Chol 0 mg; Sod 159 mg.

Evelyn M. Freemire, Battle Creek

Butterscotch Frosting

2 cups packed brown sugar
1/2 cup milk

3 tablespoons butter
1 teaspoon vanilla extract

Combine brown sugar and milk in saucepan. Cook over medium heat to 234 to 240 degrees on candy thermometer, soft-ball stage. Remove from heat. Add butter and vanilla; beat until thick. **Yield: 15 servings.**

Approx Per Serving: Cal 163; Prot <1 g; Carbo 36 g; Fiber 0 g;
   T Fat 3 g; 14% Calories from Fat; Chol 7 mg; Sod 39 mg.

Betty L. Menhennick, Marquette

Fluffy Frosting

2 tablespoons (heaping) flour
1/2 cup milk
1/2 cup butter

1/2 cup sugar
1/2 teaspoon salt
1 teaspoon vanilla extract

Combine flour and milk in saucepan. Cook over medium heat until thickened, stirring constantly. Remove from heat. Combine flour mixture, butter, sugar, salt and vanilla in mixer bowl. Beat for 15 to 20 minutes or until very fluffy.
Yield: 15 servings.

Approx Per Serving: Cal 90; Prot <1 g; Carbo 8 g; Fiber <1 g;
   T Fat 6 g; 63% Calories from Fat; Chol 18 mg; Sod 126 mg.

Case Schoo, Falmouth

Grandma's Chocolate Sauce

1 ounce unsweetened chocolate
1/2 cup sugar
2 tablespoons butter
1 cup water

Salt to taste
1 teaspoon vanilla extract
1 tablespoon cornstarch

Combine chocolate, sugar, butter, water, salt, vanilla and cornstarch in saucepan. Cook over medium heat until thickened, stirring constantly. May serve hot over white cake squares. **Yield: 6 servings.**

Approx Per Serving: Cal 129; Prot 1 g; Carbo 19 g; Fiber 1 g;
   T Fat 6 g; 42% Calories from Fat; Chol 10 mg; Sod 33 mg.

Karen Kay Boss, Kalamazoo

ADOPT - A - HIGHWAY

Bonbons

2 1-pound packages confectioners' sugar
1 cup butter, softened
4 cups flaked coconut

1 14-ounce can sweetened condensed milk
30 ounces chocolate chips
2 bars paraffin wax

Combine confectioners' sugar, butter, coconut and condensed milk in bowl; mix well. Shape into bite-sized balls. Melt chocolate chips and paraffin in top of double boiler, stirring frequently. Dip coconut balls in chocolate mixture. Place on waxed paper to cool. **Yield: 172 servings.**

Approx Per Serving: Cal 74; Prot <1 g; Carbo 11 g; Fiber <1 g;
    T Fat 4 g; 41% Calories from Fat; Chol 4 mg; Sod 13 mg.

Shirley A. Cook, Lansing

Debbie Z.'s Caramels

1 cup butter
2 cups sugar
1 cup light corn syrup

1 14-ounce can sweetened condensed milk
1/2 teaspoon vanilla extract

Combine butter, sugar, corn syrup and condensed milk in saucepan. Bring to a boil over medium heat. Cook to 240 degrees on candy thermometer, soft-ball stage. Remove from heat. Stir in vanilla. Pour into buttered 9x13-inch dish. Let stand until cool. Cut into squares; wrap in waxed paper. **Yield: 96 servings.**

Approx Per Serving: Cal 56; Prot <1 g; Carbo 9 g; Fiber 0 g;
    T Fat 2 g; 35% Calories from Fat; Chol 7 mg; Sod 23 mg.

Elizabeth Kempher, Skandia

Caramels

1 cup margarine
2 1/2 cups packed brown sugar
1 14-ounce can sweetened condensed milk

1 cup light corn syrup
3/4 cup walnuts

Melt margarine in saucepan over low heat. Add brown sugar, condensed milk and corn syrup; mix well. Bring to a boil over medium heat. Reduce heat to low. Simmer for 30 minutes. Stir in walnuts. Pour into greased 9x13-inch dish. Chill overnight. Cut into squares; wrap in waxed paper. **Yield: 96 servings.**

Approx Per Serving: Cal 73; Prot <1 g; Carbo 12 g; Fiber <1 g;
    T Fat 3 g; 34% Calories from Fat; Chol 1 mg; Sod 32 mg.

Becky Cartwright, Lansing

Bun Candy Bars

2 cups chocolate chips
2 cups butterscotch chips
2 cups peanut butter
1 cup margarine
1/4 cup vanilla instant pudding mix

1/2 cup evaporated milk
1 teaspoon vanilla or maple extract
2   1-pound packages confectioners'
   sugar
16 ounces Spanish peanuts

Melt chocolate chips, butterscotch chips and peanut butter in double boiler over medium heat. Spread half the mixture in 10x15-inch dish. Chill until firm. Bring margarine, pudding mix and evaporated milk to a boil in saucepan over medium heat. Cook for 1 minute. Stir in vanilla. Combine with confectioners' sugar in mixer bowl. Beat until smooth. Spread over chocolate layer. Chill until firm. Stir peanuts into remaining warm chocolate mixture. Pour over pudding layer. Chill until firm. Cut into bars. **Yield: 36 servings.**

Approx Per Serving: Cal 411; Prot 8 g; Carbo 46 g; Fiber 2 g;
    T Fat 24 g; 50% Calories from Fat; Chol 1 mg; Sod 143 mg.

Cindy Fogg, Otsego

Church Windows

2 cups semisweet chocolate chips
1/2 ounce bar paraffin
1   10-ounce package miniature
   marshmallows

1   6-ounce package flaked coconut
1 cup chopped walnuts
1 tablespoon vanilla extract

Melt chocolate and paraffin in saucepan, stirring frequently; cool. Fold in remaining ingredients. Shape into logs. Chill until firm. Slice to serve. **Yield: 48 servings.**

Approx Per Serving: Cal 87; Prot 1 g; Carbo 11 g; Fiber 1 g;
    T Fat 5 g; 50% Calories from Fat; Chol 0 mg; Sod 7 mg.

Autumn Nicole Kessinger, Eau Claire

Chocolate Marshmallow Bars

2 cups semisweet chocolate chips
2 cups butterscotch chips
1 cup chunky peanut butter

1   10-ounce package colored
   miniature marshmallows

Combine first 3 ingredients in glass bowl. Microwave on High for 3 minutes or until melted; stir well. Add marshmallows, stirring to coat. Spoon into buttered 9x13-inch dish. Chill until firm. Cut into bars. **Yield: 36 servings.**

Approx Per Serving: Cal 147; Prot 3 g; Carbo 17 g; Fiber 1 g;
    T Fat 9 g; 50% Calories from Fat; Chol 0 mg; Sod 51 mg.

Betty Gingrass, Iron Mountain

Coconut Joys

¹/₂ cup melted butter
2 cups confectioners' sugar
3 cups flaked coconut

2 ounces unsweetened chocolate,
  melted

Mix melted butter, confectioners' sugar and coconut in bowl. Shape by rounded teaspoonfuls into small balls; place on waxed paper-lined dish. Make indentation in center of each; fill with melted chocolate. Chill until firm; store in refrigerator. **Yield: 36 servings.**

Approx Per Serving: Cal 85; Prot <1 g; Carbo 10 g; Fiber 1 g;
    T Fat 5 g; 55% Calories from Fat; Chol 7 mg; Sod 23 mg.

Shirley A. Cook, Lansing

No-Fail Divinity

¹/₂ cup water
2 cups sugar
¹/₈ teaspoon salt

1 7-ounce jar marshmallow creme
¹/₂ cup chopped pecans
1 teaspoon vanilla extract

Combine water, sugar and salt in saucepan. Bring to a rolling boil for 2 minutes, stirring constantly. Place marshmallow creme in large bowl; pour hot syrup over top. Beat until mixture loses gloss. Fold in pecans and vanilla. Drop by spoonfuls onto waxed paper; cool. **Yield: 24 servings.**

Approx Per Serving: Cal 107; Prot <1 g; Carbo 24 g; Fiber <1 g;
    T Fat 2 g; 14% Calories from Fat; Chol 0 mg; Sod 16 mg.

Cathy Schwartzfisher, Petoskey

Christmas Fudge

4¹/₂ cups sugar
¹/₂ cup margarine
1 12-ounce can evaporated milk
12 ounces German's sweet chocolate
2 cups semisweet chocolate chips

1 16-ounce milk chocolate bar
1 13-ounce jar marshmallow creme
1¹/₂ teaspoons salt
2 tablespoons vanilla extract
2 cups chopped walnuts

Combine sugar, margarine and evaporated milk in saucepan; mix well. Bring to a boil; reduce heat. Simmer for 6 minutes, stirring constantly. Pour hot syrup over mixture of German's chocolate, chocolate chips, chocolate bar, marshmallow creme, salt and vanilla in large bowl. Beat until stiff. Fold in walnuts. Pour into buttered 10x15-inch dish; chill. Cut into small squares. **Yield: 80 servings.**

Approx Per Serving: Cal 166; Prot 2 g; Carbo 24 g; Fiber <1 g;
    T Fat 8 g; 41% Calories from Fat; Chol 2 mg; Sod 67 mg.

Betty Boyd, Hemlock

Easy Fudge

2 cups semisweet chocolate chips
1 14-ounce can sweetened
   condensed milk

1¼ cups chopped walnuts
1 teaspoon vanilla extract

Combine chocolate chips and condensed milk in top of double boiler. Cook over hot water until smooth, stirring frequently. Add walnuts and vanilla; mix well. Spread into 8x8-inch dish lined with foil. Chill for 2 hours; cut into squares. **Yield: 24 servings.**

Approx Per Serving: Cal 165; Prot 3 g; Carbo 18 g; Fiber 1 g;
    T Fat 10 g; 53% Calories from Fat; Chol 6 mg; Sod 24 mg.

Sally Taylor, Marquette

Peanut Brittle

1½ teaspoons baking soda
1 teaspoon water
1 teaspoon vanilla extract
1½ cups sugar

1 cup water
1 cup light corn syrup
3 tablespoons butter
1 pound raw peanuts

Combine baking soda, 1 teaspoon water and vanilla in small bowl; mix well and set aside. Combine sugar, 1 cup water and corn syrup in large saucepan; mix well. Cool over medium heat to 240 degrees on candy thermometer, soft ball stage, stirring occasionally. Stir in butter and peanuts. Cook to 300 degrees on candy thermometer, hard crack stage, stirring constantly. Remove from heat; stir in baking soda mixture. Pour onto warm buttered baking sheets, spreading to ¼ inch thick. Cool; break into pieces. **Yield: 60 servings.**

Approx Per Serving: Cal 82; Prot 2 g; Carbo 11 g; Fiber 1 g;
    T Fat 4 g; 43% Calories from Fat; Chol 2 mg; Sod 29 mg.

Cyndi Sechler, Grass Valley, California

Choose a cool dry day to make candy. Hard candies, divinities, fondants and nougats are especially sensitive to humid conditions.

Microwave Peanut Brittle

1 cup raw peanuts
1/2 cup light corn syrup
1 teaspoon butter
1 cup sugar

1/8 teaspoon salt
1 teaspoon baking soda
1 teaspoon vanilla extract

Combine peanuts, corn syrup, butter, sugar and salt in microwave-safe bowl; mix well. Microwave on High for 2 minutes; stir. Microwave for 2 minutes longer or to 300 degrees on candy thermometer, hard crack stage. Beat in baking soda and vanilla. Pour mixture onto foil. Cool; break into pieces. **Yield: 28 servings.**

Approx Per Serving: Cal 76; Prot 1 g; Carbo 13 g; Fiber <1 g;
     T Fat 3 g; 30% Calories from Fat; Chol <1 mg; Sod 43 mg.

Margaret Shurlow, Vassar

Crispy Peanut Butter Balls

3 cups crisp rice cereal
2 cups confectioners' sugar
2 1/4 cups peanut butter

1/4 cup melted margarine
1/3 bar paraffin wax
2 cups milk chocolate chips

Combine cereal, confectioners' sugar, peanut butter and margarine in bowl; mix well. Shape into small balls; place on tray. Chill until firm. Melt paraffin and chocolate over low heat in saucepan, stirring frequently. Dip balls into mixture to coat using spoon or fork. Place on waxed paper to cool. **Yield: 60 servings.**

Approx Per Serving: Cal 105; Prot 3 g; Carbo 9 g; Fiber 1 g;
     T Fat 7 g; 55% Calories from Fat; Chol 0 mg; Sod 70 mg.

Carolyn Devers, Laingsburg

Coconut-Peanut Butter Balls

2 1/2 cups crushed graham crackers
3 1/2 cups confectioners' sugar
1 cup margarine, softened
1 cup peanut butter

1 3-ounce can shredded coconut
1 cup chopped walnuts
2 cups chocolate chips
1/2 bar paraffin

Combine crushed graham crackers, confectioners' sugar, margarine, peanut butter, coconut and walnuts in bowl; mix well. Shape into small balls; place on tray in refrigerator to chill. Melt chocolate chips and paraffin over low heat in heavy saucepan, stirring frequently. Dip balls into hot chocolate mixture to coat using wooden picks. Place on waxed paper to cool. **Yield: 72 servings.**

Approx Per Serving: Cal 125; Prot 2 g; Carbo 13 g; Fiber 1 g;
     T Fat 8 g; 54% Calories from Fat; Chol 0 mg; Sod 74 mg.

Sean Travis Doty, Eau Claire

Grace's Famous Peanut Butter Candy

3 cups sugar
1/2 teaspoon vanilla extract
1/8 teaspoon salt

1/2 teaspoon margarine
2 tablespoons milk
3/4 cup peanut butter

Mix first 5 ingredients in medium saucepan. Bring to a boil over high heat. Reduce heat to medium. Cook to 240 degrees on candy thermometer, soft-ball stage, stirring constantly. Remove from heat. Stir in peanut butter, beating until mixture loses gloss. Spread on buttered waxed paper; cool. Cut into squares. **Yield: 24 servings.**

Approx Per Serving: Cal 146; Prot 2 g; Carbo 26 g; Fiber 1 g;
   T Fat 4 g; 25% Calories from Fat; Chol <1 mg; Sod 46 mg.

Grace M. Taylor, East Grand Rapids

Peanut Butter Fudge

4 cups peanut butter chips
1   7-ounce jar marshmallow creme
1 1/2 cups chopped pecans
1 tablespoon vanilla extract

4 1/2 cups sugar
1   12-ounce can evaporated milk
1/3 cup butter

Mix first 4 ingredients in mixer bowl. Mix sugar, evaporated milk and butter in saucepan. Bring to a rolling boil over medium heat. Boil for 4 minutes, stirring occasionally. Pour over chip mixture. Beat at medium speed until blended. Pour onto greased tray; cool. Cut into squares. **Yield: 35 servings.**

Approx Per Serving: Cal 285; Prot 5 g; Carbo 41 g; Fiber <1 g;
   T Fat 12 g; 36% Calories from Fat; Chol 8 mg; Sod 78 mg.

Edith Kalohn, Lake Orion

Mexican Pecan Patties

3 cups sugar
1 cup milk
1 1/2 teaspoons butter

1 cup chopped pecans
1 tablespoon vanilla extract

Caramelize 1 cup sugar in large cast-iron skillet over medium heat, stirring constantly to avoid burning. Combine remaining 2 cups sugar with milk in saucepan. Bring to a boil, stirring until sugar is dissolved. Pour gradually into caramelized sugar. Cook over medium high heat to 240 degrees on candy thermometer, soft-ball stage, stirring constantly. Remove from heat; stir in butter, pecans and vanilla. Beat until mixture is stiff. Drop by spoonfuls onto waxed paper; cool. **Yield: 32 servings.**

Approx Per Serving: Cal 105; Prot 1 g; Carbo 20 g; Fiber <1 g;
   T Fat 3 g; 25% Calories from Fat; Chol 2 mg; Sod 5 mg.

Peggy St. Louis, Kingsford

No-Bake Pralines

1 3-ounce package butterscotch
  pudding and pie filling mix
1½ cups pecan halves

1 cup packed brown sugar
½ cup evaporated milk
1 tablespoon margarine

Combine pudding mix, pecans, brown sugar, evaporated milk and margarine in saucepan; mix well. Cook over medium high heat for 3 to 4 minutes, stirring constantly; cool. Stir gently. Drop by teaspoonfuls onto waxed paper; cool. **Yield: 24 servings.**

Approx Per Serving: Cal 112; Prot 1 g; Carbo 16 g; Fiber <1 g;
    T Fat 5 g; 42% Calories from Fat; Chol 2 mg; Sod 40 mg.

Barb Miltibarger

Raisin Clusters

8 ounces German's sweet chocolate
⅔ cup sweetened condensed milk

1 cup raisins

Melt chocolate in top of double boiler over hot water, stirring frequently. Remove from heat. Add sweetened condensed milk, stirring until smooth. Stir in raisins. Drop by teaspoonfuls onto foil. Let stand for 3 hours or until firm, turning once. Store in airtight containers. **Yield: 24 servings.**

Approx Per Serving: Cal 95; Prot 1 g; Carbo 16 g; Fiber <1 g;
    T Fat 4 g; 34% Calories from Fat; Chol 3 mg; Sod 12 mg.

Shirley A. Cook, Lansing

Easy Rocky Road

2 cups semisweet chocolate chips
¼ cup butter
2 tablespoons shortening

3 cups miniature marshmallows
½ cup chopped pecans

Combine chocolate chips, butter and shortening in large microwave-safe bowl. Microwave on Medium for 5 to 7 minutes or until chips are melted, stirring once. Add marshmallows and pecans, stirring to coat. Spread into buttered 8x8-inch dish. Chill, covered, until firm; cut into squares. **Yield: 24 servings.**

Approx Per Serving: Cal 137; Prot 1 g; Carbo 14 g; Fiber 1 g;
    T Fat 10 g; 59% Calories from Fat; Chol 5 mg; Sod 24 mg.

Sally Taylor, Marquette

Applesauce Jumbles

2³/4 cups flour
1¹/2 cups packed brown sugar
¹/2 cup shortening
³/4 cup applesauce
1 teaspoon vanilla extract
1 cup chopped pecans

¹/2 teaspoon baking soda
1 teaspoon cinnamon
¹/4 teaspoon ground cloves
1 teaspoon salt
2 eggs, beaten
1 cup semisweet chocolate chips

Mix flour and brown sugar in bowl. Cut in shortening until mixture is crumbly. Add applesauce, vanilla, pecans, baking soda, cinnamon, cloves, salt, eggs and chocolate chips; mix well. Drop by heaping tablespoonfuls 2 inches apart on ungreased cookie sheet. Bake at 375 degrees for 10 minutes. **Yield: 40 cookies.**

Approx Per Cookie: Cal 142; Prot 2 g; Carbo 21 g; Fiber 1 g;
    T Fat 6 g; 40% Calories from Fat; Chol 11 mg; Sod 73 mg.

Alice Kathy DeVries, Pierson

Banana Nugget Cookies

1 cup sugar
³/4 cup margarine, softened
1 egg, beaten
1¹/2 cups flour
¹/2 teaspoon salt
¹/2 teaspoon baking soda

¹/4 teaspoon nutmeg
³/4 teaspoon cinnamon
1 cup mashed bananas
1³/4 cups quick-cooking oats
2 cups semisweet chocolate chips
³/4 cup chopped pecans

Cream sugar and margarine in mixer bowl until light and fluffy. Add egg, flour, salt, baking soda, nutmeg, cinnamon, bananas and oats; mix well. Fold in chocolate chips and pecans. Drop by heaping tablespoonfuls onto greased cookie sheets. Bake at 400 degrees for 10 to 12 minutes or until golden brown. **Yield: 40 cookies.**

Approx Per Cookie: Cal 146; Prot 2 g; Carbo 18 g; Fiber 1 g;
    T Fat 8 g; 49% Calories from Fat; Chol 5 mg; Sod 80 mg.

Suzanne K. Clark, Saginaw

Cool cookies completely in a single layer on a wire rack before storing. Store soft and chewy cookies in an airtight container and crisp cookies in a jar with a loose-fitting lid.

Banana-Oatmeal Cookies

1½ cups sifted flour
½ teaspoon baking soda
1 teaspoon baking powder
1 teaspoon salt
¼ teaspoon nutmeg
¾ teaspoon cinnamon
¾ cup shortening

1 cup sugar
1 egg, beaten
1 cup mashed bananas
1¾ cups rolled oats
½ cup chopped pecans
1½ teaspoons lemon juice

Sift flour, baking soda, baking powder, salt, nutmeg and cinnamon into large bowl. Cream shortening and sugar in mixer bowl until light and fluffy. Add egg and bananas; beat well. Stir in oats, pecans, lemon juice and sifted dry ingredients. Drop by heaping tablespoonfuls 2 inches apart on cookie sheets. Bake at 400 degrees for 15 minutes. May omit baking powder for crisper cookie. **Yield: 40 cookies.**

Approx Per Cookie: Cal 100; Prot 1 g; Carbo 12 g; Fiber 1 g;
    T Fat 5 g; 47% Calories from Fat; Chol 5 mg; Sod 74 mg.

Nellie Thompson, Romulus

Big Cookie

¾ ounce oats
½ teaspoon baking powder
2 packets artificial sweetener
1 tablespoon crunchy peanut butter

2 tablespoons plus 2 teaspoons dry
  milk powder
2 tablespoons water
2 tablespoons raisins

Combine oats, baking powder, sweetener and peanut butter in bowl; mix well. Add milk powder and water, stirring to moisten. Fold in raisins. Drop onto center of cookie sheet sprayed with nonstick cooking spray. Bake at 350 degrees for 8 to 10 minutes or until brown. **Yield: 1 serving.**

Approx Per Serving: Cal 289; Prot 12 g; Carbo 43 g; Fiber 4 g;
    T Fat 10 g; 28% Calories from Fat; Chol 2 mg; Sod 316 mg.

Berdina Holford, Jackson

Christmas Butter Cookies

1/2 cup butter, softened
1/2 cup sugar
1 egg, beaten
3/4 teaspoon vanilla extract

2 cups sifted flour
1/2 teaspoon baking powder
1/4 teaspoon salt

Cream butter and sugar in mixer bowl until light and fluffy. Beat in egg and vanilla. Sift in flour, baking powder and salt; mix well. Chill dough for 30 minutes. Roll out to 1/8-inch thickness on lightly floured surface. Cut with assorted Christmas cookie cutters. Place on ungreased cookie sheet. Bake at 350 degrees for 10 minutes. Decorate as desired. **Yield: 36 cookies.**

Approx Per Cookie: Cal 59; Prot 1 g; Carbo 8 g; Fiber <1 g;
    T Fat 3 g; 42% Calories from Fat; Chol 13 mg; Sod 43 mg.

Marian Kasper, Saginaw

Soft Butter Cookies

1 1/3 cups margarine
1 cup sugar
2 eggs, beaten

1 teaspoon vanilla extract
3 1/2 cups flour
1 teaspoon baking powder

Cream margarine, sugar, eggs and vanilla in mixer bowl until light and fluffy. Stir in flour and baking powder. Pat out gently to desired thickness. Cut out with cookie cutters. Bake at 350 degrees for 8 to 12 minutes or until light brown. Cool and frost with favorite frosting. Use hard Blue Bonnet-type margarine for soft cookies. Doubling recipe may result in harder cookies. **Yield: 36 cookies.**

Approx Per Cookie: Cal 131; Prot 2 g; Carbo 15 g; Fiber <1 g;
    T Fat 7 g; 49% Calories from Fat; Chol 12 mg; Sod 92 mg.

Sally Kennamer, Kent City

Famous Neiman-Marcus Chocolate Chip Cookies

5 cups oats
2 cups butter, softened
2 cups sugar
2 cups packed brown sugar
4 eggs, beaten
2 teaspoons vanilla extract
4 cups flour

1 teaspoon salt
2 teaspoons baking powder
2 teaspoons baking soda
4 cups semisweet chocolate chips
1   8-ounce dark chocolate candy bar,
  grated
3 cups chopped pecans

Process oats in blender container until powdered; set aside. Cream butter with sugars in mixer bowl. Beat in eggs and vanilla. Add powdered oats, flour, salt, baking powder, baking soda, chocolate chips, grated chocolate and pecans; mix well. Roll into balls; place 2 inches apart on ungreased cookie sheet. Bake at 375 degrees for 8 minutes. **Yield: 112 cookies.**

Approx Per Cookie: Cal 157; Prot 2 g; Carbo 19 g; Fiber 1 g;
  T Fat 9 g; 48% Calories from Fat; Chol 17 mg; Sod 75 mg.

Vivian Olson, Traverse City

Oatmeal-Chocolate-Chocolate Chip Cookies

1½ cups sugar
1 cup margarine, softened
1 egg, beaten
¼ cup water
1 teaspoon vanilla extract
1¼ cups flour

⅓ cup baking cocoa
½ teaspoon salt
½ teaspoon baking soda
3 cups oats
2 cups chocolate chips

Cream sugar and margarine in mixer bowl until light and fluffy. Beat in egg, water and vanilla. Combine flour, baking cocoa, salt and baking soda in bowl. Add to creamed mixture; mix well. Stir in oats and chocolate chips. Drop by rounded teaspoonfuls onto ungreased cookie sheet. Bake at 350 degrees for 10 to 12 minutes. Cool for 1 minute on cookie sheet; remove to wire racks to cool completely. Store in airtight container. **Yield: 72 cookies.**

Approx Per Cookie: Cal 86; Prot 1 g; Carbo 11 g; Fiber 1 g;
  T Fat 5 g; 46% Calories from Fat; Chol 3 mg; Sod 52 mg.

Sharon R. Seibel, Freeland

*When baking large batches of cookies, use a refrigerator shelf
or extra oven rack as an oversize cooling rack.*

Low-Cholesterol Cookies

1 cup cholesterol-free margarine,
  softened
³/₄ cup sugar
¹/₂ teaspoon baking powder

¹/₂ teaspoon baking soda
¹/₂ teaspoon vanilla extract
¹/₂ teaspoon vinegar
1¹/₂ cups flour

Beat margarine, sugar, baking powder and baking soda in mixer bowl for 15 minutes until light and fluffy. Stir in vanilla and vinegar. Stir in flour gently. Drop by tablespoonfuls onto nonstick cookie sheet. Bake at 300 degrees for 15 minutes. **Yield: 45 cookies.**

Approx Per Cookie: Cal 64; Prot <1 g; Carbo 7 g; Fiber <1 g;
    T Fat 4 g; 57% Calories from Fat; Chol 0 mg; Sod 61 mg.

Juanita Kenyon, Plainwell

Chow Mein Cookies

2 3-ounce cans chow mein noodles
1 cup cashews

1 cup butterscotch chips
1 cup semisweet chocolate chips

Combine noodles and cashews in bowl. Melt butterscotch and chocolate chips over low heat in heavy saucepan, stirring frequently. Pour over noodle mixture, stirring to coat. Drop by teaspoonfuls onto greased waxed paper. Chill until firm. **Yield: 60 cookies.**

Approx Per Cookie: Cal 55; Prot 1 g; Carbo 6 g; Fiber <1 g;
    T Fat 4 g; 57% Calories from Fat; Chol <1 mg; Sod 30 mg.

Michelle Richards, Lansing

Homemade Oreo Cookies

1 2-layer package dark chocolate
  cake mix
¹/₂ cup melted margarine
1 egg, beaten

2 cups confectioners' sugar
1 teaspoon vanilla extract
1 egg white
¹/₄ cup shortening

Combine cake mix, margarine and egg in bowl; mix well. Shape into balls; place on ungreased cookie sheet. Bake at 350 degrees for 8 minutes. Invert onto wire rack to cool completely. Cream confectioners sugar, vanilla, egg white and shortening in mixer bowl until light and fluffy. Spread over half the cookies; top with remaining cookies. **Yield: 24 cookies.**

Approx Per Cookie: Cal 187; Prot 1 g; Carbo 28 g; Fiber 0 g;
    T Fat 8 g; 38% Calories from Fat; Chol 9 mg; Sod 181 mg.

Mary Lucas, Rockford

Pure-Fruit Cookies

1¹/₂ cups mashed bananas
¹/₃ cup oil
1 teaspoon vanilla extract
1¹/₂ cups rolled oats
¹/₂ cup oatbran
¹/₂ cup chopped dried apricots

¹/₄ cup chopped dates
¹/₄ cup raisins
¹/₄ cup chopped dried papaya
¹/₄ cup chopped dried unsweetened
   pineapple
¹/₂ cup chopped walnuts

Beat bananas, oil and vanilla in large bowl. Add oats, oatbran, apricots, dates, raisins, papaya, pineapple and walnuts; mix well. Drop by rounded tablespoonfuls 1 inch apart onto greased cookie sheets; flatten slightly. Bake at 325 degrees for 20 to 25 minutes until edges are light brown. Cool on wire rack; store in refrigerator. May substitute other dried fruits, as preferred. **Yield: 24 cookies.**

Approx Per Cookie: Cal 108; Prot 2 g; Carbo 16 g; Fiber 2 g;
   T Fat 5 g; 39% Calories from Fat; Chol 0 mg; Sod 2 mg.

Frances Peeks, Holland

Haystacks

¹/₄ cup butter
¹/₂ cup creamy peanut butter
2 cups butterscotch chips

6 cups cornflakes
²/₃ cup miniature semisweet
   chocolate chips

Melt butter, peanut butter and butterscotch chips over very low heat in large saucepan, stirring constantly; remove from heat. Pour over cornflakes in bowl, stirring until coated. Add chocolate chips; mix well. Drop by ¹/₄ cupfuls onto waxed paper-lined trays. Chill until firm. Garnish with chopped nuts or chocolate jimmies. **Yield: 36 servings.**

Approx Per Serving: Cal 111; Prot 2 g; Carbo 11 g; Fiber 1 g;
   T Fat 8 g; 57% Calories from Fat; Chol 3 mg; Sod 74 mg.

Ruth C. Rhode, Stevensville

Healthwise Cookies

2 cups oats
1 cup cholesterol-free margarine,
  softened

1 cup flour
1/2 cup sugar

Combine oats, margarine, flour and sugar in bowl; mix well. Shape into balls. Place on ungreased cookie sheet; flatten slightly. Bake at 350 degrees for 10 to 12 minutes. May add 1/2 cup chocolate chips, 1/3 cup chopped walnuts, 1/3 cup slivered almonds or 1/2 teaspoon almond extract. **Yield: 30 cookies.**

Approx Per Cookie: Cal 103; Prot 1 g; Carbo 10 g; Fiber 1 g;
  T Fat 6 g; 56% Calories from Fat; Chol 0 mg; Sod 72 mg.

Dorothy Contois, Marquette

Mom's Old-Fashioned Icebox Cookies

2 cups packed brown sugar
1 cup sugar
1 cup shortening
1 teaspoon vanilla extract
1/2 teaspoon salt
4 eggs, beaten

1 teaspoon baking soda
1 teaspoon cream of tartar
6 cups flour
2 cups chopped walnuts
6 ounces chopped dates

Cream brown sugar, sugar and shortening in mixer bowl until light and fluffy. Add vanilla, salt, eggs, baking soda, cream of tartar and flour; mix well. Fold in walnuts and dates. Shape into 2-inch diameter rolls; wrap with waxed paper. Chill in refrigerator overnight. Slice dough to desired thickness. Arrange on nonstick cookie sheet. Bake at 350 degrees for 6 to 8 minutes or until golden brown.
Yield: 100 cookies.

Approx Per Cookie: Cal 97; Prot 1 g; Carbo 15 g; Fiber <1 g;
  T Fat 4 g; 35% Calories from Fat; Chol 9 mg; Sod 25 mg.

Karen Fitting, Saginaw

Gelatin Cookies

³/₄ cup margarine, softened
1/2 cup sugar
1 3-ounce package flavored gelatin
2 eggs, beaten

1 teaspoon vanilla extract
2¹/₂ cups flour
1 teaspoon baking powder
1 teaspoon salt

Cream margarine, sugar and gelatin in mixer bowl until light and fluffy. Add eggs and vanilla; beat well. Sift in flour, baking powder and salt; mix well. Shape into ³/₄-inch balls. Place on ungreased cookie sheet 3 inches apart. Flatten with glass dipped in sugar. Bake at 400 degrees for 6 to 8 minutes or until edges are light brown. **Yield: 48 cookies.**

Approx Per Cookie: Cal 67; Prot 1 g; Carbo 9 g; Fiber <1 g;
     T Fat 3 g; 42% Calories from Fat; Chol 9 mg; Sod 93 mg.

Nancy Briolat, St. Ignace

German Lebkuchen

3¹/₂ cups flour
1 teaspoon baking soda
1/4 teaspoon salt
1 teaspoon cinnamon
1/2 teaspoon ground cloves
1/2 teaspoon ground allspice
1/2 teaspoon nutmeg
1/2 cup molasses
1/2 cup sour cream
1/2 cup sugar

1/4 cup butter, softened
1 egg, slightly beaten
1/4 cup chopped walnuts
1/4 cup finely chopped citron
1/4 cup finely chopped candied
     orange peel
1 teaspoon grated lemon peel
1/2 teaspoon aniseed
30 whole peanuts, halved

Sift flour, baking soda, salt, cinnamon, cloves, allspice and nutmeg together; set aside. Combine molasses, sour cream and sugar in saucepan. Bring to a boil over medium heat, stirring occasionally. Pour into large bowl; cool. Add butter, egg, walnuts, citron, orange peel, lemon peel and aniseed; mix well. Stir in sifted dry ingredients, adding additional flour if needed to make stiff dough. Chill, covered, for 12 hours to overnight. Turn out onto floured surface. Roll out half the dough into 1/4-inch thick rectangle; cut into 1¹/₂x2-inch portions. Place 1 inch apart on greased cookie sheet; press peanut half into center of each cookie. Repeat with remaining dough. Bake at 400 degrees for 10 to 12 minutes. Turn onto wire rack to cool. **Yield: 60 servings.**

Approx Per Serving: Cal 65; Prot 1 g; Carbo 11 g; Fiber <1 g;
     T Fat 2 g; 28% Calories from Fat; Chol 6 mg; Sod 38 mg.

Marian Kasper, Saginaw

Soft Oatmeal Cookies

1 cup raisins
1 cup shortening
1 cup sugar
3 eggs
2 cups flour
3/4 teaspoon baking soda

1 teaspoon salt
1 teaspoon cinnamon
1/2 teaspoon allspice
2 cups quick-cooking oats
1 cup chopped pecans

Combine raisins and boiling water to cover in saucepan. Simmer for 3 to 4 minutes; drain, reserving 6 tablespoons liquid. Cream shortening, sugar and eggs in mixer bowl until light and fluffy. Add mixture of flour, baking soda, salt and spices; mix well. Stir in oats and reserved raisin liquid. Add pecans; mix well. Drop by tablespoonfuls onto greased cookie sheet. Bake at 350 degrees for 10 to 12 minutes or until brown. Remove to wire rack to cool. **Yield: 36 cookies.**

Approx Per Cookie: Cal 156; Prot 2 g; Carbo 17 g; Fiber 2 g;
    T Fat 9 g; 52% Calories from Fat; Chol 18 mg; Sod 84 mg.

Jean Schillings, Freeland

Orange Chews

5 tablespoons margarine, softened
1/4 cup sugar
1/2 cup packed brown sugar
1 egg, beaten
1 cup flour
1/2 teaspoon baking soda

1/2 teaspoon salt
2 tablespoons sour milk
1/2 to 3/4 cup candied orange slices
1 tablespoon flour
1/2 cup chopped pecans
1/2 cup chopped raisins

Cream margarine, sugar and brown sugar in mixer bowl until light and fluffy. Add egg; beat well. Stir in 1 cup flour, baking soda, salt and sour milk; mix well. Toss orange slices with 1 tablespoon flour. Fold into mixture with pecans and raisins. Chill for 2 hours to overnight. Drop by tablespoonfuls onto nonstick cookie sheets. Bake at 350 degrees for 12 to 15 minutes. **Yield: 20 servings.**

Approx Per Serving: Cal 152; Prot 1 g; Carbo 25 g; Fiber 1 g;
    T Fat 5 g; 31% Calories from Fat; Chol 11 mg; Sod 121 mg.

Jennie Badelt, Sault Ste. Marie

Peanut Cups

1 20-ounce package peanut butter cookie dough	48 miniature peanut butter cups, wrappers discarded

Cut cookie dough into 12 slices; cut into quarters. Place one portion of dough into each paper-lined cup of miniature muffin pan. Bake at 350 degrees until dough begins to puff up. Place 1 peanut butter cup on top of each portion. Return to oven. Bake just until brown. **Yield: 48 servings.**

Approx Per Serving: Cal 101; Prot 2 g; Carbo 11 g; Fiber <1 g;
    T Fat 6 g; 50% Calories from Fat; Chol <1 mg; Sod 83 mg.

Clara E. Hancock, Midland

Peanut Butter Cookies

2 cups sifted flour	1/2 cup peanut butter
3/4 teaspoon baking soda	1/2 cup packed brown sugar
1/2 teaspoon baking powder	1/2 cup sugar
1/4 teaspoon salt	1 egg, beaten
1/2 cup shortening	1/4 cup orange juice

Sift flour, baking soda, baking powder and salt together. Cream shortening, peanut butter, brown sugar and sugar in mixer bowl until light and fluffy. Beat in egg. Sift in flour mixture alternately with orange juice, stirring until stiff dough forms. Chill until firm. Shape into small balls; place 3 inches apart on ungreased cookie sheet. Make crisscross pattern on tops with fork. Bake at 375 degrees for 12 minutes. **Yield: 60 cookies.**

Approx Per Cookie: Cal 59; Prot 1 g; Carbo 7 g; Fiber <1 g;
    T Fat 3 g; 44% Calories from Fat; Chol 4 mg; Sod 33 mg.

Lisa Ann McCullough

Always leave 1 to 2 inches between cookies dropped on baking sheet to allow room to spread. Thin doughs will spread more than thicker doughs.

Peanut Butter-Oatmeal Cookies

³/₄ cup butter-flavored shortening
1 cup peanut butter
1¹/₂ cups packed brown sugar
¹/₂ cup water
1 egg

1 teaspoon vanilla extract
3 cups quick-cooking oats
1¹/₂ cups flour
¹/₂ teaspoon baking soda

Cream shortening, peanut butter and brown sugar in mixer bowl until light and fluffy. Beat in water, egg and vanilla. Stir in oats, flour and baking soda. Chill, covered, for 2 hours. Shape into 1-inch balls. Place on ungreased cookie sheet; flatten with fork dipped in sugar to form crisscross pattern. Bake at 350 degrees for 9 to 11 minutes or until edges are golden brown. Cool for 1 minute on cookie sheet; remove to wire rack to cool completely. **Yield: 90 cookies.**

Approx Per Cookie: Cal 68; Prot 2 g; Carbo 8 g; Fiber 1 g;
    T Fat 3 g; 44% Calories from Fat; Chol 2 mg; Sod 19 mg.

Ruth Rhode, Stevensville

Pineapple Drop Cookies

¹/₂ cup shortening
³/₄ cup sugar
2 eggs
1 cup crushed pineapple
2 cups flour
2 teaspoons baking powder
¹/₂ teaspoon salt

¹/₄ teaspoon baking soda
¹/₂ cup chopped pecans
6 tablespoons butter
1¹/₂ cups confectioners' sugar
1 teaspoon vanilla extract
3 tablespoons pineapple juice

Cream shortening and sugar in mixer bowl until light and fluffy. Add eggs 1 at a time, beating well after each addition. Fold in pineapple. Sift flour, baking powder, salt and baking soda together in bowl; add to creamed mixture. Stir in pecans. Drop by spoonfuls onto greased cookie sheet. Bake at 350 degrees for 10 minutes. Remove to wire rack to cool. Melt butter in skillet until golden; remove from heat. Add confectioners' sugar, vanilla and pineapple juice, stirring until smooth. Spread over cooled cookies. **Yield: 36 cookies.**

Approx Per Cookie: Cal 125; Prot 1 g; Carbo 16 g; Fiber <1 g;
    T Fat 6 g; 44% Calories from Fat; Chol 17 mg; Sod 74 mg.

Jeanne DeLaney, Traverse City

Pineapple-Raisin Drops

1/2 cup raisins
3/4 cup crushed pineapple with juice
1 cup packed brown sugar
1/2 cup butter, softened
1 egg
1 teaspoon vanilla extract

2 cups flour
1 teaspoon baking powder
1/2 teaspoon baking soda
1/2 teaspoon salt
1/2 cup pecans

Combine raisins and pineapple with juice in bowl; set aside. Cream brown sugar, butter, egg and vanilla in mixer bowl until light and fluffy. Stir in raisins and pineapple. Combine flour, baking powder, baking soda and salt in bowl; mix well. Add to creamed mixture, stirring well. Fold in pecans. Drop by spoonfuls onto greased cookie sheet. Bake at 375 degrees for 12 to 15 minutes or until light brown. **Yield: 36 cookies.**

Approx Per Cookie: Cal 101; Prot 1 g; Carbo 16 g; Fiber <1 g;
T Fat 4 g; 34% Calories from Fat; Chol 13 mg; Sod 77 mg.

Carol Lyons, Horton

Potato Chip-Oatmeal Cookies

1 cup sugar
1 cup packed brown sugar
1 cup margarine, softened
2 eggs, beaten
1 teaspoon vanilla extract

13/4 to 2 cups flour
1 teaspoon baking soda
2 cups oats
2 cups crushed potato chips

Cream sugar, brown sugar, margarine, eggs and vanilla in mixer bowl until light and fluffy. Combine flour, baking soda, oats and potato chips in large bowl; mix well. Stir into creamed mixture. Drop by spoonfuls 2 inches apart onto greased cookie sheet. Bake at 375 degrees for 10 to 12 minutes or until light brown. **Yield: 56 cookies.**

Approx Per Cookie: Cal 102; Prot 1 g; Carbo 15 g; Fiber 1 g;
T Fat 4 g; 38% Calories from Fat; Chol 8 mg; Sod 67 mg.

Nina Cawley, Saginaw

*You can reduce the shortening in oatmeal cookies by 1/3 or
more without affecting the quality.*

Potato Chip Cookies

1 cup butter, softened
1/2 cup sugar
1 teaspoon vanilla extract

1³/4 cups flour
1 cup crushed potato chips
1/2 cup chopped pecans

Cream butter, sugar and vanilla in mixer bowl until light and fluffy. Stir in flour, potato chips and pecans. Drop by spoonfuls onto ungreased cookie sheet; press lightly with fork to make ridges in each cookie. Bake at 350 degrees for 12 to 15 minutes or until golden brown. **Yield: 24 cookies.**

Approx Per Cookie: Cal 146; Prot 1 g; Carbo 13 g; Fiber 1 g;
    T Fat 10 g; 62% Calories from Fat; Chol 21 mg; Sod 76 mg.

Betty Berglund, Marquette

Pudding Cookies

1/2 cup sugar
³/4 cup packed brown sugar
1 cup butter, softened
2 eggs, beaten
1 teaspoon vanilla extract
2¹/4 cups flour

1 teaspoon baking soda
1 3-ounce package vanilla instant
    pudding mix
2 cups semisweet chocolate chips
1/2 cup chopped pecans

Cream sugar, brown sugar, butter, eggs and vanilla in mixer bowl until light and fluffy. Add flour, baking soda, and pudding mix, stirring until smooth. Fold in chocolate chips and pecans. Drop by spoonfuls onto ungreased cookie sheet. Bake at 375 degrees for 10 minutes or until golden brown. **Yield: 36 cookies.**

Approx Per Cookie: Cal 178; Prot 2 g; Carbo 22 g; Fiber 1 g;
    T Fat 10 g; 48% Calories from Fat; Chol 26 mg; Sod 90 mg.

Kristy Little, Eau Claire

Rum Balls

1 cup confectioners' sugar
1¹/2 tablespoons baking cocoa
1/8 teaspoon salt
2¹/2 cups finely crushed vanilla wafers

1/2 cup rum
2¹/2 tablespoons light corn syrup
1 cup finely chopped walnuts
1/2 cup confectioners' sugar

Mix first 4 ingredients in bowl. Add rum and corn syrup, stirring until moistened. Fold in walnuts. Shape into small balls. Roll in 1/2 cup confectioners' sugar to coat. Store in airtight container or in freezer. **Yield: 36 servings.**

Approx Per Serving: Cal 81; Prot 1 g; Carbo 11 g; Fiber <1 g;
    T Fat 3 g; 37% Calories from Fat; Chol 4 mg; Sod 31 mg.

Carolyn Devers, Laingsburg

McDougall's Shortbread

2 cups flour
1/4 teaspoon salt
1/4 teaspoon baking powder

1 cup butter, softened
1/2 cup confectioners' sugar
1 teaspoon vanilla extract

Sift flour, salt and baking powder together. Cream butter, confectioners' sugar and vanilla in mixer bowl until light and fluffy. Stir in sifted dry ingredients. Roll into 8x12-inch rectangle 1/2 inch thick on lightly floured surface. Cut into 2-inch squares. Place 1 inch apart on buttered cookie sheet. Bake at 375 degrees for 10 to 12 minutes or until light brown. **Yield: 24 servings.**

Approx Per Serving: Cal 116; Prot 1 g; Carbo 11 g; Fiber <1 g;
    T Fat 8 g; 60% Calories from Fat; Chol 21 mg; Sod 90 mg.

Dani Peterson, Lansing

Snickerdoodles

1/2 cup margarine, softened
1/2 cup shortening
1 1/2 cups sugar
2 eggs, beaten
2 3/4 cups flour

2 teaspoons cream of tartar
1 teaspoon baking soda
1/4 teaspoon salt
2 tablespoons sugar
2 teaspoons cinnamon

Cream margarine, shortening, 1 1/2 cups sugar and eggs in mixer bowl until light and fluffy. Stir in flour, cream of tartar, baking soda and salt until smooth. Shape by teaspoonfuls into balls. Roll in mixture of 2 tablespoons sugar and cinnamon. Place on ungreased cookie sheet. Bake at 400 degrees for 8 to 10 minutes or until brown. **Yield: 72 servings.**

Approx Per Serving: Cal 61; Prot 1 g; Carbo 8 g; Fiber <1 g;
    T Fat 3 g; 42% Calories from Fat; Chol 6 mg; Sod 36 mg.

Barb Buskirk, Portland

Pack homemade refrigerator cookie dough into clean 6-ounce
frozen juice cans. Freeze until needed. Thaw for about 15
minutes, remove bottom of can and push dough up,
using the top edge as a cutting guide.

Snickerdoodles with Peanuts

2 cups shortening
3 cups sugar
4 eggs, beaten
5¹/₂ cups flour

4 teaspoons cream of tartar
2 teaspoons baking soda
2 cups Spanish peanuts

Cream shortening, sugar and eggs in mixer bowl until light and fluffy. Stir in flour, cream of tartar, baking soda and peanuts. Chill in refrigerator until firm. Shape dough into small balls. Arrange on cookie sheet, flattening slightly with fork dipped in water. Bake at 400 degrees for 8 to 10 minutes or until brown. **Yield: 100 servings.**

Approx Per Serving: Cal 104; Prot 2 g; Carbo 12 g; Fiber <1 g;
 T Fat 6 g; 49% Calories from Fat; Chol 9 mg; Sod 20 mg.

Peg Landfair, Dimondale

Sour Cream Cookies

3 cups packed brown sugar
1¹/₂ cups shortening
3 eggs, beaten
1¹/₂ cups sour cream
2 teaspoons vanilla extract
6 cups flour
1¹/₂ teaspoons baking powder
1 tablespoon baking soda

1¹/₂ teaspoons salt
2 teaspoons grated nutmeg
1 1-pound package confectioners'
 sugar
2 tablespoons margarine, softened
1¹/₂ teaspoons vanilla extract
¹/₄ cup (scant) evaporated milk

Cream brown sugar and shortening in mixer bowl until light and fluffy. Beat in eggs, sour cream and vanilla. Add flour, baking powder, baking soda, salt and nutmeg, stirring until smooth. Roll out on lightly floured surface to ¹/₂-inch thickness. Cut with cookie cutter into desired shapes; arrange on greased cookie sheet. Bake at 350 degrees for 10 to 12 minutes. Remove to wire rack to cool. Beat confectioners' sugar, margarine, vanilla and enough evaporated milk to make of spreading consistency in small bowl. Spread over cooled cookies. May add red or green food coloring to frosting for Christmas cookies. **Yield: 72 cookies.**

Approx Per Cookie: Cal 166; Prot 2 g; Carbo 27 g; Fiber <1 g;
 T Fat 6 g; 32% Calories from Fat; Chol 11 mg; Sod 101 mg.

Anita Edick, Lansing

Chocolate-Sour Cream Drop Cookies

1/2 cup margarine, softened
11/2 cups sugar
2 eggs, beaten
2 ounces unsweetened chocolate,
 melted
1 cup sour cream

1 teaspoon vanilla extract
23/4 cups flour
1 teaspoon baking soda
1/2 teaspoon baking powder
1/2 teaspoon salt

Cream margarine, sugar, eggs and melted chocolate in mixer bowl until light and fluffy. Add sour cream, vanilla, flour, baking soda, baking powder and salt, stirring until smooth. Chill dough for 2 hours to overnight. Drop by tablespoonfuls onto greased cookie sheet. Bake at 400 degrees for 8 to 10 minutes or until light brown. **Yield: 40 cookies.**

Approx Per Cookie: Cal 104; Prot 2 g; Carbo 15 g; Fiber <1 g;
 T Fat 5 g; 39% Calories from Fat; Chol 13 mg; Sod 85 mg.

Kimberly Trosien, Essexville

Crisp Sugar Cookies

1 cup confectioners' sugar
1 cup sugar
1 cup margarine, softened
1 cup oil
2 eggs, beaten

1 teaspoon vanilla extract
41/4 cups flour
1 teaspoon salt
1 teaspoon baking soda
1 teaspoon cream of tartar

Cream confectioners' sugar, sugar and margarine in mixer bowl until light and fluffy. Add oil, eggs and vanilla, beating well. Sift flour, salt, baking soda and cream of tartar together. Stir into creamed mixture until smooth. Chill in refrigerator overnight. Shape into balls; arrange on ungreased cookie sheet. Flatten with glass dipped in sugar. Bake at 375 degrees for 10 to 15 minutes or until edges are light brown. **Yield: 48 cookies.**

Approx Per Cookie: Cal 143; Prot 1 g; Carbo 15 g; Fiber <1 g;
 T Fat 9 g; 54% Calories from Fat; Chol 9 mg; Sod 109 mg.
 Nutritional information does not include additional sugar for dipping.

Ruth Hayden, Kalamazoo

Soft Sugar Cookies

1/2 cup shortening	1 cup sour cream
31/2 cups sugar	2 teaspoons baking soda
2 teaspoons vanilla extract	8 cups flour
4 eggs, beaten	

Cream shortening and sugar in mixer bowl until light and fluffy. Add vanilla, eggs and sour cream, beating well. Add baking soda and flour, stirring until smooth. Roll out on lightly floured surface; cut to desired shapes with cookie cutter. Place on ungreased cookie sheet. Bake at 325 degrees for 9 minutes. **Yield: 72 cookies.**

Approx Per Cookie: Cal 112; Prot 2 g; Carbo 20 g; Fiber <1 g;
T Fat 3 g; 20% Calories from Fat; Chol 13 mg; Sod 29 mg.

Karla S. Holcomb, Lansing

Sugar-Free Pineapple Cookies

1/2 cup shortening	Grated rind of 1 orange
1 egg, beaten	2 cups flour
1 8-ounce can crushed juice-pack	1 teaspoon baking soda
pineapple, drained	1 teaspoon cinnamon
1 cup chopped pecans	1/2 teaspoon ground cloves
1/3 cup chopped apricots	1 teaspoon nutmeg
1/3 cup chopped prunes	1/2 teaspoon salt
1/3 cup chopped dates	

Mix shortening and egg in bowl. Add pineapple, pecans, apricots, prunes, dates and orange rind; mix well. Sift flour, baking soda, cinnamon, cloves, nutmeg and salt together. Stir into fruit mixture. Drop by spoonfuls onto nonstick cookie sheet. Bake at 350 degrees for 10 to 12 minutes or until light brown. **Yield: 40 cookies.**

Approx Per Cookie: Cal 84; Prot 1 g; Carbo 10 g; Fiber 1 g;
T Fat 5 g; 50% Calories from Fat; Chol 5 mg; Sod 49 mg.

Bonnie Pierce, Ionia

Sugarless Cookies

2 tablespoons sugar-free peanut
  butter
2 tablespoons sugar-free chocolate
  drink mix

1 teaspoon vanilla extract
1 banana, mashed
1/2 cup Grape Nuts flakes

Combine peanut butter, chocolate drink mix, vanilla and banana in bowl, beating until smooth. Stir in Grape Nuts flakes. Drop by spoonfuls onto tray. Cover and freeze. **Yield: 24 cookies.**

Approx Per Cookie: Cal 22; Prot 1 g; Carbo 4 g; Fiber <1 g;
    T Fat 1 g; 28% Calories from Fat; Chol 0 mg; Sod 25 mg.

Mrs. Max Osborn, Jackson

Old-Fashioned Tea Cakes

1 cup butter, softened
1½ cups sugar
3 eggs, beaten

2 teaspoons vanilla extract
3 cups flour

Cream butter and sugar in mixer bowl until light and fluffy. Add eggs and vanilla, beating well. Stir in flour until smooth. Drop by spoonfuls onto ungreased cookie sheet. Bake at 350 degrees for 15 to 20 minutes or until light brown. **Yield: 36 servings.**

Approx Per Serving: Cal 123; Prot 2 g; Carbo 16 g; Fiber <1 g;
    T Fat 6 g; 42% Calories from Fat; Chol 32 mg; Sod 49 mg.

Dorothy Beauch, Saginaw

Waffle Turtle Cookies

1½ cups sugar
1 cup margarine, softened
2 teaspoons vanilla extract
4 eggs

2 cups flour
1/2 cup baking cocoa
1/4 teaspoon salt
1/2 cup chopped pecans

Cream sugar, margarine and vanilla in mixer bowl until light and fluffy. Add eggs 1 at a time, beating well after each addition. Sift flour, baking cocoa and salt together. Add to creamed mixture, stirring until smooth. Fold in pecans. Drop by heaping spoonfuls onto hot waffle iron. Bake for 2 minutes. Store in airtight container. **Yield: 36 cookies.**

Approx Per Cookie: Cal 126; Prot 2 g; Carbo 15 g; Fiber 1 g;
    T Fat 7 g; 49% Calories from Fat; Chol 24 mg; Sod 83 mg.

Nancy Shirah, Kalamazoo

Danish Apple Bars

2½ cups flour
1 teaspoon salt
1 cup margarine
1 egg yolk
½ cup (about) milk
1 cup crushed cornflakes

8 to 10 tart apples, peeled and sliced
1 cup sugar
1 teaspoon cinnamon
1 egg white
1 cup confectioners' sugar
4 teaspoons milk

Combine flour and salt in bowl. Cut in margarine until mixture is crumbly. Beat egg yolk with enough milk to measure ⅔ cup. Stir into flour mixture. Roll out half the dough into 12x17-inch rectangle on floured surface. Press into 10x15-inch baking pan. Sprinkle with cornflakes. Layer with apples. Sprinkle apples with mixture of sugar and cinnamon. Roll out remaining dough; place over apples, sealing edges and cutting vents. Beat egg white in mixer bowl until frothy. Brush over pastry. Bake at 375 degrees for 40 to 50 minutes; cool slightly. Combine confectioners' sugar and 4 teaspoons milk in small bowl, stirring until smooth. Spread over top crust; cut into bars. May bake in 9x13-inch pan using only 5 apples. **Yield: 36 servings.**

Approx Per Serving: Cal 143; Prot 1 g; Carbo 23 g; Fiber 1 g;
    T Fat 6 g; 34% Calories from Fat; Chol 6 mg; Sod 146 mg.

Cathy DeGoede, Grand Rapids
Eileen Schrader, Reese

Brickle Bars

½ cup margarine
2 ounces unsweetened chocolate
1 cup sugar
2 eggs, beaten
1 teaspoon vanilla extract

¾ cup flour
¾ cup almond brickle chips
½ cup miniature semisweet
    chocolate chips

Melt margarine with chocolate over low heat in 2-quart saucepan. Remove from heat and cool slightly. Add sugar, eggs and vanilla, beating with wooden spoon until mixed. Stir in flour. Spread in greased 8x8-inch baking pan. Sprinkle brickle chips and chocolate chips over top. Bake at 350 degrees for 30 minutes. Cool in pan on rack. Cut into bars. **Yield: 16 servings.**

Approx Per Serving: Cal 176; Prot 2 g; Carbo 21 g; Fiber 1 g;
    T Fat 10 g; 50% Calories from Fat; Chol 27 mg; Sod 77 mg.
    Nutritional information does not include almond brickle chips.

Cathy DeGoede, Grand Rapids

Crunchy Caramel-Chocolate Chews

¹/4 cup margarine
¹/4 cup molasses
2 cups crushed crispy rice squares
  cereal

40 caramels
3 tablespoons milk
1 cup semisweet chocolate chips
1 cup chopped walnuts

Melt margarine with molasses in saucepan over low heat; remove from heat. Stir in cereal. Press into greased 9x9-inch pan. Bake at 350 degrees for 10 minutes. Melt caramels with milk in heavy saucepan over low heat until smooth, stirring constantly. Pour over prepared crust. Sprinkle with chocolate chips and walnuts. Cool; cut into squares. **Yield: 16 servings.**

Approx Per Serving: Cal 256; Prot 3 g; Carbo 33 g; Fiber 1 g;
  T Fat 14 g; 47% Calories from Fat; Chol 1 mg; Sod 141 mg.

Sally Taylor, Marquette

Chocolate Fudge Brownies with Icing

2 cups sugar
1 cup butter, softened
2 eggs, beaten
1 tablespoon light corn syrup
1 teaspoon vanilla extract
¹/2 cup baking cocoa
2 cups cake flour

1 cup chopped walnuts
2¹/4 cups confectioners' sugar
3 tablespoons baking cocoa
¹/4 cup butter, softened
1 teaspoon vanilla extract
¹/4 cup (about) hot black coffee

Cream sugar and 1 cup butter in mixer bowl until light and fluffy. Beat in eggs, corn syrup and 1 teaspoon vanilla. Add baking cocoa and flour, stirring well. Fold in walnuts. Pour into 9x13-inch baking pan. Bake at 350 degrees for 30 minutes. Combine confectioners' sugar, 3 tablespoons baking cocoa, ¹/4 cup butter, 1 teaspoon vanilla and enough hot coffee to make of spreading consistency in bowl; mix well. Spread over warm brownies; cut into squares. **Yield: 24 servings.**

Approx Per Serving: Cal 274; Prot 2 g; Carbo 38 g; Fiber 1 g;
  T Fat 14 g; 43% Calories from Fat; Chol 44 mg; Sod 89 mg.

Eileen M. Haywood, Traverse City

Double Fudge-Cream Cheese Brownies

1 cup butter
4 ounces unsweetened chocolate
2 cups sugar
4 eggs, slightly beaten
1 teaspoon salt
1 teaspoon baking powder
2 teaspoons vanilla extract
1½ cups flour

1 cup semisweet chocolate chips
¼ cup sugar
2 tablespoons butter, softened
3 ounces cream cheese, softened
1 egg, beaten
1 tablespoon flour
½ teaspoon vanilla extract

Melt 1 cup butter with chocolate over medium heat in 2-quart saucepan, stirring frequently; remove from heat. Add 2 cups sugar, 4 eggs, salt, baking powder, 2 teaspoons vanilla and 1½ cups flour, stirring until smooth. Fold in chocolate chips. Spread half the batter into greased 9x13-inch baking pan. Combine ¼ cup sugar, 2 tablespoons butter, cream cheese, 1 egg, 1 tablespoon flour and ½ teaspoon vanilla in small bowl; mix well. Spread over batter in pan; spoon remaining batter over top. Bake at 350 degrees for 30 to 35 minutes or until edges pull away from sides of pan. Cool and cut into squares. **Yield: 24 servings.**

Approx Per Serving: Cal 268; Prot 3 g; Carbo 31 g; Fiber 1 g;
    T Fat 16 g; 52% Calories from Fat; Chol 72 mg; Sod 202 mg.

Debby Uhrik, Stevensville

Basic Brownies

2 cups sugar
6 tablespoons baking cocoa
4 eggs, slightly beaten
2 teaspoons vanilla extract

1½ cups flour
¾ cup melted margarine
1 cup chopped pecans

Combine sugar and baking cocoa in bowl. Add eggs and vanilla, beating well. Stir in flour, margarine and pecans. Pour into 9x13-inch baking pan. Bake at 350 degrees for 25 to 30 minutes or until edges pull away from sides of pan. Cool in pan; cut into squares. May frost with favorite frosting. **Yield: 24 servings.**

Approx Per Serving: Cal 194; Prot 3 g; Carbo 24 g; Fiber 1 g;
    T Fat 10 g; 46% Calories from Fat; Chol 36 mg; Sod 79 mg.

Carolyn Devers, Laingsburg

Easy Brownies

2 cups sugar
¹/₈ teaspoon salt
²/₃ cup baking cocoa
1 cup melted margarine
4 eggs
2 teaspoons vanilla extract
1¹/₂ cups flour

1 cup chopped pecans
1   1-pound package confectioners'
    sugar
5 tablespoons baking cocoa
1 teaspoon vanilla extract
2 tablespoons margarine

Combine sugar, salt and ²/₃ cup baking cocoa in bowl. Add melted margarine, eggs and 2 teaspoons vanilla, stirring until smooth. Stir in flour and pecans. Pour into greased 9x13-inch baking pan. Bake at 325 degrees for 30 to 35 minutes; cool slightly. Combine confectioners' sugar, 5 tablespoons baking cocoa, 1 teaspoon vanilla and 2 tablespoons margarine in bowl. Add enough hot water to make of spreading consistency. Spread over warm brownies; cut into squares. **Yield: 24 servings.**

Approx Per Serving: Cal 313; Prot 3 g; Carbo 48 g; Fiber 2 g;
    T Fat 14 g; 37% Calories from Fat; Chol 36 mg; Sod 124 mg.

Janet Sandon, Saginaw

Fudge Squares

2 cups sugar
2 cups flour
3¹/₂ tablespoons baking cocoa
1 cup water
¹/₄ cup margarine

¹/₂ cup oil
1 cup buttermilk
1 teaspoon baking soda
2 eggs, beaten
1 teaspoon vanilla extract

Combine sugar and flour in bowl; set aside. Combine baking cocoa, water, margarine and oil in large saucepan; mix well. Bring to a boil; remove from heat. Add flour mixture, buttermilk, baking soda, eggs and vanilla, stirring until smooth. Pour into 10x15-inch baking pan. Bake at 350 degrees for 20 to 25 minutes or until edges pull away from sides of pan. Cut into squares. **Yield: 48 servings.**

Approx Per Serving: Cal 86; Prot 1 g; Carbo 13 g; Fiber <1 g;
    T Fat 4 g; 37% Calories from Fat; Chol 9 mg; Sod 37 mg.

Lena Hill, Fremont

Fudge Philly Brownies

2¹/₄ cups sugar
6 eggs, beaten
2 teaspoons vanilla extract
2 cups flour
1¹/₂ cups chopped pecans

1¹/₂ cups margarine
6 ounces unsweetened chocolate
3¹/₂ cups sugar
16 ounces cream cheese, softened
2 eggs, beaten

Combine sugar, eggs, vanilla, flour and pecans in large bowl; mix well. Melt margarine with chocolate in saucepan over low heat, stirring frequently. Pour into flour mixture; mix well. Reserve 2 cups mixture; pour remaining mixture into 12x17-inch baking pan. Cream 3¹/₂ cups sugar, cream cheese and eggs in mixer bowl until light and fluffy. Pour over flour mixture; top with reserved mixture. Swirl with knife to marbleize. Bake at 350 degrees for 45 to 50 minutes or until sides pull away from edges of pan. Let stand until cool. Cut into squares. **Yield: 60 servings.**

Approx Per Serving: Cal 201; Prot 2 g; Carbo 24 g; Fiber 1 g;
    T Fat 12 g; 50% Calories from Fat; Chol 37 mg; Sod 86 mg.

Joan Keeney, Haslett

Zucchini Brownies

3 cups flour
¹/₄ cup baking cocoa
1 teaspoon baking soda
1 teaspoon cinnamon
1 cup oil
1³/₄ cups sugar

2 cups grated zucchini
2 eggs, beaten
1 teaspoon vanilla extract
¹/₂ cup buttermilk
1 cup semisweet chocolate chips
1 cup chopped pecans

Combine flour, baking cocoa, baking soda and cinnamon in large bowl. Add oil, sugar, zucchini, eggs, vanilla and buttermilk; mix well. Pour into greased 11x15-inch baking pan. Sprinkle with chocolate chips and pecans. Bake at 350 degrees for 25 to 30 minutes. Let stand until cool. Cut into squares. **Yield: 48 servings.**

Approx Per Serving: Cal 138; Prot 2 g; Carbo 16 g; Fiber 1 g;
    T Fat 8 g; 50% Calories from Fat; Chol 9 mg; Sod 24 mg.

Carolyn Juckett, Jackson

Butterfinger Bars

1 cup margarine, softened
1 cup packed brown sugar
4 cups quick-cooking oats

1 cup semisweet chocolate chips
³/4 cup peanut butter

Combine margarine, brown sugar and oats in bowl; mix well. Press into buttered 9x13-inch pan. Bake at 350 degrees for 15 minutes. Melt chocolate chips and peanut butter in saucepan over low heat, stirring constantly. Spread over cooled crust. Chill; cut into bars. **Yield: 24 servings.**

Approx Per Serving: Cal 246; Prot 5 g; Carbo 26 g; Fiber 2 g;
T Fat 15 g; 53% Calories from Fat; Chol 0 mg; Sod 128 mg.

Ron Uhrik, Stevensville

Christmas Butterfingers

2 cups sweet butter, softened
¹/2 cup confectioners' sugar
1 egg yolk

2 tablespoons whiskey
4 cups sifted flour

Beat butter in mixer bowl until light and fluffy. Add confectioners' sugar, egg yolk and whiskey; mix well. Stir in flour gradually until well mixed. Chill dough until firm. Shape into 2-inch long pencil-shaped rolls. Form into crescents; place on baking sheet. Bake at 375 degrees for 10 to 12 minutes or until golden brown. Remove to wire rack to cool. Dust with additional confectioners' sugar while warm if desired. May substitute 2 tablespoons vanilla extract for whiskey. **Yield: 32 servings.**

Approx Per Serving: Cal 165; Prot 2 g; Carbo 13 g; Fiber <1 g;
T Fat 12 g; 65% Calories from Fat; Chol 38 mg; Sod 97 mg.

Fran Lubic, Kalamazoo

*To add colorful sparkle to your holiday dessert tray, roll refrigerator
cookie dough into a log and mix in a combination of candied
fruit and chopped almonds or walnuts. Refrigerate until firm, then
slice and bake using package directions.*

Caramel Rocky Road Bars

1 cup flour
3/4 cup quick-cooking oats
1/2 cup sugar
1/2 cup butter, softened
1/2 teaspoon baking soda
1/4 teaspoon salt

1/4 cup chopped salted peanuts
1/2 cup caramel dessert topping
1/2 cup salted peanut halves
1 1/2 cups miniature marshmallows
1/2 cup milk chocolate chips

Combine flour, oats, sugar, butter, baking soda and salt in bowl, stirring until mixture is crumbly. Stir in peanuts. Reserve 3/4 cup crumb mixture. Press remaining mixture into greased and floured 9x9-inch baking dish. Bake at 350 degrees for 12 to 17 minutes or until light brown. Spread caramel topping over warm crust. Sprinkle with peanut halves, marshmallows, chocolate chips and reserved crumb mixture. Bake for 20 to 25 minutes longer or until light brown. Chill, covered, until firm. Cut into bars. **Yield: 24 servings.**

Approx Per Serving: Cal 144; Prot 2 g; Carbo 19 g; Fiber 1 g;
    T Fat 7 g; 41% Calories from Fat; Chol 10 mg; Sod 113 mg.

Mrs. Edward Cherry, Maple City

Chocolate-Cherry Squares

1 2-layer package chocolate cake mix
1 21-ounce can cherry pie filling
2 eggs, beaten
1 teaspoon almond extract

1 cup sugar
1/3 cup milk
5 tablespoons butter
1 cup semisweet chocolate chips

Combine cake mix, pie filling, eggs and almond extract in large bowl, stirring well to mix. Pour into greased 10x15-inch pan. Bake at 350 degrees for 15 to 20 minutes or until edges pull away from sides of pan. Combine sugar, milk and butter in saucepan. Bring to a boil for 1 minute, stirring constantly; remove from heat. Add chocolate chips, stirring until melted. Spread over warm crust. Cool and cut into squares. May bake in 9x13-inch pan for 20 to 30 minutes. **Yield: 36 servings.**

Approx Per Serving: Cal 142; Prot 1 g; Carbo 25 g; Fiber <1 g;
    T Fat 5 g; 30% Calories from Fat; Chol 17 mg; Sod 111 mg.

Esther Lowe, Traverse City

Crispy Bars

1/2 cup margarine, softened	1/8 teaspoon salt
2 eggs, beaten	1 tablespoon vanilla extract
3/4 cup sugar	5 ounces miniature marshmallows
2 tablespoons baking cocoa	1 cup semisweet chocolate chips
3/4 cup flour	1 cup peanut butter
1/4 teaspoon baking powder	1 cup crisp rice cereal

Combine margarine, eggs and sugar in mixer bowl. Beat until light and fluffy. Stir in baking cocoa, flour, baking powder, salt and vanilla. Spread into 9x13-inch pan. Bake at 350 degrees for 15 to 20 minutes or until brown. Sprinkle with marshmallows. Bake for 1 to 2 minutes longer or until marshmallows are puffy. Melt chocolate chips and peanut butter in saucepan over low heat, stirring constantly; remove from heat. Stir in cereal. Spread over cooled marshmallow layer. Chill in refrigerator until firm. Cut into bars. **Yield: 24 servings.**

Approx Per Serving: Cal 205; Prot 5 g; Carbo 21 g; Fiber 1 g;
    T Fat 12 g; 52% Calories from Fat; Chol 18 mg; Sod 129 mg.

Florence Wigg, Negaunae

Dream Bars

1/2 cup margarine, softened	1/4 cup flour
1/2 cup packed brown sugar	1/4 teaspoon salt
1 1/2 cups flour	1 teaspoon vanilla extract
3 eggs	1 1/2 cups flaked coconut
1 1/2 cups packed brown sugar	1 cup chopped pecans

Cream margarine and 1/2 cup brown sugar in bowl. Stir in 1 1/2 cups flour. Press mixture into 9x13-inch pan. Bake at 350 degrees for 15 minutes. Beat eggs in bowl until foamy. Add 1 1/2 cups brown sugar gradually; beat well. Stir in 1/4 cup flour, salt and vanilla. Fold in coconut and pecans. Pour over prepared crust. Bake for 20 to 25 minutes longer; cool. Cut into bars. May add 1 cup chocolate chips to crust mixture or 2 teaspoons lemon peel and 2 tablespoons lemon juice to coconut mixture. **Yield: 24 servings.**

Approx Per Serving: Cal 217; Prot 2 g; Carbo 32 g; Fiber 1 g;
    T Fat 9 g; 38% Calories from Fat; Chol 27 mg; Sod 87 mg.

Donna Cass, Wyoming

Footprint Squares

1 cup margarine, softened
1 cup sugar
2 eggs, beaten

2 cups flour
1/2 teaspoon almond extract
1   21-ounce can cherry pie filling

Cream margarine and sugar in mixer bowl until light and fluffy. Beat in eggs. Add flour and almond extract, stirring well. Spread on 10x15-inch baking sheet. Score for 24 squares. Place a spoonful of pie filling in center of each square. Bake at 350 degrees for 25 to 30 minutes or until light brown. Cut into 24 squares; cool. May dust with confectioners' sugar. May substitute blueberry pie filling for cherry pie filling and substitute lemon extract for almond extract. **Yield: 24 servings.**

Approx Per Serving: Cal 168; Prot 2 g; Carbo 23 g; Fiber 1 g;
     T Fat 8 g; 43% Calories from Fat; Chol 18 mg; Sod 103 mg.

Lee Capron, Battle Creek

Graham Ditties

20 whole graham crackers
3/4 cup margarine
1 cup sugar
1   5-ounce can evaporated milk
1 egg, beaten
1 cup graham cracker crumbs

1 cup chopped walnuts
1 cup flaked coconut
1 cup confectioners' sugar
1/4 cup margarine, softened
1/2 teaspoon milk

Line ungreased 10x15-inch baking pan with half the graham crackers. Combine margarine, sugar, evaporated milk and egg in saucepan; mix well. Cook over medium heat until thickened, stirring constantly; remove from heat. Add graham cracker crumbs, walnuts and coconut; mix well. Spread over graham cracker layer. Top with remaining whole graham crackers. Cream confectioners' sugar with 1/4 cup margarine until light and fluffy. Add enough milk to make of spreading consistency; spread over top layer of graham crackers. Chill in refrigerator until firm; cut into bars. May sprinkle with additional coconut or walnuts. **Yield: 36 servings.**

Approx Per Serving: Cal 149; Prot 2 g; Carbo 16 g; Fiber 1 g;
     T Fat 9 g; 53% Calories from Fat; Chol 7 mg; Sod 111 mg.

Catherine Wojnaroski, Goetzville

Kit Kat Bars

1 cup margarine
1/3 cup milk
2 cups graham cracker crumbs
1 cup packed brown sugar

1/2 cup sugar
1 12-ounce package butter crackers
1 cup semisweet chocolate chips
1/2 cup peanut butter

Combine margarine, milk, graham cracker crumbs, brown sugar and sugar in saucepan; mix well. Bring to a boil. Cook for 5 minutes, stirring constantly. Line bottom of 9x13-inch pan with butter crackers. Alternate layers of sugar mixture and crackers, 1/2 at a time, ending with crackers. Combine chocolate chips and peanut butter in saucepan. Cook over medium heat until melted, stirring constantly. Spread over top layer. Chill until firm; cut into bars. **Yield: 24 servings.**

Approx Per Serving: Cal 310; Prot 4 g; Carbo 38 g; Fiber 1 g;
    T Fat 19 g; 50% Calories from Fat; Chol <1 mg; Sod 322 mg.

Betty L. Menhennick, Marquette

Layered Bar Cookies

1/2 cup butter
1 cup graham cracker crumbs
1 cup semisweet chocolate chips
1 cup butterscotch chips

1 1/3 cups flaked coconut
1/2 cup chopped walnuts
1 5-ounce can sweetened condensed
  milk

Melt butter in 9x13-inch baking pan; sprinkle evenly with graham cracker crumbs. Layer with chocolate chips, butterscotch chips, coconut and walnuts. Pour condensed milk over top. Bake at 350 degrees for 35 minutes; cool. Cut into bars. **Yield: 24 servings.**

Approx Per Serving: Cal 170; Prot 2 g; Carbo 16 g; Fiber 1 g;
    T Fat 12 g; 59% Calories from Fat; Chol 12 mg; Sod 78 mg.

Vickie L. Tackelbury, Saginaw

Easy Lemon-Angel Bars

1 package angel food cake mix
1 21-ounce can lemon pie filling

1 16-ounce can prepared lemon
  frosting

Combine cake mix and pie filling in bowl; mix well. Spread over greased 10x15-inch baking sheet. Bake at 350 degrees for 20 minutes; cool slightly. Frost with lemon frosting. Cut into bars. **Yield: 36 servings.**

Approx Per Serving: Cal 114; Prot 1 g; Carbo 22 g; Fiber <1 g;
    T Fat 2 g; 17% Calories from Fat; Chol 0 mg; Sod 75 mg.

Sally Taylor, Marquette

Lemon Bars

2 cups flour
1 cup margarine, softened
1/2 cup confectioners' sugar
4 eggs, slightly beaten
2 cups sugar

6 tablespoons lemon juice
Grated rind of 1 lemon
1/4 cup flour
1 teaspoon baking powder

Combine flour, margarine and confectioners' sugar in bowl; mix until crumbly. Pat into 9x13-inch pan. Bake at 350 degrees for 20 minutes. Combine eggs, sugar, lemon juice, lemon rind, 1/4 cup flour and baking powder in bowl; mix well. Spread over baked crust. Bake for 25 minutes longer. Cool and cut into bars. May sprinkle with additional confectioners' sugar while warm. **Yield: 24 servings**

Approx Per Serving: Cal 199; Prot 2 g; Carbo 29 g; Fiber <1 g;
    T Fat 9 g; 39% Calories from Fat; Chol 36 mg; Sod 115 mg.

Florence Wigg, Negaunee

Lemon Pudding Bars

1 cup flour
1/2 cup margarine, softened
1/2 cup chopped pecans
8 ounces cream cheese, softened
8 ounces whipped topping

1 cup confectioners' sugar
2 3-ounce packages lemon instant
    pudding mix
3 cups cold milk

Combine flour, margarine and pecans in bowl, stirring until crumbly. Pat into 9x13-inch pan. Bake at 350 degrees for 10 to 12 minutes or until golden brown; cool. Cream together cream cheese, half the whipped topping and confectioners' sugar in bowl until light and fluffy. Spread over cooled crust. Beat pudding mix with milk in bowl until thickened. Spread over cream cheese layer. Top with remaining whipped topping. Garnish with additional chopped pecans. Cut into bars. Store in refrigerator. **Yield: 24 servings.**

Approx Per Serving: Cal 197; Prot 3 g; Carbo 20 g; Fiber <1 g;
    T Fat 12 g; 55% Calories from Fat; Chol 14 mg; Sod 135 mg.

Dorothy Morin, Houghton

Use a pizza cutter to slice bar cookies.

Zucchini-Lemon Bars

³/₄ cup butter, softened
³/₄ cup sugar
1 egg, beaten
Grated rind of 1 lemon
2 cups flour
1 teaspoon baking powder

¹/₂ teaspoon salt
1 cup shredded zucchini
1 cup chopped walnuts
1 cup confectioners' sugar
1 to 1¹/₂ tablespoons lemon juice

Cream butter and sugar in mixer bowl until light and fluffy. Beat in egg and lemon rind. Sift flour, baking powder and salt together layer; stir into creamed mixture. Add zucchini and walnuts; mix well. Pour into 9x13-inch baking pan. Bake at 375 degrees for 15 to 20 minutes or until layer tests done. Combine confectioners' sugar with enough lemon juice to make of spreading consistency. Spread over baked layer; cut into bars. **Yield: 24 servings.**

Approx Per Serving: Cal 170; Prot 2 g; Carbo 21 g; Fiber 1 g;
 T Fat 9 g; 48% Calories from Fat; Chol 24 mg; Sod 111 mg.

Michelle Richards, Lansing

Marble Squares

8 ounces cream cheese, softened
¹/₃ cup sugar
1 egg
³/₄ cup water
¹/₂ cup margarine
1 ounce unsweetened chocolate
2 cups sugar

2 cups flour
2 eggs
¹/₂ cup sour cream
1 teaspoon baking soda
¹/₂ teaspoon salt
1 cup semisweet chocolate chips

Beat cream cheese with ¹/₃ cup sugar in mixer bowl. Add 1 egg, beating until smooth; set aside. Combine water, margarine and chocolate in saucepan. Bring to a boil; remove from heat. Stir in mixture of 2 cups sugar and flour. Add 2 eggs, sour cream, baking soda and salt; mix well. Pour into greased and floured 10x15-inch baking pan. Spoon cream cheese mixture over chocolate batter. Swirl with knife to marbleize. Sprinkle with chocolate chips. Bake at 375 degrees for 25 to 30 minutes or until wooden pick inserted in center comes out clean. Cool and cut into squares. **Yield: 36 servings.**

Approx Per Serving: Cal 161; Prot 2 g; Carbo 21 g; Fiber <1 g;
 T Fat 8 g; 43% Calories from Fat; Chol 26 mg; Sod 109 mg.

Marjorie Madol, Bay City

Nanaimo Bars

2 cups graham cracker crumbs
1 cup flaked coconut
1/2 cup chopped walnuts
1/2 cup margarine
1/4 cup sugar
3 tablespoons baking cocoa

1 egg, beaten
1 teaspoon vanilla extract
1/4 cup margarine, softened
2 cups confectioners' sugar
2 tablespoons hot water
2/3 cup chocolate chips

Mix graham cracker crumbs, coconut and walnuts in bowl; set aside. Combine margarine and sugar in saucepan. Heat until margarine is melted; stir in baking cocoa. Cook over medium-low heat until smooth, stirring constantly; remove from heat. Beat egg with vanilla in bowl. Stir 1 tablespoon chocolate mixture into egg mixture. Pour egg mixture into chocolate mixture, beating well. Mix with crumb mixture. Press mixture into oiled 8x8-inch pan. Place in freezer until firm. Mix 1/4 cup margarine with confectioners's sugar and hot water in bowl, stirring to obtain spreading consistency. Spread over top of chilled layer. Melt chocolate chips in top of double boiler or microwave in glass bowl until melted. Spread over top layer. Chill, covered, for 30 minutes. Cut into bars. **Yield: 15 servings.**

Approx Per Serving: Cal 320; Prot 3 g; Carbo 39 g; Fiber 2 g;
    T Fat 18 g; 49% Calories from Fat; Chol 14 mg; Sod 213 mg.

Margaret A. Voet, Marquette

Chocolate-Filled Oatmeal Bars

3/4 cup margarine
1 cup packed brown sugar
1/2 teaspoon baking soda
1 tablespoon hot water
1 1/4 cups oats

1 1/2 cups flour
1   14-ounce can sweetened
    condensed milk
1 cup semisweet chocolate chips

Melt margarine with brown sugar in saucepan, stirring frequently; remove from heat. Dissolve baking soda in hot water; add to sugar mixture. Stir in oats and flour, mixing well. Press 2/3 of mixture into 9x13-inch pan. Heat condensed milk and chocolate chips in saucepan. Cook until chocolate is melted and mixture is smooth, stirring constantly. Pour over prepared crust; top with remaining mixture. Bake at 350 degrees for 20 minutes. Cool and cut into bars. **Yield: 24 servings.**

Approx Per Serving: Cal 227; Prot 3 g; Carbo 33 g; Fiber 1 g;
    T Fat 10 g; 38% Calories from Fat; Chol 6 mg; Sod 111 mg.

Kenna Dobson, Ishpeming

Pineapple Bars

1 2-layer package yellow cake mix
3 egg yolks
3 tablespoons margarine, softened
3 egg whites
½ cup sugar

2 cups flaked coconut
1 8-ounce can crushed pineapple, drained
½ cup chopped pecans

Combine cake mix, egg yolks and margarine in bowl, stirring until crumbly. Press into greased 9x13-inch baking pan. Beat egg whites in bowl until soft peaks form; add sugar. Beat until stiff peaks form. Fold in coconut and pineapple; spread over prepared crust. Sprinkle with pecans. Bake at 350 degrees for 30 minutes. Let stand until cool. Cut into bars. Store in refrigerator. **Yield: 24 servings.**

Approx Per Serving: Cal 180; Prot 2 g; Carbo 26 g; Fiber 1 g;
    T Fat 8 g; 37% Calories from Fat; Chol 27 mg; Sod 156 mg.

Lois Elliott, Escanaba

Pumpkin Bars

4 eggs, beaten
1⅔ cups sugar
1 cup oil
1 16-ounce can pumpkin
2 cups flour
2 teaspoons baking powder
2 teaspoons cinnamon

1 teaspoon salt
1 teaspoon baking soda
3 ounces cream cheese, softened
½ cup margarine, softened
1 teaspoon vanilla extract
2 cups sifted confectioners' sugar

Combine eggs, sugar, oil and pumpkin in mixer bowl. Beat until light and fluffy. Mix flour, baking powder, cinnamon, salt and baking soda together. Add to pumpkin mixture, stirring to mix. Spread in ungreased 10x15-inch baking pan. Bake at 350 degrees for 25 to 30 minutes; cool. Beat cream cheese, margarine and vanilla in mixer bowl until light and fluffy. Stir in confectioners' sugar gradually until smooth. Spread over cooled layer. Cut into bars. **Yield: 48 servings.**

Approx Per Serving: Cal 135; Prot 1 g; Carbo 16 g; Fiber <1 g;
    T Fat 8 g; 50% Calories from Fat; Chol 20 mg; Sod 109 mg.

Teather Uhrik, Stevensville

Rice Crispy Bars

1 cup sugar
1 cup light corn syrup
1 cup peanut butter

6 cups crisp rice cereal
2 cups semisweet chocolate chips,
  melted

Combine sugar and corn syrup in large saucepan. Bring to a boil; remove from heat. Add peanut butter, stirring until smooth. Stir in rice cereal. Spoon into buttered 9x13-inch pan. Melt chocolate chips in glass bowl in microwave or in top of double boiler. Spread melted chocolate over cereal layer. Cool and cut into bars. May substitute honey for corn syrup and prepared chocolate frosting for chocolate chips. **Yield: 24 servings.**

Approx Per Serving: Cal 233; Prot 4 g; Carbo 35 g; Fiber 1 g;
    T Fat 11 g; 38% Calories from Fat; Chol 0 mg; Sod 137 mg.

Alice Burrows, Petoskey

Rice Chex Junior Bars

4 2-ounce Snickers candy bars
6 cups frosted Rice Chex Juniors
  cereal

36 marshmallows
3 tablespoons margarine

Chop 3 candy bars into 1/2-inch pieces. Combine with cereal in large bowl. Melt marshmallows, margarine and remaining candy bar over low heat in large saucepan, stirring constantly; remove from heat. Add cereal mixture, stirring until coated. Spread into buttered 9x13-inch pan; cool. Cut into bars. **Yield: 36 servings.**

Approx Per Serving: Cal 85; Prot 1 g; Carbo 15 g; Fiber <1 g;
    T Fat 2 g; 25% Calories from Fat; Chol 0 mg; Sod 79 mg.

Mary Lucas, Rockford

Scotcheroos

1 cup light corn syrup
1 cup sugar
1 cup creamy peanut butter

6 cups crisp rice cereal
1 cup butterscotch chips
1 cup semisweet chocolate chips

Combine corn syrup and sugar in large saucepan. Bring to a boil, stirring constantly. Add peanut butter, stirring until smooth; remove from heat. Add rice cereal, stirring to coat. Press mixture into greased 9x13-inch pan. Melt butterscotch and chocolate chips in small saucepan over very low heat, stirring frequently. Spread over cereal mixture. Cool and cut into bars. **Yield: 36 servings.**

Approx Per Serving: Cal 148; Prot 3 g; Carbo 22 g; Fiber 1 g;
    T Fat 6 g; 36% Calories from Fat; Chol 0 mg; Sod 94 mg.

Cathy DeGoede, Grand Rapids

Snickers Bars

1 cup milk chocolate chips
¼ cup butterscotch chips
¼ cup peanut butter
1 cup sugar
¼ cup milk
¼ cup margarine
¼ cup peanut butter
1   7-ounce jar marshmallow creme

1 teaspoon vanilla extract
2 cups dry roasted peanuts
1   14-ounce package caramels
2 tablespoons hot water
1 cup milk chocolate chips
¼ cup butterscotch chips
¼ cup peanut butter

Melt 1 cup chocolate chips, ¼ cup butterscotch chips and ¼ cup peanut butter in top of double boiler, stirring frequently. Spread in greased 9x13-inch pan. Combine sugar, milk and margarine in small saucepan. Bring to a boil for 5 minutes, stirring constantly; remove from heat. Add ¼ cup peanut butter, marshmallow creme and vanilla, stirring well. Spread over chocolate layer. Sprinkle with peanuts. Melt caramels with 2 tablespoons hot water in saucepan, stirring constantly. Drizzle over peanuts. Melt 1 cup chocolate chips, ¼ cup butterscotch chips and ¼ cup peanut butter in top of double boiler. Spread over caramel layer. Let cool and cut into bars. **Yield: 36 servings.**

Approx Per Serving: Cal 216; Prot 4 g; Carbo 26 g; Fiber <1 g;
    T Fat 11 g; 46% Calories from Fat; Chol 1 mg; Sod 140 mg.

Barb Kubont, Escanaba

Sour Cream-Rhubarb Squares

1½ cups packed brown sugar
½ cup shortening
1 egg, beaten
1 teaspoon baking soda
2 cups flour
½ teaspoon salt

1 cup sour cream
3 cups chopped rhubarb
½ cup sugar
½ cup chopped pecans
1 tablespoon melted margarine
1 teaspoon cinnamon

Cream brown sugar and shortening in mixer bowl until light and fluffy. Beat in egg. Sift baking soda, flour and salt together. Stir into creamed mixture alternately with sour cream. Stir in rhubarb. Spoon into greased and floured 9x13-inch baking pan. Combine sugar, pecans, melted margarine and cinnamon in small bowl, stirring until crumbly. Sprinkle over rhubarb mixture. Bake at 350 degrees for 50 to 60 minutes or until brown. Cool and cut into squares. **Yield: 24 servings.**

Approx Per Serving: Cal 204; Prot 2 g; Carbo 30 g; Fiber 1 g;
    T Fat 9 g; 38% Calories from Fat; Chol 13 mg; Sod 101 mg.

Sally Taylor, Marquette

Sugarless Fruit Bars

8 ounces chopped apricots
8 ounces prunes
1   10-ounce can crushed juice-pack
    pineapple, drained
1/4 cup water
1 cup oats
1/2 cup orange juice
1/4 cup shredded coconut
Grated rind of 1 orange
1 cup chopped pecans

Combine apricots, prunes, pineapple and water in bowl. Cover and let stand overnight. Add oats, orange juice, coconut, orange rind and pecans, stirring well. Spoon into greased 9x13-inch baking pan. Bake at 400 degrees for 30 minutes. Cool and cut into bars. May substitute chopped dates for part of the fruit. **Yield: 24 servings.**

Approx Per Serving: Cal 88; Prot 1 g; Carbo 13 g; Fiber 2 g;
    T Fat 4 g; 38% Calories from Fat; Chol 0 mg; Sod 3 mg.

Bonnie Pierce, Ionia

Mexican Wedding Bars

2 cups flour
2 teaspoons baking soda
1 1/2 cups sugar
1 teaspoon salt
3 eggs, beaten
1 teaspoon vanilla extract
1   20-ounce can crushed pineapple
1 cup chopped pecans
1 cup shredded coconut
1/2 cup margarine, softened
1 teaspoon vanilla extract
2 cups confectioners' sugar
8 ounces cream cheese, softened

Combine flour, baking soda, sugar and salt in bowl. Add eggs, 1 teaspoon vanilla, pineapple with juice, pecans and coconut; mix well. Spread in 10x15-inch baking pan. Bake at 350 degrees for 30 minutes; cool. Cream margarine, 1 teaspoon vanilla, confectioners' sugar and cream cheese in mixer bowl until light and fluffy. Spread over cooled layer. Cut into bars. **Yield: 48 servings.**

Approx Per Serving: Cal 137; Prot 2 g; Carbo 19 g; Fiber 1 g;
    T Fat 6 g; 41% Calories from Fat; Chol 19 mg; Sod 125 mg.

Lois Elliott, Escanaba

Twix Bars

60 butter crackers
1 cup crushed graham crackers
1/2 cup butter, softened
1/4 cup milk
1/2 cup sugar
2/3 cup packed brown sugar
1/2 cup chocolate chips
1/2 cup butterscotch chips
2/3 cup peanut butter

Place half the crackers in 9x13-inch pan. Mix graham cracker crumbs, butter, milk, sugar and brown sugar in saucepan. Bring to a boil for 3 to 5 minutes, stirring frequently. Pour over cracker layer. Top with remaining crackers. Melt chocolate chips, butterscotch chips and peanut butter over low heat in saucepan, stirring frequently. Pour over crackers. Let stand for several hours to overnight. Cut into bars. **Yield: 36 servings.**

Approx Per Serving: Cal 141; Prot 2 g; Carbo 17 g; Fiber 1 g;
    T Fat 8 g; 49% Calories from Fat; Chol 7 mg; Sod 116 mg.

Carol Goodson, Traverse City

Yummy Bars

1   2-layer package white cake mix
1/3 cup margarine, softened
1 egg, beaten
3 cups miniature marshmallows
2/3 cup light corn syrup
1/4 cup margarine
2 teaspoons vanilla extract
2 cups peanut butter chips
2 cups salted peanuts
2 cups crisp rice cereal

Combine cake mix, 1/3 cup margarine and egg in bowl, stirring until crumbly. Press into ungreased 9x13-inch baking pan. Bake at 350 degrees for 12 to 18 minutes or until golden brown. Sprinkle with marshmallows. Bake for 1 to 2 minutes or until marshmallows puff up. Combine corn syrup, 1/4 cup margarine, vanilla and peanut butter chips in heavy saucepan. Cook over low heat until chips are melted, stirring frequently; remove from heat. Stir in peanuts and rice cereal. Pour over marshmallow layer; chill. Cut into bars. **Yield: 36 servings.**

Approx Per Serving: Cal 225; Prot 5 g; Carbo 27 g; Fiber 1 g;
    T Fat 11 g; 44% Calories from Fat; Chol 6 mg; Sod 202 mg.

Peggy St. Louis, Kingsford

GLEN SHAFFER TELEPHONE PIONEER MUSEUM

Pies

Telephone Directory 1948

Bell Telephone

SKN

Caramel-Apple Pie

24 caramels
1 tablespoon milk
1 9-inch graham cracker pie shell
1/3 cup chopped pecans
8 ounces cream cheese, softened
1/2 cup sour cream

2 tablespoons sugar
1/2 cup chunky applesauce
2 teaspoons vanilla extract
1/2 teaspoon cinnamon
8 ounces whipped topping

Place caramels and milk in glass dish. Microwave on High for 1 to 1½ minutes or until caramels melt. Stir until smooth. Spoon into pie shell. Sprinkle with pecans. Let stand until cool. Beat cream cheese, sour cream and sugar in mixer bowl until smooth. Stir in applesauce, vanilla and cinnamon. Fold in half the whipped topping gently. Spread over caramel layer. Chill for 4 hours or longer. Top with remaining whipped topping. Garnish with apple slices and additional melted caramels. **Yield: 8 servings.**

Approx Per Serving: Cal 596; Prot 6 g; Carbo 62 g; Fiber 2 g;
     T Fat 37 g; 55% Calories from Fat; Chol 39 mg; Sod 400 mg.

Brenda Buss, Grand Rapids

Apple Cream Pies

Wolf River apples
2 unbaked 9-inch pie shells
Salt to taste
1 cup sugar
1 cup packed brown sugar

1/2 cup flour
Half and half or whipping cream
Butter to taste
Cinnamon to taste

Cut apples into halves. Cut an X on curved sides of halves. Place cut sides down in pie shells. Sprinkle with salt. Mix sugar, brown sugar and flour in bowl. Sprinkle over apples. Pour in enough half and half to fill pie shells. Dot with butter; sprinkle with cinnamon. Bake at 375 degrees for 1 hour. **Yield: 16 servings.**

Nutritional analysis for this recipe is not available.

T. C. Smorgasbroads, Traverse City

*Prevent a soggy lower pie crust by brushing it with egg white
or melted butter before adding the filling.*

Apple-Peach Pie

2 cups sliced apples
1 recipe 2-crust pie pastry
1 cup sugar
1/4 cup flour

2 teaspoons cinnamon
1/8 teaspoon ground cloves
1/4 teaspoon salt
2 cups sliced peaches

Arrange apple slices in pastry-lined pie plate. Mix sugar, flour, cinnamon, cloves and salt in bowl. Sprinkle half the mixture over apples. Top with peaches and remaining sugar mixture. Top with remaining pastry; seal edge and cut vents. Bake at 425 degrees for 10 minutes. Reduce oven temperature to 375 degrees. Bake for 20 to 30 minutes or until apples are tender. **Yield: 8 servings.**

Approx Per Serving: Cal 347; Prot 3 g; Carbo 54 g; Fiber 2 g;
    T Fat 14 g; 35% Calories from Fat; Chol 0 mg; Sod 343 mg.

Sally Taylor, Marquette

Cheddar-Apple Pie

1/2 to 3/4 cup sugar
1/4 cup flour
1 teaspoon cinnamon

5 cups sliced apples
1 recipe 2-crust pie pastry
1 cup shredded Cheddar cheese

Combine sugar, flour, cinnamon and apples in bowl; toss to mix. Arrange mixture in pastry-lined 9-inch pie plate. Sprinkle cheese over top. Top with remaining pastry; seal edge and cut vents. Bake at 400 degrees for 45 minutes or until apples are tender. **Yield: 8 servings.**

Approx Per Serving: Cal 386; Prot 7 g; Carbo 49 g; Fiber 2 g;
    T Fat 18 g; 42% Calories from Fat; Chol 15 mg; Sod 364 mg.

Sally Taylor, Marquette

Apricot-Crumb Pie

4 cups sliced fresh apricots
1/2 cup sugar
1/4 teaspoon nutmeg
1 unbaked 9-inch pie shell

3/4 cup flour
1/4 cup packed brown sugar
1/3 cup butter

Toss apricot slices with sugar and nutmeg in bowl. Arrange mixture in pie shell. Mix flour and brown sugar in bowl. Cut in butter until crumbly. Sprinkle over apricots. Bake at 400 degrees for 45 minutes. **Yield: 8 servings.**

Approx Per Serving: Cal 339; Prot 4 g; Carbo 48 g; Fiber 2 g;
    T Fat 16 g; 40% Calories from Fat; Chol 21 mg; Sod 206 mg.

Sally Taylor, Marquette

Banana-Apple Pie

2 cups sliced bananas
1 baked 9-inch pie shell
1 tablespoon lemon juice

2 cups sweetened applesauce
1 cup whipping cream
1 tablespoon sugar

Arrange banana slices in pie shell. Sprinkle with lemon juice. Spoon applesauce over top. Beat whipping cream with sugar in mixer bowl until soft peaks form. Spoon over applesauce layer. Chill completely. **Yield: 8 servings.**

Approx Per Serving: Cal 305; Prot 3 g; Carbo 34 g; Fiber 2 g;
    T Fat 19 g; 54% Calories from Fat; Chol 41 mg; Sod 151 mg.

Sally Taylor, Marquette

Banana Parfait Pie

1   3-ounce package strawberry
    gelatin
1¼ cups hot water

1 pint vanilla ice cream
1½ cups sliced bananas
1 baked 9-inch pie shell

Dissolve gelatin in hot water in 2-quart saucepan. Stir in ice cream until melted. Chill for 15 minutes or until partially set. Fold in banana slices gently. Spoon into pie shell. Chill for 10 minutes or until set. Garnish with whipped cream and additional banana slices. **Yield: 8 servings.**

Approx Per Serving: Cal 245; Prot 4 g; Carbo 34 g; Fiber 1 g;
    T Fat 11 g; 40% Calories from Fat; Chol 15 mg; Sod 201 mg.

Sally Taylor, Marquette

Caramel Pies

8 ounces coconut
½ cup chopped pecans
¼ cup butter
1   14-ounce can sweetened
    condensed milk

8 ounces cream cheese, softened
16 ounces whipped topping
1   12-ounce jar caramel ice cream
    topping
3   9-inch graham cracker pie shells

Brown coconut and pecans in butter in skillet over low heat. Let stand until cool. Beat condensed milk, cream cheese and whipped topping in mixer bowl until smooth. Layer cream cheese mixture, caramel topping and coconut mixture alternately in pie shells until all ingredients are used. Freeze until firm. Let stand at room temperature for 10 minutes before serving. **Yield: 24 servings.**

Approx Per Serving: Cal 470; Prot 5 g; Carbo 55 g; Fiber 2 g;
    T Fat 27 g; 51% Calories from Fat; Chol 21 mg; Sod 354 mg.

Lee Capron, Battle Creek

Impossible Cheesecake Pie

³/₄ cup milk
2 eggs
¹/₂ cup baking mix
2 teaspoons vanilla extract
1 cup sugar
16 ounces cream cheese, softened, cut
    into cubes

1 cup sour cream
2 tablespoons sugar
2 teaspoons vanilla extract
1   21-ounce can cherry pie filling

Combine milk, eggs, baking mix, 2 teaspoons vanilla and 1 cup sugar in blender container. Process at high speed for 15 seconds. Add cream cheese. Process for 2 minutes. Spoon into 9-inch pie plate. Bake at 350 degrees for 40 to 45 minutes or until center is firm. Let stand until cool. Spread mixture of sour cream, 2 tablespoons sugar and 2 teaspoons vanilla over baked layer. Top with pie filling. Chill until serving time. **Yield: 8 servings.**

Approx Per Serving: Cal 513; Prot 8 g; Carbo 57 g; Fiber 1 g;
    T Fat 29 g; 50% Calories from Fat; Chol 131 mg; Sod 332 mg.

June Adams, Sault Ste. Marie

Country Kitchen Cherry Pie

2   16-ounce cans juice-pack, pitted
    tart cherries
2¹/₂ tablespoons quick-cooking
    tapioca
¹/₄ teaspoon salt
¹/₄ teaspoon almond extract

1 teaspoon lemon juice
4 drops of red food coloring
1 cup sugar
1 recipe 2-crust pie pastry
1 tablespoon butter
¹/₄ cup sugar

Drain cherries, reserving ¹/₃ cup liquid. Combine reserved liquid with tapioca, salt, almond flavoring, lemon juice and food coloring; mix well. Stir in cherries and 1 cup sugar. Let stand for several minutes. Spoon mixture into 9-inch pastry-lined pie plate. Dot with butter; sprinkle with remaining ¹/₄ cup sugar. Cut remaining pastry into strips; arrange lattice-fashion on top. Bake at 425 degrees for 40 to 45 minutes. May fit foil collar around edge of pie plate before baking to prevent crust from burning. **Yield: 8 servings.**

Approx Per Serving: Cal 387; Prot 3 g; Carbo 62 g; Fiber 1 g;
    T Fat 15 g; 34% Calories from Fat; Chol 4 mg; Sod 363 mg.

Dani Peterson, Lansing

Hershey Pie

7 or 8 1½-ounce chocolate candy
   bars

8 ounces whipped topping
1 9-inch graham cracker pie shell

Melt candy bars in top of double boiler over medium heat, stirring frequently. Fold melted chocolate gently into whipped topping in bowl. Spoon into pie shell. Chill for 1 to 2 hours. **Yield: 8 servings.**

Approx Per Serving: Cal 512; Prot 5 g; Carbo 56 g; Fiber 2 g;
   T Fat 32 g; 54% Calories from Fat; Chol 9 mg; Sod 280 mg.

Pat Fiebig, Grand Rapids

Kathy's Family Secret

¼ cup flour
¼ cup butter
1 teaspoon vanilla extract
¼ cup baking cocoa
1 12-ounce can evaporated milk
½ cup milk

¾ cup sugar
½ teaspoon salt
3 egg yolks
2 baked 9-inch pie shells
3 egg whites
6 tablespoons sugar

Combine flour, butter, vanilla, baking cocoa, evaporated milk, milk, ¾ cup sugar, salt and egg yolks in saucepan. Cook over medium heat until thickened, stirring constantly. Spoon into pie shells. Beat egg whites in mixer bowl until soft peaks form. Add 6 tablespoons sugar gradually, beating until stiff peaks form. Spread meringue over pies, sealing to edges. Broil until golden brown. **Yield: 16 servings.**

Approx Per Serving: Cal 252; Prot 5 g; Carbo 29 g; Fiber 1 g;
   T Fat 14 g; 48% Calories from Fat; Chol 55 mg; Sod 266 mg.

Kathy Lambert, Lansing

Cottage Cheese Pie

4 cups cottage cheese
2 eggs
1 teaspoon vanilla extract

½ cup sugar
1 unbaked 9-inch pie shell
Cinnamon to taste

Combine cottage cheese, eggs, vanilla and sugar in bowl; mix well. Spoon into pie shell. Sprinkle with cinnamon. Bake at 400 degrees for 15 minutes. Reduce oven temperature to 350 degrees. Bake for 45 minutes. Let stand until cool. Chill completely. **Yield: 8 servings.**

Approx Per Serving: Cal 290; Prot 16 g; Carbo 26 g; Fiber <1 g;
   T Fat 13 g; 42% Calories from Fat; Chol 69 mg; Sod 580 mg.

Virginia Piechowiak, Saginaw

Coconut Cream Pies

1 cup sugar
3 tablespoons cornstarch
5 egg yolks
1 cup cold milk
4 cups warm milk
1 tablespoon vanilla extract

2 tablespoons butter
1 cup coconut
1 recipe Holland Rusk Pie Shells
  (page 356)
3 egg whites
4 to 5 teaspoons sugar

Combine 1 cup sugar, cornstarch and egg yolks in bowl; mix well. Add 1 cup cold milk gradually, stirring constantly. Add 4 cups warm milk gradually, stirring constantly. Pour mixture into large saucepan. Cook over medium heat until thickened, stirring constantly. Stir in vanilla, butter and coconut. Let stand until cool. Spoon into Holland Rusk Pie Shells. Beat egg whites in mixer bowl until soft peaks form. Add 4 to 5 teaspoons sugar gradually, beating until stiff peaks form. Spoon over pie fillings, sealing to edge. Bake at 350 degrees until meringue is golden brown.
Yield: 16 servings.

Approx Per Serving: Cal 224; Prot 3 g; Carbo 36 g; Fiber 1 g;
  T Fat 8 g; 32% Calories from Fat; Chol 78 mg; Sod 67 mg.

Tillie Luikes, Kentwood

Cranberry-Pineapple Pie

1 cup sugar
3 tablespoons flour
1/4 teaspoon salt
1/2 cup corn syrup
1/2 cup pineapple syrup

4 cups cranberries
4 slices canned pineapple, chopped
1 teaspoon grated lemon rind
1 unbaked 9-inch pie shell

Combine sugar, flour, salt, corn syrup and pineapple syrup in saucepan. Bring to a boil over low heat. Add cranberries. Simmer until berries pop. Stir in pineapple and lemon rind. Cool slightly. Do not stir. Spoon into pie shell. Bake at 425 degrees for 10 minutes. Reduce oven temperature to 350 degrees. Bake for 30 minutes.
Yield: 8 servings.

Approx Per Serving: Cal 331; Prot 2 g; Carbo 66 g; Fiber 3 g;
  T Fat 8 g; 20% Calories from Fat; Chol 0 mg; Sod 215 mg.

Sally Taylor, Marquette

Pies with cream or custard filling should be cooled to room temperature and then refrigerated to prevent spoilage.

Christmas Pies

1 20-ounce can pitted sour cherries
1 20-ounce can crushed pineapple
1 cup sugar
1/3 cup flour
1 3-ounce package lemon gelatin

1 teaspoon red food coloring
1 cup chopped pecans
1 cup mashed bananas
2 baked 9-inch pie shells
8 ounces whipped topping

Combine undrained cherries, undrained pineapple, sugar and flour in saucepan. Cook over medium heat until thickened, stirring constantly. Stir in gelatin. Let stand until cool. Stir in food coloring, pecans and bananas. Spoon into pie shells. Spread whipped topping over tops of pies. Chill until serving time. **Yield: 16 servings.**

Approx Per Serving: Cal 338; Prot 4 g; Carbo 47 g; Fiber 2 g;
T Fat 17 g; 42% Calories from Fat; Chol 0 mg; Sod 162 mg.

Elaine Hartwig, Gaylord

Lemon and Sour Cream Pie

1 cup sugar
3 tablespoons cornstarch
1/8 teaspoon salt
1 cup milk
3 egg yolks, beaten
1/4 cup butter
1 teaspoon grated lemon rind

1/4 cup lemon juice
1 cup sour cream
1 baked 9-inch pie shell
3 egg whites
1/4 teaspoon cream of tartar
1/2 teaspoon vanilla extract
6 tablespoons sugar

Mix 1 cup sugar, cornstarch and salt in saucepan. Stir in milk gradually. Cook over medium heat until thickened, stirring constantly. Stir a small amount of hot liquid into beaten egg yolks; stir egg yolk mixture into hot mixture. Cook for 2 minutes longer, stirring constantly. Stir in butter, lemon rind and lemon juice. Remove from heat. Let stand, covered, until cool. Fold in sour cream gently. Spoon into pie shell. Beat egg whites until soft peaks form. Add cream of tartar and vanilla. Add sugar gradually, beating until stiff peaks form. Spread meringue over pie, sealing to edge. Bake at 350 degrees for 12 to 15 minutes or until meringue is golden brown. Chill until serving time. **Yield: 8 servings.**

Approx Per Serving: Cal 425; Prot 7 g; Carbo 51 g; Fiber 1 g;
T Fat 22 g; 47% Calories from Fat; Chol 112 mg; Sod 293 mg.

Lydia Engstrom, Reed City

Sugar-Free Lemon Pie

1 package Sweet Pretenders vanilla
  cookies, crushed
1 tablespoon margarine, softened
Grated rind of 1 lemon
Juice of 1 lemon
³/₄ cup egg substitute
2 tablespoons (heaping) cornstarch

1 tablespoon margarine
2 cups boiling water
18 packets artificial sweetener
3 egg whites
¹/₄ teaspoon cream of tartar
2 packets artificial sweetener

Mix crumbs with margarine in bowl. Press over bottom and side of 9-inch glass pie plate. Bake at 350 degrees for 8 minutes. Cool completely. Mix lemon rind, lemon juice, egg substitute, cornstarch and margarine in top of double boiler over medium heat. Add boiling water gradually, stirring constantly. Cook until thickened, stirring constantly. Remove from heat. Stir in 18 packets of artificial sweetener. Spoon into cooled pie shell. Beat egg whites until soft peaks form. Add cream of tartar and 2 packets of artificial sweetener. Beat until stiff peaks form. Spread meringue over pie, sealing to edge. Microwave on High for 1 to 2¹/₂ minutes or until meringue is set. Chill until serving time. **Yield: 8 servings.**

Approx Per Serving: Cal 194; Prot 7 g; Carbo 22 g; Fiber <1 g;
  T Fat 9 g; 42% Calories from Fat; Chol <1 mg; Sod 104 mg.

Bonnie Pierce, Ionia

Oatmeal Pie

3 eggs, beaten
²/₃ cup quick-cooking oats
²/₃ cup sugar
1 cup packed brown sugar

²/₃ cup coconut
2 tablespoons butter, softened
2 teaspoons vanilla extract
1 unbaked 9-inch pie shell

Combine eggs, oats, sugar, brown sugar, coconut, butter and vanilla in bowl; mix well. Spoon into pie shell. Bake at 350 degrees for 30 to 35 minutes. **Yield: 8 servings.**

Approx Per Serving: Cal 416; Prot 5 g; Carbo 67 g; Fiber 2 g;
  T Fat 15 g; 32% Calories from Fat; Chol 88 mg; Sod 205 mg.

Alice (Kathy) DeVries, Pierson

Orange Chiffon Pie

1   3-ounce package vanilla instant
    pudding mix
½ cup frozen orange juice
    concentrate

½ cup water
8 ounces whipped topping
1   9-inch graham cracker pie shell

Combine pudding mix, orange juice concentrate and water in bowl; mix well. Fold in whipped topping gently. Spoon into pie shell. Chill until serving time. **Yield: 8 servings.**

Approx Per Serving: Cal 362; Prot 3 g; Carbo 49 g; Fiber 1 g;
    T Fat 18 g; 44% Calories from Fat; Chol 0 mg; Sod 318 mg.

Dorothy A. Beisel, Saginaw

Peanut Butter Pie

4 ounces cream cheese, softened
1 cup confectioners' sugar
⅓ cup smooth or crunchy peanut
    butter

½ cup milk
9 ounces whipped topping
1   8-inch graham cracker pie shell

Beat cream cheese with confectioners' sugar in mixer bowl until smooth. Add peanut butter and milk; mix well. Fold in whipped topping gently. Spoon into pie shell. Freeze until serving time. **Yield: 8 servings.**

Approx Per Serving: Cal 463; Prot 7 g; Carbo 48 g; Fiber 1 g;
    T Fat 29 g; 54% Calories from Fat; Chol 18 mg; Sod 312 mg.

Nelda R. Murphy, Clare

Double Peanut Butter Pie

15 graham crackers, crushed
1 tablespoon honey
½ cup melted butter
¾ cup chunky peanut butter
8 ounces cream cheese, softened

⅓ cup plus 2 tablespoons peanut
    butter
1 cup sifted confectioners' sugar
½ cup milk
12 ounces whipped topping

Mix cracker crumbs with honey, butter and ¾ cup peanut butter in bowl. Press over bottom and side of 9-inch pie plate. Freeze. Beat cream cheese and ⅓ cup plus 2 tablespoons peanut butter until smooth. Add confectioners' sugar and milk gradually, beating constantly. Fold in whipped topping gently. Spoon into prepared pie shell. Freeze; let stand at room temperature for 20 minutes before serving. **Yield: 8 servings.**

Approx Per Serving: Cal 685; Prot 14 g; Carbo 44 g; Fiber 2 g;
    T Fat 54 g; 68% Calories from Fat; Chol 64 mg; Sod 455 mg.

Jessie Wojnaroski, Goetzville

Microwave Pecan Pie

1 unbaked 9-inch pie shell
1 egg yolk, beaten
2 tablespoons dark corn syrup
1/4 cup butter
3 eggs
1 egg white

1 cup dark corn syrup
1/3 cup packed brown sugar
1 tablespoon flour
1 teaspoon vanilla extract
1 1/2 cups pecan halves

Press pie shell into glass pie plate. Brush pie shell with mixture of egg yolk and 2 tablespoons corn syrup. Microwave on High for 5 to 7 minutes, turning once. Place butter in 4-cup glass bowl. Microwave on High for 30 to 60 seconds or until butter melts. Add eggs and egg white; mix well. Stir in 1 cup corn syrup, brown sugar, flour and vanilla. Fold in pecans. Spoon into prepared pie shell. Microwave on High for 12 to 15 minutes or until surface of pie is dry and filling is set. **Yield: 8 servings.**

Approx Per Serving: Cal 518; Prot 6 g; Carbo 60 g; Fiber 2 g;
   T Fat 30 g; 50% Calories from Fat; Chol 122 mg; Sod 256 mg.

June B. Brown, Bradenton, Florida

Pumpkin-Lemon Cream Pie

2 eggs, slightly beaten
1   16-ounce can pumpkin
1/2 cup sugar
1 teaspoon cinnamon
1/2 teaspoon salt
1/2 teaspoon ginger
1 1/3 cups half and half

1 unbaked 9-inch pie shell
1 cup sour cream
2 tablespoons brown sugar
1 tablespoon lemon juice
Grated rind of 1 lemon
1/4 cup chopped pecans

Combine eggs, pumpkin, sugar, cinnamon, salt, ginger and half and half in bowl; mix well. Spoon into pie shell. Bake at 425 degrees for 15 minutes. Reduce oven temperature to 350 degrees. Bake for 45 minutes or until knife inserted near center comes out clean. Cool for 20 minutes. Mix sour cream, brown sugar, lemon juice and lemon rind in bowl. Spread over pie evenly. Bake for 10 minutes longer. Sprinkle with pecans. Serve warm or cold. **Yield: 8 servings.**

Approx Per Serving: Cal 352; Prot 6 g; Carbo 34 g; Fiber 2 g;
   T Fat 22 g; 55% Calories from Fat; Chol 81 mg; Sod 324 mg.

Mary M. Gouin, Mattawan

Pumpkin-Ice Cream Pies

1 cup packed brown sugar
1   16-ounce can pumpkin
2 teaspoons cinnamon
1 teaspoon ginger
1/2 teaspoon nutmeg

1/2 teaspoon cloves
1 teaspoon salt
1 gallon vanilla ice cream, softened
3 graham cracker pie shells

Combine brown sugar, pumpkin, cinnamon, ginger, nutmeg, cloves and salt in saucepan. Bring to a simmer, stirring to mix well. Cool to room temperature. Combine with ice cream in mixer bowl; beat until smooth. Spoon into pie shells. Freeze until firm. Let stand at room temperature for several minutes before serving. May add pecans if desired. **Yield: 18 servings.**

Approx Per Serving: Cal 577; Prot 7 g; Carbo 79 g; Fiber 1 g;
    T Fat 27 g; 42% Calories from Fat; Chol 52 mg; Sod 548 mg.

Betty Boyd, Hemlock

Pumpkin Pies

3 cups canned pumpkin
2 1/2 cups nondairy instant coffee
    creamer
2 cups packed brown sugar
1 teaspoon salt
2 teaspoons cinnamon
1 teaspoon ginger

1/2 teaspoon ground cloves
1/4 cup margarine
1 cup egg substitute
2 egg whites, stiffly beaten
1 teaspoon lemon extract
1 teaspoon orange extract
2 unbaked 9-inch pie shells

Combine pumpkin, coffee creamer powder, brown sugar, salt, cinnamon, ginger, cloves and margarine in saucepan. Cook over low heat until margarine melts. Add egg substitute gradually, stirring constantly. Fold in egg whites and flavorings gently. Spoon into pie shells. Bake at 500 degrees for 15 minutes. Reduce oven temperature to 325 degrees. Bake for 25 to 30 minutes. **Yield: 16 servings.**

Approx Per Serving: Cal 379; Prot 5 g; Carbo 55 g; Fiber 1 g;
    T Fat 16 g; 38% Calories from Fat; Chol <1 mg; Sod 385 mg.

Joanne Homer, Lansing

*Fruit, mince and chiffon pies freeze well. Custard
and meringue pies do not freeze well.*

Pumpkin-Pecan Pie

4 eggs, slightly beaten
2 cups canned pumpkin
1 cup sugar
1/2 cup dark corn syrup
1 teaspoon vanilla extract

1 1/2 teaspoons cinnamon
1/4 teaspoon salt
1 unbaked 9-inch pie shell
1 cup chopped pecans

Combine eggs, pumpkin, sugar, corn syrup, vanilla, cinnamon and salt in bowl; mix well. Spoon into pie shell. Top with pecans. Bake at 350 degrees for 40 minutes or until set. **Yield: 8 servings.**

Approx Per Serving: Cal 429; Prot 6 g; Carbo 58 g; Fiber 3 g;
T Fat 21 g; 42% Calories from Fat; Chol 106 mg; Sod 256 mg.

Shirley A. Cook, Lansing

Squash Pie

1 1/2 cups cooked chopped squash
1 cup packed brown sugar
2 tablespoons molasses
2 teaspoons cinnamon
1 teaspoon ginger

1/2 teaspoon salt
3 eggs, slightly beaten
1 cup evaporated milk
1 unbaked 9-inch pie shell

Combine first 6 ingredients in bowl; mix until smooth. Beat in eggs and evaporated milk. Spoon into pie shell. Bake at 425 degrees for 40 to 45 minutes or until knife inserted in center comes out clean. **Yield: 8 servings.**

Approx Per Serving: Cal 330; Prot 6 g; Carbo 51 g; Fiber 1 g;
T Fat 12 g; 33% Calories from Fat; Chol 89 mg; Sod 346 mg.

Sally Taylor, Marquette

Sweet Potato Pie

3 eggs
1 1/4 cups sugar
1 teaspoon cinnamon
1/2 teaspoon allspice
1/4 teaspoon nutmeg

Salt to taste
1 cup whipping cream
3 cups mashed cooked sweet potatoes
1 unbaked 9-inch pie shell

Beat eggs in mixer bowl. Add sugar, cinnamon, allspice, nutmeg and salt; mix well. Stir in cream. Add sweet potatoes; mix well. Spoon into pie shell. Bake at 350 degrees for 1 hour or until set. **Yield: 8 servings.**

Approx Per Serving: Cal 494; Prot 6 g; Carbo 72 g; Fiber 2 g;
T Fat 21 g; 38% Calories from Fat; Chol 121 mg; Sod 191 mg.

Jackie Adams, Lansing

Zucchini-Mock Apple Pies

8 cups sliced, seeded and peeled
  zucchini
2/3 cup lemon juice
1 cup sugar
1/4 teaspoon nutmeg
1 tablespoon flour
2 tablespoons water

1/2 cup sugar
1 teaspoon baking powder
1 cup flour
3/4 teaspoon salt
1 egg
1/3 cup shortening

Mix zucchini with lemon juice in saucepan. Cook over medium heat until squash is tender. Stir in 1 cup sugar, nutmeg, 1 tablespoon flour and water. Spoon into 2 pie plates. Mix 1/2 cup sugar, baking powder, 1 cup flour and salt in bowl. Add egg and shortening, stirring until crumbly. Sprinkle over zucchini mixtures. Bake at 350 degrees for 20 to 30 minutes or until golden brown. Garnish with whipped topping. **Yield: 16 servings.**

Approx Per Serving: Cal 157; Prot 2 g; Carbo 28 g; Fiber 1 g;
  T Fat 5 g; 27% Calories from Fat; Chol 14 mg; Sod 107 mg.

Anna J. Sells, Battle Creek

Mom's Pie Pastry

2 cups flour
1 teaspoon salt

2/3 cup shortening
1/2 cup water

Mix flour with salt in bowl. Reserve 1/3 of mixture. Cut shortening into remaining mixture until crumbly. Combine reserved flour and water to make smooth paste. Stir paste into shortening mixture. Divide into halves. Shape into balls. Roll on floured surface. Fit into 2 pie plates. Pierce shells with fork for baked shells. Bake at 425 degrees for 10 minutes. **Yield: 2 pie shells.**

Approx Per Pie Shell: Cal 1053; Prot 13 g; Carbo 95 g; Fiber 3 g;
  T Fat 69 g; 59% Calories from Fat; Chol 0 mg; Sod 1068 mg.

Dani Peterson, Lansing

Holland Rusk Pie Shells

1 4-ounce package Holland Rusk
   toast, crushed

1/2 to 1 cup sugar
3 to 4 tablespoons melted butter

Combine toast crumbs with sugar in bowl. Stir in butter. Press pastry into 2 pie plates. **Yield: 2 pie shells.**

Approx Per Pie Shell: Cal 828; Prot 8 g; Carbo 140 g; Fiber 0 g;
  T Fat 28 g; 30% Calories from Fat; Chol 62 mg; Sod 335 mg.

Tillie Luikes, Kentwood

Quick Coconut Crust

3 tablespoons butter, softened   **1¹/₂ cups shredded coconut**

Spread butter evenly in 9-inch pie plate. Sprinkle with coconut. Press into bottom and side of pie plate. Bake at 300 degrees for 15 to 20 minutes. Let stand until cool. **Yield: 1 pie shell.**

Approx Per Pie Shell: Cal 656; Prot 4 g; Carbo 85 g; Fiber 14 g;
    T Fat 37 g; 48% Calories from Fat; Chol 0 mg; Sod 23 mg.

Sally Taylor, Marquette

Gingersnap Crust

1¹/₄ cups gingersnap crumbs   **¹/₂ teaspoon cinnamon**
3 tablespoons sugar   **¹/₂ cup butter, softened**

Combine cookie crumbs with sugar and cinnamon in bowl. Stir in butter. Press crumb mixture into bottom and side of 9-inch pie plate, using back of a spoon. Bake at 350 degrees for 10 minutes. Let stand until cool. **Yield: 1 pie shell.**

Approx Per Pie Shell: Cal 1990; Prot 15 g; Carbo 233 g; Fiber 0 g;
    T Fat 113 g; 51% Calories from Fat; Chol 248 mg; Sod 2175 mg.

Sally Taylor, Marquette

Mayonnaise Pie Shell

1 cup sifted flour   **1¹/₂ tablespoons water**
¹/₄ teaspoon salt   **¹/₂ teaspoon grated lemon rind**
¹/₃ cup mayonnaise

Mix flour and salt in bowl. Stir in mayonnaise with fork. Add water and lemon rind; mix well. Roll into 12-inch circle on lightly floured surface. Fit into 9-inch pie plate. May fit dough into 6 tart shells. **Yield: 1 pie shell.**

Approx Per Pie Shell: Cal 940; Prot 13 g; Carbo 90 g; Fiber 3 g;
    T Fat 59 g; 56% Calories from Fat; Chol 43 mg; Sod 948 mg.

Sally Taylor, Marquette

No-Roll Pie Shell

1½ cups flour
½ teaspoon salt

½ cup oil
2 tablespoons cold milk

Mix flour and salt in 9-inch pie plate. Whip oil and milk together with fork. Pour over flour mixture. Mix with fork just until moistened. Press evenly over bottom and side of pie plate. Prick bottom of dough with fork. Bake at 425 degrees for 12 to 15 minutes. Let stand until cool. **Yield: 1 pie shell.**

Approx Per Pie Shell: Cal 1665; Prot 21 g; Carbo 144 g; Fiber 5 g;
    T Fat 112 g; 60% Calories from Fat; Chol 4 mg; Sod 1082 mg.

Margaret Shurlow, Vassar

Quick Oatmeal Pie Crust

2 cups quick-cooking oats
⅓ cup melted butter
¼ teaspoon salt

2 teaspoons grated lemon rind
3 tablespoons light corn syrup

Mix oats and butter in bowl. Stir in salt, lemon rind and corn syrup. Press into bottom and side of 9-inch pie plate. Bake at 375 degrees for 15 to 20 minutes or until light brown. Let stand until cool. **Yield: 1 pie shell.**

Approx Per Pie Shell: Cal 1332; Prot 27 g; Carbo 155 g; Fiber 18 g;
    T Fat 71 g; 47% Calories from Fat; Chol 164 mg; Sod 1076 mg.

Sally Taylor, Marquette

Pie Pastries

4 cups flour
1 teaspoon salt
1 tablespoon sugar
1½ cups shortening

½ cup water
1 egg
1 tablespoon vinegar

Combine flour, salt and sugar in bowl. Cut in shortening until crumbly. Mix water, egg and vinegar in small bowl. Stir into flour mixture. Divide into 4 portions. Roll on floured surface. **Yield: 4 pie shells.**

Approx Per Pie Shell: Cal 1167; Prot 15 g; Carbo 99 g; Fiber 3 g;
    T Fat 80 g; 61% Calories from Fat; Chol 53 mg; Sod 553 mg.

T. C. Smorgasbroads, Traverse City

Contributors, Charts and Index

Contributors

Adams, Jackie
Adams, June
Adamski, Janet
Alpers, Jeanne L.
Anderson, Karen
Andrus, Ruth
Aros, Audrey M.
Augustine, Jerold
Avery, Barb
Badelt, Jennie
Bailey, Astrid
Bailey, Janice
Baird, Elaine
Baker, Florence
Balzer, Dorothy
Barlett, Jennie Hill
Barton, Dorothy
Bastian, Colleen
Beauch, Dorothy
Bedell, Paula
Bedore, Evelyn
Beechner, Julie
Beisel, Dorothy A.
Bell, Margaret
Bergeron, Hazel M.
Berglund, Betty
Berry, Ruth
Bethune, Leore
Bezemek, Marilyn
Bigford, Karen
Biolat, Nancy
Bittner, Vikki
Blaser, Ann
Boog, Martha
Boss, Karen Kay
Bossche, Pam
Bouwman, Joann
Boyd, Betty
Bradford, Gladys D.

Bradley, Pauline
Brana, Jacqueline
Brassar, June
Brechtelsbauer, Alice
Brechtelsbauer, Michele
Brock, Marilyn
Brokob, Katherine
Brown, Genevieve
Brown, June B.
Budd, Gert
Burrows, Alice
Buskirk, Barb
Buss, Brenda
Butenschden, A. L.
Byers, Helen
Cameron, Grace
Campbell, Alice
Candelaria, Edwin L.
Canterbury, Florence H.
Capron, Lee
Carey, Mary
Carpenter, Nancy
Carter, Marlene
Carter, Wayne
Cartwright, Becky
Cass, Donna
Cavitch, Julius L.
Cawley, Nina
Champlin, Aurelia
Chase, Florence
Cherry, Mrs. Edward
Christensen, Elaine
Christensen, Ruth
Clark, Carl N.
Clark, Suzanne K.
Clements, Julie
Clemo, Kathy
Cohn, Margaret L.
Cohoon, Bessie Stuhr

Cohoon, Zelma
Colgan, Juanita
Colley, Evelyn D.
Collins, Kay
Contois, Barbara
Contois, Dorothy
Cook, Shirley A.
Coombs, Marilyn
Coronado, Naomi S.
Couture, Karla
Coyne, Joan
Crampton, June
Cramton, Rosemary
Crampton-Snider, Shelby
Creamer, Mrs. William
Crocker, Alice
Crouse, Margaret
Curtis, JoAnn E.
Davis, Jan
Debri, Gloria J.
DeBruyn, Nancy K.
DeFeyta, Dorothy
DeGoede, Cathy
DeGraff, Helen
Dehn Sr., Mrs. William
DeLaney, Jeanne
De Laski, Estella
De Laski, Marcia
DenBeste, Therese
DeNooyer, Frances
Devers, Bill
Devers, Carolyn
De Vries, Alice (Kathy)
De Vries, Harriett
Dewitt, Betty
Deyaert, Norma
Dobwon, Kenna
Dohm-Beiser, Kathy
Dopierala, Jennie

Dorman, Jan
Doty, Karen
Doty, Sean Travis
Dragicevich, Waneta
Duvall, Alice
Duvall, Balicia
Duvall, Billie Jo
Duvall, Cliff
Ebelt, Judy
Edge, Sara F.
Edick, Anita
Edwards, Nancy
Eisenzimmer, Deanna
Elliott, Lois
Emelander, Jan
Emmons, Joan
Engstrom, Lydia
Erickson, Esther
Evans, Grace
Fairley, Janice Sweet
Farago, Laszlo
Ferguson, Barb
Fiebig, Pat
Fineout, Carol
Fineout, Marie
Finner, Helen
Fischrupp, Esther
Fitting, Karen
Flanagan, Ruth
Fogg, Cindy
Fox, Evelyn
Fox, Karon
Freemire, Evelyn M.
French, Howard
Frydel, Joyce
Furney, Nancy J.
Gabel, Hannah
Gabel, Vera
Gabrion, Mary

Gardner, Mike
Garter, E. Fern
Gee, Phyllis
Gilmore, Geraldine
Gingrass, Betty
Goodson, Carol
Gordon, Mary
Gothro, Mabel
Goudreau, Dana
Gouin, Mary M.
Hallam, Lucy
Hamilton, Jim
Hammond, Bonnie
Hamstra, Pam
Hancock, Clara E.
Hancock, Leo
Handley, Tom
Harmon, Robin
Harper, Jennifer
Hartman, Judy
Hartwig, Elaine
Hatch, Arlene E.
Haubenstricker, Linda
Hayden, Mrs. L.
Hayden, Mark
Hayden, Ruth
Haynack, Mrs. Ed
Haywood, Eileen M.
Heighes, Margaret
Heikkinen, Patti
Heil, Marion
Helmer, Evelyn
Helsten, Elizabeth
Helt, Sandy
Hendershot, Pat
Herman, Mary
Hill, Lena
Hilson, Ilene
Hines, Sandy

Hodges, Fran
Hoermann, Helen
Holcomb, Karla S.
Holcomb, Rose M.
Holford, Berdina
Holmes, Donna
Holt, Etta
Homer, Joanne
Hooker, Ethel
Hopp, Donna J.
Hoult, Amy
Howard, Joan
Huff, Louise
Hull, Ann
Hyland, Pat
Idalski, Marcy
Idalski, Pat
Izel, Rita
Jacobs, Helen E.
Jankoviak, Irene A.
Janson, Kathleen Laude
Jaquays, Clara
Jarvinen, Valerie
Johan, Bernadine A.
Johnson, Albina
Johnson, Esther M.
Johnson, Winifred
Joseph, Rose
Juckett, Carolyn
Juskewicz, Diane
Kalohn, Edith
Kammerer, Ann M.
Kasper, Marian
Kauppila, Bertha
Keckritz, Lucile
Keeney, Helen
Keeney, Joan
Keeney, Mary
Keith, Roseannah

Kempher, Elizabeth
Kennamer, Sally
Kenney, Joan
Kenyon, Juanita
Kessinger, Autumn Nicole
Kessinger, Ruby
Kesson, Margorie
Kilderhouse, Hazel
King, Carroll
Kirkpatrick, Craig
Kloko, Vi
Knapp, Pat
Kobie, Etta Jo
Kolenda, Stanley
Kolton, Edna A.
Konoski, Mary J.
Kubont, Barb
Lake, Kay
Lambert, Kathy
Landfair, Peg
Latin, Violet
Leaby, Loraynne
Leach, Betty
Lindsey, Tanya
Lintemuth, Mary Alice
Linton, Nancy
Lippens, Judy
Little, Dennis
Little, Erik
Little, Kristy
Little, Mike
Little, Nova
Lomashewich, Donna
Lowe, Esther
Lubic, Fran
Lucas, Mary
Lueder, Pat
Luikes, Tillie
Lyons, Carol

Madol, Marjorie
Mansfield, Juanita
Marlatt, Virginia C.
Marshall, Jo
Martin, Charlotte
Martin, Dorothy
Martin, Reg & Pat
Massman, Elsa
Mast, Esther
McCauley, Virginia
McComb, Patricia A.
McConnell, Cereda
McCullough, Lisa Ann
McKenna, John
McLain, Florence
McLeod-Hill, Karen
McMeel, Sheila
McPherson, Aileen
Menhennick, Betty L.
Mercier, Barbara A.
Metzger, Loraine
Miller, Robert
Miltibarger, Barb
Miner, Susan
Misner, Edith
Momier, Irene
Morin, Dorothy
Morrin, Dorothy
Moss, Helen Lorraine
Muhlenbeck, Fred
Muhlenbeck, Marion
Murdock, Donna
Murphy, Evon
Murphy, Nelda R.
Murray, Betty
Murray, Melanie
Nabozny, Barbara
Nadeau, Ed
Nealy, Sandy

Nearing, Ruth
Nelson, Ruth
Neuhaus, Nancy
Norlock, Geri
Nothelfer, Helen
Nowlin, Nancy
Noyce, Helen
O'Berry, Marlea
O'Rourke, Kathy
Oliver, Sharon Conner
Olson, Joyce
Olson, Vivian
Ondovcsik, Althea
Osborn, Mrs. Max
Palmiteer, Ruth
Pancheri, Aileen
Parrish, Lorraine
Patrick, Donna
Peeks, Frances
Perkins, Bobbie N.
Perry, Pat
Peterson, Dani
Phillips, Ralph E.
Piechowiak, Gaye
Piechowiak, Virginia
Pierce, Bonnie
Prieur, Renee
Ramey, Nancy
Ratell, Doris
Raternink, Rosemarie
Reinert, Carolyn
Reinholm, Sharon
Rhode, Ruth C.
Richards, Michelle
Rieger, Julia M.
Riggle, Mary Helen
Rizzio, Patti
Robbins, Jim & Maureen
Robinson, Eloise

Robinson, Frances
Rock, Agnes
Roekle, Janet A.
Rogers, Marilyn
Rogers, Nellie K.
Roggenbeck, Lois
Rothenthaler, Diane
Rothenthaler, Rocky
Rummel, Ruth
Ruppert, Oneta
Russell, E. Eugene
Ryan, Jackie
Ryba, Carolyn
Sampier, Luci
Sandon, Janet
Sandstedt, Janell
Sarvello, Joan
Schillings, Jean
Scholten, Mark
Schoo, Case
Schrader, Eileen
Schulte, Pat
Schultz, Vivian
Schulz, Jeanette L.
Schwartzfisher, Cathy
Scibior, Jean
Scofield, Laura
Sechler, Cyndi
Secore, Elna A.
Seibel, Sharon R.
Sells, Anna J.
Sevenski, Dee
Shadduck, Marylyn
Shafer, Judy
Shaw, Mrs. E. A.
Shearer, Marilyn
Sherman, Arlene
Sherman, Pete & Jan
Shillings, Virginia M.

Shirah, Nancy
Shurlow, Margaret
Smith, Ardith
Smith, Barbara
Smith, Leo
Smorgasbroads, T. C.
Snider, Pat
Sommer, Marquita
Sprow, Mary Ann
St. John, Marion
St. Louis, Peggy
Steffes, Jean A.
Stevens, Sue
Stewart, Nila
Stone, Beverly J.
Sudol, Lois
Swaney, Lu
Tackebury, Dixie L.
Tackelbury, Vickie L.
Tanner, Maralynn
Taylor, Grace M.
Taylor, Robert
Taylor, Sally
Thelen, Barbara
Thomas, Sue
Thompson, Nellie
Thurston, Mary Ann
Tonka, Lynn
Toogood, Denise
Town, June A.
Tracy, Eleanor
Trosien, Kimberly
Uhrik, Debby

Uhrik, Jason
Uhrik, Ron
Uhrik, Teather
Underhill, Marion
Valeski, Carol J.
Van Oort, Joanne
Venable, Marge
Villanueva, Sue
Virch, Patricia
Vitale, Mary
Voet, Margaret A.
Walls, Lois
Ward, Beverly
Watson, Lorraine B.
Wellington, Shirley Sullivan
West, Anne
Wigg, Florence
Wilhelm, Karen
Wojnaroski, Catherine
Wojnaroski, Jessie
Wojnaroski, Ray
Wolf, Joan
Woodford, Emma M.
Wright, Sue
Wykes, Beverly
Yarrow, Peggy
Yeager, Judy
Yerrick, Leanore E.
Zeedyk, Teddy
Zeller, Dorothy Louise
Zervan, Agnes R.
Ziebart, Butch
Zimmerman, Marilyn

Equivalent Chart

	When the recipe calls for	Use
Baking	½ cup butter	4 ounces
	2 cups butter	1 pound
	4 cups all-purpose flour	1 pound
	4½ to 5 cups sifted cake flour	1 pound
	1 square chocolate	1 ounce
	1 cup semisweet chocolate chips	6 ounces
	4 cups marshmallows	1 pound
	2¼ cups packed brown sugar	1 pound
	4 cups confectioners' sugar	1 pound
	2 cups granulated sugar	1 pound
Cereal – Bread	1 cup fine dry bread crumbs	4 to 5 slices
	1 cup soft bread crumbs	2 slices
	1 cup small bread cubes	2 slices
	1 cup fine cracker crumbs	28 saltines
	1 cup fine graham cracker crumbs	15 crackers
	1 cup vanilla wafer crumbs	22 wafers
	1 cup crushed cornflakes	3 cups uncrushed
	4 cups cooked macaroni	8 ounces uncooked
	3½ cups cooked rice	1 cup uncooked
Dairy	1 cup shredded cheese	4 ounces
	1 cup cottage cheese	8 ounces
	1 cup sour cream	8 ounces
	1 cup whipped cream	½ cup heavy cream
	⅔ cup evaporated milk	1 small can
	1⅔ cups evaporated milk	1 13-ounce can
Fruit	4 cups sliced or chopped apples	4 medium
	1 cup mashed bananas	3 medium
	2 cups pitted cherries	4 cups unpitted
	2½ cups shredded coconut	8 ounces
	4 cups cranberries	1 pound
	1 cup pitted dates	1 8-ounce package
	1 cup candied fruit	1 8-ounce package
	3 to 4 tablespoons lemon juice plus 1 tablespoon grated lemon rind	1 lemon
	⅓ cup orange juice plus 2 teaspoons grated orange rind	1 orange
	4 cups sliced peaches	8 medium
	2 cups pitted prunes	1 12-ounce package
	3 cups raisins	1 15-ounce package

	When the recipe calls for	Use
Meats	4 cups chopped cooked chicken 3 cups chopped cooked meat 2 cups cooked ground meat	1 5-pound chicken 1 pound, cooked 1 pound, cooked
Nuts	1 cup chopped nuts	4 ounces shelled 1 pound unshelled
Vegetables	2 cups cooked green beans 2½ cups lima beans or red beans 4 cups shredded cabbage 1 cup grated carrot 8 ounces fresh mushrooms 1 cup chopped onion 4 cups sliced or chopped potatoes 2 cups canned tomatoes	½ pound fresh or 1 16-ounce can 1 cup dried, cooked 1 pound 1 large 1 4-ounce can 1 large 4 medium 1 16-ounce can

Measurement Equivalents

1 tablespoon = 3 teaspoons
2 tablespoons = 1 ounce
4 tablespoons = ¼ cup
5⅓ tablespoons = ⅓ cup
8 tablespoons = ½ cup
12 tablespoons = ¾ cup
16 tablespoons = 1 cup
1 cup = 8 ounces or ½ pint
4 cups = 1 quart
4 quarts = 1 gallon

1 6½ to 8-ounce can = 1 cup
1 10½ to 12-ounce can = 1¼ cups
1 14 to 16-ounce can = 1¾ cups
1 16 to 17-ounce can = 2 cups
1 18 to 20-ounce can = 2½ cups
1 29-ounce can = 3½ cups
1 46 to 51-ounce can = 5¾ cups
1 6½ to 7½-pound can or Number
   10 = 12 to 13 cups

Metric Equivalents

Liquid		Dry	
1 teaspoon	= 5 milliliters	1 quart	= 1 liter
1 tablespoon	= 15 milliliters	1 ounce	= 30 grams
1 fluid ounce	= 30 milliliters	1 pound	= 450 grams
1 cup	= 250 milliliters	2.2 pounds	= 1 kilogram
1 pint	= 500 milliliters		

NOTE: The metric measures are approximate benchmarks for purposes of home food preparation.

Substitution Chart

	Instead of	Use
Baking	1 teaspoon baking powder	¼ teaspoon baking soda plus ½ teaspoon cream of tartar
	1 tablespoon cornstarch (for thickening)	2 tablespoons flour or 1 tablespoon tapioca
	1 cup sifted all-purpose flour	1 cup plus 2 tablespoons sifted cake flour
	1 cup sifted cake flour	1 cup minus 2 tablespoons sifted all-purpose flour
	1 cup dry bread crumbs	¾ cup cracker crumbs
Dairy	1 cup buttermilk	1 cup sour milk or 1 cup yogurt
	1 cup heavy cream	¾ cup skim milk plus ⅓ cup butter
	1 cup light cream	⅞ cup skim milk plus 3 tablespoons butter
	1 cup sour cream	⅞ cup sour milk plus 3 tablespoons butter
	1 cup sour milk	1 cup milk plus 1 tablespoon vinegar or lemon juice or 1 cup buttermilk
Seasoning	1 teaspoon allspice	½ teaspoon cinnamon plus ⅛ teaspoon cloves
	1 cup catsup	1 cup tomato sauce plus ½ cup sugar plus 2 tablespoons vinegar
	1 clove of garlic	⅛ teaspoon garlic powder or ⅛ teaspoon instant minced garlic or ¾ teaspoon garlic salt or 5 drops of liquid garlic
	1 teaspoon Italian spice	¼ teaspoon each oregano, basil, thyme, rosemary plus dash of cayenne pepper
	1 teaspoon lemon juice	½ teaspoon vinegar
	1 tablespoon mustard	1 teaspoon dry mustard
	1 medium onion	1 tablespoon dried minced onion or 1 teaspoon onion powder
Sweet	1 1-ounce square chocolate	¼ cup cocoa plus 1 teaspoon shortening
	1⅔ ounces semisweet chocolate	1 ounce unsweetened chocolate plus 4 teaspoons granulated sugar
	1 cup honey	1 to 1¼ cups sugar plus ¼ cup liquid or 1 cup corn syrup or molasses
	1 cup granulated sugar	1 cup packed brown sugar or 1 cup corn syrup, molasses or honey minus ¼ cup liquid

Glossary of Cooking Techniques

Bake: To cook by dry heat in an oven, or under hot coals.

Bard: To cover lean meats with bacon or pork fat before cooking to prevent dryness.

Baste: To moisten, especially meats, with melted butter, pan drippings, sauce, etc. during cooking time.

Beat: To mix ingredients by vigorous stirring or with electric mixer.

Blanch: To immerse, usually vegetables or fruit, briefly into boiling water to inactivate enzymes, loosen skin, or soak away excess salt.

Blend: To combine 2 or more ingredients, at least 1 of which is liquid or soft, to produce a mixture of uniform consistency quickly.

Boil: To heat liquid until bubbly; the boiling point for water is about 212 degrees, depending on altitude and atmospheric pressure.

Braise: To cook, especially meats, covered, in a small amount of liquid.

Brew: To prepare a beverage by allowing boiling water to extract flavor and/or color from certain substances.

Broil: To cook by direct exposure to intense heat such as a flame or an electric heating unit.

Caramelize: To melt sugar in heavy pan over low heat until golden, stirring constantly.

Chill: To cool in the refrigerator or in cracked ice.

Clarify: To remove impurities from melted butter by allowing the sediment to settle, then pouring off clear yellow liquid. Other fats may be clarified by straining.

Cream: To blend butter, margarine, shortening, usually softened, or sometimes oil, with a granulated or crushed ingredient until the mixture is soft and creamy. Usually described in method as light and fluffy.

Curdle: To congeal milk with rennet or heat until solid lumps or curds are formed.

Cut in: To disperse solid shortening into dry ingredients with a knife or pastry blender. Texture of the mixture should resemble coarse cracker meal. Described in method as crumbly.

Decant: To pour a liquid such as wine or melted butter carefully from 1 container into another leaving the sediment in the original container.

Deep-fry: To cook in a deep pan or skillet containing hot cooking oil. Deep-fried foods are generally completely immersed in the hot oil.

Deglaze: To heat stock, wine or other liquid in the pan in which meat has been cooked, mixing with pan juices and sediment to form a gravy or sauce base.

Degorger: To remove strong flavors or impurities before cooking, i.e. soaking ham in cold water or sprinkling vegetables with salt, then letting stand for a period of time and pressing out excess fluid.

Degrease: To remove accumulated fat from surface of hot liquids.

Dice: To cut into small cubes about 1/4-inch in size. Do not use dice unless ingredient can truly be cut into cubes.

Dissolve: To create a solution by thoroughly mixing a solid or granular substance with a liquid until no sediment remains.

Dredge: To coat completely with flour, bread crumbs, etc.

Filet: To remove bones from meat or fish. (Pieces of meat, fish or poultry from which bones have been removed are called filets.)

Flambé: To pour warmed Brandy or other spirits over food in a pan, then ignite and continue cooking briefly.

Fold in: To blend a delicate frothy mixture into a heavier one so that none of the lightness or volume is lost. Using a rubber spatula, turn under and bring up and over, rotating bowl 1/4 turn after each folding motion.

Fry: To cook in a pan or skillet containing hot cooking oil. The oil should not totally cover the food.

Garnish: To decorate food before serving.

Glaze: To cover or coat with sauce, syrup, egg white, or a jellied substance. After applying, it becomes firm; adding color and flavor.

Grate: To rub food against a rough, perforated utensil to produce slivers, chunks, curls, etc.

Gratiné: To top a sauced dish with crumbs, cheese or butter, then brown under a broiler.

Grill: To broil, usually over hot coals or charcoal.

Grind: To cut, crush, or force through a chopper to produce small bits.

Infuse: To steep herbs or other flavorings in a liquid until liquid absorbs flavor.

Julienne: To cut vegetables, fruit, etc. into long thin strips.

Knead: To press, fold, and stretch dough until smooth and elastic. Method usually notes time frame or result.

Lard: To insert strips of fat or bacon into lean meat to keep it moist and juicy during cooking. Larding is an internal basting technique.

Leaven: To cause batters and doughs to rise, usually by means of a chemical leavening agent. This process may occur before or during baking.

Marinate: To soak, usually in a highly seasoned oil-acid solution, to flavor and/or tenderize food.

Melt: To liquefy solid foods by the action of heat.

Mince: To cut or chop into very small pieces.

Mix: To combine ingredients to distribute uniformly.

Mold: To shape into a particular form.

Panbroil: To cook in a skillet or pan using a very small amount of fat to prevent sticking.

Panfry: To cook in a skillet or pan containing only a small amount of fat.

Parboil: To partially cook in boiling water. Most parboiled foods require additional cooking with or without other ingredients.

Parch: To dry or roast slightly through exposure to intense heat.

Pit: To remove the hard inedible seed from peaches, plums, etc.

Plank: To broil and serve on a board or wooden platter.

Plump: To soak fruits, usually dried, in liquid until puffy and softened.

Poach: To cook in a small amount of gently simmering liquid.

Preserve: To prevent food spoilage by pickling, salting, dehydrating, smoking, boiling in syrup, etc. Preserved foods have excellent keeping qualities when properly prepared.

Purée: To reduce the pulp of cooked fruit and vegetables to a smooth and thick liquid by straining or blending.

Reduce: To boil stock, gravy or other liquid until volume is reduced, liquid is thickened and flavor is intensified.

Refresh: To place blanched drained vegetables or other food in cold water to halt cooking process.

Render: To cook meat or meat trimmings at low temperature until fat melts and can be drained and strained.

Roast: (1) To cook by dry heat either in an oven or over hot coals. (2) To dry or parch by intense heat.

Sauté: To cook in a skillet containing a small amount of hot cooking oil. Sautéed foods should never be immersed in the oil. Should be stirred frequently.

Scald: (1) To heat a liquid almost to the boiling point. (2) To soak; usually vegetables or fruit; in boiling water until the skins are loosened; see blanch, which is our preferred term.

Scallop: To bake with a sauce in a casserole. The food may either be mixed or layered with the sauce.

Score: To make shallow cuts diagonally in parallel lines, especially meat.

Scramble: To cook and stir simultaneously, especially eggs.

Shirr: To crack eggs into individual buttered baking dishes, then bake or broil until whites are set. Chopped meats or vegetables, cheese, cream, or bread crumbs may also be added.

Shred: To cut or shave food into slivers.

Shuck: To remove the husk from corn or the shell from oysters, clams, etc.

Sieve: To press a mixture through a closely meshed metal utensil to make it homogeneous.

Sift: To pass, usually dry ingredients, through a fine wire mesh in order to produce a uniform consistency.

Simmer: To cook in or with a liquid at or just below the boiling point.

Skewer: (1) To thread; usually meat and vegetables; onto a sharpened rod (as in shish kabob). (2) To fasten the opening of stuffed fowl closed with small pins.

Skim: To ladle or spoon off excess fat or scum from the surface of a liquid.

Smoke: To preserve or cook through continuous exposure to wood smoke for a long time.

Steam: To cook with water vapor in a closed container, usually in a steamer, on a rack, or in a double boiler.

Sterilize: To cleanse and purify through exposure to intense heat.

Stew: To simmer, usually meats and vegetables, for a long period of time. Also used to tenderize meats.

Stir-fry: To cook small pieces of vegetables and/or meat in a small amount of oil in a wok or skillet over high heat, stirring constantly, until tender-crisp.

Strain: To pass through a strainer, sieve, or cheesecloth in order to break down or remove solids or impurities.

Stuff: To fill or pack cavities especially those of meats, vegetables and poultry.

Toast: To brown and crisp, usually by means of direct heat or to bake until brown.

Toss: To mix lightly with lifting motion using 2 forks or spoons.

Truss: To bind poultry legs and wings close to body before cooking.

Whip: To beat a mixture until air has been thoroughly incorporated and the mixture is light and fluffy, volume is greatly increased, and mixture holds its shape.

Wilt: To apply heat to cause dehydration, and a droopy appearance.

Index

382 INDEX

To Order Additional Copies of

Great Cooking from the Great Lakes

Makes checks payable to:
Great Cooking from the Great Lakes

Please send me _____ copies of *Great Cooking from the Great Lakes*

Great Cooking from the Great Lakes   @ $ 12.00 each $_____

Postage and Handling   @ $ 2.00 each $_____

Total $_____

Name _____

Address _____

City/State/Zip _____

Mail to:
Great Lakes Chapter #90
Telephone Pioneers of America
3566 Michael Ave. S.W.
Grand Rapids, Michigan 49509

Great Lakes Chapter #90
Telephone Pioneers of America
3566 Michael Ave. S.W.
Grand Rapids, Michigan 49509